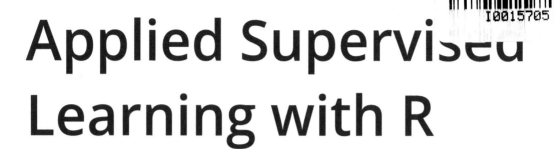

Applied Supervised Learning with R

Use machine learning libraries of R to build models that solve business problems and predict future trends

Karthik Ramasubramanian and Jojo Moolayil

Applied Supervised Learning with R

Authors: Karthik Ramasubramanian and Jojo Moolayil

Technical Reviewer: Pulkit Khandelwal

Managing Editor: Vishal Mewada

Acquisitions Editor: Aditya Date

Production Editor: Shantanu Zagade

Editorial Board: David Barnes, Mayank Bhardwaj, Ewan Buckingham, Simon Cox, Mahesh Dhyani, Taabish Khan, Manasa Kumar, Alex Mazonowicz, Douglas Paterson, Dominic Pereira, Shiny Poojary, Erol Staveley, Ankita Thakur, Mohita Vyas, and Jonathan Wray

First Published: May 2019

Production Reference: 1310519

ISBN: 978-1-83855-633-4

Published by Packt Publishing Ltd.

Livery Place, 35 Livery Street

Birmingham B3 2PB, UK

Table of Contents

Exploratory Analysis of Data   61

Model Improvements   325

Preface

About

This section briefly introduces the authors, the coverage of this book, the technical skills you'll need to get started, and the hardware and software requirements required to complete all of the included activities and exercises.

About the Book

R was one of the first programming languages developed for statistical computing and data analysis with excellent support for visualization. With the rise of data science, R emerged as an undoubtedly good choice of programming language among many data science practitioners. Since R was open source and extremely powerful in building sophisticated statistical models, it quickly found adoption in both industry and academia.

Applied Supervised Learning with R covers the complete process of using R to develop applications using supervised machine learning algorithms that cater to your business needs. Your learning curve starts with developing your analytical thinking to create a problem statement using business inputs or domain research. You will learn about many evaluation metrics that compare various algorithms, and you will then use these metrics to select the best algorithm for your problem. After finalizing the algorithm you want to use, you will study hyperparameter optimization techniques to fine-tune your set of optimal parameters. To avoid overfitting your model, you will also be shown how to add various regularization terms. You will also learn about deploying your model into a production environment.

When you have completed the book, you will be an expert at modeling supervised machine learning algorithms to precisely fulfill your business needs.

About the Authors

Karthik Ramasubramanian completed his M.Sc. in Theoretical Computer Science at PSG College of Technology, India, where he pioneered the application of machine learning, data mining, and fuzzy logic in his research work on computer and network security. He has over seven years' experience of leading data science and business analytics in retail, Fast-Moving Consumer Goods, e-commerce, information technology, and the hospitality industry for multinational companies and unicorn start-ups.

He is a researcher and a problem solver with diverse experience of the data science life cycle, starting from data problem discovery to creating data science proof of concepts and products for various industry use cases. In his leadership roles, Karthik has been instrumental in solving many ROI-driven business problems via data science solutions. He has mentored and trained hundreds of professionals and students globally in data science through various online platforms and university engagement programs. He has also developed intelligent chatbots based on deep learning models that understand human-like interactions, customer segmentation models, recommendation systems, and many natural language processing models.

He is an author of the book *Machine Learning Using* R, published by Apress, a publishing house of Springer Business+Science Media. The book was a big success with more than 50,000 online downloads and hardcover sales. The book was subsequently published as a second edition with extended chapters on *Deep Learning and Time Series Modeling*.

Jojo Moolayil is an artificial intelligence, deep learning, machine learning, and decision science professional with over six years of industrial experience. He is the author of *Learn Keras for Deep Neural Networks*, published by Apress, and *Smarter Decisions – The Intersection of IoT and Decision Science*, published by Packt Publishing. He has worked with several industry leaders on high-impact, critical data science and machine learning projects across multiple verticals. He is currently associated with Amazon Web Services as a research scientist in Canada.

Apart from writing books on AI, decision science, and the internet of things, Jojo has been a technical reviewer for various books in the same fields published by Apress and Packt Publishing. He is an active data science tutor and maintains a blog at http://blog. jojomoolayil.com.

Learning Objectives

- Develop analytical thinking to precisely identify a business problem

- Wrangle data with dplyr, tidyr, and reshape2

- Visualize data with ggplot2

- Validate your supervised machine learning model using the k-fold algorithm

- Optimize hyperparameters with grid and random search and Bayesian optimization

- Deploy your model on AWS Lambda with Plumber

- Improve a model's performance with feature selection and dimensionality reduction

Audience

This book is specially designed for novice and intermediate data analysts, data scientists, and data engineers who want to explore various methods of supervised machine learning and its various use cases. Some background in statistics, probability, calculus, linear algebra, and programming will help you thoroughly understand and follow the content of this book.

Approach

Applied Supervised Learning with R perfectly balances theory and exercises. Each module is designed to build on the learning of the previous module. The book contains multiple activities that use real-life business scenarios for you to practice and apply your new skills in a highly relevant context.

Minimum Hardware Requirements

For the optimal student experience, we recommend the following hardware configuration:

- **Processor**: Intel or AMD 4-core or better
- **Memory**: 8 GB RAM
- **Storage**: 20 GB available space

Software Requirements

You'll need the following software installed in advance:

- **Operating systems**: Windows 7, 8.1, or 10, Ubuntu 14.04 or later, or macOS Sierra or later
- **Browser**: Google Chrome or Mozilla Firefox
- RStudio
- RStudio Cloud

You'll also need the following software, packages, and libraries installed in advance:

- `dplyr`
- `tidyr`
- `reshape2`
- `lubridate`
- `ggplot2`
- `caret`
- `mlr`
- `OpenML`

Conventions

Code words in text, database table names, folder names, filenames, file extensions, pathnames, dummy URLs, user input, and Twitter handles are shown as follows: "The `Location`, `WindDir`, and `RainToday` variables and many more are categorical, and the remainder are continuous."

A block of code is set as follows:

```
temp_df<-as.data.frame(
  sort(
  round(
  sapply(df, function(y) sum(length(which(is.na(y)))))/dim(df)[1],2)
  )
)
colnames(temp_df) <- "NullPerc"
```

New terms and important words are shown in bold. Words that you see on the screen, for example, in menus or dialog boxes, appear in the text such as this: "Click on the **Next** button and navigate to the **Details** page."

Installation and Setup

To install a package on the RStudio Cloud, you can use the following syntax:

```
install.packages("Package_Name")
```

For example:

```
install.packages("ggplot2")
```

To verify the installation, run the following command:

```
library(Package_Name)
```

For example:

```
library(ggplot2)
```

Installing the Code Bundle

Copy the code bundle for the class to the `C:/Code` folder.

Additional Resources

The code bundle for this book is also hosted on GitHub at: https://github.com/TrainingByPackt/Applied-Supervised-Learning-with-R.

We also have other code bundles from our rich catalog of books, videos, and E-learning products available at https://github.com/PacktPublishing/ and https://github.com/TrainingByPackt. Check them out!

R for Advanced Analytics

Learning Objectives

By the end of this chapter, you will be able to:

- Explain advanced R programming constructs
- Print the summary statistics of a real-world dataset
- Read data from CSV, text, and JSON files
- Write R markdown files for code reproducibility
- Explain R data structures such as data.frame, data.table, lists, arrays, and matrices
- Implement the cbind, rbind, merge, reshape, aggregate, and apply functions
- Use packages such as dplyr, plyr, caret, tm, and many more
- Create visualizations using ggplot

In this chapter, we will set the foundation for programming with R and understand the various syntax and data structures for advanced analytics.

Introduction

R was one of the early programming languages developed for statistical computing and data analysis with good support for visualization. With the rise of data science, R emerged as an undoubted choice of programming language among many data science practitioners. Since R was open-source and extremely powerful in building sophisticated statistical models, it quickly found adoption in both industry and academia.

Tools and software such as SAS and SPSS were only affordable by large corporations, and traditional programming languages such as C/C++ and Java were not suitable for performing complex data analysis and building model. Hence, the need for a much more straightforward, comprehensive, community-driven, cross-platform compatible, and flexible programming language was a necessity.

Though Python programming language is increasingly becoming popular in recent times because of its industry-wide adoption and robust production-grade implementation, R is still the choice of programming language for quick prototyping of advanced machine learning models. R has one of the most populous collection of packages (a collection of functions/methods for accomplishing a complicated procedure, which otherwise requires a lot of time and effort to implement). At the time of writing this book, the **Comprehensive R Archive Network** (**CRAN**), a network of FTP and web servers around the world that store identical, up-to-date, versions of code and documentation for R, has more than 13,000 packages.

While there are numerous books and online resources on learning the fundamentals of R, in this chapter, we will limit the scope only to cover the important topics in R programming that will be used extensively in many data science projects. We will use a real-world dataset from the UCI Machine Learning Repository to demonstrate the concepts. The material in this chapter will be useful for learners who are new to R Programming. The upcoming chapters in supervised learning concepts will borrow many of the implementations from this chapter.

Working with Real-World Datasets

There are plenty of open datasets available online these days. The following are some popular sources of open datasets:

- **Kaggle**: A platform for hosting data science competitions. The official website is https://www.kaggle.com/.

- **UCI Machine Learning Repository**: A collection of databases, domain theories, and data generators that are used by the machine learning community for the empirical analysis of machine learning algorithms. You can visit the official page via navigating to https://archive.ics.uci.edu/ml/index.php URL.

- **data.gov.in**: Open Indian government data platform, which is available at https://data.gov.in/.

- **World Bank Open Data**: Free and open access to global development data, which can be accessed from https://data.worldbank.org/.

Increasingly, many private and public organizations are willing to make their data available for public access. However, it is restricted to only complex datasets where the organization is looking for solutions to their data science problem through crowd-sourcing platforms such as Kaggle. There is no substitute for learning from data acquired internally in the organization as part of a job that offers all kinds of challenges in processing and analyzing.

Significant learning opportunity and challenge concerning data processing comes from the public data sources as well, as not all the data from these sources are clean and in a standard format. JSON, Excel, and XML are some other formats used along with CSV, though CSV is predominant. Each format needs a separate encoding and decoding method and hence a reader package in R. In our next section, we will discuss various data formats and how to process the available data in detail.

Throughout this chapter and in many others, we will use the direct marketing campaigns (phone calls) of a Portuguese banking institution dataset from UCI Machine Learning Repository. (https://archive.ics.uci.edu/ml/datasets/bank+marketing). The following table describes the fields in detail:

No	Field Name	Detail
1	age	age (numeric)
2	job	job : type of job (categorical: 'admin.','blue-collar','entrepreneur','housemaid','management','retired','self-employed','services','student','technician','unemployed','unknown')
3	marital	marital : marital status (categorical: 'divorced','married','single','unknown'; note: 'divorced' means divorced or widowed)
4	education	education (categorical: 'basic.4y','basic.6y','basic.9y','high.school','illiterate','professional.course','university.degree','unknown')
5	housing	housing: has a housing loan? (categorical: 'no','yes','unknown')
6	loan	loan: has a personal loan? (categorical: 'no','yes','unknown')
7	contact	contact: contact communication type (categorical: 'cellular','telephone')
8	month	month: last contact month of year (categorical: 'jan', 'feb', 'mar', ..., 'nov', 'dec')

Figure 1.1: Portuguese banking institution dataset from UCI Machine Learning Repository (Part 1)

9	duration	duration: last contact duration, in seconds (numeric). Important note: this attribute highly affects the output target (e.g., if duration=0 then y='no'). Yet, the duration is not known before a call is performed. Also, after the end of the call y is obviously known. Thus, this input should only be included for benchmark purposes and should be discarded if the intention is to have a realistic predictive model.
10	campaign	campaign: number of contacts performed during this campaign and for this client (numeric, includes the last contact)
11	pdays	pdays: number of days that passed by after the client was last contacted from a previous campaign (numeric; 999 means the client was not previously contacted)
12	previous	previous: number of contacts performed before this campaign and for this client (numeric)
13	poutcomes	poutcome: outcome of the previous marketing campaign (categorical: 'failure', 'nonexistent', 'success')
14	Y	y - has the client subscribed a term deposit? (binary: 'yes','no')
15	default	default: has credit in default? (categorical: 'no','yes','unknown')

Figure 1.2: Portuguese banking institution dataset from UCI Machine Learning Repository (Part 2)

In the following exercise, we will download the **bank.zip** dataset as a ZIP file and unzip it using the **unzip** method.

Exercise 1: Using the unzip Method for Unzipping a Downloaded File

In this exercise, we will write an R script to download the Portuguese Bank Direct Campaign dataset from UCI Machine Learning Repository and extract the content of the ZIP file in a given folder using the **unzip** function.

Preform these steps to complete the exercise:

1. First, open R Studio on your system.

2. Now, set the working directory of your choice using the following command:

```
wd <- "<WORKING DIRECTORY>"
setwd(wd)
```

> **Note**
>
> R codes in this book are implemented using the R version 3.2.2.

3. Download the ZIP file containing the datasets using the **download.file()** method:

```
url <- "https://archive.ics.uci.edu/ml/machine-learning-databases/00222/
bank.zip"
destinationFileName <- "bank.zip"
download.file(url, destinationFileName,method = "auto", quiet=FALSE)
```

4. Now, before we unzip the file in the working directory using the **unzip()** method, we need to choose a file and save its file path in R (for Windows) or specify the complete path:

```
zipFile<-file.choose()
```

5. Define the folder where the ZIP file is unzipped:

```
outputDir <- wd
```

6. Finally, unzip the ZIP file using the following command:

```
unzip(zipFile, exdir=outputDir)
```

The output is as follows:

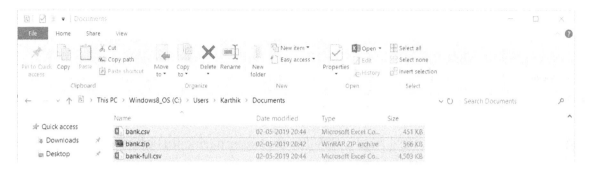

Figure 1.3: Unzipping the bank.zip file

Reading Data from Various Data Formats

Data from digital systems is generated in various forms: browsing history on an e-commerce website, clickstream data, the purchase history of a customer, social media interactions, footfalls in a retail store, images from satellite and drones, and numerous other formats and types of data. We are living in an exciting time when technology is significantly changing lives, and enterprises are leveraging it to create their next data strategy to make better decisions.

It is not enough to be able to collect a huge amount of different types of data; we also need to leverage value out of it. A CCTV footage captured throughout a day will help the law and order teams of the government in improving the real-time surveillance of public places. The challenge remains in how we will process a large volume of heterogeneous data formats within a single system.

Transaction data in the **Customer Relationship Management (CRM)** application would mostly be tabular and feed in social media is mostly text, audio, video, and images.

We can categorize the data formats as structured—tabular data such as CSV and database tables; unstructured—textual data such as tweets, FB posts, and word documents; and semi-structured. Unlike textual, which is hard for machines to process and understand, semi-structured provides associated metadata, which makes it easy for computers to process it. It's popularly used with many web applications for data exchange, and JSON is an example of the semi-structured data format.

In this section, we will see how to load, process, and transform various data formats in R. Within the scope of this book, we will work with CSV, text, and JSON data.

CSV Files

CSV files are the most common type of data storage and exchange formats for structured data. R provides a method called **read.csv()** for reading data from a CSV file. It will read the data into a **data.frame** (more about it in the next section). There are many arguments that the method takes; the two required arguments are a path to the **filename** and **sep**, which specifies the character that separates the column values. The **summary()** method describes the six summary statistics, **min**, **first quartile**, **median**, **mean**, **third quartile**, and **max**.

In the following exercise, we'll read a CSV file and summarize its column.

Exercise 2: Reading a CSV File and Summarizing its Column

In this exercise, we will read the previously extracted CSV file and use the **summary** function to print the min, max, mean, median, 1st quartile, and 3rd quartile values of numeric variables and count the categories of the categorical variable.

Carry out these steps to read a CSV file and later summarize its columns:

1. First, use the **read.csv** method and load the **bank-full.csv** into a DataFrame:

    ```
    df_bank_detail <- read.csv("bank-full.csv", sep = ';')
    ```

2. Print the summary of the DataFrame:

    ```
    summary(df_bank_detail)
    ```

    The output is as follows:

    ```
    ##        age                      job             marital            education
    ##  Min.   :18.00    blue-collar:9732    divorced: 5207    primary   : 6851
    ##  1st Qu.:33.00    management :9458    married :27214    secondary:23202
    ##  Median :39.00    technician :7597    single  :12790    tertiary :13301
    ##  Mean   :40.94    admin.     :5171                      unknown   : 1857
    ##  3rd Qu.:48.00    services   :4154
    ##  Max.   :95.00    retired    :2264
    ```

JSON

JSON is the next most commonly used data format for sharing and storing data. It is unlike CSV files, which only deal with rows and columns of data where each has a definite number of columns. For example, in the e-commerce data of the customers, each row could be representing a customer with their information stored in separate columns. For a customer, if a column has no value, the field is stored as NULL.

JSON provides an added flexibility of having a varying number of fields for each customer. This type of flexibility relieves the developer from the burden of maintaining a schema as we have in traditional relational databases, wherein the same customer data might be spread across multiple tables to optimize for storage and querying time.

JSON is more of a key-value store type of storage, where all we care about is the keys (such as the name, age, and DOB) and their corresponding values. While this sounds flexible, proper care has to be taken, otherwise manageability might at times, go out of control. Fortunately, with the advent of big data technologies in recent days, many document stores (a subclass of the key-value store), popularly also known as **NoSQL** databases, are available for storing, retrieving, and processing data in such formats.

In the following exercise, the JSON file has data for cardamom (spices and condiments) cultivation district-wise in Tamil Nadu, India, for the year 2015-16. The keys include **area** (hectare), **production** (in quintals), and **productivity** (average yield per hectare).

The **jsonlite** package provides an implementation to read and convert a JSON file into DataFrame, which makes the analysis simpler. The **fromJSON** method reads a JSON file, and if the **flatten** argument in the **fromJSON** function is set to TRUE, it gives a DataFrame.

Exercise 3: Reading a JSON file and Storing the Data in DataFrame

In this exercise, we will read a JSON file and store the data in the DataFrame.

Perform the following steps to complete the exercise:

1. Download the data from https://data.gov.in/catalog/area-production-productivity-spices-condiments-district-wise-tamil-nadu-year-2015-16.

2. First, use the following command to install the packages required for the system of read the JSON file:

    ```
    install jsonlite package
    install.packages("jsonlite")
    library(jsonlite)
    ```

3. Next, read the JSON file using the **fromJSON** method, as illustrated here:

    ```
    json_file <- "crop.json"
    json_data <- jsonlite::fromJSON(json_file, flatten = TRUE)
    ```

4. The second element in the list contains the DataFrame with crop production value. Retrieve it from **json_data** and store as a DataFrame named **crop_production**:

    ```
    crop_production <- data.frame(json_data[[2]])
    ```

5. Next, use the following command to rename the columns:

```
colnames(crop_production) <- c("S.
No","District","Area","Production","PTY")
```

6. Now, print the top six rows using the **head()** function:

```
head(crop_production)
```

The output is as follows:

```
##    S.No    District Area Production  PTY
## 1    1     Ariyalur  NA         NA   NA
## 2    2   Coimbatore  808        26 0.03
## 3    3    Cuddalore  NA         NA   NA
## 4    4   Dharmapuri  NA         NA   NA
## 5    5     Dindigul  231         2 0.01
## 6    6        Erode  NA         NA   NA
```

Text

Unstructured data is the language of the web. All the social media, blogs, web pages, and many other sources of information are textual and untidy to extract any meaningful information. An increasing amount of research work is coming out from the **Natural Language Processing (NLP)** field, wherein computers are becoming better in understanding not only the meaning of the word but also the context in which it's used in a sentence. The rise of computer chatbot, which responds to a human query, is the most sophisticated form of understanding textual information.

In R, we will use the **tm** text mining package to show how to read, process, and retrieve meaningful information from text data. We will use a small sample of the **Amazon Food Review** dataset in Kaggle (https://www.kaggle.com/snap/amazon-fine-food-reviews) for the exercise in this section.

In the **tm** package, collections of text documents are called **Corpus**. One implementation of Corpus in the **tm** package is **VCorpus (volatile corpus)**. Volatile corpus is named after the fact that it's stored in-memory for fast processing. To check the metadata information of the **VCorpus** object, we can use the **inspect()** method. The following exercise uses the **lapply** method for looping through the first two reviews and casting the text as a character. You will learn more about the **apply** family of function in the *The Apply Family of Functions* section.

Exercise 4: Reading a CSV File with Text Column and Storing the Data in VCorpus

In this exercise, we will read a CSV file with the text column and store the data in VCorpus.

Perform the following steps to complete the exercise:

1. First, let's load the text mining package from the R into the system to read the text file:

```
library(tm)
```

2. Now, read the first top 10 reviews from the file:

```
review_top_10 <- read.csv("Reviews_Only_Top_10_Records.csv")
```

3. To store the text column in **VCorpus**, use the following command:

```
review_corpus <- VCorpus(VectorSource(review_top_10$Text))
```

4. To inspect the structure of first two reviews, execute the following command:

```
inspect(review_corpus[1:2])
```

The output is as follows:

```
## <<VCorpus>>
## Metadata:  corpus specific: 0, document level (indexed): 0
## Content:  documents: 2

## [[1]]
## <<PlainTextDocument>>
## Metadata:  7
## Content:  chars: 263

## [[2]]
## <<PlainTextDocument>>
## Metadata:  7
## Content:  chars: 190
```

5. Using **lapply**, cast the first review as character and print:

```
lapply(review_corpus[1:2], as.character)
## $'1'
## [1] "I have bought several of the Vitality canned dog food products and
have found them all to be of good quality. The product looks more like a
stew than a processed meat and it smells better. My Labrador is finicky and
she appreciates this product better than  most."

## $'2'
## [1] "Product arrived labeled as Jumbo Salted Peanuts...the peanuts were
actually small sized unsalted. Not sure if this was an error or if the
vendor intended to represent the product as \"Jumbo\"."
```

We will revisit the **review_corpus** dataset in a later section to show how to convert the unstructured textual information to structured tabular data.

Apart from CSV, Text, and JSON, there are numerous other data formats depending upon the source of data and its usage. R has a rich collection of libraries that helps with many formats. R can import not only the standard formats (apart from the previous three) such as HTML tables and XML but also formats specific to an analytical tool such as SAS and SPSS. This democratization led to a significant migration of industry experts who were earlier working in the propriety tools (costly and often found with only the large corporations) to open source analytical programming languages such as R and Python.

Write R Markdown Files for Code Reproducibility

The considerable success of analytics is a result of the way the information and knowledge network around the subject started to spread. More open source communities emerged, developers were happily sharing their work with the outer world, and many data projects were becoming reproducible. This change meant that work started by one person was soon getting adapted, improvised, and modified in many different forms by a community of people before it got adopted in an entirely different domain than the one from where it initially emerged. Imagine every research work that gets published in conference submitting a collection of code and data that is easily reproducible along with their research paper. This change is accelerating the pace at which an idea meets reality, and innovation will start to boom.

Now, let's see how to create such reproducible work in a single file that we call the **R Markdown** file. In the following activity, we will demonstrate how to create a new R Markdown file in RStudio. A detailed intro to R Markdown could be found at https://rmarkdown.rstudio.com/lesson-1.html.

In the next activity, you will recreate the code shown in *Exercise 4, Reading a CSV File with Text Column and Storing the Data in VCorpus*, into an R Markdown. Observe in *Figure* 4.2 that you have just written the explanation and the code in R Markdown, and when the **Knit to Word** action is performed, it interweaves the explanation, code, and its output neatly into a word document.

Activity 1: Create an R Markdown File to Read a CSV File and Write a Summary of Data

In this activity, we will create a R Markdown file to read a CSV file and print a small summary of the data in a word file:

Perform the following steps to complete the activity:

1. Open RStudio and navigate to the **R Markdown** option:

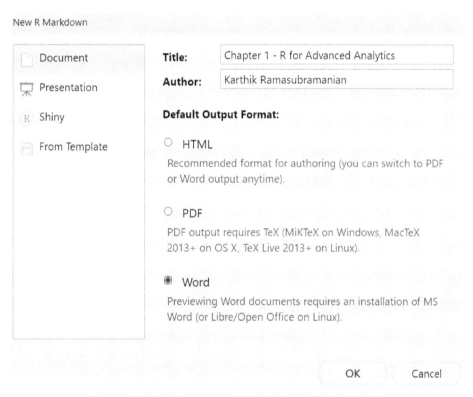

Figure 1.4: Creating a new R Markdown file in Rstudio

2. Provide the **Title** and **Author** name for the document and select the **Default Output Format** as **Word**:

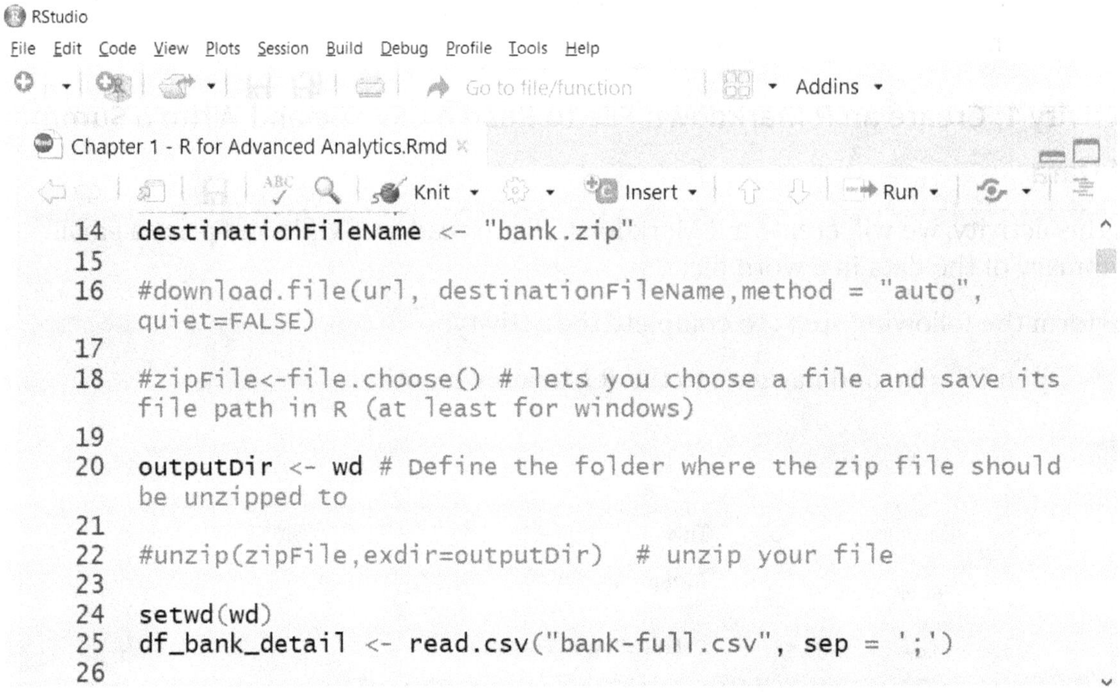

RStudio

File Edit Code View Plots Session Build Debug Profile Tools Help

Go to file/function   Addins ▾

Chapter 1 - R for Advanced Analytics.Rmd

Knit ▾   Insert ▾   Run ▾

```
14  destinationFileName <- "bank.zip"
15
16  #download.file(url, destinationFileName,method = "auto",
    quiet=FALSE)
17
18  #zipFile<-file.choose() # lets you choose a file and save its
    file path in R (at least for windows)
19
20  outputDir <- wd # Define the folder where the zip file should
    be unzipped to
21
22  #unzip(zipFile,exdir=outputDir)  # unzip your file
23
24  setwd(wd)
25  df_bank_detail <- read.csv("bank-full.csv", sep = ';')
26
```

Figure 1.5: Using the read.csv method to read the data

3. Use the **read.csv()** method to read the **bank-full.csv** file.

4. Finally, print the summary into a word file using the **summary** method.

The output is as follows:

```
##       age                    job              marital           education
## Min.   :18.00    blue-collar:9732    divorced: 5207    primary  : 6851
## 1st Qu.:33.00    management :9458    married :27214    secondary:23202
## Median :39.00    technician :7597    single  :12790    tertiary :13301
## Mean   :40.94    admin.     :5171                      unknown  : 1857
## 3rd Qu.:48.00    services   :4154
## Max.   :95.00    retired    :2264
##                  (Other)    :6835
## default         balance        housing        loan          contact
## no :44396   Min.    : -8019   no :20081   no :37967   cellular :29285
## yes:  815   1st Qu.:    72    yes:25130   yes: 7244   telephone: 2906
##             Median :    448                           unknown  :13020
##             Mean   :   1362
##             3rd Qu.:   1428
##             Max.   :102127
##
```

Figure 1.6: Final output after using the summary method

Note

The solution for this activity can be found at page 438.

Data Structures in R

In any programming language, data structures are the fundamental units of storing information and making it ready for further processing. Depending on the type of data, various forms of data structures are available for **storing** and **processing**. Each of the data structures explained in the next section has its characteristic features and applicability.

In this section, we will explore each of it and how to use it with our data.

Vector

Vector is the most fundamental of all the data structures, and the values are stored in a 1-D array. Vector is the most suitable for a single variable with a series of values. In *Exercise 3, Reading a JSON File and Storing the Data in DataFrame*, refer to step 4 where we assigned a DataFrame its column names and concatenated using the `c()` method, as shown here:

```
c_names <- c("S.No","District","Area","Production","PTY")
```

We can extract the second value in the vector by specifying the index in square brackets next to the vector name. Let's review the following code where we subset the value in the second index:

```
c_names[2]
```

The output is as follows:

```
## [1] "District"
```

The collection of string concatenated with the `c()` method is a vector. It can store a homogenous collection of characters, integers, or floating point values. While trying to store an integer with character, an implicit type cast will happen, which will convert all the values to character.

> **Caution**
>
> Note that it might not be the expected behavior every time. Caution is required, especially when the data is not clean. It may otherwise cause errors that are harder to find than the usual programming errors.

Matrix

Matrix is the higher dimension data structure used for storing n-dimensional data. It is suitable for storing tabular data. Similar to vector, the matrix also allows only homogenous collection of data in its rows and columns.

The following code generates 16 random numbers drawn from a binomial distribution with a parameter, number of trials **(size)** = **100**, and success probability equal to **0.4**. The **rbinom()** method in R is useful for generating such random numbers:

```
r_numbers <- rbinom(n = 16, size = 100, prob = 0.4)
```

Now, to store **r_number** as a matrix, use the following command:

```
matrix(r_numbers, nrow = 4, ncol = 4)
```

The output is as follows:

```
##      [,1] [,2] [,3] [,4]
## [1,]  48   39   37   39
## [2,]  34   41   32   38
## [3,]  40   34   42   46
## [4,]  37   42   36   44
```

Let's extend the text mining example we took in *Exercise 4, Reading a CSV File with Text Column and Storing the Data in VCorpus*, to understand the usage of matrix in text mining.

Consider the following two reviews. Use the **lapply** to type cast the first review to **as.character** and print:

```
lapply(review_corpus[1:2], as.character)
```

The output is as follows:

```
## $'1'
```

```
## [1] "I have bought several of the Vitality canned dog food products and
have found them all to be of good quality. The product looks more like a
stew than a processed meat, and it smells better. My Labrador is finicky, and
she appreciates this product better than  most."
```

```
## $'2'
```

```
## [1] "Product arrived labeled as Jumbo Salted Peanuts...the peanuts were
actually small sized unsalted. Not sure if this was an error or if the
vendor intended to represent the product as \"Jumbo\"."
```

Now, in the following exercise, we will transform the data to remove stopwords, whitespaces, and punctuations from these two paragraphs. We will then perform stemming (both *looking* and *looked* will be reduced to look). Also, for consistency, convert all the text into lowercase.

Exercise 5: Performing Transformation on the Data to Make it Available for the Analysis

In this exercise, we will perform the transformation on the data to make it available for further analysis.

Perform the following steps to complete the exercise:

1. First, use the following commands to convert all the characters in the data to lowercase:

    ```
    top_2_reviews <- review_corpus[1:2]
    top_2_reviews <- tm_map(top_2_reviews,content_transformer(tolower))
    lapply(top_2_reviews[1], as.character)
    ```

    The output is as follows:

    ```
    ## [1] "I have bought several of the vitality canned dog food products and
    have found them all to be of good quality. the product looks more like a
    stew than a processed meat and it smells better. my labrador is finicky,
    and she appreciates this product better than  most."
    ```

2. Next, remove the stopwords from the data, such as, **a**, **the**, **an**, and many more:

    ```
    top_2_reviews <- tm_map(top_2_reviews,removeWords, stopwords("english"))
    lapply(top_2_reviews[1], as.character)
    ```

    The output is as follows:

    ```
    ## [1] "  bought several   vitality canned dog food products    found
    good quality.  product looks   like   stew    processed meat    smells better.
    labrador   finicky   appreciates   product better    ."
    ```

3. Remove extra whitespaces between words using the following command:

    ```
    top_2_reviews <- tm_map(top_2_reviews,stripWhitespace)
    lapply(top_2_reviews[1], as.character)
    ```

    The output is as follows:

    ```
    ## [1] " bought several vitality canned dog food products found good
    quality. product looks like stew processed meat smells better. labrador
    finicky appreciates product better ."
    ```

4. Perform the stemming process, which will only keep the root of the word. For example, **looking** and **looked** will become **look**:

```
top_2_reviews <- tm_map(top_2_reviews,stemDocument)
lapply(top_2_reviews[1], as.character)
```

The output is as follows:

```
## [1] " bought sever vital can dog food product found good quality.
product look like stew process meat smell better. labrador finicki appreci
product better ."
```

Now that we have the text processed and cleaned up, we can create a document matrix that stores merely the frequency of the occurrence of distinct words in the two reviews. We will demonstrate how to count each word contained in the review. Each row of the matrix represents one review, and the columns are distinct words. Most of the values are zero because not all the words will be present in each review. In this example, we have a sparsity of 49%, which means only 51% of the matrix contains non-zero values.

5. Create **Document Term Matrix (DTM)**, in which each row will represent one tweet (also referred to as Doc) and each column a unique word from the corpus:

```
dtm <- DocumentTermMatrix(top_2_reviews)
inspect(dtm)
```

The output is as follows:

```
## <<DocumentTermMatrix (documents: 2, terms: 37)>>
## Non-/sparse entries: 38/36
## Sparsity            : 49%
## Maximal term length: 10
## Weighting           : term frequency (tf)
##
##      Terms
## Docs "jumbo". actual appreci arriv better better. bought can dog error
##    1        0      0       1     0      1       1      1   1   1     0
##    2        |      1       0     1      0       0      0   0   0     1
##      Terms
## Docs finicki food found good intend jumbo label labrador like look meat
##    1       1    1     1    1      0     0     0        1    1    1    1
##    2       0    0     0    0      1     1     1        0    0    0    0
## 0
```

We can use this document term matrix in a plenty of ways. For the sake of the brevity of this introduction to the matrix, we will skip the details of the Document Term Matric here.

The DTM shown in the previous code is in the list format. In order to convert it to the matrix, we can use the **as.matrix()** method again. The matrix contains two documents (reviews) and 37 unique words. The count of a particular word in a document is retrieved by specifying the row and column index or name in the matrix.

6. Now, store the results in a matrix using the following command:

```
dtm_matrix <- as.matrix(dtm)
```

7. To find the dimension of the matrix, that is, 2 documents and 37 words, use the following command:

```
dim(dtm_matrix)
```

The output is as follows:

```
## [1]  2 37
```

8. Now, print a subset of the matrix:

```
dtm_matrix[1:2,1:7]
```

The output is as follows:

```
##      Terms
## Docs "jumbo". actual appreci arriv better better. bought
##    1        0      0       1     0      1       1      1
##    2        1      1       0     1      0       0      0
```

9. Finally, count the word **product** in document 1 using the following command:

```
dtm_matrix[1,"product"]
```

The output is as follows:

```
## [1] 3
```

List

While vector and matrix both are useful structures to be used in various computations in a program, it might not be sufficient for storing a real-world dataset, which most often contains data of mix types, like a customer table in CRM application has the customer name and age together in two columns. The list offers a structure to allow for storing two different types of data together.

In the following exercise, along with generating 16 random numbers, we have used the **sample()** method to generate 16 characters from the English alphabet. The **list** method stores both the integers and characters together.

Exercise 6: Using the List Method for Storing Integers and Characters Together

In this exercise, we will use the **list** method to store randomly generated numbers and characters. The random numbers will be generated using the **rbinom** function, and the random characters will be selected from English alphabets A-Z.

Perform the following steps to complete the exercise:

1. First, generate 16 random numbers drawn from a binomial distribution with parameter size equals **100** and the probability of success equals **0.4**:

   ```
   r_numbers <- rbinom(n = 16, size = 100, prob = 0.4)
   ```

2. Now, select 16 alphabets from English **LETTERS** without repetition:

   ```
   #sample() will generate 16 random letters from the English alphabet
   without repetition
   r_characters <- sample(LETTERS, size = 16, replace = FALSE)
   ```

3. Put **r_numbers** and **r_characters** into a single list. The **list()** function will create the data structure list with **r_numbers** and **r_characters**:

   ```
   list(r_numbers, r_characters)
   ```

   The output is as follows:

   ```
   ## [[1]]
   ##   [1] 48 53 38 31 44 43 36 47 43 38 43 41 45 40 44 50
   ##
   ## [[2]]
   ##   [1] "V" "C" "N" "Z" "E" "L" "A" "Y" "U" "F" "H" "D" "O" "K" "T" "X"
   ```

   In the following step, we will see a list with the integer and character vectors stored together.

4. Now, let's store and retrieve integer and character vectors from a list:

```
r_list <- list(r_numbers, r_characters)
```

5. Next, retrieve values in the character vector using the following command:

```
r_list[[2]]
```

The output is as follows:

```
##   [1] "V" "C" "N" "Z" "E" "L" "A" "Y" "U" "F" "H" "D" "O" "K" "T" "X"
```

6. Finally, retrieve the first value in the character vector:

```
(r_list[[2]])[1]
```

The output is as follows:

```
## [1] "V"
```

Though this solves the requirement of storing heterogeneous data types together, its still doesn't put any integrity checks on the relationship between the values in the two vectors. If we would like to assign every *letter* to one *integer*. In the previous output, **V** represents **48**, **C** represents **53**, and so on.

A list is not robust to handle such one-to-one mapping. Consider the following code, instead of **16** characters, if we generate 18 random characters, and it still allows for storing it in a list. The last two characters have no associated mapping with the integer now.

7. Now, generate 16 random numbers drawn from a binomial distribution with parameter size equal to **100** and probability of success equal to **0.4**:

```
r_numbers <- rbinom(n = 16, size = 100, prob = 0.4)
```

8. Select any 18 alphabets from English **LETTERS** without repetition:

```
r_characters <- sample(LETTERS, 18, FALSE)
```

9. Place **r_numbers** and **r_characters** into a single list:

```
list(r_numbers, r_characters)
```

The output is as follows:

```
## [[1]]
##   [1] 48 53 38 31 44 43 36 47 43 38 43 41 45 40 44 50
##
## [[2]]
##   [1] "V" "C" "N" "Z" "E" "L" "A" "Y" "U" "F" "H" "D" "O" "K" "T" "X"
"P"  "Q"
```

Activity 2: Create a List of Two Matrices and Access the Values

In this activity, you will create two matrices and retrieve a few values using the index of the matrix. You will also perform operations such as multiplication and subtraction.

Perform the following steps to complete the activity:

1. Create two matrices of size **10 x 4** and **4 x 5** by randomly generated numbers from a binomial distribution (use **rbinom** method). Call the matrix **mat_A** and **mat_B**, respectively.

2. Now, store the two matrices in a list.

3. Using the list, access the row 4 and column 2 of **mat_A** and store it in variable **A**, and access row 2 and column 1 of **mat_B** and store it in variable **B**.

4. Multiply the **A** and **B** matrices and subtract from row 2 and column 1 of **mat_A**.

> **Note**
>
> The solution for this activity can be found at page 440.

DataFrame

With the limitation of vector, matrix, and list, a data structure suitable for real-world datasets was a much-needed requirement for data science practitioners. DataFrames are an elegant way of storing and retrieving tabular data. We have already seen how DataFrame handles the rows and columns of data in *Exercise 3, Reading a JSON File and Storing the Data in DataFrame*. DataFrames will be extensively used throughout the book.

Exercise 7: Performing Integrity Checks Using DataFrame

Let's revisit *step 6* of *Exercise 6, Using the List Method for Storing Integers and Characters Together*, where we discussed the integrity check when we attempted to store two unequal length vectors in a list and will see how DataFrame handles it differently. We will, once again, generate random numbers (**r_numbers**) and random characters (**r_characters**).

Perform the following steps to complete the exercise:

1. First, generate 16 random numbers drawn from a binomial distribution with parameter size equal to **100** and probability of success equal to **0.4**:

   ```
   r_numbers <- rbinom(n = 16, size = 100, prob = 0.4)
   ```

2. Select any 18 alphabets from English **LETTERS** without repetition:

   ```
   r_characters <- sample(LETTERS, 18, FALSE)
   ```

3. Put **r_numbers** and **r_characters** into a single DataFrame:

   ```
   data.frame(r_numbers, r_characters)
   ```

   The output is as follows:

   ```
   Error in data.frame(r_numbers, r_characters) :
     arguments imply differing number of rows: 16, 18
   ```

   As you can see, the error in the previous output shows that the last two LETTERS, that is, **P** and **Q**, have no mapping with a corresponding random **INTEGER** generated using the binomial distribution.

Accessing any particular row and column in the DataFrame is similar to the matrix. We will show many tricks and techniques to best use the power of indexing in the DataFrame, which also includes some of the filtering options.

Every row in a DataFrame is a result of the tightly coupled collection of columns. Each column clearly defines the relationship each row of data has with every other one. If there is no corresponding value available in a column, it will be filled with NA. For example, a customer in a CRM application might not have filled their marital status, whereas a few other customers filled it. So, it becomes essential during application design to specify which columns are mandatory and which are optional.

Data Table

With the growing adaption of DataFrame came a time when its limitations started to surface. Particularly with large datasets, DataFrame performs poorly. In the complex analysis, we often create many intermediate DataFrames to store the results. However, R is built on an in-memory computation architecture, and it heavily depends on RAM. Unlike disk space, RAM is limited to either 4 or 8 GB in many standard desktops and laptops. DataFrame is not built efficiently to manage the memory during the computation, which often results in **out of memory error**, especially when working with large datasets.

In order to handle this issue, **data.table** inherited the **data.frame** functionality and offers fast and memory-efficient version for the following task on top of it:

- File reader and writer

- Aggregations

- Updates

- Equi, non-equi, rolling, range, and interval joins

Efficient memory management makes the development fast and reduces the latency between operations. The following exercise shows the significant difference **data.table** makes in computation time as compared to **data.frame**. First, we read the complete **Amazon Food Review** dataset, which is close to 286 MB and contains half a million records (this is quite a big dataset for R), using the **fread()** method, which is one of the fast reading methods from **data.table**.

Exercise 8: Exploring the File Read Operation

In this exercise, we will only show file read operations. You are encouraged to test the other functionalities (https://cran.r-project.org/web/packages/data.table/vignettes/datatable-intro.html) and compare the data table capabilities over DataFrame.

Perform the following steps to complete the exercise:

1. First, load the data table package using the following command:

```
library(data.table)
```

2. Read the dataset using the **fread()** method of the **data.table** package:

```
system.time(fread("Reviews_Full.csv"))
```

The output is as follows:

```
Read 14.1% of 568454 rows
Read 31.7% of 568454 rows
Read 54.5% of 568454 rows
Read 72.1% of 568454 rows
Read 79.2% of 568454 rows
Read 568454 rows and 10 (of 10) columns from 0.280 GB file in 00:00:08
##    user  system elapsed
##    3.62    0.15    3.78
```

3. Now, read the same CSV file using the **read.csv()** method of base package:

```
system.time(read.csv("Reviews_Full.csv"))
```

The output is as follows:

```
##    user  system elapsed
##    4.84    0.05    4.91
```

Observe that **3.78** seconds elapsed for reading it through the **fread()** method, while the **read.csv** function took **4.91** seconds. The execution speed is almost 30% faster. As the size of the data increasing, this difference is even more significant.

In the previous output, the **user** time is the time spent by the current R session, and **system** time is the time spent by the operating system to complete the process. It's possible that you may get a different value after executing the **system.time** method even if you use the same dataset. It depends a lot on how busy your CPU was at the time of running the method. However, we should read the output of the **system.time** method relative to the comparison we are carrying out and not relative to the absolute values.

When the size of the dataset is too large, we have too many intermediate operations to get to the final output. However, keep in mind that **data.table** is not the magic wand that allows us to deal with a dataset of any size in R. The size of RAM still plays a significant role, and **data.table** is no substitute for distributed and parallel processing big data systems. However, even for the smaller dataset, the usage of **data.table** has shown much better performance than **data.frames**.

Data Processing and Transformation

So far, we have seen different ways to read and store data. Now, let's focus on the kind of data processing and transformation required to perform data analysis and draw insights or build models. Data in its raw form is hardly of any use, so it becomes essential to process it to make it suitable for any useful purpose. This section focuses on many methods in R that have widespread usage during data analysis.

cbind

As the name suggests, it combines two or more vector, matrix, DataFrame, or table by column. **cbind** is useful when we have more than one vector, matrix, or DataFrame that need to be combined into one for analysis or visualization. The output of **cbind** varies based on the input data. The following exercise provides a few examples of **cbind**, which combines two vectors.

Exercise 9: Exploring the cbind Function

In this exercise, we will implement the **cbind** function to combine two DataFrame objects.

Perform the following steps to complete the exercise:

1. Generate 16 random numbers drawn from a binomial distribution with parameter size equal to **100** and probability of success equal to **0.4**:

   ```
   r_numbers <- rbinom(n = 16, size = 100, prob = 0.4)
   ```

2. Next, print the **r_numbers** values using the following command:

   ```
   r_numbers
   ```

   The output is as follows:

   ```
   ##  [1] 38 46 40 42 45 39 37 35 44 39 46 41 31 32 34 43
   ```

3. Select any 16 alphabets from English **LETTERS** without repetition:

   ```
   r_characters <- sample(LETTERS, 18, FALSE)
   ```

4. Now, print the **r_characters** values using the following command:

   ```
   r_characters
   ```

   The output is as follows:

   ```
   ##  [1] "C" "K" "Z" "I" "E" "A" "X" "O" "H" "Y" "T" "B" "N" "F" "U" "V"
   "S"
   ## [18] "P"
   ```

5. Combine **r_numbers** and **r_characters** using **cbind**:

   ```
   cbind(r_numbers, r_characters)
   ```

The output is as follows:

```
## Warning in cbind(r_numbers, r_characters): number of rows of result is
not a multiple of vector length (arg 1)
##        r_numbers r_characters
## [1,] "38"       "C"
## [2,] "46"       "K"
## [3,] "40"       "Z"
## [4,] "42"       "I"
## [5,] "45"       "E"
## [6,] "39"       "A"
## [7,] "37"       "X"
## [8,] "35"       "O"
## [9,] "44"       "H"
"
```

6. Print the class (type of data structure) we obtain after using **cbind**:

    ```
    class(cbind(r_numbers, r_characters))
    ```

    The output is as follows:

    ```
    ## [1] "matrix"
    ```

    Observe a warning message in the output of **cbind** in the 5th step of this exercise:

    ```
    number of rows of result is not a multiple of vector length (arg 1)
    r_numbers r_characters
    ```

The error means that the lengths of **r_numbers** and **r_characters** are not same (16 and 18, respectively). Note that the **cbind()** method, unlike **as.data.frame()**, doesn't throw an error. Instead, it automatically performs what is known as **Recycling**, and the vector of shorter length gets recycled. In the output, the **r_numbers 38** and **48** are recycled from the top to fill the 17th and 18th index.

Consider that we write the following command instead:

```
cbind(as.data.frame(r_numbers), as.data.frame(r_characters))
```

It will now throw an error as we had shown earlier in the DataFrame section:

```
Error in data.frame(..., check.names = FALSE) :
  arguments imply differing number of rows: 16, 18
```

One needs to be careful by always checking for the dimensions and the class of data. Otherwise, it may lead to unwanted results. When we give two vectors, it creates a matrix by default on doing a **cbind**.

> **Note**
>
> Since we are not setting any seed value, the output of sample and **rbinom** will differ in each execution of the code.

rbind

rbind is like **cbind**, but it combines by row instead of column. For **rbind** to work, the number of columns should be equal in both the DataFrames. It is useful in cases when we want to append an additional set of observations with an existing dataset where all the columns of the original dataset are the same and are in the same order. Let's explore **rbind** in the following exercise.

Exercise 10: Exploring the rbind Function

In this exercise, we will combine two DataFrames using the **rbind** function.

Perform the following steps to complete the exercise:

1. Generate 16 random numbers drawn from a binomial distribution with parameter size equal to **100** and probability of success equal to 0.4:

   ```
   r_numbers <- rbinom(n = 18, size = 100, prob = 0.4)
   ```

2. Next, print the **r_numbers** values:

   ```
   r_numbers
   ```

   The output is as follows:

   ```
   ##  [1] 38 46 40 42 45 39 37 35 44 39 46 41 31 32 34 43
   ```

3. Select any 16 alphabets from English **LETTERS** without repetition:

   ```
   r_characters <- sample(LETTERS, 18, FALSE)
   ```

4. Now, print the **r_characters** using the following command:

    ```
    r_characters
    ```

    The output is as follows:

    ```
    ##   [1] "C" "K" "Z" "I" "E" "A" "X" "O" "H" "Y" "T" "B" "N" "F" "U" "V"
    "S"
    ## [18] "P"
    ```

5. Finally, use the **rbind** method to print the combined value of **r_numbers** and **r_characters**:

    ```
    rbind(r_numbers, r_characters)
    ```

    The output is as follows:

    ```
    ##                [,1] [,2] [,3] [,4] [,5] [,6] [,7] [,8] [,9] [,10] [,11]
    ## r_numbers     "37" "44" "38" "38" "41" "35" "38" "40" "38" "45"  "37"
    ## r_characters  "Q"  "Y"  "O"  "L"  "A"  "G"  "V"  "S"  "B"  "U"   "D"
    ##                [,12] [,13] [,14] [,15] [,16] [,17] [,18]
    ## r_numbers     "40"  "41"  "42"  "36"  "44"  "37"  "44"
    ## r_characters  "R"   "T"   "P"   "F"   "X"   "C"   "I"
    ```

From the last step, observe that the **rbind** function concatenates (binds) the **r_numbers** and **r_characters** as two rows of data, unlike **cbind**, where it was stacked in two columns. Except for the output, all the other rules of **cbind** apply to **rbind** as well.

The merge Function

The **merge()** function in R is particularly useful when there is more than one DataFrame to join using a common column (what we call a **primary key** in the database world). Merge has two different implementations for the DataFrame and data table, which behave mostly in the same way.

Exercise 11: Exploring the merge Function

In this exercise, we will generate two DataFrames, that is, **df_one** and **df_two**, such that the **r_numbers** column uniquely identifies each row in each of the DataFrame.

Perform the following steps to complete the exercise:

First DataFrame

1. Use the **set.seed()** method to ensure that the same random numbers are generated every time the code is run:

    ```
    set.seed(100)
    ```

2. Next, generate any 16 random numbers between 1 to 30 without repetition:

```
r_numbers <- sample(1:30,10, replace = FALSE)
```

3. Generate any 16 characters from the English alphabet with repetition:

```
r_characters <- sample(LETTERS, 10, TRUE)
```

4. Combine **r_numbers** and **r_characters** into one DataFrame named **df_one**:

```
df_one <- cbind(as.data.frame(r_numbers), as.data.frame(r_characters))
df_one
```

The output is as follows:

```
##      r_numbers r_characters
## 1           10            Q
## 2            8            W
## 3           16            H
## 4            2            K
## 5           13            T
## 6           26            R
## 7           20            F
## 8            9            J
## 9           25            J
## 10           4            R
```

Second DataFrame

1. Use the **set.seed()** method for preserving the same random numbers over multiple runs:

```
set.seed(200)
```

2. Next, generate any 16 random numbers between 1 to 30 without repetition:

```
r_numbers <- sample(1:30,10, replace = FALSE)
```

3. Now, generate any 16 characters from the English alphabet with repetition:

```
r_characters <- sample(LETTERS, 10, TRUE)
```

4. Combine **r_numbers** and **r_characters** into one DataFrame named **df_two**:

```
df_two <- cbind(as.data.frame(r_numbers), as.data.frame(r_characters))
df_two
```

The output is as follows:

```
##      r_numbers r_characters
## 1          17            L
## 2          30            Q
## 3          29            D
## 4          19            Q
## 5          18            J
## 6          21            H
## 7          26            O
## 8           3            D
## 9          12            X
## 10          5            Q
```

Once we create the **df_one** and **df_two** DataFrames using the **cbind()** function, we are ready to perform some merge (will use the word JOIN, which means the same as **merge()**).

Now, let's see how different type of joins give different results.

In the world of databases, JOINs are used to combine two or more than two tables using a common primary key. In databases, we use Structured Query Language (SQL) to perform the JOINs. In R, the **merge()** function helps us with the same functionality as SQL offers in databases. Also, instead of tables, we have DataFrames here, which is again a table with rows and columns of data.

Inner Join

In *Exercise 11, Exploring the merge Function*, we created two DataFrames: **df_one** and **df_two**. We will now join the two DataFrames using **Inner Join**. Observe that only the value **26** (row number **7**) in the **r_numbers** column is common between the two DataFrames, where the corresponding character in the **r_characters** column is **R** in **df_one** and character **O** in **df_two**. In the output, **X** corresponds to the **df_one** DataFrame and **Y** correspond to the **df_two** DataFrame.

To merge the **df_one** and **df_two** DataFrames using the **r_numbers** column, use the following command:

```
merge(df_one, df_two, by = "r_numbers")
##      r_numbers r_characters.x r_characters.y
## 1           26              R              O
```

Left Join

Left Join gives all the values of **df_one** in the **r_numbers** column and adds **<NA>** as a value wherever the corresponding value in **df_two** is not found. For example, for **r_number = 2**, there is no value in **df_two**, whereas for **r_number = 26**, values in **df_one** and **df_two**, for the **r_characters** column is **R** and **0**, respectively.

To merge the **df_one** and **df_two** DataFrames using the **r_numbers** column, use the following command:

```
merge(df_one, df_two, by = "r_numbers", all.x = TRUE)
##    r_numbers r_characters.x r_characters.y
## 1          2              K           <NA>
## 2          4              R           <NA>
## 3          8              W           <NA>
## 4          9              J           <NA>
## 5         10              Q           <NA>
## 6         13              T           <NA>
## 7         16              H           <NA>
## 8         20              F           <NA>
## 9         25              J           <NA>
## 10        26              R              0
```

Right Join

Right Joins works just like Left Join, except for that the values in the **r_character** columns of **df_one** are **<NA>** wherever a match is not found. Again, **r_numbers = 26** is the only match.

To merge the **df_one** and **df_two** DataFrames using the **r_numbers** column, use the following command:

```
merge(df_one, df_two, by = "r_numbers", all.y = TRUE)
##     r_numbers r_characters.x r_characters.y
## 1          3           <NA>              D
## 2          5           <NA>              Q
## 3         12           <NA>              X
## 4         17           <NA>              L
## 5         18           <NA>              J
## 6         19           <NA>              Q
## 7         21           <NA>              H
## 8         26              R              O
## 9         29           <NA>              D
## 10        30           <NA>              Q
```

Full Join

Unlike Left and Right Join, **Full Join** gives all the unique values of the **r_numbers** column from both the DataFrames and adds **<NA>** in the **r_characters** column from the respective DataFrame. Observe that only the **r_number** = **26** row has values from both the DataFrame.

To merge the **df_one** and **df_two** DataFrames using the **r_numbers** column, use the following command:

```
merge(df_one, df_two, by = "r_numbers", all = TRUE)
##     r_numbers r_characters.x r_characters.y
## 1          2              K           <NA>
## 2          3           <NA>              D
## 3          4              R           <NA>
## 4          5           <NA>              Q
## 5          8              W           <NA>
## 6          9              J           <NA>
## 7         10              Q           <NA>
```

## 8	12	<NA>	X
## 9	13	T	<NA>
## 10	16	H	<NA>
## 11	17	<NA>	L
## 12	18	<NA>	J
## 13	19	<NA>	Q

...

The reshape Function

Data is known to be in a **wide** format if each subject has only a single row, with each measurement present as a different variable or column. Similarly, it is a **long** format if each measurement has a single observation (thus, multiple rows per subject). The reshape function is used often to convert between wide and long formats for a variety of operations to make the data useful for computation or analysis. In many visualizations, we use `reshape()` to convert wide format to long and vice versa.

We will use the Iris dataset. This dataset contains variables named `Sepal.Length`, `Sepal.Width`, `Petal.Length`, and `Petal.Width`, whose measurements are given in centimeters, for 50 flowers from each of 3 species of Iris, namely *setosa*, *versicolor*, and *virginica*.

Exercise 12: Exploring the reshape Function

In this exercise, we will explore the reshape function.

Perform the following steps to complete the exercise:

1. First, print the top five rows of the iris dataset using the following command:

   ```
   head(iris)
   ```

   The output of the previous command is as follows:

   ```
   ##   Sepal.Length Sepal.Width Petal.Length Petal.Width Species
   ## 1          5.1         3.5          1.4         0.2  setosa
   ## 2          4.9         3.0          1.4         0.2  setosa
   ## 3          4.7         3.2          1.3         0.2  setosa
   ## 4          4.6         3.1          1.5         0.2  setosa
   ## 5          5.0         3.6          1.4         0.2  setosa
   ## 6          5.4         3.9          1.7         0.4  setosa
   ```

2. Now, create a variable called **Type** based on the following condition. When **Sepal. Width > 2** and **Sepal Width <= 3**, we will assign **TYPE 1** or **TYPE 2**. The type column is for demo purpose only and has no particular logic:

```
iris$Type <- ifelse((iris$Sepal.Width>2 & iris$Sepal.Width <=3),"TYPE
1","TYPE 2")
```

3. Store the **Type**, **Sepal.Width**, and **Species** columns in the **df_iris** DataFrame:

```
df_iris <- iris[,c("Type","Sepal.Width","Species")]
```

4. Next, reshape **df_iris** into wide DataFrame using the following **reshape** command:

```
reshape(df_iris,idvar = "Species", timevar = "Type", direction = "wide")
```

The output is as follows:

```
##          Species Sepal.Width.TYPE 2 Sepal.Width.TYPE 1
## 1         setosa                3.5                3.0
## 51    versicolor                3.2                2.3
## 101    virginica                3.3                2.7
```

You will get a warning while running the **reshape** command, saying as follows:

```
multiple rows match for Type=TYPE 2: first taken multiple rows match for
Type=TYPE 1: first taken
```

This warning means there were multiple values for **Type 1** and **Type 2** for the three species, so the reshape has picked the first occurrence of each of the species. In this case, the **1**, **51**, and **101** row numbers. We will now see how we could handle this transformation better in the **aggregate** function.

The aggregate Function

Aggregation is a useful method for computing statistics such as count, averages, standard deviations, and quartiles, and it also allows for writing a custom function. In the following code, the formula (formula is a name of the data structure in R, not a mathematical equation) for each Iris species computes the mean of the numeric measures sepal and petal width and length. The first of the aggregate function argument is a formula that takes species and all the other measurements to compute the mean from all the observations.

```
aggregate(formula =. ~ Species, data = iris, FUN = mean)
```

The output of the previous command is as follows:

```
##       Species Sepal.Length Sepal.Width Petal.Length Petal.Width
## 1      setosa        5.006       3.428        1.462       0.246
## 2  versicolor        5.936       2.770        4.260       1.326
## 3   virginica        6.588       2.974        5.552       2.026
```

The Apply Family of Functions

If one has to debate on a few powerful features of R programming, the **apply** family of functions, would find a mention. It is used commonly to avoid using looping structures such as **for** and **while** even though they are available in R.

First, it's slow to run **for** loops in R and second, the implementation of the **apply** functions in R is based on efficient programming languages such as C/C++, which makes it extremely fast to loop.

There are many functions in the **apply** family. Depending on the structure of the input and output required, we select the appropriate function:

- **apply()**
- **lapply()**
- **sapply()**
- **vapply()**
- **mapply()**
- **rapply()**
- **tapply()**

We will discuss a few in this section.

The apply Function

The **apply()** function takes an array, including a matrix, as input and returns a vector, array, or list of values obtained by applying a function to margins of an array or matrix.

Exercise 13: Implementing the apply Function

In this exercise, we will count the number of vowels in each column of a 100 x 100 matrix of random letters from the English alphabet. The **MARGIN = 1** function will scan each row, and **MARGIN = 2** will specify the column. The same function will the count vowels in each row.

Perform the following steps to complete the exercise:

1. Create a 100 x 100 matrix of random letters (**ncol** is the number of columns and **nrow** is the number of rows) using the following command:

```
r_characters <- matrix(sample(LETTERS, 10000, replace = TRUE), ncol = 100,
nrow = 100)
```

2. Now, create a function named **c_vowel** to count the number of vowels in a given array:

```
c_vowel <- function(x_char){
  return(sum(x_char %in% c("A","I","O","U")))
}
```

3. Next, use the **apply** function to run through each column of the matrix, and use the **c_vowel** function as illustrated here:

```
apply(r_characters, MARGIN = 2, c_vowel)
```

The output is as follows:

```
##   [1] 17 16 10 11 12 25 16 14 14 12 20 13 16 14 14 20 10 12 11 16 10 20
15
##  [24] 10 14 13 17 14 14 13 15 19 18 21 15 13 19 21 24 18 13 20 15 15 15
19
##  [47] 13  6 18 11 16 16 11 13 20 14 12 17 11 14 14 16 13 11 23 14 17 14
22
##  [70] 11 18 10 18 21 19 14 18 12 13 15 16 10 15 19 14 13 16 15 12 12 14
10
##  [93] 16 16 20 16 13 22 15 15
```

The lapply Function

The **lapply** function looks similar to **apply()**, with a difference that it takes input as a *list* and returns a *list* as output. After rewriting our previous example in the following exercise, the output of class function shows that the output is a list.

Exercise 14: Implementing the lapply Function

In this exercise, we will take a list of vectors and count the number of vowels.

Perform the following steps to complete the exercise:

1. Create a list with two vector of random letters, each of size 100:

    ```
    r_characters <- list(a=sample(LETTERS, 100, replace = TRUE),
                          b=sample(LETTERS, 100, replace = TRUE))
    ```

2. Use the **lapply** function to run through on list **a** and **b**, and the **c_vowel** function to count the number of vowels from the list:

    ```
    lapply(r_characters, c_vowel)
    ```

    The output is as follows:

    ```
    ## $a
    ## [1] 19
    ## $b
    ## [1] 10
    ```

3. Check the class (type) of the output. The **class()** function provides the type of data structure:

    ```
    out_list <- lapply(r_characters, c_vowel)
    class(out_list)
    ```

    The output is as follows:

    ```
    ## [1] "list"
    ```

The sapply Function

The **sapply** function is just a wrapper on the **lapply** function, where the output is a vector or matrix instead of a list. In the following code, observe the type of the output after applying **sapply** difference. The output returns a vector of integers, as we can check with the **class()** function:

```
sapply(r_characters, c_vowel)
```

```
##  a  b
```

```
## 19 10
```

To print the class of the output, use the following command:

```
out_vector <- sapply(r_characters, c_vowel)
class(out_vector)
```

The output of the previous command is as follows:

```
## [1] "integer"
```

The tapply Function

Apply a function to each cell of a ragged array, that is, to each (non-empty) group of values given by a unique combination of the levels of certain factors. The **tapply** function is quite useful when it comes to working on a subset level of data. For example, in our **aggregate** function, if we were to get an aggregate like standard deviation for the type of Iris species, we could use **tapply**. The following code shows how to use the **tapply** function:

First, calculate the standard deviation of sepal length for each Iris species:

```
tapply(iris$Sepal.Length, iris$Species,sd)
```

The output is as follows:

```
##     setosa versicolor  virginica
##  0.3524897  0.5161711  0.6358796
```

Next, calculate the standard deviation of sepal width for each of the Iris species:

```
tapply(iris$Sepal.Width, iris$Species,sd)
```

The output of the previous command is as follows:

```
##     setosa versicolor  virginica
##  0.3790644  0.3137983  0.3224966
```

Now, let's explore some popular and useful R packages that might be of value while building complex data processing methods, machine learning models, or data visualization.

Useful Packages

While there are more than thirteen thousand packages in the CRAN repository, some of the packages have a unique place and utility for some major functionality. So far, we saw many examples of data manipulations such as join, aggregate, reshaping, and sub-setting. The R packages we will discuss next will provide a plethora of functions, providing a wide range of data processing and transformation capabilities.

The dplyr Package

The **dplyr** package helps in the most common data manipulation challenges through five different methods, namely, **mutate()**, **select()**, **filter()**, **summarise()**, and **arrange()**. Let's revisit our direct marketing campaigns (phone calls) of a Portuguese banking institution dataset from UCI Machine Learning Repository to test out all these methods.

The **%>%** symbol in the following exercise is called **chain operator**. The output of the one operation is sent to the next one without explicitly creating a new variable. Such a chaining operation is storage efficient and makes the readability of the code easy.

Exercise 15: Implementing the dplyr Package

In this exercise, we are interested in knowing the average bank balance of people doing blue-collar jobs by their marital status. Use the functions from the **dplyr** package to get the answer.

Perform the following steps to complete the exercise:

1. Import the **bank-full.csv** file into the **df_bank_detail** object using the **read.csv()** function:

    ```
    df_bank_detail <- read.csv("bank-full.csv", sep = ';')
    ```

2. Now, load the **dplyr** library:

    ```
    library(dplyr)
    ```

3. Select (filter) all the observations where the **job** column contains the value **blue-collar** and then group by the martial status to generate the summary statistic, **mean**:

    ```
    df_bank_detail %>%
      filter(job == "blue-collar") %>%
      group_by(marital) %>%
      summarise(
        cnt = n(),
        average = mean(balance, na.rm = TRUE)
      )
    ```

The output is as follows:

```
## # A tibble: 3 x 3
##     marital   cnt   average
##     <fctr> <int>     <dbl>
## 1 divorced   750  820.8067
## 2  married  6968 1113.1659
## 3   single  2014 1056.1053
```

4. Let's find out the bank balance of customers with secondary education and default as **yes**:

```
df_bank_detail %>%
  mutate(sec_edu_and_default = ifelse((education == "secondary" & default
== "yes"), "yes","no")) %>%
  select(age, job, marital,balance, sec_edu_and_default) %>%
  filter(sec_edu_and_default == "yes") %>%
  group_by(marital) %>%
  summarise(
    cnt = n(),
    average = mean(balance, na.rm = TRUE)
  )
```

The output is as follows:

```
## # A tibble: 3 x 3
##     marital   cnt    average
##     <fctr> <int>      <dbl>
## 1 divorced    64   -8.90625
## 2  married   243  -74.46914
## 3   single   151 -217.43046
```

Much of complex analysis is done with ease. Note that the `mutate()` method helps in creating custom columns with certain calculation or logic.

The tidyr Package

The **tidyr** package has three essential functions—**gather()**, **separate()**, and **spread()**— for cleaning messy data.

The **gather()** function converts **wide** DataFrame to long by taking multiple columns and gathering them into key-value pairs.

Exercise 16: Implementing the tidyr Package

In this exercise, we will explore the **tidyr** package and the functions associated with it.

Perform the following steps to complete the exercise:

1. Import the **tidyr** library using the following command:

   ```
   library(tidyr)
   ```

2. Next, set the **seed** to 100 using the following command:

   ```
   set.seed(100)
   ```

3. Create an **r_name** object and store the 5 person names in it:

   ```
   r_name <- c("John", "Jenny", "Michael", "Dona", "Alex")
   ```

4. For the **r_food_A** object, generate 16 random numbers between 1 to 30 without repetition:

   ```
   r_food_A <- sample(1:150,5, replace = FALSE)
   ```

5. Similarly, for the **r_food_B** object, generate 16 random numbers between 1 to 30 without repetition:

   ```
   r_food_B <- sample(1:150,5, replace = FALSE)
   ```

6. Create and print the data from the DataFrame using the following command:

   ```
   df_untidy <- data.frame(r_name, r_food_A, r_food_B)
   df_untidy
   ```

   The output is as follows:

   ```
   ##      r_name r_food_A r_food_B
   ## 1      John       47       73
   ## 2     Jenny       39      122
   ## 3   Michael       82       55
   ## 4      Dona        9       81
   ## 5      Alex       69       25
   ```

7. Use the **gather()** method from the **tidyr** package:

   ```
   df_long <- df_untidy %>%
     gather(food, calories, r_food_A:r_food_B)
   df_long
   ```

The output is as follows:

```
##       r_name      food calories
## 1       John r_food_A       47
## 2      Jenny r_food_A       39
## 3    Michael r_food_A       82
## 4       Dona r_food_A        9
## 5       Alex r_food_A       69
## 6       John r_food_B       73
## 7      Jenny r_food_B      122
## 8    Michael r_food_B       55
## 9       Dona r_food_B       81
## 10      Alex r_food_B       25
```

8. The **spread()** function works the other way around of **gather()**, that is, it takes a long format and converts it into wide format:

```
df_long %>%
   spread(food,calories)
##       r_name r_food_A r_food_B
## 1      Alex       69       25
## 2      Dona        9       81
## 3     Jenny       39      122
## 4      John       47       73
## 5 Michael       82       55
```

9. The **separate()** function is useful in places where columns are a combination of values and is used for making it a key column for other purposes. We can separate out the key if it has a common separator character:

```
key <- c("John.r_food_A", "Jenny.r_food_A", "Michael.r_food_A", "Dona.r_
food_A", "Alex.r_food_A", "John.r_food_B", "Jenny.r_food_B", "Michael.r_
food_B", "Dona.r_food_B", "Alex.r_food_B")
calories <- c(74, 139, 52, 141, 102, 134, 27, 94, 146, 20)
df_large_key <- data.frame(key,calories)
df_large_key
```

The output is as follows:

```
##                    key calories
## 1        John.r_food_A       74
## 2       Jenny.r_food_A      139
## 3     Michael.r_food_A       52
## 4        Dona.r_food_A      141
## 5        Alex.r_food_A      102
## 6        John.r_food_B      134
## 7       Jenny.r_food_B       27
## 8     Michael.r_food_B       94
## 9        Dona.r_food_B      146
## 10       Alex.r_food_B       20
df_large_key %>%
  separate(key, into = c("name","food"), sep = "\\.")
##         name       food calories
## 1       John   r_food_A       74
## 2      Jenny   r_food_A      139
## 3    Michael   r_food_A       52
## 4       Dona   r_food_A      141
## 5       Alex   r_food_A      102
## 6       John   r_food_B      134
## 7      Jenny   r_food_B       27
## 8    Michael   r_food_B       94
## 9       Dona   r_food_B      146
## 10      Alex   r_food_B       20
```

Activity 3: Create a DataFrame with Five Summary Statistics for All Numeric Variables from Bank Data Using dplyr and tidyr

This activity will make you accustomed to selecting all numeric fields from the bank data and produce the summary statistics on numeric variables.

Perform the following steps to complete the activity:

1. Extract all numeric variables from bank data using **select()**.

2. Using the **summarise_all()** method, compute min, 1st quartile, 3rd quartile, median, mean, max, and standard deviation.

> **Note**
>
> You can learn more about the **summarise_all** function at https://www. rdocumentation.org/packages/dplyr/versions/0.5.0/topics/summarise_all.

3. Store the result in a DataFrame of wide format named **df_wide**.

4. Now, to convert wide format to deep, use the gather, separate, and spread functions of the **tidyr** package.

5. The final output should have one row for each variable and one column each of min, 1st quartile, 3rd quartile, median, mean, max, and standard deviation.

   Once you complete the activity, you should have the final output as follows:

```
## # A tibble: 4 x 8
##           var   min   q25 median   q75    max       mean          sd
## *       <chr> <dbl> <dbl>  <dbl> <dbl>  <dbl>      <dbl>       <dbl>
## 1         age    18    33     39    48     95   40.93621    10.61876
## 2     balance -8019    72    448  1428 102127 1362.27206 3044.76583
## 3    duration     0   103    180   319   4918  258.16308  257.52781
## 4       pdays    -1    -1     -1    -1    871   40.19783  100.12875
```

> **Note**
>
> The solution for this activity can be found on page 440.

The plyr Package

What we saw with the **apply** functions could be done through the **plyr** package on a much bigger scale and robustness. The **plyr** package provides the ability to split the dataset into subsets, apply a common function to each subset, and combine the results into a single output. The advantage of using **plyr** over the **apply** function is features like the following:

- Speed of code execution
- Parallelization of processing using **foreach** loop
- Support for list, DataFrame, and matrices
- Better debugging of errors

All the function names in **plyr** are clearly defined based on input and output. For example, if an input is a DataFrame and output is list, the function name would be **dlply**.

The following figure from the *The Split-Apply-Combine Strategy for Data Analysis* paper displays all the different **plyr** functions:

Input \ Output	Array	Data frame	List	Discarded
Array	aaply	adply	alply	a_ply
Data frame	daply	ddply	dlply	d_ply
List	laply	ldply	llply	l_ply

Figure 1.7: Functions in the plyr packages

The _ means the output will be discarded.

Exercise 17: Exploring the plyr Package

In this exercise, we will see how split-apply-combine makes things simple with the flexibility of controlling the input and output.

Perform the following steps to complete the exercise:

1. Load the **plyr** package using the following command:

```
library(plyr)
```

2. Next, use the slightly tweaked version of the **c_vowel** function we created in the earlier example in *Exercise 13, Exploring the apply Function*:

```
c_vowel <- function(x_char){
    return(sum(as.character(x_char[,"b"]) %in% c("A","I","O","U")))
}
```

3. Set the **seed** to **101**:

```
set.seed(101)
```

4. Store the value in the **r_characters** object:

```
r_characters <- data.frame(a=rep(c("Split_1","Split_2","Split_3"),1000),
                    b= sample(LETTERS, 3000, replace = TRUE))
```

> **Note**
>
> `Input = DataFrame to output = list`

5. Use the **dlply()** function and print the split in the row format:

```
dlply(r_characters, c_vowel)
```

The output is as follows:

```
## $Split_1
## [1] 153
##
## $Split_2
## [1] 154
##
## $Split_3
## [1] 147
```

> **Note**
>
> `Input = data.frame to output = array`

6. We can simply replace dlply with the **daply()** function and print the split in the column format as an array:

```
daply(r_characters, c_vowel)
```

The output is as follows:

```
## Split_1 Split_2 Split_3
##     153     154     147
```

> **Note**
>
> Input = DataFrame to output = DataFrame

7. Use the **ddply()** function and print the split:

```
ddply(r_characters, c_vowel)
```

The output is as follows:

```
##          a  V1
## 1 Split_1 153
## 2 Split_2 154
## 3 Split_3 147
```

In steps 5, 6, and 7, observe how we created a list, array, and data as an output for DataFrame input. All we must do is use a different function from **plyr**. This makes it easy to type cast between many possible combinations.

The caret Package

The **caret** package is particularly useful for building a predictive model, and it provides a structure for seamlessly following the entire process of building a predictive model. Starting from splitting data to training and testing dataset and variable importance estimation, we will extensively use the **caret** package in our chapters on regression and classification. In summary, **caret** provides tools for:

- Data splitting
- Pre-processing
- Feature selection
- Model training
- Model tuning using resampling
- Variable importance estimation

We will revisit the caret package with examples in *Chapter 4, Regression*, and *Chapter 5, Classification*.

Data Visualization

An essential part of what we call **Exploratory Data Analysis (EDA)**, more on this in *Chapter 2, Exploratory Analysis of Data*, is the ability to visualize data in a way that communicates insights elegantly and makes storytelling far more comprehensible. Not only does data visualization help us in communicating better insights, but it also helps with spotting anomalies. Before we get there, let's look at some of the most common visualizations that we often use in data analysis. All the examples in this section will be in **ggplot2**, a powerful package in R. Just like **dplyr** and **plyr**, **ggplot2** is built on the **Grammar of Graphics**, which is a tool that enables us to describe the components of a graphic concisely.

> **Note**
>
> Good grammar will allow us to gain insight into the composition of complicated graphics and reveal unexpected connections between seemingly different graphics.
>
> (Cox 1978) [Cox, D. R. (1978), "Some Remarks on the Role in Statistics of Graphical Methods," Applied Statistics, 27 (1), 4–9. [3,26].

Scatterplot

A scatterplot is a type of plot or mathematical diagram using Cartesian coordinates to display values for typically two variables for a set of data. If the points are color-coded, an additional variable can be displayed.

It is the most common type of chart and is extremely useful in spotting patterns in the data, especially between two variables. We will use our bank data again to do some EDA. Let's use the Portuguese bank direct campaign dataset for the visualizations:

```
df_bank_detail <- read.csv("bank-full.csv", sep = ';')
```

ggplot works in a layered way of stacking different elements of the plot. In the following example of this section, in the first layer, we provide the data to the **ggplot()** method and then map it with aesthetic details like *x* and *y*-axis, in the example, the **age** and **balance** values, respectively. Finally, to be able to identify some reasoning associated with few high bank balances, we added a color based on the type of job.

Execute the following command to plot the scatterplot of age and balance:

```
ggplot(data = df_bank_detail) +
  geom_point(mapping = aes(x = age, y = balance, color = job))
```

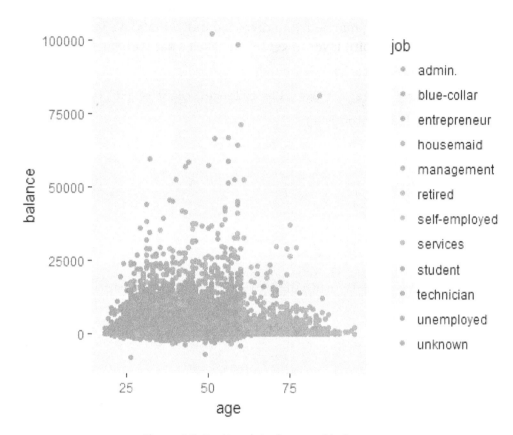

Figure 1.8: Scatterplot of age and balance.

From *Figure* 1.8, the distribution of bank balance with age looks much normal, with middle age showing a high bank balance whereas youngsters and old people are on the lower side of the spectrum.

Interestingly, some outlier values seem to be coming from management and retired professionals.

In data visualization, it's always tempting to see a graph and jump to a conclusion. A data visual is for consuming the data better and not for drawing causal inference. Usually, an interpretation by an analyst is always vetted by a business. Graphs that are aesthetically pleasing often tempt you to put it into presentation deck. So, next time a beautiful chart gets into your presentation deck, carefully analyze what you are going to say.

Scatter Plot between Age and Balance split by Marital Status

In this section, we will draw three scatter plots in a single plot between age and balance split by marital status (one for each single, divorced, and married individuals).

Now, you could split the distribution by marital status. The patterns seem to be consistent among the single, married, and divorced individuals. We used a method called `facet_wrap()` as the third layer in **ggplot**. It takes a `marital` variable as a formula:

```
ggplot(data = df_bank_detail) +
  geom_point(mapping = aes(x = age, y = balance, color = job)) +
  facet_wrap(~ marital, nrow = 1)
```

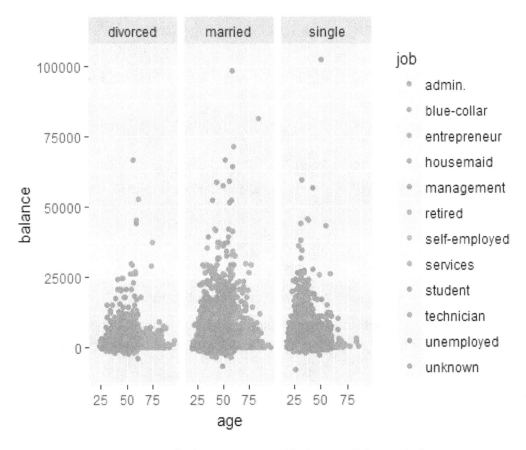

Figure 1.9: Scatter plot between age and balance split by marital status

Line Charts

A line chart or line graph is a type of chart that displays information as a series of data points called **markers** connected by straight line segments.

ggplot uses an elegant **geom()** method, which helps in quickly switching between two visual objects. In the previous example, we saw **geom_point()** for the scatterplot. In line charts, the observations are connected by a line in the order of the variable on the x-axis. The shaded area surrounding the line represents the 95% confidence interval, that is, there is 95% confidence that the actual regression line lies within the shaded area. We will discuss more on this idea in *Chapter 4, Regression*.

In the following plot, we show the line chart of age and bank balance for single, married, and divorced individuals. It is not clear whether there is some trend, but one can see the pattern among the three categories:

```
ggplot(data = df_bank_detail) +
   geom_smooth(mapping = aes(x = age, y = balance, linetype = marital))
## 'geom_smooth()' using method = 'gam'
```

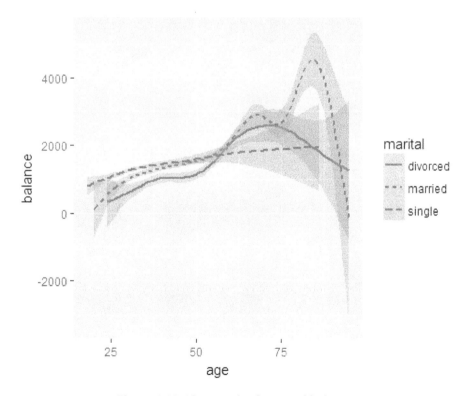

Figure 1.10: Line graph of age and balance

Histogram

A histogram is a visualization consisting of rectangles whose area is proportional to the frequency of a variable and whose width is equal to the class interval.

The height of the bar in a histogram represents the number of observations in each group. In the following example, we are counting the number of observations for each type of job and marital status. **y** is a binary variable checking whether the client subscribed a term deposit or not (**yes**, **no**) as a response to the campaign call.

It looks like blue-collar individuals are responding to the campaign calls the least, and individuals in management jobs are subscribing to the term deposit the most:

```
ggplot(data = df_bank_detail) +
  geom_bar(mapping = aes(x=job, fill = y)) +
  theme(axis.text.x = element_text(angle=90, vjust=.8, hjust=0.8))
```

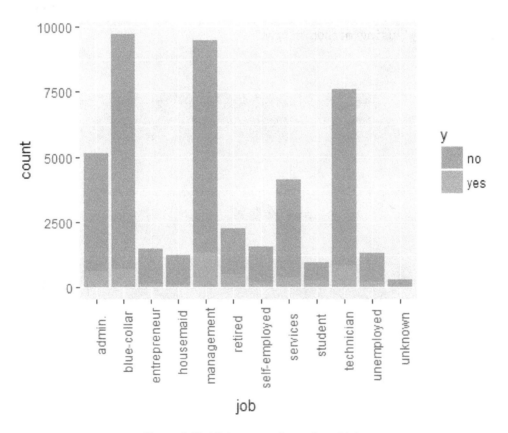

Figure 1.11: Histogram of count and job

Boxplot

A boxplot is a standardized way of displaying the distribution of data based on a five number summary (minimum, first quartile (Q1), median, third quartile (Q3), and maximum). Probably, boxplot is the only chart that encapsulates much information in a beautiful looking representation compared to any other charts. Observe the summary of the **age** variable by each **job** type. The five summary statistics, that is, min, first quartile, median, mean, third quartile, and max, are described succinctly by a boxplot.

The 25th and 75th percentiles, in the first and third quartiles, are shown by lower and upper hinges, respectively. The upper whisker, which extends from the hinges to the maximum value, is within an IQR of 1.5 *, from the hinge. This is where the IQR is the inter-quartile range or distance between the two quartiles. This is similar in case of the lower hinge. All the points that are outside the hinges are called **outliers**:

```
tapply(df_bank_detail$age, df_bank_detail$job, summary)
```

The output is as follows:

```
## $admin.
##     Min. 1st Qu.  Median    Mean 3rd Qu.    Max.
##    20.00   32.00   38.00   39.29   46.00   75.00
##
## $'blue-collar'
##     Min. 1st Qu.  Median    Mean 3rd Qu.    Max.
##    20.00   33.00   39.00   40.04   47.00   75.00
##
## $entrepreneur
##     Min. 1st Qu.  Median    Mean 3rd Qu.    Max.
##    21.00   35.00   41.00   42.19   49.00   84.00
##
## $housemaid
##     Min. 1st Qu.  Median    Mean 3rd Qu.    Max.
##    22.00   38.00   47.00   46.42   55.00   83.00
##
## $management
```

```
##      Min. 1st Qu.  Median    Mean 3rd Qu.    Max.
##     21.00   33.00   38.00   40.45   48.00   81.00
##
## $retired
##      Min. 1st Qu.  Median    Mean 3rd Qu.    Max.
##     24.00   56.00   59.00   61.63   67.00   95.00
##
## $'self-employed'
##      Min. 1st Qu.  Median    Mean 3rd Qu.    Max.
##     22.00   33.00   39.00   40.48   48.00   76.00
##
0
```

In the following boxplot, we are looking at the summary of age with respect to each job type. The size of the box that is set to **varwidth = TRUE** in **geom_boxplot** shows the number of observations in the particular job type. The wider the box, the larger the number of observations:

```
ggplot(data = df_bank_detail, mapping = aes(x=job, y = age, fill = job)) +
   geom_boxplot(varwidth = TRUE) +
   theme(axis.text.x = element_text(angle=90, vjust=.8, hjust=0.8))
```

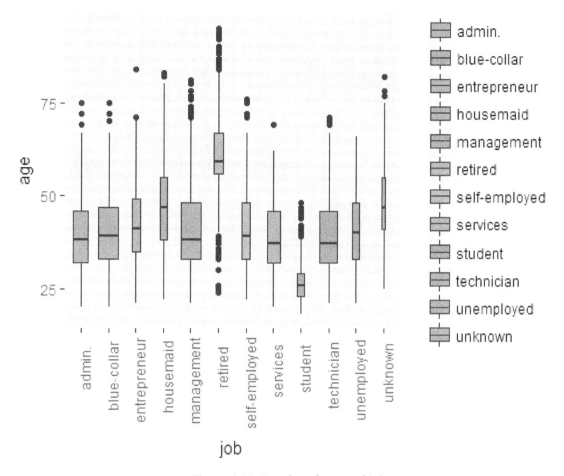

Figure 1.12: Boxplot of age and job

Summary

In this chapter, we visited some basics of R programming data types, data structures, and important functions and packages. We described vectors, matrix, list, DataFrame, and data tables as different forms of storing data. In the data processing and transformation space, we explore the **cbind**, **rbind**, `merge`, `reshape`, `aggregate`, and `apply` family of functions.

We also discussed the most important packages in R such as **dplyr**, `tidyr`, and `plyr`. In the end, the `ggplot2` data visualization package was used to demonstrate various types of visualization and how to draw insights from them.

In the next chapter, we will use all that you have learned in this chapter for performing Exploratory Data Analysis (EDA). In EDA, data transformation and visualization you learned here will be useful for drawing inferences from data.

Exploratory Analysis of Data

Learning Objectives

By the end of this chapter, you will be able to:

- Define a problem statement with industry standard frameworks
- Perform univariate and bivariate analysis
- Explain multivariate analysis
- Perform hypothesis testing
- Perform data wrangling using the dplyr and reshape2 packages
- Visualize data using the ggplot2 package

In this chapter, we will acquaint learners with techniques to clean, transform, and visualize data in order to get useful insights.

Introduction

Chapter 1, R for Advanced Analytics, introduced to you the R language and its ecosystem for data science. We are now ready to enter a crucial part of data science and machine learning, that is, **Exploratory Data Analysis (EDA)**, the art of understanding the data.

In this chapter, we will approach EDA with the same banking dataset used in the previous chapter, but in a more problem-centric way. We will start by defining the problem statement with industry standard artifacts, design a solution for the problem, and learn how EDA fits in the larger problem framework. We will then tackle the EDA for the direct marketing campaigns (phone calls) of a Portuguese banking institution use case using a combination of data engineering, data wrangling, and data visualization techniques in R, backed up by a business-centric approach.

In any data science use case, understanding the data consumes the bulk of the time and effort. Most data science professionals spend around 80% of their time understanding data. Given that this is the most crucial part of your journey, it is important to have a macro-view of the overall process for any data science use case.

A typical data science use case takes the path of a core business-analytics problem or a machine-learning problem. With either path approached, EDA is inevitable. *Figure 2.1* demonstrates the life cycle of a basic data science use case. It starts by defining the problem statement using one or more standard frameworks, and then it delves into data gathering and reaches EDA. The majority of efforts and time in any project is consumed in EDA. Once the process of understanding the data is complete, a project may take a different path based on the scope of the use case. In most business analytics-based use cases, the next step is to assimilate all the observed patterns into meaningful insights. Though this might sound trivial, it is an iterative and arduous task. This step then evolves into story-telling, where the condensed insights are tailored into a meaningful story for the business stakeholders. Similarly, in scenarios where the objective is to develop a predictive model, the next step would be to actually develop a machine learning model and then deploy it into a production system/product.

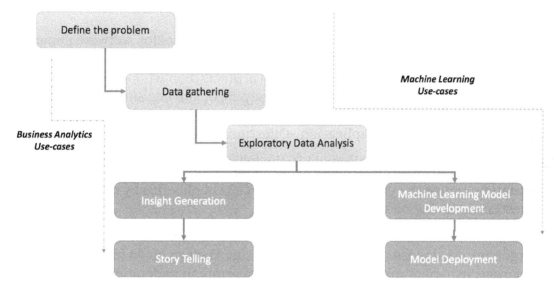

Figure 2.1: Life cycle of a data science use case

Let's take a brief look at the first step, *Defining the Problem Statement.*

Defining the Problem Statement

If you recollect the data we explored in *Chapter 1, R for Advanced Analytics*, bank marketing data, we have a dataset that captures the telemarketing campaigns conducted by a bank to attract customers.

A large multinational bank is designing a marketing campaign to achieve its growth target by enticing customers for bank deposits. The campaign has been ineffective in luring customers, and the marketing team wants to understand how the campaign can be improved to achieve the growth targets.

We can reframe the problem from the business stakeholders' perspective and try to see what kind of solution would best fit here.

Problem-Designing Artifacts

Just like there are several frameworks, templates, and artifacts for software engineering and other industrial projects, data science and business analytics projects can also be effectively represented using industry standard artifacts. Some popular choices are available from consulting giants such as McKinsey, BCG, and decision sciences giants such as Mu Sigma. We will use a popular framework based on the **Minto Pyramid** principle called **Situation – Complication –Question Analysis (SCQ)**.

Let's try defining the problem statement in the following construct:

- **Situation**: Define the current situation. We can simplify this by answering the question—what happened?

  A large multinational bank is designing a marketing campaign to achieve its growth target by enticing customers for bank deposits. The campaign has been ineffective in luring customers, and the marketing team wants to understand how the campaign can be improved to achieve the growth targets.

In the previous section, we saw a hypothetical business problem framed for the banking data's use case. Though this might be different in reality, we are definitely trying to solve a valid use case. By representing the problem statement in the format demonstrated as in the previous format, we have a clear area to focus on and solve. This solves the first step in the life cycle of a typical data science use case. The second step is data gathering, which we explored in the previous chapter. We will refer to the same dataset provided by UCI machine learning repository at https://archive.ics.uci.edu/ml/datasets/Bank%20Marketing.

> **Note**
>
> [Moro et al., 2014] S. Moro, P. Cortez, and P. Rita. A Data-Driven Approach to Predict the Success of Bank Telemarketing. Decision Support Systems, Elsevier, 62:22-31, June 2014.

This brings us to the final step: EDA. In this use case, we want to understand the various factors that are leading to the poor performance of the campaign. Before we delve into the actual exercise, let's take a moment to understand the concept of EDA in a more intuitive way.

Understanding the Science Behind EDA

In layman's terms, we can define EDA as the science of understanding data. A more formal definition is the process of analyzing and exploring datasets to summarize its characteristics, properties, and latent relationships using statistical, visual, analytical, or a combination of techniques.

To cement our understanding, let's break down the definition further. The dataset is a combination of numeric and categorical features. To study the data, we might need to explore features individually, and to study relationships, we might need to explore features together. Depending on the number of features and the type of features, we may cross paths with different types of EDA.

To simplify, we can broadly classify the process of EDA as follows:

- **Univariate analysis**: Studying a single feature
- **Bivariate analysis**: Studying the relationship between two features
- **Multivariate analysis**: Studying the relationship between more than two features

For now, we will restrict the scope of the chapter to **univariate** and **bivariate** analysis. A few forms of multivariate analysis, such as regression, will be covered in the upcoming chapters.

To accomplish each of the previously mentioned analyses, we can use visualization techniques such as boxplots, scatter plots, and bar charts; statistical techniques such as hypothesis testing; or simple analytical techniques such as averages, frequency counts, and so on.

Breaking this further down, we have another dimension to cater to, that is, the types of features–**numeric** or **categorical**. In each of the type of analysis mentioned–**univariate** and **bivariate**–based on the type of the feature, we might have a different visual technique to accomplish the study. So, for univariate analysis of a numeric variable, we could use a histogram or a boxplot, whereas we might use a frequency bar chart for a categorical variable. We will get into the details of the overall exercise of EDA using a *lazy programming* approach, that is, we will explore the context and details of the analysis as and when it occurs in the book.

With the basic background context set for the exercise, let's get ready for a specific EDA exercise.

Exploratory Data Analysis

We will get started with the dataset available to download from UCI ML Repository at https://archive.ics.uci.edu/ml/datasets/Bank%20Marketing.

Download the ZIP file and extract it to a folder in your workspace and use the file named **bank-additional-full.csv**. Ask the students to start a new Jupyter notebook or an IDE of their choice and load the data into memory.

Exercise 18: Studying the Data Dimensions

Let's quickly ingest the data using the simple commands we explored in the previous chapter and take a look at a few essential characteristics of the dataset.

We are exploring the length and breadth of the data, that is, the number of rows and columns, the names of each column, the data type of each column, and a high-level view of what is stored in each column.

Perform the following steps to explore the bank dataset:

1. First, import all the required libraries in RStudio:

```
library(dplyr)
library(ggplot2)
library(repr)
library(cowplot)
```

2. Now, use the **option** method to set the **width** and **height** of the plot as **12** and **4**, respectively:

```
options(repr.plot.width=12, repr.plot.height=4)
```

Ensure that you download and place the **bank-additional-full.csv** file in the appropriate folder. You can access the file from http://bit.ly/2DR4P9I.

3. Create a DataFrame object and read the CSV file using the following command:

```
df <- read.csv("/Chapter 2/Data/bank-additional/bank-additional-full.
csv",sep=';')
```

4. Now, use the following command to display the data from the dataset:

```
str(df)
```

The output is as follows:

```
'data.frame':    41188 obs. of  21 variables:
 $ age            : int  56 57 37 40 56 45 59 41 24 25 ...
 $ job            : Factor w/ 12 levels "admin.","blue-collar",..: 4 8 8 1 8 8 1 2 10 8 ...
 $ marital        : Factor w/ 4 levels "divorced","married",..: 2 2 2 2 2 2 2 2 3 3 ...
 $ education      : Factor w/ 8 levels "basic.4y","basic.6y",..: 1 4 4 2 4 3 6 8 6 4 ...
 $ default        : Factor w/ 3 levels "no","unknown",..: 1 2 1 1 1 2 1 2 1 1 ...
 $ housing        : Factor w/ 3 levels "no","unknown",..: 1 1 3 1 1 1 1 1 3 3 ...
 $ loan           : Factor w/ 3 levels "no","unknown",..: 1 1 1 1 3 1 1 1 1 1 ...
 $ contact        : Factor w/ 2 levels "cellular","telephone": 2 2 2 2 2 2 2 2 2 2 ...
 $ month          : Factor w/ 10 levels "apr","aug","dec",..: 7 7 7 7 7 7 7 7 7 7 ...
 $ day_of_week    : Factor w/ 5 levels "fri","mon","thu",..: 2 2 2 2 2 2 2 2 2 2 ...
 $ duration       : int  261 149 226 151 307 198 139 217 380 50 ...
 $ campaign       : int  1 1 1 1 1 1 1 1 1 1 ...
 $ pdays          : int  999 999 999 999 999 999 999 999 999 999 ...
 $ previous       : int  0 0 0 0 0 0 0 0 0 0 ...
 $ poutcome       : Factor w/ 3 levels "failure","nonexistent",..: 2 2 2 2 2 2 2 2 2 2 ...
 $ emp.var.rate   : num  1.1 1.1 1.1 1.1 1.1 1.1 1.1 1.1 1.1 1.1 ...
 $ cons.price.idx : num  94 94 94 94 94 ...
 $ cons.conf.idx  : num  -36.4 -36.4 -36.4 -36.4 -36.4 -36.4 -36.4 -36.4 -36.4 -36.4 ...
 $ euribor3m      : num  4.86 4.86 4.86 4.86 4.86 ...
 $ nr.employed    : num  5191 5191 5191 5191 5191 ...
 $ y              : Factor w/ 2 levels "no","yes": 1 1 1 1 1 1 1 1 1 1 ...
```

Figure 2.2: Bank data from the bank-additional-full CSV file

In the preceding example, we used the traditional **read.csv** function that's available in R to read the file into memory. We added an argument to the **sep=";"** function since the file is semicolon separated. The **str** function prints the high-level information we require about the dataset. If you carefully observe the output snippet, you can see that the first line denotes the shape of data, that is, the number of rows/observations and the number of columns/variables.

The next 21 lines in the output snippet give us a sneak-peek of each variable in dataset. It displays the name of the variable, its datatype, and the first few values in the dataset. We have one line for each column. The **str** function practically gives us a macro-view of the entire dataset.

As you can see from the dataset, we have 20 independent variables, such as **age**, **job**, and **education**, and one outcome/dependent variable—**y**. Here, the outcome variable defines whether the campaign call made to the client resulted in a successful deposit sign-up with **yes** or **no**. To understand the overall dataset, we now need to study each variable in the dataset. Let's first hop on to univariate analysis.

Univariate Analysis

Univariate analysis is the study of a single feature/variable. Here, we describe the data to help us get an overall view of how it is organized. For numeric features, such as **age**, **duration**, **nr.employed** (numeric features in the dataset) and many others, we look at summary statistics such as min, max, mean, standard deviation, and percentile distribution. These measures together help us understand the spread of the data. Similarly, for categorical features such as **job**, **marital**, and **education**, we need to study the distinct values in the feature and the frequency of these values. To accomplish this, we can implement a few analytical, visual, and statistical techniques. Let's take a look at the analytical and visual techniques for exploring numeric features.

Exploring Numeric/Continuous Features

If you explored the previous output snippet, you might have noted that we have a mix of numeric and categorical features in the dataset. Let's start by looking at the first feature in the dataset, which is a numeric feature named **age**. As the name suggests, it denotes the age of the customer being targeted. Let's take a look at the summary statistics of the feature and visualize it using a simple boxplot.

Exercise 19: Visualizing Data Using a Box Plot

In this exercise, we will explore using a boxplot for univariate analysis, explain how to interpret the boxplot, and walk through the code.

Perform the following steps to visualize the data using a boxplot:

1. First, import the ggplot2 package using the following command:

   ```
   library(ggplot2)
   ```

2. Create a DataFrame object, **df**, and use the **bank-additional-full.csv** file using the following command:

   ```
   df <- read.csv("/Chapter 2/Data/bank-additional/bank-additional-full.
   csv",sep=';')
   ```

3. Print the **age** data, such as **mean** and **max**, using the following command:

   ```
   print(summary(df$age))
   ```

   The output is as follows:

   ```
   Min. 1st Qu.  Median   Mean 3rd Qu.   Max.
   17.00   32.00   38.00   40.02   47.00   98.00
   ```

4. Next, print the standard deviation of age as follows:

```
print(paste("Std.Dev:",round(sd(df$age),2)))
```

The output is as follows:

```
[1] "Std.Dev: 10.42"
```

5. Now, plot the boxplot using of age with following parameters:

```
ggplot(data=df,aes(y=age)) + geom_boxplot(outlier.colour="black")
```

The output is as follows:

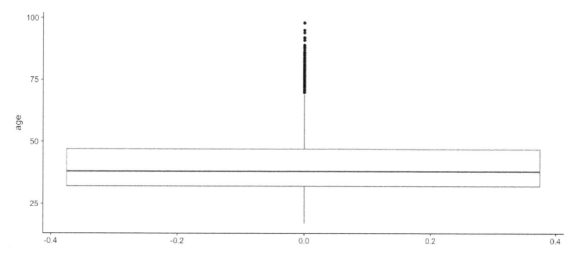

Figure 2.3: Boxplot of age.

We first load the **ggplot2** library, which provides handy functions for visualizing the data. R provides a simple function called **summary**, which prints summary statistics such as min, max, median, mean, 75th percentile, and 25th percentile values. The next line uses the **sd** function to compute the standard deviation, and, lastly, the final line uses the **ggplot** library to plot the boxplot for the data.

If you explore the variable with the output from the summary statistics, we can see that age has a minimum value of 17, a max of 98, and a mean of 42. If you take a close look at the gap between the 75th percentile (3rd quartile) and the 100th percentile (max), we can see a huge jump. This indicates that there are outliers present in the age variable. The presence of outliers will incorrectly change your conclusions from the analysis. In some cases, when there is just one data point with a value of **1000x** the 75th percentile, your mean will shift toward the right. In scenarios where you would use just mean as a ballpark figure to give an estimate of the variable, the whole understanding of the feature might be misleading.

The boxplot, on the other hand, helps us visually consume this information in a simple and lucid way. The boxplot splits the data into three quartiles. The lower quartile, that is, the line below the box, represents the min and the 25th percentile. The middle quartile represents the 25th to 50th to 75th percentile. The upper quartile represents the 75th to the 100th percentile. The dots above the 100th percentile are outliers determined by the internal functions. As we can see, the observation from the summary statistics are in line with the boxplots. We do see outliers, marked as dots above the upper quartile.

In the next exercise, we will perform an EDA on the age variable using a histogram. Let's see what insight we can get from the histogram plot.

Exercise 20: Visualizing Data Using a Histogram

In this exercise, we will discuss how to interpret the histogram and outliers. Let's continue from the previous exercise.

In order to get a more detailed view of the data and closely understand how the **age** variable is organized, we can use histograms. A histogram is a special bar plot, where the data is grouped and sequentially arranged into equal intervals called **bins**, and the frequency of data points in the respective bins are plotted. The histogram helps us to understand the distribution of the data more effectively. The exercise plots the histogram to help us visualize the data more effectively.

Perform the following steps:

1. First, import the ggplot2 package using the following command:

```
library(ggplot2)
```

2. Create a DataFrame object, **df**, and use the **bank-additional-full.csv** file using the following command:

```
df <- read.csv("/Chapter 2/Data/bank-additional/bank-additional-full.csv",sep=';')
```

3. Now, use the following command to plot the histogram for age using the provided parameters:

```
ggplot(data=df,aes(x=age)) +
        geom_histogram(bins=10,fill="blue", color="black", alpha =0.5)  +
        ggtitle("Histogram for Age") +
        theme_bw()
```

The output is as follows:

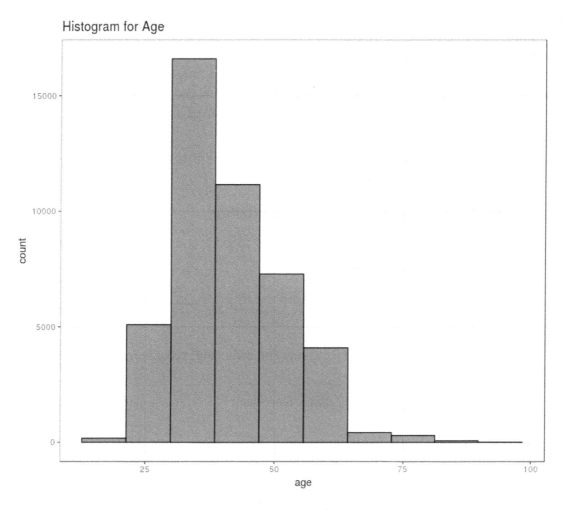

Figure 2.4: Histogram for age

The **ggplot** function defines the base layer for visualization, which is then followed by the **geom_histogram** function with parameters that define the histogram-related aspects such as the number of bins, color to fill, alpha (opacity), and many more. The number of bins is also calculated by default, but it can be overridden by passing a value to the **bin** parameter, such as **bin=10**. The next function, **ggtitle**, is used to add a title to the plot, and the **theme_bw** function is added to change the theme to black and white instead of the default. The **theme** function is optional and is added here for only visually appealing plots.

As you can clearly see, the histogram gives us a more granular view of the data distribution for the feature. We can understand that the number of records drastically reduce after 65 and only a few records have values beyond 75. In some cases, choosing the number of bins for the histogram becomes important as higher number of bins make the distribution messy and a smaller number of bins make the distribution less informative. In scenarios where we would want to see a much more granular view of the distribution, instead of increasing the number of bins for the histogram, we can opt for visualizing using a density plot that visualizes the plot over a continuous interval while using kernel smoothing to smooth out the noise.

We can also visualize the age variable using a density plot rather a histogram. The next exercise goes into the details of how to do it.

Exercise 21: Visualizing Data Using a Density Plot

In this exercise, we will demonstrate the density plot for the same feature, **age**.

Perform the following steps:

1. First, import the ggplot2 package using the following command:

```
library(ggplot2)
```

2. Create a DataFrame object, **df**, and use the **bank-additional-full.csv** file using the following command:

```
df <- read.csv("/Chapter 2/Data/bank-additional/bank-additional-full.csv",sep=';')
```

3. Now, use the following command to plot the density plot for age:

```
ggplot(data=df,aes(x=age)) + geom_density(fill="red",alpha =0.5) +
                             ggtitle("Density Plot for Age") +
                             theme_bw()
```

The output is as follows:

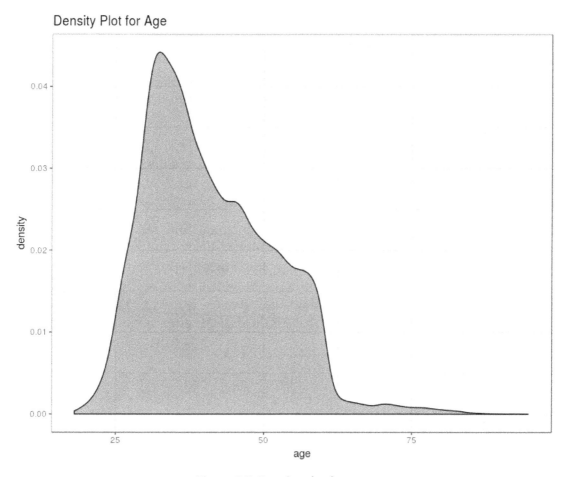

Figure 2.5: Density plot for age.

Similar to the previous exercise, we use the same base for the visualization with the **ggplot** function and use a different **geom_density** function for the density plot. The rest of the additional functions used for the visualization remain the same.

Density plots give finer details than a histogram. While this level of detail can also be achieved using higher number of bins for a histogram, there is often a hit and try method required to get the best number of bins. In such cases, an easier option to opt for would be density plots.

Now that we have understood the idea of univariate analysis for numeric variables, let's speed up the data exploration for other variables. We have a total of 10 categorical features and 10 numeric columns. Let's try to take a look at four numeric variables together using a histogram.

Just like we plotted the histogram for age, we can do it for multiple variables at the same time by defining a custom function. The next exercise shows how to do this.

Exercise 22: Visualizing Multiple Variables Using a Histogram

In this exercise, we will combine the four histograms, one for each of the variables of interest, into a single plot. We have **campaign**, which indicates the number of contacts performed during the campaign, and **pdays**, which indicates the number of days since the client was last contacted by the previous campaign; a value of 999 indicates that the client was never contacted before. **previous** indicates the number of contacts previously made for this client, and lastly, **emp.var.rate** indicates the employment variance rate.

Let's perform the following steps to complete the exercise:

1. First, import the **cowplot** package using the following command:

   ```
   library(cowplot)
   ```

   Ensure that the **cowplot** package is installed.

2. Next, define a function to plot histograms for all numeric columns:

   ```
   plot_grid_numeric <- function(df,list_of_variables,ncols=2){
       plt_matrix<-list()
       i<-1
       for(column in list_of_variables){
           plt_matrix[[i]]<-ggplot(data=df,aes_string(x=column)) +
               geom_histogram(binwidth=2,fill="blue", color="black",
                       alpha =0.5)  +
               ggtitle(paste("Histogram for variable: ",column)) + theme_bw()
               i<-i+1
               }
       plot_grid(plotlist=plt_matrix,ncol=2)
   }
   ```

3. Now, use the **summary** function to print the mean, max, and other parameters for the **campaign**, **pdays**, **previous**, and **emp.var.rate** columns:

```
summary(df[,c("campaign","pdays","previous","emp.var.rate")])
```

The output is as follows:

```
    campaign              pdays           previous          emp.var.rate
 Min.   : 1.000    Min.   :  0.0    Min.   :0.000    Min.   :-3.40000
 1st Qu.: 1.000    1st Qu.:999.0    1st Qu.:0.000    1st Qu.:-1.80000
 Median : 2.000    Median :999.0    Median :0.000    Median : 1.10000
 Mean   : 2.568    Mean   :962.5    Mean   :0.173    Mean   : 0.08189
 3rd Qu.: 3.000    3rd Qu.:999.0    3rd Qu.:0.000    3rd Qu.: 1.40000
 Max.   :56.000    Max.   :999.0    Max.   :7.000    Max.   : 1.40000
```

4. Call the function we defined earlier to plot the histogram:

```
plot_grid_numeric(df,c("campaign","pdays","previous","emp.var.rate"),2)
```

The output is as follows:

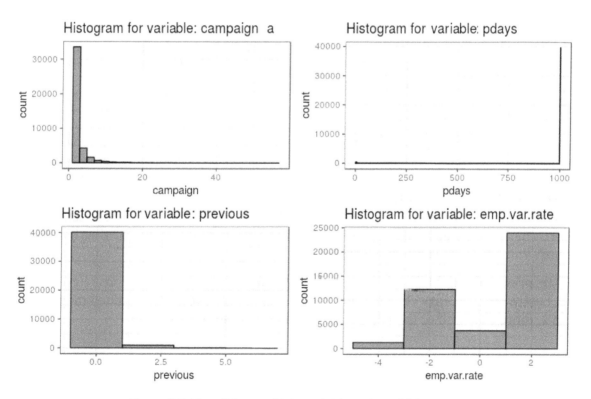

Figure 2.6: Visualizing multiple variables using a histogram

In this exercise, we automated the process of stacking multiple plots of the same kind into a consolidated plot. We first load the required **cowplot** library. This library provides handy functions for creating a plot grid for plots rendered by the **ggplot** library. If you do not have the library loaded, install the packages using the **install. packages('cowplot')** command. We then define a function called **plot_grid_numeric**, which accepts the parameters dataset, a list of features to plot, and the number of columns to be used in the grid. If you observe the internals of the function, you will see that we simply traverse through the list of provided variables using a **for** loop and collect the individual plots into a list called **plt_matrix**. Later, we use the **plot_grid** function provided by the **cowplot** library to arrange the plots into a grid with two columns.

The same function can be used to display a grid of any number of histograms; use a number based on your screen size. The current number has been restricted to 4 for best results. We also use the **summary** function to display the overall statistics for the same set of numeric variables in conjunction with the histogram plots.

> **Note**
>
> There is no exception handling code used in the previous function. We have ignored implementing sophisticated code for now in order to focus on the topic of interest. In the event of using the function for non-numeric variables, the error messages will not be the most effective to solve it.

As we can see in the previous plot, we now have four variables together for analysis. Studying the summary statistics in tandem with the histogram plots helps us uncover the underlying variable better. **Campaign** has 75% of the values below or equal to 3. We can see that there is an outlier at 56, but a significant majority of the records have values less than 5. **pdays** seems to not be a useful variable for our analysis as almost all records have the default value of 999. The tall bar in 1000 makes it clear that barely any records will have values other than 999.

For the **previous** variable, we see the exact opposite of **pdays**; most records have a value of 0. Lastly, **emp.var.rate** shows us an interesting result. Though the values range from **-4** to 2, more than half of the records have a positive value.

So, with the analysis of these four variables, we can roughly conclude that the previously conducted campaigns didn't communicate very often by phone with the clients, or it could also mean that close to none of the clients targeted in the previous campaign were contacted for the current campaign. Also, the ones who were contacted earlier were contacted seven times at most. The number of days since the client was last contacted naturally is in sync with the results from the previous campaign, because hardly any have been contacted earlier. However, for the current campaign, clients have been contacted an average of 2.5 times, 75% of the clients have been contacted up to 3 times, and some clients have been contacted as high as 56 times. The employment variance rate is an indicator of how many people are hired or fired due to macro-economic situations. We understand that the economic situation has been fairly steady for most of the time during the campaigns.

Similar to the function created in the previous section to stack histograms together, in this activity, we will create another function to stack density plots and another for boxplots.

Activity 4: Plotting Multiple Density Plots and Boxplots

In this activity, we will create a function to stack density plots, and another for boxplots. Use the newly created functions to visualize the same set of variables as in the previous section and study the most effective way to analyze numeric variables.

By end of this activity, you will learn how to plot multiple variables in density plot at the same time. Doing so makes it easy to compare the different variables in one go and draw insights about the data.

Perform the following steps to complete this activity:

1. First, load the necessary libraries and packages in RStudio.

2. Read the **bank-additional-full.csv** dataset into a DataFrame named **df**.

3. Define the **plot_grid_numeric** function for the density plot:

```
plot_grid_numeric <- function(df,list_of_variables,ncols=2){
  plt_matrix<-list()
  i<-1
  }
  plot_grid(plotlist=plt_matrix,ncol=2)
}
```

4. Plot the density plot for the **campaign**, **pdays**, **previous**, and **emp.var.rate** variables:

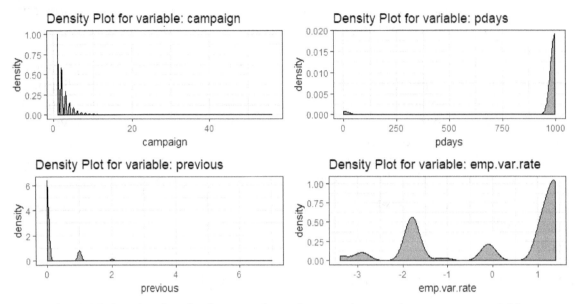

Figure 2.7: Density plots for the campaign, pdays, previous, and emp.var.rate variables

Observe that the interpretations we obtained using the histogram are visibly true in the density plot as well. Hence, this serves as another alternative plot for looking at the same trend.

5. Repeat the steps for the boxplot:

```
plot_grid_numeric <- function(df,list_of_variables,ncols=2){
  plt_matrix<-list()
  i<-1
}
plot_grid_numeric(df,c("campaign","pdays","previous","emp.var.rate"),2)
```

The plot is as follows:

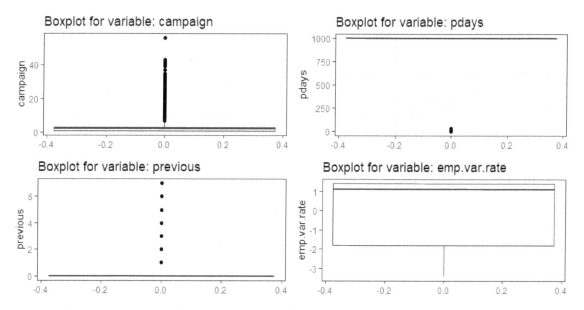

Figure 2.8: Boxplots for the campaign, pdays, previous, and emp.var.rate variables

An additional point to note in the boxplot is that it shows the clear presence of outliers in the **campaign** variable, which wasn't very visible in the other two plots. A similar observation could be made for **previous** and **pdays** variables as well. Students should try to plot boxplots after removing the outliers and see how different they look then.

Note

You can find the solution for this activity on page 442.

Exercise 23: Plotting a Histogram for the nr.employed, euribor3m, cons.conf. idx, and duration Variables

In this exercise, we will move to the next and the last set of four numeric variables. We have **nr.employed**, which indicates the number of employees employed at the bank, and **euribor3m**, which indicates the 3-month euro interbank rates for average interest rates. Also, we have **cons.conf.index**, which is the consumer confidence indicator measured as the degree of optimism on the state by consumers by expressing through the activities of savings and spending. Lastly, there is **duration**, which indicates the last contact duration. As per the metadata provided by UCI, this variable is highly correlated with the outcome and will lead to possible data leakage. Therefore, we will drop this variable from our future analysis.

Perform the following steps to study the next set of numeric variables:

1. First, import the **cowplot** package using the following command:

    ```
    library(cowplot)
    ```

2. Create a DataFrame object, **df**, and use the **bank-additional-full.csv** file using the following command:

    ```
    df <- read.csv("/Chapter 2/Data/bank-additional/bank-additional-full.
    csv",sep=';')
    ```

3. Print the details using the **summary** method:

    ```
    summary(df[,c("nr.employed","euribor3m","cons.conf.idx","duration")])
    ```

    The output is as follows:

    ```
       nr.employed       euribor3m        cons.conf.idx        duration
     Min.   :4964     Min.    :0.634    Min.    :-50.8    Min.    :   0.0
     1st Qu.:5099     1st Qu.:1.344     1st Qu.:-42.7     1st Qu.: 102.0
     Median :5191     Median :4.857     Median :-41.8     Median :  180.0
     Mean   :5167     Mean    :3.621    Mean    :-40.5    Mean    :  258.3
     3rd Qu.:5228     3rd Qu.:4.961     3rd Qu.:-36.4     3rd Qu.: 319.0
     Max.   :5228     Max.    :5.045    Max.    :-26.9    Max.    :4918.0
    ```

4. Plot the histogram for the defined variables, as illustrated in the following command:

    ```
    plot_grid_numeric(df,c("nr.employed","euribor3m","cons.conf.
    idx","duration"),2)
    ```

The output is as follows:

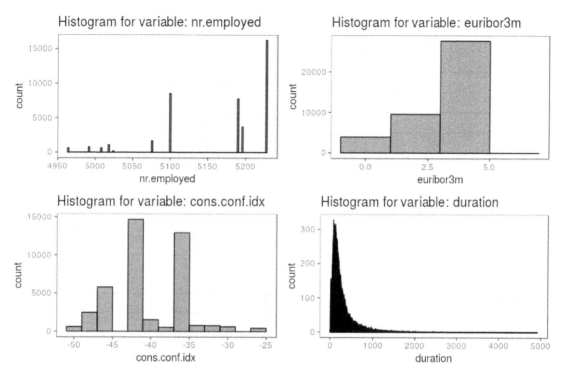

Figure 2.9: Histogram of count and duration for various variables

Just like *Exercise 5, Visualizing Multiple Variables Using a Histogram*, we first perform the summary statistics on our desired set of variables with the **summary** function, and then plot the combined histogram for all the desired variables together by calling the same functions we defined earlier.

As we can see, the number of employees employed has been mostly constant at **5228**, but it has also decreased during the time period to different values. This number is measured quarterly, and hence the frequency is not very dynamic, which is why we can see values centered around only a few bins. The euro interbank interest rate has been mostly between **2.5** and **5**. There are just 1 or 2 records that have values above 5, and we can see that the max value measured for this variable is **5.045**. The consumer confidence index is mostly negative, which means that the consumers mostly perceived the state of the economy negatively during this time. We see two peaks in the bins of the histogram, which calls for the most common confidence index during the time and vaguely suggests limited variation in the index during the length of the campaign. The duration of the call, in seconds, shall be ignored from our analysis for now.

To summarize, we understand that the bank's number of employees increased and decreased during the campaigns in a range of ~250, which is ~5% of the total employees. It ranged between **4964** and **5228** and mostly had little variation. The consumer confidence index remained mostly negative and with little variation during the time period, and the euro interbank rates had an average of 3.6, with most of the records between 2.5 and 5.

Now, let's move on to study the categorical variables using univariate analysis.

Exploring Categorical Features

Categorical features differ from numeric or continuous features in nature, and therefore the traditional methods used earlier aren't applicable here. We can analyze the number of different classes within a categorical variable and the frequency associated with each. This can be achieved using either simple analytical techniques or visual techniques. Let's explore a list of categorical features using a combination of both.

Exercise 24: Exploring Categorical Features

In this exercise, we will start with a simple variable, that is, **marital**, which indicates the marital status of the client. Let's use the **dplyr** library to perform grouped data aggregation.

Perform the following steps to complete the exercise:

1. First, import the **dplyr** library in the system using the following command:

    ```
    library(dplyr)
    ```

2. Next, we will create an object named **marital_distribution** and store the value based on the following condition:

    ```
    marital_distribution <- df %>% group_by(marital) %>%
                            summarize(Count = n()) %>%
                            mutate(Perc.Count = round(Count/
    sum(Count)*100))
    ```

3. Now, print the value stored in the **marital_distribution** object:

    ```
    print(marital_distribution)
    ```

The output is as follows:

```
# A tibble: 4 x 3
  marital  Count Perc.Count
  <fct>    <int>      <dbl>
1 divorced  4612         11
2 married  24928         61
3 single   11568         28
4 unknown     80          0
```

To count the distinct number of classes within the categorical column and to get the count of records within each of the individual classes, we use the **group_by** functions available under the **dplyr** library. The **%>%**, also called the **concatenation command**, is analogous to the Linux piped operations. It extracts output from the left of the operator, passes on to the right of the operator, and concatenates the entire series of operations. Here, we first group the DataFrame by the variable of our interest, that is, **marital** and then pass the output to the **summarize** function, which aggregates the DataFrame to the grouped level using the aggregation function we provide; in this case, **n()** is a simple **count** equivalent. Finally, we use the **mutate** function to calculate the percentage of counts for each of the individual group members.

We see that majority of the campaign calls were made to married clients, around 61%, followed by calls to single clients at 28% and so on.

Exercise 25: Exploring Categorical Features Using a Bar Chart

In this exercise, we will plot a bar chart with the frequency counts for each class visualized. We could also use the bar chart to represent the frequency distribution of each of these individual categories with a plot.

Perform the following steps to complete the exercise:

1. First, import the **ggplot2** package using the following command:

    ```
    library(ggplot2)
    ```

2. Create a DataFrame object, **df**, and use the **bank-additional-full.csv** file using the following command:

    ```
    df <- read.csv("/Chapter 2/Data/bank-additional/bank-additional-full.
    csv",sep=';')
    ```

3. Now, plot the bar chart of marital status per count using the following command:

```
ggplot(data = marital_distribution,aes(x=marital,y=Perc.Count)) +
                geom_bar(stat="identity",fill="blue",alpha=0.6) +
                geom_text(aes(label=marital_distribution$Perc.Count, vjust =
    -0.3))
```

The output is as follows:

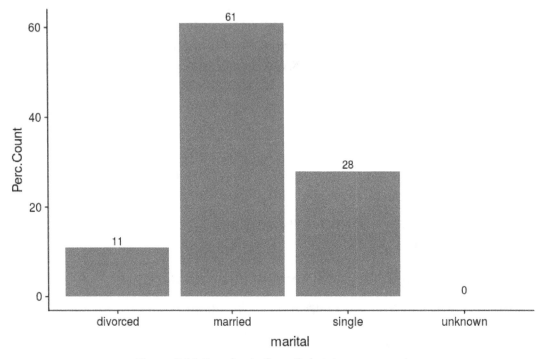

Figure 2.10: Bar chart of marital status per count

We use the same dataset engineered in the previous snippet, which calculates the frequency of each class and its relative percentage. To plot the bar chart, we use the same base function of **ggplot**, where we define the aesthetics of the x and y variables and append the bar plot using the **geom_bar** function. The **geom_text** function allows us to add labels to each bar in the plot.

We can now see the same numbers displayed in the previous exercise visualized here with a bar plot. In scenarios where we have a large number of classes within the variable, glancing through each individual class to study them might not be the most effective method. A simple plot easily helps us to understand the frequency distribution of the categorical variable in an easy-to-consume way.

Exercise 26: Exploring Categorical Features using Pie Chart

In this exercise, we will define the pie chart and the various components within it.

Similar to the bar plot, we also have a pie chart that makes understanding the percentage distribution of the classes easier. Perform the following steps to visualize the same variable, that is, marital status using a pie chart:

1. First, import the **ggplot2** package using the following command:

    ```
    library(ggplot2)
    ```

2. Create a DataFrame object, **df**, and use the **bank-additional-full.csv** file using the following command:

    ```
    df <- read.csv("/Chapter 2/Data/bank-additional/bank-additional-full.
    csv",sep=';')
    ```

3. Next, define the label positions using the following command:

    ```
    plot_breaks = 100 - (cumsum(marital_distribution$Perc.Count) -
                        marital_distribution$Perc.Count/2)
    ```

4. Now, define labels for the plots:

    ```
    plot_labels = paste0(marital_distribution$marital,"-",marital_
    distribution$Perc.Count,"%")
    ```

5. Set the plot size for better visuals:

    ```
    options(repr.plot.width=12, repr.plot.height=8)
    ```

6. Create the pie chart using the following command:

    ```
    ggplot(data = marital_distribution,aes(x=1,y=Perc.Count, fill=marital)) +
                geom_bar(stat="identity") + #Creates the base bar visual
                coord_polar(theta ="y")  + #Creates the pie chart
                scale_y_continuous(breaks=plot_breaks, labels = plot_
    labels,position = "left") +
                theme(axis.text.x = element_text(angle = 30, hjust =1)) +
    #rotates the labels
                theme(text = element_text(size=15)) + #increases the font
    size for the legend
                ggtitle("Percentage Distribution of Marital Status") #Adds
    the plot title
    ```

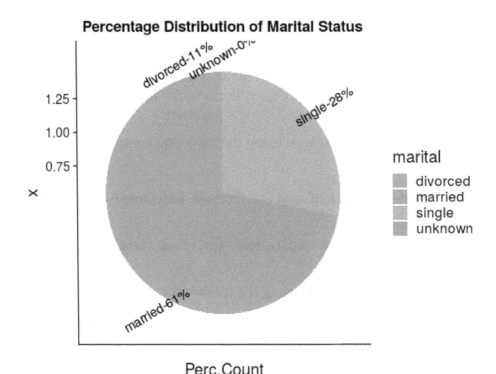

Figure 2.11: Pie chart for the percentage distribution for the marital status

We first define a few extra variables that will help us to get the plot in an easier way. In order to label the pie chart, we would need the break points and the actual labels. The break point should ideally be located in the middle part of the pie piece. So, we take a cumulative sum of the percentage distribution and subtract half of each category to find the mid-point of the section. We then subtract the entire number from 100 to arrange the labels in a clockwise direction.

The next step defines the label for each pie piece; we use the **paste** function to concatenate the label name and the actual percentage values. The pie chart functionality in **ggplot** works by constructing elements on top of a bar chart. We first use the base from **ggplot** and **geom_bar** to render the base for a stacked bar plot and use the **coord_polar** function to transform this into the required pie chart. The **scale_y_continuous** function helps in placing the labels on the pie distribution. The next line adds a rotation angle to the positioning of the text. The **size** parameter inside the **element_text** portion of the **theme** function defines the font size for the text in the plot. The rest is the same as we studied in the earlier plots.

We can see that the pie chart provides us with an intuitive way to explore the percentage distribution for the categories within each variable. A word of caution to choose the pie chart over bar plot would be based on the number of distinct categories within a variable. Though pie charts are visually more appealing, with many distinct classes, pie charts become overcrowded.

> **Note**
>
> Pie charts are best avoided when the number of distinct classes within a categorical variable is high. There is no definite rule, but anything that makes visually cluttered pie charts would not be ideal to study.

Exercise 27: Automate Plotting Categorical Variables

In this exercise, we will automate the plotting of categorical variables.

Just like numeric variables, we also have 10 categorical variables, excluding the target variable. Similar to automating the exploration of numeric features, let's now create a function for categorical variables. To keep things simple, we will primarily use boxplots with a percentage distribution instead of a pie chart. We will start with four categorical features and then move to the next remainder set.

Perform the following steps to complete the exercise:

1. First, import the **cowplot** package using the following command:

    ```
    library(cowplot)
    ```

2. Define a function to plot histograms for all numeric columns:

    ```
    plot_grid_categorical <- function(df,list_of_variables,ncols=2){
        plt_matrix <- list()
        i<-1
        #Iterate for each variable
        for(column in list_of_variables){
            #Creating a temporary DataFrame with the aggregation
            var.dist <- df %>% group_by_(column) %>%
                           summarize(Count = n()) %>%
                           mutate(Perc.Count = round(Count/
    sum(Count)*100,1))
    ```

```
            options(repr.plot.width=12, repr.plot.height=10)
            plt_matrix[[i]]<-ggplot(data = var.dist,aes_
    string(x=column,y="Perc.Count")) +
                geom_bar(stat="identity",fill="blue",alpha=0.6) + #Defines the
    bar plot
                geom_text(label=var.dist$Perc.Count,vjust=-0.3)+  #Adds the
    labels
                theme(axis.text.x = element_text(angle = 90, vjust = 1)) +
    #rotates the labels
                ggtitle(paste("Percentage Distribution of variable: ",column))
    #Creates the title +
                i<-i+1
        }
            plot_grid(plotlist=plt_matrix,ncol=ncols) #plots the grid
    }
```

3. Next, call the **summary** statistics using the following command:

```
summary(df[,c("job","education","default","contact")])
```

The output is as follows:

```
                  job                        education          default
    contact
    admin.      :10422    university.degree  :12168    no       :32588    cellular
    :26144
    blue-collar: 9254    high.school         : 9515    unknown: 8597
    telephone:15044
    technician : 6743    basic.9y            : 6045    yes     :    3
    services   : 3969    professional.course: 5243
    management : 2924    basic.4y            : 4176
    retired     : 1720    basic.6y            : 2292
    (Other)     : 6156    (Other)             : 1749
```

4. Call the function we defined earlier to plot the histogram:

```
plot_grid_categorical(df,c("job","education","default","contact"),2)
```

The output is as follows:

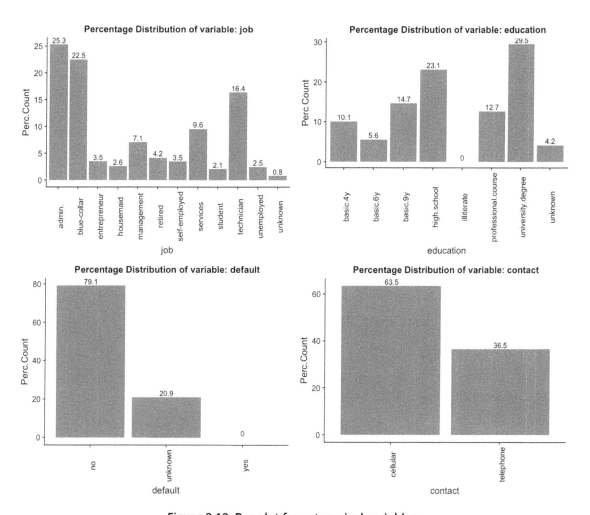

Figure 2.12: Bar plot for categorical variables

Similar to the earlier function we created for the numeric features visual automation, we have created a simple function to explore the percentage distribution for categorical features. Some additions to the function are the creation of the temporary aggregation dataset and some additional cosmetic enhancements to the plot. We add the labels and rotate them by 30 degrees so that they can neatly align with the plot, and the rest remains the same. We get the frequency count by calling the **summary** function on the **categorical** column. Similar to numeric columns, we explore the categorical columns first using the **summary** function and then use the defined function to visualize the collated bar plots.

Exploring the **job** feature, we can see 12 distinct values, with most of the records for admin, blue-collar, and technician. Overall, the **job** category seems to have a fairly diverse distribution of values. Education level of the client also has a diverse set of values, with ~50% of the values from high school and university. For the **default** variable, which indicates whether the client has defaulted in credit previously, we have ~80% of the values as **no** and around ~20% unknown. This doesn't seem to be useful information. Finally, **contact**, which defines the mode of contact used for the campaign communication, shows that 64% was through cellular phones, and the rest through landlines.

Let's move on and repeat the same analysis for the next set of features.

Exercise 28: Automate Plotting for the Remaining Categorical Variables

In this exercise, we will reuse the same function for the next set of four categorical variables. Remember that you need to use the frequency count generated using the **summary** command in conjunction with the plots to interpret the value.

Let's perform the following procedure to complete the exercise:

1. First, import the **cowplot** package using the following command:

   ```
   library(cowplot)
   ```

2. Create a DataFrame object, **df**, and use the **bank-additional-full.csv** file using the following command:

   ```
   df <- read.csv("/Chapter 2/Data/bank-additional/bank-additional-full.
   csv",sep=';')
   ```

3. Next, call the **summary** statistics using the following command:

   ```
   summary(df[,c("loan","month","day_of_week","poutcome")])
   ```

   The output is as follows:

   ```
         loan              month         day_of_week           poutcome
    no     :33950    may    :13769    fri:7827    failure    : 4252
    unknown:  990    jul    : 7174    mon:8514    nonexistent:35563
    yes    : 6248    aug    : 6178    thu:8623    success    : 1373
                     jun    : 5318    tue:8090
                     nov    : 4101    wed:8134
                     apr    : 2632
                     (Other): 2016
   ```

4. Call the defined function to plot the histogram:

```
plot_grid_categorical(df,c("loan","month","day_of_week","poutcome"),2)
```

The output is as follows:

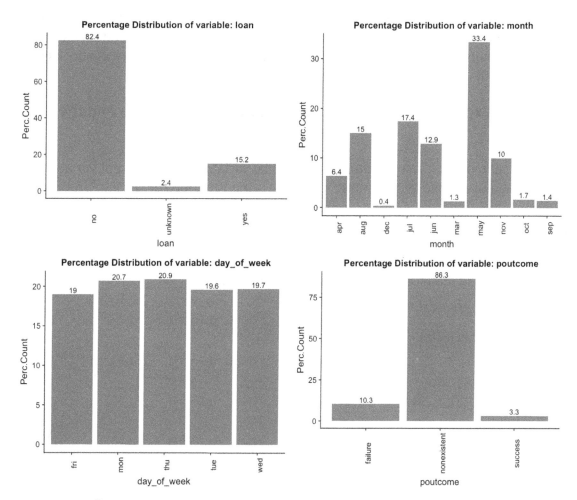

Figure 2.13: Automate plotting for the remaining categorical variables

We reuse the previously defined functions to explore the new set of four variables just like we explored the previous set of features.

The **loan** variable indicates whether the client has a personal loan. We have ~86.6% of clients with no personal loan, 10.3% with a loan, and 3.3% unknown. Similarly, the **month** variable indicates the actual month when the campaign calls were executed. We see that the majority of communication was conducted in the month of **may**, followed by **jul** and **aug**. Overall, the **month** feature also seems to be a fairly diverse variable with a good distribution of values. The **day_of_week** variable shows a consistent distribution across all days of the week. **poutcome** indicates the result of the previously executed campaign; a significant majority was non-existent, a small chunk of around 3.3% was successful, and ~10% failed.

Exercise 29: Exploring the Last Remaining Categorical Variable and the Target Variable

Finally, let's explore the last remaining categorical variable and the target variable. Since both are categorical, we can continue using the same function for the exploration.

Repeat the same process for the last independent categorical variable and the dependent variable (which is also categorical):

1. First, after importing the required packages and creating DataFrame object, call the summary statistics using the following command:

    ```
    summary(df[,c("y","housing")])
    ```

    The output is as follows:

    ```
         y                 housing
     no :36548    no      :18622
     yes: 4640    unknown:  990
                  yes     :21576
    ```

2. Call the defined function to plot the histogram:

    ```
    plot_grid_categorical(df,c("y","housing"),2)
    ```

The output is as follows:

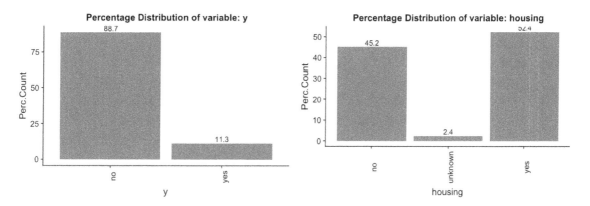

Figure 2.14: Histogram of housing per count

If we carefully look at the distribution of the outcome variable, we can see that a large majority of the clients have negatively responded to the campaign calls. Only ~11% of the overall campaign base have positively responded to the campaign. Similarly, if we look at the **housing** variable, we can see that roughly 50% of the clients had a housing loan.

To summarize, we can distill our observations as follows:

- The campaign was conducted with a major focus of new customers who had not been previously contacted.

- Around 60% of the client base are married and 80% have not defaulted in credit history.

- Roughly 50% of the client base has a housing loan and over 80% has never opted for a personal loan.

- The campaign was the most active during the month of May and demonstrated fairly strong momentum in July and August.

- More than 60% of the communication of the campaign was through cellular phones, and over 50% of the client base at least had a high school degree.

- Overall, only 11% of the campaign calls had a positive response.

With the univariate analysis of all the numeric and categorical variables complete, we now have a fair understanding of the story the data conveys. We almost understand each data dimension and its distribution. Let's move on to explore another interesting facet of EDA: bivariate analysis.

Bivariate Analysis

In **bivariate analysis**, we extend our analysis to study two variables together. In our use case, we have around 20 independent variables. It is indeed possible to study all permutation combinations of the available 20 variables, but we won't go to that extent in this chapter. In our use case, we are more interested in studying all the factors that led to the poor performance of the campaign. Therefore, our primary focus will be to perform bivariate analysis and study the relationship between all the independent variables and our dependent target variable. Again, depending on the type of variable, we will have a different type of visual or analytical technique to analyze the relationship between the two variables. The possible combinations are numeric and numeric, and numeric and categorical. Given that our dependent variable is a categorical variable, we might have to explore the relationship between two independent variables in our list to study the relationship between two numeric variables. Let's get started.

Studying the Relationship between Two Numeric Variables

To understand how we can study the relationship between two numeric variables, we can leverage scatter plots. It is a 2-dimensional visualization of the data, where each variable is plotted on an axis along its length. Relationships between the variables are easily identified by studying the trend across the visualization. Let's take a look at an example in the following exercise.

Exercise 30: Studying the Relationship between Employee Variance Rate and Number of Employees

Let's study the relationship between employee variance rate and the number of employees. Ideally, the number of employees should increase as the variation rate increases.

Perform the following steps to complete the exercise:

1. First, import the **ggplot2** package using the following command:

   ```
   library(ggplot2)
   ```

2. Create a DataFrame object, **df**, and use the **bank-additional-full.csv** file using the following command:

   ```
   df <- read.csv("/Chapter 2/Data/bank-additional/bank-additional-full.
   csv",sep=';')
   ```

3. Now, plot the scatter plot using the following command:

```
ggplot(data=df,aes(x=emp.var.rate,y=nr.employed)) + geom_point(size=4) +
ggtitle("Scatterplot of Employment variation rate v/s Number of
Employees")
```

The output is as follows:

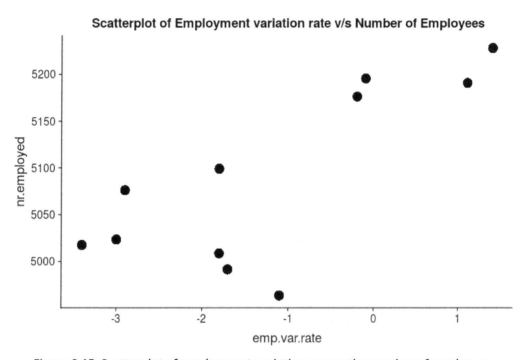

Figure 2.15: Scatterplot of employment variation versus the number of employees

We use the same base function, **ggplot**, with a new wrapper for the scatterplot. The **geom_point** function in **ggplot** provides the necessary constructs for using a scatterplot.

We can see an overall increasing trend, that is, as employment variance rate increases, we see the number of employees also increases. The fewer number of dots are due to repetitive records in **nr.employed**.

Studying the Relationship between a Categorical and a Numeric Variable

Let's first recall the methods discussed to study the relationship between the numeric and categorical variable and discuss the approach to execute it.

In this section, we will discuss the different aggregation metrics that we can use for summarizing the data. So far, we have used **avg**, but a better approach would be to use a combination of **avg**, **min**, **max**, and other metrics.

Exercise 31: Studying the Relationship between the y and age Variables

We have a categorical dependent variable and nine numeric variables to explore. To start small, we will first explore the relationship between our target, **y**, and **age**. To study the relationship between a categorical and numeric variable, we can choose a simple analytical technique where we calculate the average age across each target outcome; if we see stark differences, we can make insights from the observations.

In this exercise, we will calculate the average age across each target outcome and also count the number of records in each bucket, followed by a visual representation.

Perform the following steps:

1. First, import the **ggplot2** package using the following command:

   ```
   library(ggplot2)
   ```

2. Create a DataFrame object, **df**, and use the **bank-additional-full.csv** file using the following command:

   ```
   df <- read.csv("/Chapter 2/Data/bank-additional/bank-additional-full.
   csv",sep=';')
   ```

3. Create a **temp** object and store the value using the following command:

   ```
   temp <- df %>% group_by(y) %>%
                       summarize(Avg.Age = round(mean(age),2),
                              Num.Records = n())
   ```

4. Print the value stored in the **temp** object:

   ```
   print(temp)
   ```

The output is as follows:

```
# A tibble: 2 x 3
  y       Avg.Age Num.Records
  <fct>     <dbl>       <int>
1 no         39.9       36548
2 yes        40.9        4640
```

5. Now, create a plot using the **ggplot** command:

```
ggplot(data= temp, aes(x=y, y=Avg.Age)) +
      geom_bar(stat="identity",fill="blue",alpha= 0.5) +   #Creates the
bar plot
      geom_text(label=temp$Avg.Age,vjust=-0.3)+  #Adds the label
      ggtitle(paste("Average Age across target outcome"))  #Creates the
title
```

The output is as follows:

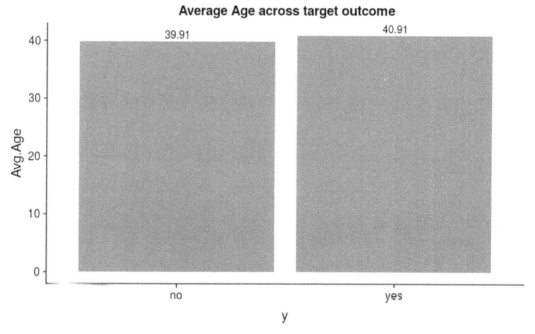

Figure 2.16: Histogram for the average age across target outcome

The first line of code creates the temporary aggregation datasets, which summarizes the average age and the number of records in each category. The plotting functionality used is on the lines of our previous visuals. We extend the **ggplot** function with the **geom_bar** to render the bar plots.

We can see that there is barely any difference between the two outcomes. We don't see any interesting patterns.

> **Note**
>
> In bivariate analysis, we need to be careful before concluding any interesting patterns as insights. In many cases, due to the skewed distribution of data, the patterns would seem surprisingly interesting.

Let's move on to the next set of variables.

Exercise 32: Studying the Relationship between the Average Value and the y Variable

In this exercise, we will study the relationship between the next set of variables: **average** and **y**.

Perform the following steps to complete the exercise:

1. Import the required libraries and create the DataFrame object.

2. Next, create the **plot_bivariate_numeric_and_categorical** object using the following command:

```
plot_bivariate_numeric_and_categorical <- function(df,target,list_of_
variables,ncols=2){
    target<-sym(target) #Defined for converting text to column names
    plt_matrix <- list()
    i<-1
```

```
for(column in list_of_variables){
        col <-sym(column) #defined for converting text to column name
        temp <- df %>% group_by(!!sym(target)) %>%
                    summarize(Avg.Val = round(mean(!!sym(col)),2))
        options(repr.plot.width=12, repr.plot.height=8) #Defines plot size
          plt_matrix[[i]]<-ggplot(data= temp, aes(x=!!sym(target), y=Avg.
Val)) +
          geom_bar(stat="identity",fill="blue",alpha= 0.5) +
          geom_text(label=temp$Avg.Val,vjust=-0.3)+  #Adds the labels
          ggtitle(paste("Average",column,"across target outcomes"))
  #Creates the title
            i<-i+1
    }
    plot_grid(plotlist = plt_matrix,ncol=ncols)
}
```

3. Now, print the distribution of records across target outcomes:

```
print("Distribution of records across target outcomes-")
print(table(df$y))
```

The output is as follows:

```
[1] "Distribution of records across target outcomes-"
    no    yes
36548  4640
```

4. Now, plot the histogram using the following command for the defined variables:

```
plot_bivariate_numeric_and_
categorical(df,"y",c("campaign","pdays","previous","emp.var.rate"),2)
```

The output is as follows:

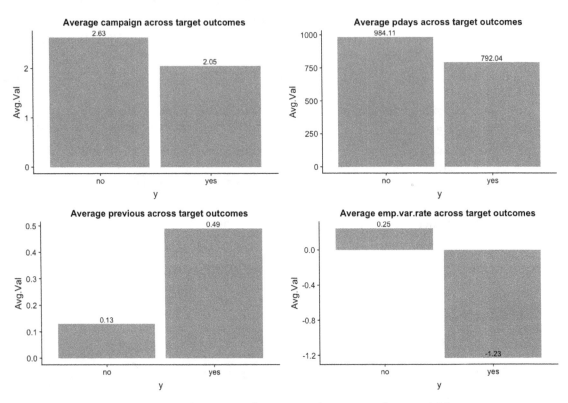

Figure 2.17: Histogram of average value versus the y variable

In order to automate the data exploration task for bivariate analysis between a categorical and a numeric variable, we have defined a function similar to the one we defined in the previous exercise. We have additionally used the **sym** function, which will help us use dynamic column names in the function. Using **!!sym(column)** converts a string to a real column name that's analogous to passing the actual value. The previous function first aggregates the average value of the target across the variable of interest. The **plot** function then uses the information to plot the bar chart with the average values across the target outcomes.

In bivariate analysis, it is important to carefully validate the patterns observed before concluding a specific insight. In some cases, outliers might skew the results and therefore deliver incorrect findings. Additionally, fewer of records for a particular pattern might also be a risky pattern to conclude. It is always recommended to collect all the insights observed and further validate them with additional extensive EDA or statistical techniques for significance.

Here, we don't see any prominent results to conclude. In the `campaign` variable, the average number of contacts made during the campaign is a bit lower for successful campaigns, but the difference is too small to make any possible conclusions. `pdays`, which indicate the number of days since the last contact in the previous campaign shows a big difference between the outcomes for the target.

However, this difference is purely due to most clients being not contacted in the previous campaign. All of those records have values set to 999. The same holds true for `previous`; though there is a decent difference between the two, most clients were contacted for the first time in the current campaign. The employment variance rate, however, shows counter-intuitive results. We would actually expect the variance rate to be higher when the outcome is **yes**, but we see it the other way around. This sounds interesting, we will make a note of this insight for now and later come back for more validation before making any conclusions.

Let's move on to the next set of categorical dependent variables to be studied with the categorical dependent variable.

Exercise 33: Studying the Relationship between the cons.price.idx, cons.conf. idx, curibor3m, and nr.employed Variables

Let's move on to the next set of categorical dependent variables to be studied with the categorical dependent variable. For this exercise, we will explore the relationship between `cons.price.idx`, `cons.conf.idx`, `euribor3m`, and `nr.employed`, with the target variable **y** using histogram.

1. Import the required libraries and create the DataFrame object.

2. Next, create a `plot_bivariate_numeric_and_categorical` function and plot the histogram:

```
plot_bivariate_numeric_and_categorical(df,"y",
                c("cons.price.idx","cons.conf.idx", "euribor3m", "nr.
employed"),2)
```

The output is as follows:

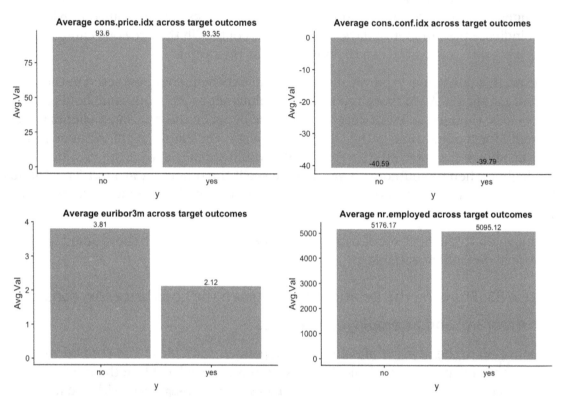

Figure 2.18: Histogram of the cons.price.idx, cons.conf.idx, euribor3m, and nr.employed variables

Again, for most cases, we don't see any prominent patterns. However, the `euribor3m` variable demonstrates some good differences between the average values for **yes** and **no** outcomes of the campaign and, again, seems counter-intuitive. We ideally expected higher bank deposits with higher interest rates. Therefore, let's make a note of the insight and validate it later.

Moving on, let's now explore the relationship between two categorical variables.

Studying the Relationship Between Two Categorical Variables

To study the relationship and patterns that exist between two categorical variables, we can first explore the frequency distribution across each category of the variables. A higher concentration in any outcome might be a potential insight. The most effective way to visualize this is using stacked bar charts.

A stacked bar chart will help us to observe the distribution of the target variable across multiple categorical variables. The distribution will reveal whether a specific category in a categorical variable dominates the target variable, **y**. If yes, we can further explore its influence on our problem.

In the next few exercises, we will explore various categorical variables across target variable **y** using stacked bar chart. We will plot absolute count and percentage to understand the distribution better.

Exercise 34: Studying the Relationship Between the Target y and marital status Variables

In this exercise, we will demonstrate the study between two categorical variables using plain frequency counts and then show how inconvenient it is.

To start simple, let's begin with exploring the relationship between the target, **y**, and **marital status**.

1. First, import the **ggplot2** package using the following command:

   ```
   library(ggplot2)
   ```

2. Create a DataFrame object, **df**, and use the **bank-additional-full.csv** file using the following command:

   ```
   df <- read.csv("/Chapter 2/Data/bank-additional/bank-additional-full.
   csv",sep=';')
   ```

3. Next, create a **temp** aggregation dataset:

   ```
   temp <- df %>% group_by(y,marital) %>% summarize(Count = n())
   ```

4. Define plot size, as illustrated here:

   ```
   options(repr.plot.width=12, repr.plot.height=4)
   ```

5. Plot the chart with frequency distribution:

```
ggplot(data = temp,aes(x=marital,y=Count,fill=y)) +
        geom_bar(stat="identity") +
        ggtitle("Distribution of target 'y' across Marital Status")
```

The output is as follows:

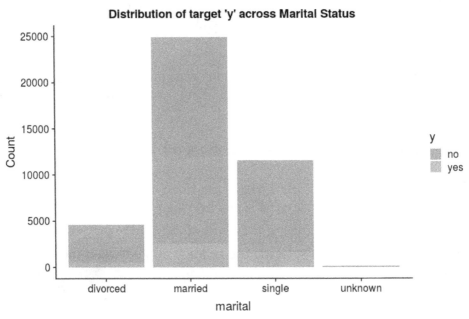

Figure 2.19: Using ggplot to study the relationship between the target y and marital status variables

We first aggregate the categorical columns using the **group_by** function. This would help us cross frequency count for each category combination. We now use this temporary dataset to plot the frequency distribution across the independent variable.

As we can see, the **yes** frequency is highest for married clients, but this may be true just because the number of married clients is high. To understand the relationship better, we can further break this down using a stacked bar chart with percentage distribution, where each bar represents the percentage of **yes** and **no**, respectively.

6. Create a **temp** aggregation dataset:

```
temp <- df %>% group_by(y,marital) %>%
               summarize(Count = n()) %>%
               ungroup() %>%  #This function ungroups the previously
grouped dataframe
               group_by(marital) %>%
               mutate(Perc = round(Count/sum(Count)*100)) %>%
               arrange(marital)
```

7. Define the plot size using the **options** method:

```
options(repr.plot.width=12, repr.plot.height=4)
```

8. Plot the percentage distribution using the **ggplot** method:

```
ggplot(data = temp,aes(x=marital,y=Perc,fill=y)) +
    geom_bar(stat="identity") +
    geom_text(aes(label = Perc), size = 5, hjust = 0.5, vjust = 0.3,
position = "stack") +
    ggtitle("Distribution of target 'y' percentage across Marital Status")
```

The output is as follows:

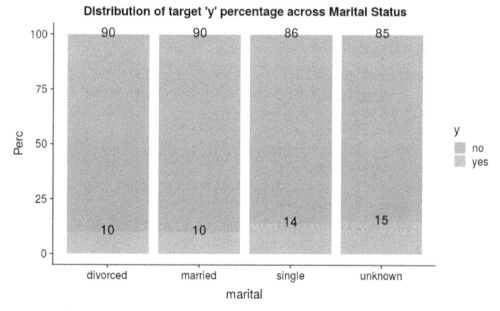

Figure 2.20: Distribution of target y percentage across marital status

We can now see counter-intuitive results compared to the previous plot. After we normalize the results, we see that **single** clients are more responsive to the campaign than those who are married. This is true for **unknown** too, but given the uncertainty of the value and the extremely low number of records, we should ignore this. We cannot directly conclude the result that single customers are more effective in responding to campaigns, but we can validate this later.

Exercise 35: Studying the Relationship between the job and education Variables

In this exercise, we will accelerate our exploration. Let's build a custom function where we can combine the two charts, that is, frequency distribution as well percentage distribution, for categorical variable's bivariate analysis.

Perform the following steps:

1. First, import the **ggplot2** package using the following command:

   ```
   library(ggplot2)
   ```

2. Create a DataFrame object, **df**, and use the **bank-additional-full.csv** file using the following command:

   ```
   df <- read.csv("/Chapter 2/Data/bank-additional/bank-additional-full.
   csv",sep=';')
   ```

3. Create a **temp** aggregation dataset:

   ```
   plot_bivariate_categorical <-  function(df, target, list_of_variables){
       target <- sym(target) #Converting the string to a column reference
       i <-1
       plt_matrix <- list()
       for(column in list_of_variables){
           col <- sym(column)
           temp <- df %>% group_by(!!sym(target),!!sym(col)) %>%
               summarize(Count = n()) %>%
               ungroup() %>% #This fucntion ungroups the previously grouped
   dataframe
               group_by(!!sym(col)) %>%
               mutate(Perc = round(Count/sum(Count)*100)) %>%
               arrange(!!sym(col))
   ```

4. Define the plot size:

```
options(repr.plot.width=14, repr.plot.height=12)
```

5. Plot the chart with a frequency distribution:

```
plt_matrix[[i]]<- ggplot(data =
temp,aes(x=!!sym(col),y=Count,fill=!!sym(target))) +
        geom_bar(stat="identity") +
        geom_text(aes(label = Count), size = 3, hjust = 0.5, vjust = -0.3,
position = "stack") +
        theme(axis.text.x = element_text(angle = 90, vjust = 1)) +
#rotates the labels
        ggtitle(paste("Distribution of target 'y'  frequency
across",column))
        i<-i+1
```

6. Plot the percentage distribution:

```
plt_matrix[[i]] <- ggplot(data =
temp,aes(x=!!sym(col),y=Perc,fill=!!sym(target))) +
        geom_bar(stat="identity") +
        geom_text(aes(label = Perc), size = 3, hjust = 0.5, vjust = -1,
position = "stack") +
        theme(axis.text.x = element_text(angle = 90, vjust = 1)) +
#rotates the labels
        ggtitle(paste("Distribution of target 'y' percentage
across",column))
        i <- i+1

    }
    plot_grid(plotlist = plt_matrix, ncol=2)
}
```

7. Plot the **plot_bivariate_categorical** using the following command:

```
plot_bivariate_categorical(df,"y",c("job","education"))
```

The output is as follows:

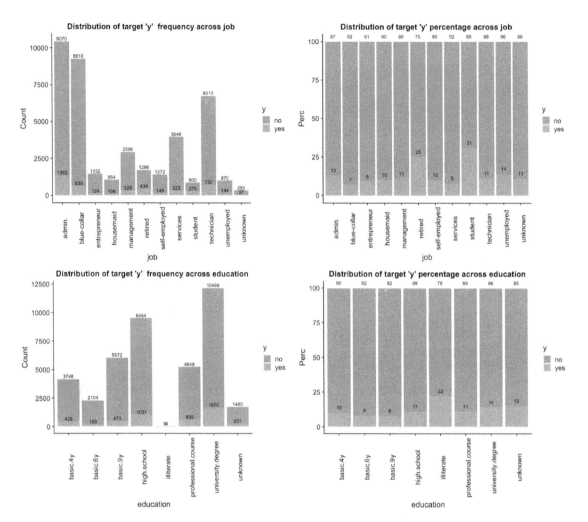

Figure 2.21: Studying the relationship between the job and education variables

We use the same principles to define the function that would plot the charts together. The additional difference here would be two plots for each combination. The first (left) is the frequency plot across the category combinations, and the right-hand side plot showcases the percentage distribution (normalized across category) visual. Studying both the plots together helps validate results more effectively. The creation of temporary aggregated datasets has an additional step with the use of the **ungroup** function. This is used to enable the relative percentage distribution of target outcome within the categorical levels of independent variable, that is, distribution of **y** across each level within **marital**.

If we observe the results from the previous output plots, we can see that the highest response rates for the campaign are from student and retired professionals, but this comes with a caveat. We see that both of these categories have far less observations as compared to the other categories. Therefore, we would need additional validation before making further conclusions. We, therefore, make a note of this insight too. From education levels, we don't see any interesting trends. Though **illiterate** clients have a high response rate, the number of observations are far too low to conclude anything tangible.

8. Let's take a look at credit default and housing loan categories:

```
plot_bivariate_categorical(df,"y",c("default","housing"))
```

The output is as follows:

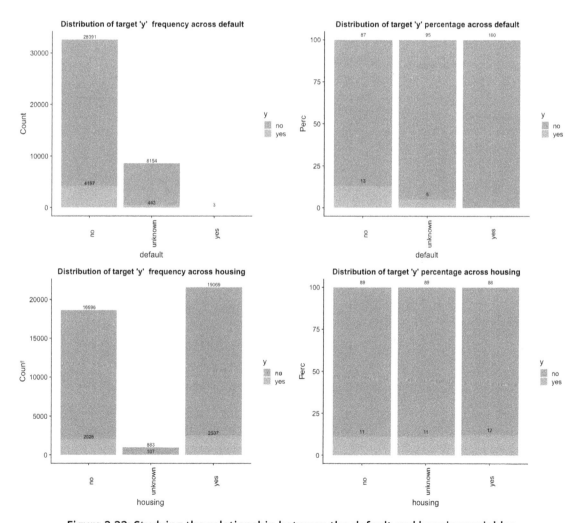

Figure 2.22: Studying the relationship between the default and housing variables

9. Again, we don't see any interesting trends. Let's continue the exploration for personal loan and contact mode:

```
plot_bivariate_categorical(df,"y",c("loan","contact"))
```

The output is as follows:

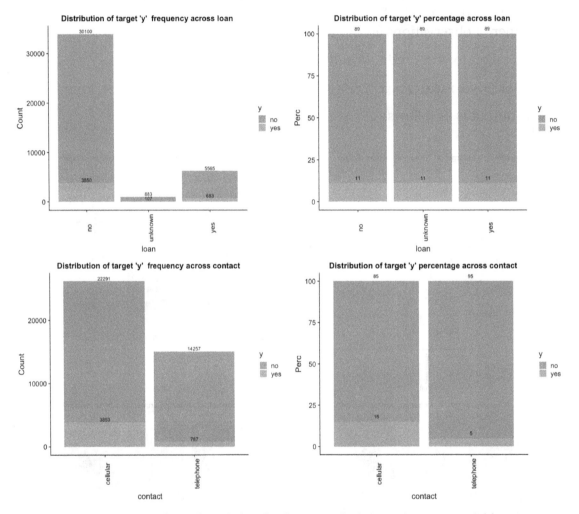

Figure 2.23: Studying the relationship between the loan and contact variables

Here, we can see an interesting trend for the mode of contact used. There is generally a higher response rate when the mode of campaign communication is cellular rather than landline. Let's make a note of this trend too and huddle back with further validation.

I encourage you to explore the relationships between our target variable and the remaining dependent categorical variables: month, day of week, and the previous outcome of the campaign.

Multivariate Analysis

Multivariate analysis is the process of studying the relationships between more than two variables; essentially, one dependent variable and more than one independent variable. Bivariate analysis is a form of multivariate analysis. There are several forms of multivariate analysis that are important, but we will skip the details for now to restrict the scope of the chapter. In the next few chapters, we will take a closer look at linear and logistic regression, which are two popular multivariate analysis techniques.

Some of the most common techniques used in multivariate analysis are as follows:

- Multiple linear regression (studying the impact of more than one independent variable on a numeric/continuous target variable)

- Logistic regression (studying the impact of more than one independent variable on a categorical target variable)

- Factor analysis

- MANOVA

Validating Insights Using Statistical Tests

Throughout the journey of EDA, we have collected and noted some interesting patterns for further validation. It is now the right time to test whether whatever we observed previously are actually valid patterns or just appeared to be interesting due to random chance. The most effective and straightforward way to approach this validation is by performing a set of statistical tests and measuring the statistical significance of the pattern. We have a ton of options in the available set of tests to choose from. The options vary based on the type of independent and dependent variable. The following is a handy reference diagram that explains the types of statistical test that we can perform to validate our observed patterns:

		Dependent	
		Categorical	Continuous
Independent	Categorical	Chi Squared test	T test/anova
	Continuous	Logistic Regression	Linear Regression

Figure 2.24: Validating dependent and independent variables

Let's collect all our interesting patterns into one place here:

- The campaign outcome has a higher chance of **yes** when the employee variance rate is low.

- The campaign outcome has a higher chance of **yes** when the euro interest rates are low.

- Single clients have a higher chance of responding positively to the campaign.

- Student and retired clients have a higher chance of responding positively to the campaign.

- Cellular contacts have a higher chance of responding positively to the campaign.

If you try to categorize these hypotheses, we can see that we have a categorical dependent variable in all cases. So, we should use a chi-squared test or logistic regression test to validate our results.

Let's perform these tests one by one.

Categorical Dependent and Numeric/Continuous Independent Variables

Hypotheses 1 and 2 have a continuous independent variable. Referring to the figure in the previous section, we will opt for the chi-squared test. In the process of hypothesis testing, we start by defining a null hypothesis and an alternate hypothesis. Start with a negative approach, that is, assume the null hypothesis to be what we don't want to happen. The hypothesis test examines the chances that the pattern observed happens due to random chance or there if is certainty about the observation. This measure is quantified as probability. If the probability of the significance of the null hypothesis to happen is less than 5% (or a suitable cut-off), we reject the null hypothesis and confirm the validity of the alternate hypothesis.

Let's begin; for hypothesis 1, we define the following:

- **Null hypothesis**: The campaign outcome has no relationship with the employee variance rate.

- **Alternate hypothesis**: The campaign outcome has a relationship with employee variance rate.

We test the validity of our null hypothesis with simple logistic regression. We will discuss this topic in more detail in the following chapters. For now, we will quickly perform a simple check to test our hypothesis. The following exercise leverages R's built-in function for performing logistic regression.

Exercise 36: Hypothesis 1 Testing for Categorical Dependent Variables and Continuous Independent Variables

To perform hypothesis testing for categorical dependent variables and continuous independent variables, we will use the `glm()` function to fit the logistic regression model (more on this in *Chapter 5, Classification*). This exercise will help us statistically test whether a categorical dependent variable (for example, **y**) has any relationship with a continuous independent variable, for example,

`emp.var.rate`.

Perform the following steps to complete the exercise:

1. Import the required libraries and create the DataFrame objects.

2. First, convert the dependent variable into a **factor** type:

    ```
    df$y <- factor(df$y)
    ```

3. Next, perform logistic regression:

    ```
    h.test <- glm(y ~ emp.var.rate, data = df, family = "binomial")
    ```

4. Print the test summary:

    ```
    summary(h.test)
    ```

    The output is as follows:

    ```
    Call:
    glm(formula = y ~ emp.var.rate, family = "binomial", data = df)

    Deviance Residuals:
        Min       1Q    Median       3Q       Max
    -1.0047   -0.4422   -0.3193   -0.2941    2.5150

    Coefficients:
                  Estimate Std. Error z value Pr(>|z|)
    (Intercept)  -2.33228     0.01939 -120.31   <2e-16 ***
    emp.var.rate -0.56222     0.01018  -55.25   <2e-16 ***
    ---
    Signif. codes:  0 '***' 0.001 '**' 0.01 '*' 0.05 '.' 0.1 ' ' 1

    (Dispersion parameter for binomial family taken to be 1)
    ```

```
        Null deviance: 28999  on 41187  degrees of freedom
    Residual deviance: 25597  on 41186  degrees of freedom
    AIC: 25601

Number of Fisher Scoring iterations: 5
```

We convert the target variable, **y**, as a **factor** (if it was not already). We use the **glm** function provided by R for logistic regression. The **glm** function also performs other forms of regression, and we specify the **family = 'binomial'** parameter for using the function as a logistic regression. The formula in the first place of the function defines the dependent and independent variables.

There are quite a few results shared in the output. We will ignore most of them for now and focus only on the final output. One of the results provided is the significance probability, which confirms that there is less than a **2e-16** chance that our null hypothesis is true, and therefore we can reject it. Therefore, the target outcome has a statistically significant relationship with the employee variance rate and, as we can see, there is a higher chance of campaign conversion as the rate decreases.

Similarly, let's repeat the same test for our second hypothesis. We define the following:

- **Null hypothesis**: The campaign outcome has no relationship with the euro interest rate.

- **Alternate hypothesis**: The campaign outcome has a relationship with the euro interest rate.

Exercise 37: Hypothesis 2 Testing for Categorical Dependent Variables and Continuous Independent Variables

Once again, we will use logistic regression to statistically test whether there is a relationship between the target variable, **y**, and the independent variable. In this exercise, we will use the **euribor3m** variable.

Perform the following steps:

1. Import the required libraries and create the DataFrame objects.

2. First, convert the dependent variable into a **factor** type:

```
df$y <- factor(df$y)
```

3. Next, perform logistic regression:

```
h.test2 <- glm(y ~ euribor3m, data = df, family = "binomial")
```

4. Print the test summary:

```
summary(h.test2)
```

The output is as follows:

```
Call:
glm(formula = y ~ euribor3m, family = "binomial", data = df)

Deviance Residuals:
    Min      1Q   Median       3Q      Max
-0.8568  -0.3730  -0.2997  -0.2917   2.5380

Coefficients:
              Estimate Std. Error z value Pr(>|z|)
(Intercept) -0.472940   0.027521  -17.18   <2e-16 ***
euribor3m   -0.536582   0.009547  -56.21   <2e-16 ***
---
Signif. codes:  0 '***' 0.001 '**' 0.01 '*' 0.05 '.' 0.1 ' ' 1

(Dispersion parameter for binomial family taken to be 1)

    Null deviance: 28999  on 41187  degrees of freedom
Residual deviance: 25343  on 41186  degrees of freedom
AIC: 25347

Number of Fisher Scoring iterations: 5
```

Focusing exclusively on the previous output, we can confirm that we can reject the null hypothesis and accept the alternative hypothesis. Therefore, the target outcome has a statistically significant relationship with the Euro Interest rate and, as we can see, there is a higher chance of campaign conversion as the rate decreases.

Categorical Dependent and Categorical Independent Variables

Moving on, let's take a look at the third hypothesis. To test the relationship between the categorical dependent variable and categorical independent variable, we can use the chi squared test.

For hypothesis 3, we define the following:

- **Null hypothesis**: The campaign outcome has no relationship with clients who never married.

- **Alternate hypothesis**: The campaign outcome has a relationship with clients who never married.

In the following exercise, we will leverage R's chi-square test function to validate the hypothesis..

Exercise 38: Hypothesis 3 Testing for Categorical Dependent Variables and Categorical Independent Variables

In this exercise, we will perform a statistical test using the chi-squared test. We use the chi-squared test because both the independent and dependent variables are categorical, particularly when testing the relationship between **y** and marital status.

Perform the following steps:

1. Import the required libraries and create the DataFrame objects.

2. First, convert the dependent variable into a **factor** type:

   ```
   df$y <- factor(df$y)
   ```

3. Create a flag for **single** clients:

   ```
   df$single_flag <- as.factor(ifelse(df$marital ==
   "single","single","other"))
   ```

4. Create a **sample** object and print the value:

   ```
   sample <- table(df$y, df$single_flag)
   print(sample)
   ```

   The output is as follows:

   ```
        other single
   no   26600   9948
   yes   3020   1620
   ```

5. Perform the chi-squared test:

   ```
   h.test3 <- chisq.test(sample)
   ```

6. Print the test summary:

   ```
   print(h.test3)
   ```

The output is as follows:

```
Pearson's Chi-squared test with Yates' continuity correction

data:  sample
X-squared = 120.32, df = 1, p-value < 2.2e-16
```

We first create a new variable/flag for this test where we define whether a client is **single** or not. Since we are exclusively defining our relationship between the target and client's **single** marital status, we mask all other classes within marital status.

The **table** command creates a new DataFrame with a simple frequency distribution between each individual class. Finally, we use this DataFrame to perform the chi-squared test.

As we can see, the p-value or the chance of the null hypothesis being true is far less than 5%. Therefore, we can accept our alternate hypothesis, which confirms the fact that the campaign's outcome is positively influenced by single clients rather than other clients.

Moving on, let's take a quick look at the validity of our 4th and 5th hypotheses.

For the 4th and 5th hypotheses, we define the following:

- **Null hypothesis**: The campaign outcome has no relationship with clients who are students or retired. The campaign outcome has no relationship with the contact mode used.

- **Alternate hypothesis**: The campaign outcome has no relationship with clients who are students or retired. The campaign outcome has a relationship with the contact mode used.

Exercise 39: Hypothesis 4 and 5 Testing for a Categorical Dependent Variable and a Categorical Independent Variable

Once again, let's use the chi-squared test to statistically check whether there is a relationship between the target variable, **y**, the categorical independent variable **job_flag**, and **contact**.

Perform the following steps:

1. Import the required libraries and create the DataFrame objects.

2. First, convert the dependent variable into a **factor** type:

```
df$y <- factor(df$y)
```

3. Prepare the independent variable:

```
df$job_flag <- as.factor(ifelse(df$job %in% c("student","retired"),as.
character(df$job),"other"))
df$contact <- as.factor(df$contact)
```

4. Create an object named **sample4** and print the value:

```
sample4 <- table(df$y, df$job_flag)
print("Frequency table for Job")
print(sample4)
```

The output is as follows:

```
[1] "Frequency table for Job"
   other retired student
no  34662    1286     600
yes  3931     434     275
```

5. Perform the test for the 4th hypothesis:

```
h.test4 <- chisq.test(sample4)
```

6. Print the test summary for the 4th hypothesis:

```
print("Hypothesis #4 results")
print(h.test4)
```

The output is as follows:

```
[1] "Hypothesis #4 results"
Pearson's Chi-squared test

data:  sample4
X-squared = 736.53, df = 2, p-value < 2.2e-16
```

7. Now, create a new **sample5** object and print the value:

```
print("Frequency table for Contact")
sample5 <- table(df$y, df$contact)
print(sample5)
```

The output is as follows:

```
[1] "Frequency table for Contact"
   cellular telephone
no    22291     14257
yes    3853       787
```

8. Perform the test on the **test5** variable:

```
h.test5 <- chisq.test(sample5)
```

9. Print the test summary for the 5th hypothesis:

```
print("Hypothesis #5 results")
print(h.test5)
```

The output is as follows:

```
[1] "Hypothesis #5 results"
Pearson's Chi-squared test with Yates' continuity correction

data:  sample5
X-squared = 862.32, df = 1, p-value < 2.2e-16
```

We can see that results have been validated in our favor. We can also see that there is definitely a relationship between student and retired clients and the cellular mode of communication with a positive outcome in the campaign.

Collating Insights – Refine the Solution to the Problem

We have now traversed the length and breadth of EDA. In the different sections, we studied the data in varying levels of depth. Now that we have valid answers for the data exploration problem, we can touch base again with the initial problem defined. If you recall the **complication** and **question** section in the problem statement, we had *What are factors that lead to poor performance of the campaign*. Well, we now have an answer based on the patterns we discovered during the bivariate analysis and validated with statistical tests.

Collating all the hypotheses validated with the correct story brings about the solution to our problem. Spend good time with the outcome of each of the hypothesis test results to knit the story together. Each hypothesis tells us whether an independent variable has a relationship with a dependent variable.

Summary

In this chapter, we explored EDA using a practical use case and traversed the business problem. We started by understanding the overall process of executing a data science problem and then defined our business problem using an industry standard framework. With the use case being cemented with appropriate questions and complications, we understood the role of EDA in designing the solution for the problem. Exploring the journey of EDA, we studied univariate, bivariate, and multivariate analysis. We performed the analysis using a combination of analytical as well as visual techniques. Through this, we explored the R packages for visualization, that is, **ggplot** and some packages for data wrangling through **dplyr**. We also validated our insights with statistical tests and, finally, collated the insights noted to loop back with the original problem statement.

In the next chapter, we will lay the foundation for various machine learning algorithms, and discuss supervised learning in depth.

3

Introduction to Supervised Learning

Learning Objectives

By the end of this chapter, you will be able to:

- Explain supervised learning and machine learning workflow

- Use and explore the Beijing PM2.5 dataset

- Explain the difference between continuous and categorical dependent variables

- Implement the basic regression and classification algorithms in R

- Identify the key differences between supervised learning and other types of machine learning

- Work with the evaluation metrics of supervised learning algorithms

- Perform model diagnostics for avoiding biased coefficient estimates and large standard errors

In this chapter, we will introduce supervised learning and demonstrate the workflow of building machine learning models with real-world examples.

Introduction

In the previous chapters, we explored some of packages of R, such as the `dplyr`, `plyr`, `lubridate`, and `ggplot2`, where we discussed the basics of storing and processing data in R. Later, the same ideas were used in Exploratory Data Analysis (EDA) to understand the ways to break data into smaller parts, extract insights from data, and explore other ways to understand the data better, before venturing into advanced modeling techniques.

In this chapter, we will take one step further toward introducing machine learning ideas. While broadly laying the foundation for thinking about various algorithms in machine learning, we will discuss supervised learning at length.

Supervised learning is based on data that is well labeled by domain experts. For classifying cats and dogs from images, an algorithm first needs to see the images labeled as cats and dogs and then learn the features based on the label. Most enterprises with a good volume of historical data are the biggest beneficiaries of the wealth of knowledge they can extract from such data. If the data is clean and annotated well, supervised learning can result in a high accuracy of prediction, unlike other machine learning algorithms, which generally produce large errors in the beginning. In the absence of the right labels, it becomes difficult to derive any meaning out of data, other than just being able to do exploratory analysis and clustering.

The standard component in solving real-world problems like predicting loan default (yes/no), failure of manufacturing machines in factories (yes/no), object detection in driverless cars (road, car, signal), predicting stock market prices (numeric) is a set of inputs (features) and a given output (label), which is usually obtained from historical data. When we predict the quantitative output, we call it **regression**, and when we predict the qualitative output, we call it **classification**.

Summary of the Beijing PM2.5 Dataset

In the urban and rural parts of many nations, the primary pollutant, fine particulate matter, is the cause of many health risks in humans and also affects climate change. In particular, PM2.5, defined as an airborne particle with an aerodynamic diameter of less than 2.5 µm, is the major category of atmospheric particulate matter. Various studies have linked PM2.5 with serious health problems such as heart attack and lung morbidity. The table in this section shows the types of atmospheric particulate matter and their size distribution in micrometers.

In this and the remaining chapters, we will use the dataset published by the authors of the research paper, *Assessing Beijing's PM2.5 pollution: severity, weather impact, APEC and winter heating*, where they use hourly PM2.5 readings taken at the US Embassy in Beijing located at 116.47 E, 39.95 N in conjunction with hourly meteorological measurements at **Beijing Capital International Airport (BCIA)**, obtained from weather. nocrew.org. Their study claims to be the first to combine PM2.5 and meteorological data for an extended period in China's PM2.5 pollution. The following table describes the attributes in the dataset:

S.No.	Attribute Name	Description
1	No	row number
2	Year	year of data in this row
3	Month	month of data in this row
4	day	day of data in this row
5	hour	hour of data in this row
6	pm2.5	PM2.5 concentration (ug/m^3)
7	DEWP	Dew Point ()
8	TEMP	Temperature ()
9	PRES	Pressure (hPa)
10	cbwd	Combined wind direction
11	Iws	Cumulated wind speed (m/s)
12	Is	Cumulated hours of snow
13	Ir	Cumulated hours of rain

Figure 3.1: Attributes in Beijing's PM2.5 dataset.

Exercise 40: Exploring the Data

In this exercise, we will learn the structure of the data with sample values for each attribute and use the **summary** function. We will see the five number summary statistics for numeric variables.

Perform the following steps to complete this exercise:

1. First, use the following command to read the Beijing PM2.5 dataset into the PM25 DataFrame object:

```
PM25 <- read.csv("https://raw.githubusercontent.com/TrainingByPackt/
Applied-Supervised-Learning-with-R/master/Lesson03/PRSA_data_2010.1.1-
2014.12.31.csv")
```

2. Next, print the structure of data with sample values using the **str** command:

```
str(PM25)
```

The output of the previous command is as follows:

```
'data.frame':       43824 obs. of  13 variables:
 $ No    : int  1 2 3 4 5 6 7 8 9 10 ...
 $ year  : int  2010 2010 2010 2010 2010 2010 2010 2010 2010 2010 ...
 $ month : int  1 1 1 1 1 1 1 1 1 1 ...
 $ day   : int  1 1 1 1 1 1 1 1 1 1 ...
 $ hour  : int  0 1 2 3 4 5 6 7 8 9 ...
 $ pm2.5 : int  NA NA NA NA NA NA NA NA NA NA ...
 $ DEWP  : int  -21 -21 -21 -21 -20 -19 -19 -19 -19 -20 ...
 $ TEMP  : num  -11 -12 -11 -14 -12 -10 -9 -9 -9 -8 ...
 $ PRES  : num  1021 1020 1019 1019 1018 ...
 $ cbwd  : Factor w/ 4 levels "cv","NE","NW",..: 3 3 3 3 3 3 3 3 3 3 ...
 $ Iws   : num  1.79 4.92 6.71 9.84 12.97 ...
 $ Is    : int  0 0 0 0 0 0 0 0 0 0 ...
 $ Ir    : int  0 0 0 0 0 0 0 0 0 0 ...
```

> **Note**
>
> Observe that the dataset contains **43824** observations and 13 attributes.
> Observe that the dataset contains data from 2010 to 2014. The values of pm2.5,
> temperature, pressure, combined wind direction, cumulated wind speed,
> cumulated hours of snow, and cumulated hours of rain are aggregated at every
> hour of the day.

3. Now, let's show the summary statistics of the dataset:

```
summary(PM25)
```

The output is as follows:

```
      No              year           month           day            hour
pm2.5
 Min.   :    1  Min.   :2010   Min.   : 1.000  Min.   : 1.00   Min.   :
0.00   Min.   :   0.00
 1st Qu.:10957  1st Qu.:2011   1st Qu.: 4.000  1st Qu.: 8.00   1st Qu.:
5.75   1st Qu.:  29.00
 Median :21912  Median :2012   Median : 7.000  Median :16.00   Median
:11.50   Median :  72.00
 Mean   :21912  Mean   :2012   Mean   : 6.524  Mean   :15.73   Mean
:11.50   Mean   :  98.61
 3rd Qu.:32868  3rd Qu.:2013   3rd Qu.:10.000  3rd Qu.:23.00   3rd
Qu.:17.25   3rd Qu.: 137.00
 Max.   :43824  Max.   :2014   Max.   :12.000  Max.   :31.00   Max.
:23.00   Max.   : 994.00

 NA's   :2067
      DEWP            TEMP            PRES         cbwd            Iws
Is
 Min.   :-40.000  Min.   :-19.00   Min.   : 991   cv: 9387   Min.   :
0.45   Min.   : 0.00000
 1st Qu.:-10.000  1st Qu.:  2.00   1st Qu.:1008   NE: 4997   1st Qu.:
1.79   1st Qu.: 0.00000
 Median :  2.000  Median : 14.00   Median :1016   NW:14150   Median :
5.37   Median : 0.00000
 Mean   :  1.817  Mean   : 12.45   Mean   :1016   SE:15290   Mean   :
23.89   Mean   : 0.05273
 3rd Qu.: 15.000  3rd Qu.: 23.00   3rd Qu.:1025              3rd Qu.:
21.91   3rd Qu.: 0.00000
 Max.   : 28.000  Max.   : 42.00   Max.   :1046              Max.
:585.60   Max.   :27.00000

      Ir
 Min.   : 0.0000
 1st Qu.: 0.0000
 Median : 0.0000
 Mean   : 0.1949
 3rd Qu.: 0.0000
 Max.   :36.0000
```

The following image is a graphical representation of the size distribution (in micrometers) of atmospheric particulate matter:

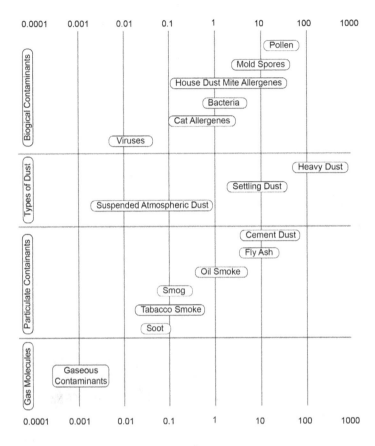

Figure 3.2: Types and size distribution (in micrometers) of atmospheric particulate matter.

Source: https://en.wikipedia.org/wiki/File:Airborne-particulate-size-chart.svg

Note

The authors of the article "The impact of PM2.5 on the human respiratory system" published in the **Journal of Thoracic Disease (JTD)** discuss the association of air pollution with respiratory system diseases. They offer a comprehensive data-driven approach for explaining the factors causing such respiratory diseases. Special attention is given to Beijing, where the adverse effect of rising PM2.5 has been studied extensively by researchers and has become a mainstream discussion point in the various climate change forums around the world. One can find more detail in the article at https://www.ncbi.nlm.nih.gov/pmc/articles/PMC4740125/.

Regression and Classification Problems

We see classification and regression problems all around us in our daily life. The chances of rain from https://weather.com, our emails getting filtered into the spam mailbox and inbox, our personal and home loans getting accepted or rejected, deciding to pick our next holiday destination, exploring the options for buying a new house, investment decisions to gain short- and long-term benefits, purchasing the next book from Amazon; the list goes on and on. The world around us today is increasingly being run by algorithms that help us with our choices (which is not always a good thing).

As discussed in *Chapter 2, Exploratory Analysis of Data*, we will use the **Minto Pyramid** principle called **Situation–Complication–Question (SCQ)** to define our problem statement. The following table shows the SCQ approach for Beijing's PM2.5 problem:

Situation Define the current situation. We can simplify this by answering the question—What happened?	Beijing and a substantial part of China are experiencing persistent air pollution. The principal pollutants are fine particulate matter and PM2.5 in particular.
Complication Define the roadblock faced by the team in achieving their desired outcomes.	An important step to remedy the situation is to measure the PM2.5 levels with certainty. Also, the relationship between PM2.5 and all the confounding factors from metrological data needs to be established. Both require diligent planning and thorough analysis.
Question Define the question that would need answers to solve the problem.	What are the factors affecting (with their strength) the PM2.5 levels in the atmosphere?

Figure 3.3: Applying SCQ on Beijing's PM2.5 problem.

Now, in the SCQ construct described in the previous table, we can do a simple correlation analysis to establish the factors affecting the PM2.5 levels or create a predictive problem (prediction means finding an approximate function that maps from input variables to an output) that estimates the PM2.5 levels using all the factors. For the clarity of terminology, we will refer to factors as input variables. Then, PM2.5 becomes the dependent variable (often referred to as output variable). The dependent variable could be either categorical or continuous.

For example, in the email classification into **SPAM/NOT SPAM** problem, the dependent variable is categorical. The following table highlights some critical differences between regression and classification problems:

S.No.	Regression	Classification
1	The dependent variable is a continuous quantity.	The dependent variable is categorical (also referred to as a discrete label).
2	Regression algorithm's effectiveness could be measured with metrics like **Root Mean Square Error (RMSE)**.	Classification algorithms are usually evaluated using accuracy, precision, and recall.
3	It's possible to convert a continuous dependent variable into a discrete label. For e.g. continuous temperature values could be represented as HIGH, MEDIUM and LOW.	It's usually not possible to convert a categorical value into continuous scale unless there is an ordinal relationship.
4	The output of the regression algorithm is the estimate of the dependent variable.	The output of a classification algorithm is in terms of probabilities. The category with the highest probability is predicted as the output.

Figure 3.4: Difference between regression and classification problems.

Machine Learning Workflow

In order to demonstrate the end-to-end process of building a predictive model (machine learning or supervised learning), we have created an easy-to-comprehend workflow. The first step is to design the problem, then source and prepare the data, which leads to coding the model for training and evaluation, and, finally, deploying the model. In the scope of this chapter, we will keep the model explanation to a bare minimum, as it will be covered again in detail in chapters 4 and 5.

The following figure describes the workflow required to build a predictive model starting from preparing the data to deploying the model:

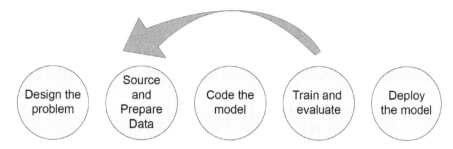

Figure 3.5: Machine learning workflow.

Design the Problem

Once we identify the domain of work, brainstorming on the designing of the problem is carried out. The idea is to first define the problem as a regression or classification problem. Once that is done, we choose the right target variable, along with identifying the features. The target variable is important because it decides how the training will take place. A supervised learning algorithm keeps the target variable at the center, while it tries to find a pattern from the given set of features.

Source and Prepare Data

Data gathering and preparation is a painstaking job, mainly when the data sources are diverse and many. With each data source, the challenges are different and hence the time taken to process it varies. Data sources with tabular data are the easiest to process provided they do not contain a lot of garbage information, whereas textual data is the hardest to clean because of its free-flowing nature.

Code the Model

Once the data is prepared and ready, we take up the task of choosing the right model. Most often, the experts first go with one baseline model to gauge the predictability power of the algorithm using input features and the target variable. Then, one can either directly try the state-of-the-art algorithms or decide to go with a trial-and-error method (of trying to use all the possible models). One must understand that there is no right or wrong model, and everything depends on the data. In coding, the data is randomly divided into training and testing. The code is written to train the model on the training dataset, and evaluation happens on the testing data. This ensures that the model does not underperform when it is deployed in the real world.

Train and Evaluate

Model evaluation is the important part of the model, where its usability in practice is decided. Based on a given set of model evaluation metrics, we need to decide, after all the trial and error, the best model. In each iteration, metrics such as the R-squared value, accuracy, precision, and F-score are computed. Usually, the entire data is divided into training and testing data (with a third split for validation set also often included). The model is trained on the training data and tested on the testing data. This separation ensures that the model is not doing any rote learning. In more technical terms, the model is not overfitting (more on this in the *Evaluation Metrics* section in this chapter). Usually, at this stage of the workflow, one could decide to go back and include more variables, train the model, and redeploy. The process is repeated until the accuracy (or the other metrics of importance) of the model reaches a plateau.

We use a random number generator function like **sample()** in R for splitting the data randomly into different parts as done in the next exercise 2, step 2.

Exercise 41: Creating a Train-and-Test Dataset Randomly Generated by the Beijing PM2.5 Dataset

In this exercise, we will create a randomly generated train-and-test dataset from the Beijing PM2.5 dataset. We will reuse the **PM25** object created in the earlier exercise.

Perform the following steps:

1. Create a **num_index** variable and set it to a value equal to the number of observations in the Beijing's PM2.5 dataset:

    ```
    num_index <- nrow(PM25)
    ```

2. Using the **sample()** function, randomly select 70% of the **num_index** values, and store them in **train_index**:

    ```
    train_index <- sample(1:num_index, 0.7*nrow(PM25))
    ```

3. Use **train_index** to select a random subset of rows from the Beijing PM2.5 dataset and store them in a DataFrame named **PM25_Train**:

    ```
    PM25_Train <- PM25[train_index,]
    ```

4. Store the remaining observation into a DataFrame named **PM25_Test**:

    ```
    PM25_Test <- PM25[-train_index,]
    ```

The exercise shows a simple example for creating the train-and-test set. A randomly selected set for training and testing ensures that the model has no bias and learns well from all the possible examples before being used in the real world on unseen data.

Deploy the Model

Once the best model is selected, the next step is to enable the model output to be used by a business application. The model is hosted as a **REpresentational State Transfer (REST)** API. These APIs are a way to host a web application as an endpoint that listens to any request for a model call and usually returns a JSON object as a response.

Deployment of the model is becoming an essential part of all machine learning projects in the industry. A model that is not deployable is no good for a company, and perhaps, merely serves the purpose of R&D. An increasing number of professionals are specializing in model deployment, which is sometimes a tedious and complicated process. In order to give the model deployment its due importance, we have given it a dedicated chapter, that is *Chapter 8, Model Deployment*.

Regression

Now that we have seen the machine learning workflow, we will take two widely used types of machine learning algorithms: regression and classification; both employ supervised learning to train the models. The entire theme of this book revolves around these two types of algorithms. The Beijing PM2.5 dataset will be used extensively in demonstrating both these types. The dataset will help in understanding how one can convert a regression problem into a classification problem and vice versa.

Simple and Multiple Linear Regression

Regression is one of the most useful and essential tools in analytics and econometrics (the branch of economics concerned with the use of mathematical methods, especially statistics, in describing economic systems). In many ways, modern machine learning has its roots in statistics, and one can attribute that mostly to Sir Francis Galton's work. Galton was an English Victorian-era statistician and polymath with deep interest and expertise in fields such as genetics, psychology, and anthropology. He was the first to apply statistical methods to study human behavior and intelligence. Notably, his publication, *Regression Towards Mediocrity in Hereditary Stature*, had many insightful findings based on regression.

In this section, we will briefly analyze the various factors that affect the PM2.5 levels using the Beijing dataset. In particular, the effect of variables such as dew point, temperature, wind speed, and pressure on PM2.5 will be explored.

Assumptions in Linear Regression Models

As regression borrows many of its concepts from applied statistics to model the data, it comes with many assumptions. One should not apply regression algorithms to any dataset or problem. Let's examine the assumptions for linear regression before we build any model.

The following table shows the assumptions and how we can statistically test whether the linear regression model follows the assumption or not. The table also shows some corrective actions if the assumption is violated. We will take up an elaborate discussion on these assumptions and perform diagnostic analysis to identify the violation in much detail in *Chapter 4, Regression*.

S.No.	Assumption	Statistical Test	Visual Test	Corrective Step
1	A linear relationship between the dependent and independent variable.	Observed better in visual tests than a statistical test.	Residual versus predicted plot (scatterplot).	Usually, a non-linear transformation like a natural log on dependent variable helps.
2	Normality—all the variables are normality distributed.	The goodness of fit test like the Kolmogorov-Smirnov test.	Histogram or Q-Q Plot.	Usually, a non-linear transformation like a natural log on dependent variable helps.
3	Multicollinearity—occurs when two or more independent variables are highly correlated.	Correlation, Tolerance, Variance Inflation Factor (VIF).	Correlation plot.	Remove the variables with high VIF score.

Figure 3.6: Various assumptions in a linear regression model (Part 1).

4	No Autocorrelation —Occurs when one value of an independent variable is correlated with another. For example, stock prices.	Durbin-Watson test.	Scatterplot of residuals (the difference between the actual and predicted value of a dependent variable).	Adding lags of dependent or/and independent variables help.
5	Homoscedasticity— Occurs when the residuals are equal throughout the regression line.	Goldfeld-Quandt Test can also be used to test for heteroscedasticity (not homoscedastic).	Scatterplot of residuals should show random spread.	Natural log transformation on the dependent variable usually helps.

Figure 3.7: Various assumptions in a linear regression model (Part 2).

Exploratory Data Analysis (EDA)

Building regression models requires an in-depth analysis of the patterns and relationship between target and input variables. The Beijing dataset provides a magnitude of different environmental factors that may affect the PM2.5 levels in the atmosphere.

Exercise 42: Exploring the Time Series Views of PM2.5, DEWP, TEMP, and PRES variables of the Beijing PM2.5 Dataset

In this exercise, we will visualize the pm2.5, DEWP, TEMP, and PRES variables in a time series plot and observe any patterns that may emerge over the years in these variables.

Perform the following steps to complete the exercise:

1. Import all the required libraries in the system:

    ```
    library(dplyr)
    library(lubridate)
    library(tidyr)
    library(grid)
    library(ggplot2)
    ```

2. Next, transform year, month, and hour into datetime using the **lubridate** package function named **ymd_h**:

```
PM25$datetime <- with(PM25, ymd_h(sprintf('%04d%02d%02d%02d', year, month,
day,hour)))
```

3. Plot the PM2.5, TEMP, DEWP, and PRES for all the years using the following command:

```
plot_pm25 <- PM25 %>%
  select(datetime, pm2.5) %>%
  na.omit() %>%
  ggplot() +
  geom_point(aes(x = datetime, y = pm2.5), size = 0.5, alpha = 0.75) +
  ylab("PM2.5")

plot_TEMP <- PM25 %>%
  select(datetime, TEMP) %>%
  na.omit() %>%
  ggplot() +
  geom_point(aes(x = datetime, y = TEMP), size = 0.5, alpha = 0.75) +
  ylab("TEMP")

plot_DEWP <- PM25 %>%
  select(datetime, DEWP) %>%
  na.omit() %>%
  ggplot() +
  geom_point(aes(x = datetime, y = DEWP), size = 0.5, alpha = 0.75) +
  ylab("DEWP")

plot_PRES <- PM25 %>%
  select(datetime, PRES) %>%
  na.omit() %>%
  ggplot() +
  geom_point(aes(x = datetime, y = PRES), size = 0.5, alpha = 0.75) +
  ylab("PRES")
```

4. Now, use the following command to plot the graphs:

```
grid.newpage()
grid.draw(rbind(ggplotGrob(plot_pm25), ggplotGrob(plot_
TEMP),ggplotGrob(plot_DEWP),ggplotGrob(plot_PRES), size = "last"))
```

The plot is as follows:

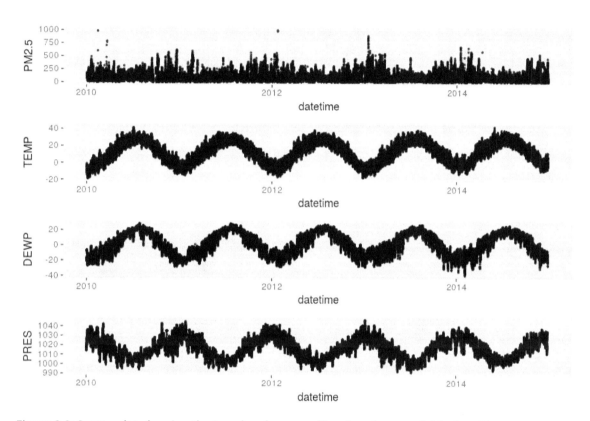

Figure 3.8: Scatterplot showing the trend and seasonality of environmental factors like temperature, dew point, and pressure, along with PM2.5 levels in Beijing from 2010 to 2014 end.

In this exercise, we first show a time series view of the PM2.5, DEWP, TEMP, and PRES variables from the dataset and observe the pattern. As shown in *Figure* 3.8, a distinct seasonality is observed **year on year (YoY)**. While DEWP, TEMP, and PRES show seasonality (the same pattern repeating every 12 months), PM2.5 seems to have a random pattern. This is an early indication that it's highly unlikely that we will see any effect of the three variables on PM2.5. However, let's probe further to ascertain this hypothesis using a correlation plot and observe if there exits any relationship between the variables.

Exercise 43: Undertaking Correlation Analysis

In this exercise, we will undertake a correlation analysis to study the strength of the relationship between the various factors.

Perform the following steps to complete the exercise:

1. Import the **corrplot** package into the system using the following command:

    ```
    library(corrplot)
    ```

2. Now, create a new object and store the required values from **PM25** into it:

    ```
    corr <- cor(PM25[!is.
    na(PM25$pm2.5),c("pm2.5","DEWP","TEMP","PRES","Iws","Is","Ir")])
    ```

3. Use the **corrplot** package to display the graphical representation of a correlation matrix:

    ```
    corrplot(corr)
    ```

    The plot is as follows:

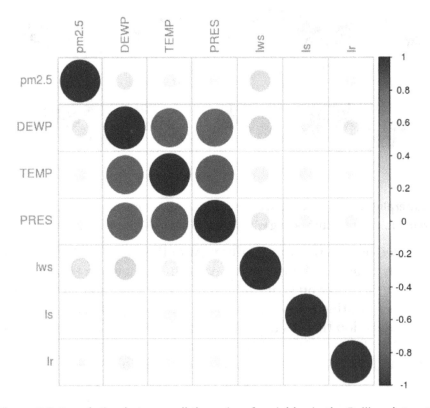

Figure 3.9: Correlation between all the pairs of variables in the Beijing dataset.

First, we compute the correlation between all the variables. The resulting correlation plot shows that there appear to be no strong correlations between PM2.5 and the other variables. However, `PM2.5` and `DEWP`, `TEMP`, and `Iws` show some mild correlation, which indicates some relationship. This should not come as a surprise, because we saw in *Figure* 3.8, that while three variables follow a seasonality trend, PM2.5 seems more random. Note here that we have not done any processing or transformation to the dataset; these findings come directly from our first level of analysis. We will go into much detail later, in *Chapter* 4, *Regression*. Now, let's also visualize the relationship between the variables using a scatterplot.

Exercise 44: Drawing a Scatterplot to Explore the Relationship between PM2.5 Levels and Other Factors

In this exercise, we will use a scatterplot to explore the relationship between `pm2.5` levels and other factors. We will like to see whether there emerge any interesting patterns or relationships. A scatterplot is a simple and effective visualization for exploratory analysis on the relationships between variables.

Perform the following steps to complete the exercise:

1. Import the **ggplot2** package into your system:

```
library(ggplot2)
```

2. Plot the scatterplot between **DEWP** and **PM2.5**, with the **month** variable used for color:

```
ggplot(data = PM25, aes(x = DEWP, y = pm2.5, color = month)) +
  geom_point() +
  geom_smooth(method='auto',formula=y~x, colour = "red", size =1.5)
```

The scatterplot is as follows:

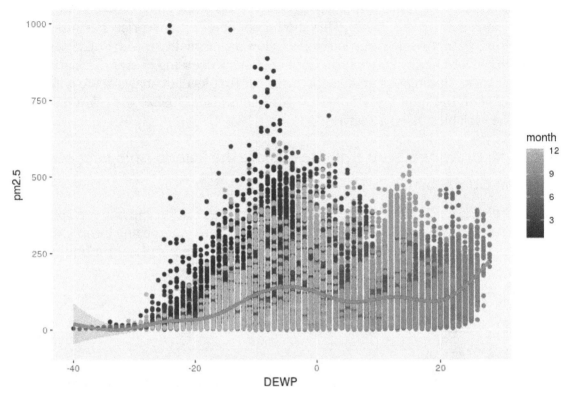

Figure 3.10: Scatterplot showing the relationship between DEWP and PM2.5 levels.

3. Plot the scatterplot between **TEMP** and **PM2.5**, with the **month** variable used for color:

```
ggplot(data = PM25, aes(x = TEMP, y = pm2.5, color = month)) +
  geom_point() +
  geom_smooth(method='auto',formula=y~x, colour = "red", size =1.5)
```

The scatterplot is as follows:

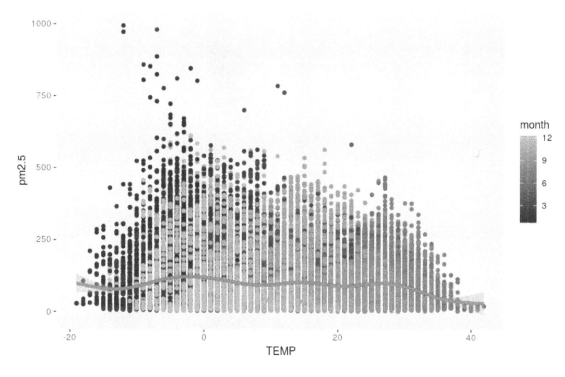

Figure 3.11: Scatterplot showing the relationship between TEMP and PM2.5 levels.

4. Create a scatterplot between **DEWP** and **PM2.5**, with an hour of the day used for color and separate views for months of the year:

```
ggplot(data = PM25, aes(x = DEWP, y = pm2.5, color = hour)) +
  geom_point() +
  geom_smooth(method='auto',formula=y~x, colour = "red", size =1) +
  facet_wrap(~ month, nrow = 4)
```

The scatterplot is as follows:

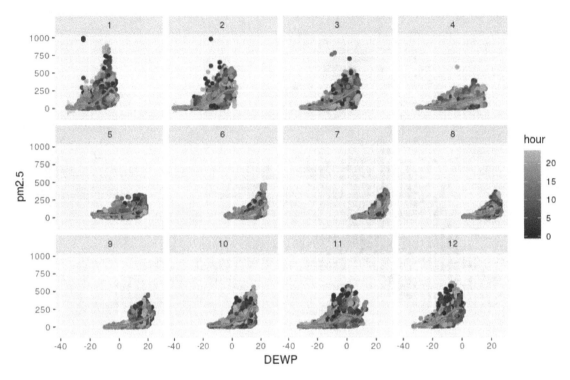

Figure 3.12: Scatterplot showing the relationship between DEWP and PM2.5 split by month of the year.

In order to gauge some relationship between variables, we used a scatterplot between **PM2.5** and **DEWP** with a line of fit. Observe that in the code, we have passed an argument to **geom_smooth()**, that is, **method = "auto"**, which automatically decides, based on the data, which model to use to fit a line. As shown in *Figure 3.10*, the line is not linear. The **geom_smooth** method chooses **generalized additive model (GAM)**. This indicates that the linear relationship assumption of the linear regression model is being violated. A similar pattern is seen with the **TEMP** and **PM2.5** plot, as shown in *Figure 3.11*. However, we could go one step further and split the scatterplot month-wise, as shown in *Figure 3.12*. This shows that a linear relationship exists, but it is highly season-dependent. For example, in April (represented by the integer **4**), the **DEWP** and **PM2.5** have a near-to-perfect straight line fit. We will extend this discussion into further details in *Chapter 4, Regression*.

So, we have seen some violation of assumption and the lack of a strong correlation between the environmental factors and PM2.5. However, there seems to be some scope for further scrutiny. In this introductory chapter on supervised learning, we will only focus on the approach based on our machine learning workflow.

> **Note**
>
> To know more about GAM, review this document: https://www.stat.cmu. edu/~cshalizi/uADA/12/lectures/ch13.pdf.

Activity 5: Draw a Scatterplot between PRES and PM2.5 Split by Months

In this activity, we will create a scatterplot between `DWEP` and `PM2.5`. Through this activity, we will learn to use the `facet_wrap()` function to create a layer on top of `ggplot()` for splitting the visualization of scatterplot into each month, thus helping to observe any seasonality pattern.

Perform the following steps to complete the activity:

1. In `ggplot`, assign the component of the `a()` method with the `PRES` variable.

2. In the next layer of the `geom_smooth()` method, set `colour = "blue"` to differentiate.

3. Finally, in the `facet_wrap()` layer, use the `month` variable to draw a separate segregation for each month.

The plot is as follows:

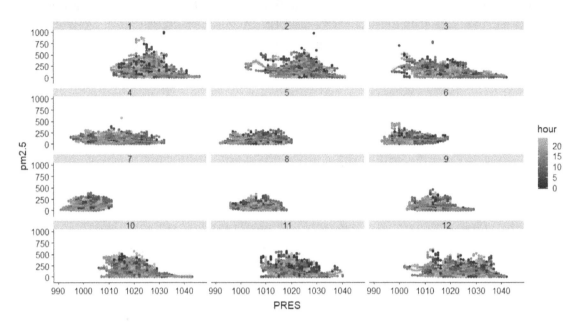

Figure 3.13: Scatterplot showing the relationship between PRES and PM2.5.

> **Note**
>
> The solution for this activity can be found on page 445.

Model Building

We have briefly explored the relationship between PM2.5 and a few factors such as TEMP and DEWP. The same analysis could be followed for other variables such as PRES, Iwd, and more. In this section, let's create a linear model. (We never hesitate to run a model even if we know the choice of model isn't the best. A trial-and-error approach in machine learning is always the best way to establish facts.)

In general, a linear regression models the linear relationship between an input variable (independent variable) and a target variable (dependent variable or explanatory variable). If we have one explanatory variable, it is called **simple linear regression**, and where there is more than one explanatory variable, it's called **multiple linear regression**. The following equation is the mathematical representation of linear regression or a linear predictor function with p explanatory variables and n observations:

$$f(X) = \beta_0 + \sum_{j=1}^{p} \beta_j X_j$$

Here, each X_j is a vector of column values (explanatory variable) for $j = 1, 2, ..., n$, and β_j is the unknown parameter or coefficient. $j = 1$ makes this equation suitable for simple linear regression. There are many algorithms to fit this function onto the data. The most popular one is **ordinary least square (OLS)**. We will discuss OLS in detail in our next chapter on regression.

Another way to think of $f(X)$ is that it's a linear predictor function that fits the observations in the $\mathbb{R}^{p+1}$–dimension space as closely as possible, minimizing the residual sum of squares (the difference in the actual value of the target value from the predicted value).

In the following exercise, we will skip the split of the dataset into train and test, as we are still in the exploration stage and have not decided to formally approach the modeling exercise. (We will touch on that in the next chapter.) We will use the `lm()` method in R for building a linear model. Again, more details on that in the next chapter. At this point, it is suffice to note that `lm()` fits a target variable to a straight line using either one or more input variables. In a simple linear regression, we use only one variable to fit the line, and in multiple linear regression, we can use more than one variable.

Exercise 45: Exploring Simple and Multiple Regression Models

In this exercise, we will explore simple and multiple regression models.

Perform the following steps to complete the exercise:

1. Import the required libraries and packages into R-Studio.

2. Next, create a DataFrame object named **simple_PM25_linear_model** and use the **lm()** method to build a linear model:

    ```
    simple_PM25_linear_model <- lm(pm2.5 ~ DEWP, data = PM25)
    ```

3. Print the summary of the object using the summary method, as illustrated here:

    ```
    summary(simple_PM25_linear_model)
    ```

    The output is as follows:

    ```
    Call:
    lm(formula = pm2.5 ~ DEWP, data = PM25)

    Residuals:
        Min      1Q  Median      3Q     Max
    -115.47  -61.26  -28.75   33.83  923.54

    Coefficients:
                Estimate Std. Error t value Pr(>|t|)
    (Intercept) 96.69984    0.44705  216.31   <2e-16 ***
    DEWP         1.09325    0.03075   35.55   <2e-16 ***
    ---
    Signif. codes:  0 '***' 0.001 '**' 0.01 '*' 0.05 '.' 0.1 ' ' 1

    Residual standard error: 90.69 on 41755 degrees of freedom
      (2067 observations deleted due to missingness)
    Multiple R-squared:  0.02939,   Adjusted R-squared:  0.02936
    F-statistic:  1264 on 1 and 41755 DF,  p-value: < 2.2e-16
    ```

4. Next, create another DataFrame object and use the **lm()** method to build a linear model:

    ```
    multiple_PM25_linear_model <- lm(pm2.5 ~ DEWP+TEMP+Iws, data = PM25)
    ```

5. Print the summary of the model object using the **summary** function:

```
summary(multiple_PM25_linear_model)
```

The output is as follows:

A)

```
-------------------------------------------------------------------
Call:
lm(formula = pm2.5 ~ DEWP + TEMP + Iws, data = PM25)

Residuals:
    Min      1Q  Median      3Q     Max
-149.02  -53.74  -16.61   34.14  877.82

-------------------------------------------------------------------
```

B)

```
-------------------------------------------------------------------
Coefficients:
              Estimate Std. Error t value Pr(>|t|)
(Intercept) 161.151207   0.768727  209.63   <2e-16 ***
DEWP          4.384196   0.051159   85.70   <2e-16 ***
TEMP         -5.133511   0.058646  -87.53   <2e-16 ***
Iws          -0.274337   0.008532  -32.15   <2e-16 ***
---
Signif. codes:  0 '***' 0.001 '**' 0.01 '*' 0.05 '.' 0.1 ' ' 1

-------------------------------------------------------------------
```

C)

```
-------------------------------------------------------------------
Residual standard error: 81.51 on 41753 degrees of freedom
  (2067 observations deleted due to missingness)
Multiple R-squared:  0.216,     Adjusted R-squared:  0.2159
F-statistic:  3834 on 3 and 41753 DF,  p-value: < 2.2e-16

-------------------------------------------------------------------
```

Model Interpretation

Now, based on the previous output of both the simple and multiple linear regression models, let's try to understand what each part of the output means. At this juncture of the book, it's sufficient to know what each part means; we will discuss the results in *Chapter 4, Regression*.

- Part **A**:

    This part shows the call to the `lm()` method with the dependent and independent variables, represented like a formula using the ~ symbol. This resembles our linear predictor function. In a simple regression model, there is only one variable– `DEWP`–and in a multiple model, there are `DEWP`, `TEMP`, and `Iws`. You also see the five summary statistics of residuals (min, first quartile, median, third quartile, and max). This indicates how far the predicted values are from the actual value.

- Part **B**:

    This part is where the core of the model output is shown. The estimates of the parameters are based on the OLS method. If we substitute the values of these estimates and `X_j` into our prediction equation, we will get the predictions. The column named `Std`. Error is the standard error of the estimate. t-value is obtained by taking the ratio of `Estimate` and `Std`. Error, and p-value highlights the statistical significance of the estimate. The visual clues, that is, the * and . symbols are based on the p-value. A value less than 0.001 gets a three star versus a value between 0.1 and 0.05, which gets a . (dot). Three stars means the best case and that the estimates corresponding to the independent variable are significant and useful in predicting (or explaining) the dependent variable. In other words, p-value helps in determining the significance of a regression model over a null model (just the mean of the dependent variable).

- Part **C**:

    This part is the one that shows the efficacy of the model. The most important values to observe are the R-squared and adjusted R-squared values, which are statistical measures that signify the percentage of variation for a dependent variable that's explained by independent variable(s) in a regression model.

Go through the section on evaluation metrics in this chapter to see the interpretation on how well the model has done on R-squared and adjusted R-squared metrics.

Classification

Similar to the regression algorithm, classification also learns from the dependent or target variables and uses all the predictor or independent variables to find the right pattern. The major difference comes from the idea that in classification, the target variable is categorical, whereas in regression, it is numeric. In this section, we will introduce logistic regression to demonstrate the concept using the Beijing PM2.5 dataset.

Logistic Regression

Logistic regression is the most favorable white-box model used for binary classification. White-box models are defined as models providing visibility into the entire reasoning done for the prediction. For each prediction made, we can leverage the model's mathematical equation and decode the reasons for the prediction made. There are also a set of classification models that are entirely black-box, that is, by no means can we understand the reasoning for the prediction leveraged by the model. In situations where we want to focus only on the end outcome, we should prefer black-box models as they are more powerful.

A Brief Introduction

Though the name ends with **regression**, logistic regression is a technique used to predict binary categorical outcomes and is hence a good choice for classification problems. As discussed in the previous section, we need a different approach to model for a categorical outcome. This can be done by transforming the outcome into the log of the odds ratio or the probability of the event to happen.

Let's distill this approach into simpler constructs. Assume that the probability of success for an event is 0.7. Then, the probability of failure for the same event would be defined as 1 − 0.7 = 0.3. The odds of success are defined as the ratio of the probability of success to the probability of failure. The odds of success would then be 0.7/0.3 = 2.33, that is, the odds of success are 2 to 1. If the probability of success is 0.5, that is, a 50-50 chance, the odds of success are 1 to 1. The logistic regression model can be mathematically represented as follows:

$$Ln\left(\frac{p}{1-p}\right) = \beta_0 + \beta_1 X_1 + \beta_2 X_2 + \ldots + \beta_n X_n$$

Here, $Ln\left(\frac{P}{1-p}\right)$ is the log of the odds ratio, which is also called the **logit** function. Solving the math further, we can deduce the probability of the outcome as shown:

$$ p = \left(\frac{e^{(\beta0\ +\ \beta1X1\ +\ \beta2X2\ +\ ...\ +\ \beta nXn)}}{1\ +\ e^{(\beta0\ +\ \beta1X1\ +\ \beta2X2\ +\ ...\ +\ \beta nXn\ )}} \right) $$

Discussing the mathematical background and derivation of the equations is beyond the scope of this chapter. However, to summarize, the logit function, which is the link function (or logic function), helps logistic regression reframe the problem (predicted outcome) intuitively as the log of the odds ratio. This, when solved, helps us to predict the probability of a binary dependent variable.

Mechanics of Logistic Regression

Just like linear regression, where the beta coefficients for the variables are estimated using the OLS method, the logistic regression model leverages the **maximum likelihood estimation (MLE)** method. The MLE function estimates the best set of values of the model parameters or beta coefficients such that it maximizes the likelihood function, that is, the probability estimates. It can also be defined as the *agreement* of the selected model with the observed data). When the best set of parameter values is estimated, plugging these values/beta coefficients into the model equation, as defined earlier, helps in estimating the probability of the outcome for a given sample. Akin to OLS, MLE is an iterative process.

Model Building

Like linear regression for building a logistic regression model in R, we have the `glm()` generalized linear model method to fit the data and logit function to score the observation.

The syntax of using the glm() function is as follows:

```
glm(Y ~ X1 + X2 + X3, data = <train_data>,family=binomial(link='logit'))
```

Here, Y is our dependent variable and X1, X2 and X3 are the independent variables. The argument data will take the training dataset. The family argument is set to binomial(link='logit'), which fits a logistic regression model.

Exercise 46: Storing the Rolling 3-Hour Average in the Beijing PM2.5 Dataset

In this exercise, we will create a new variable that stores the rolling 3-hour average of the PM2.5 variable in the Beijing PM2.5 dataset. The rolling average will smoothen any noise from a reading of PM2.5.

Let's use the **rollapply** method from the **zoo** package to complete the exercise:

1. Combine the **year**, **month**, **day**, and **hour** into a new variable called **datetime**:

   ```
   PM25$datetime <- with(PM25, ymd_h(sprintf('%04d%02d%02d%02d', year, month,
   day,hour)))
   ```

2. Remove the NAs and look at the top 6 values of the **pm2.5** variable in the PM2.5 dataset:

   ```
   PM25_subset <- na.omit(PM25[,c("datetime","pm2.5")])
   head(PM25_subset$pm2.5)
   ```

   The output is as follows:

   ```
   [1] 129 148 159 181 138 109
   ```

3. Store the **PM25_subset** into a **zoo** object of ordered observation with datetime as its index, and print the top 6 values:

   ```
   zoo(PM25_subset$pm2.5,PM25_subset$datetime)
   ```

   The output is as follows:

   ```
   2010-01-02 00:00:00 2010-01-02 01:00:00 2010-01-02 02:00:00
                   129                 148                 159
   2010-01-02 03:00:00 2010-01-02 04:00:00 2010-01-02 05:00:00
                   181                 138                 109
   ```

4. Use the **rollapply** function to create a 3-hour rolling average of the **pm2.5** variable, and print the top 6 values:

   ```
   PM25_three_hour_pm25_avg <- rollapply(zoo(PM25_subset$pm2.5,PM25_
   subset$datetime), 3, mean)
   ```

The output is as follows:

```
2010-01-02 01:00:00 2010-01-02 02:00:00 2010-01-02 03:00:00
            145.3333                162.6667                159.3333
2010-01-02 04:00:00 2010-01-02 05:00:00 2010-01-02 06:00:00
            142.6667                117.3333                112.6667
```

Observe that the **145.33** value is the average of three hours of the **pm2.5** variable, as shown in step 3 (**129**, **148**, and **159**).

Activity 6: Transforming Variables and Deriving New Variables to Build a Model

In this activity, we will perform a series of transformations and derive new variables before building the model. We need to convert the **pm2.5** variable into a categorical variable to apply a logistic regression model.

The following steps need to be performed before we can build a logistic regression classification model:

1. Combine the year, month, day, and hour into a new variable called **datetime**.

2. Using the datetime variable, calculate the average of the **pm2.5** values with a 3-hour window. Name this new variable **PM25_three_hour_pm25_avg**.

3. Create a binary variable called **pollution_level**. It gets a value **1** if **PM25_three_hour_pm25_avg** is greater than **35**, else **0**.

4. Using **pollution_level** as the dependent variable, build a logistic regression model.

5. Print the summary of the model.

   The final output is as follows:

```
Call:
glm(formula = pollution_level ~ DEWP + TEMP + Iws, family = binomial(link
= "logit"),
    data = PM25_for_class)

Deviance Residuals:
    Min       1Q   Median       3Q      Max
-2.4699  -0.5212   0.4569   0.6508   3.5824
```

```
Coefficients:
               Estimate Std. Error z value Pr(>|z|)
(Intercept)   2.5240276  0.0273353   92.34   <2e-16 ***
DEWP          0.1231959  0.0016856   73.09   <2e-16 ***
TEMP         -0.1028211  0.0018447  -55.74   <2e-16 ***
Iws          -0.0127037  0.0003535  -35.94   <2e-16 ***
---
Signif. codes:  0 '***' 0.001 '**' 0.01 '*' 0.05 '.' 0.1 ' ' 1

(Dispersion parameter for binomial family taken to be 1)

    Null deviance: 49475  on 41754  degrees of freedom
Residual deviance: 37821  on 41751  degrees of freedom
AIC: 37829

Number of Fisher Scoring iterations: 5
```

> **Note**
>
> The solution for this activity can be found on page 446.

Interpreting a Model

A large part of the **glm()** output looks similar to the **lm()** method but with a few new values, such as the following:

- **Null deviance**
- **Residual deviance**
- **Akaike Information Criterion (AIC)**
- **Fisher scoring**

In order to avoid scoring, all the above measures will be described in detail in *Chapter 5, Classification*.

Refer to0 the next section on *Evaluation Metrics* (the *Confusion Matrix Based Metrics* section) in this chapter to find an interpretation of how well the model has done on R-squared and adjusted R-squared metrics.

Evaluation Metrics

In this section, we will go through all the evaluation measures for assessing the quality of the machine learning model predictions. Based on the dependent variable, we have several choices for the evaluation measures. In the train and evaluate step of our Machine Learning Workflow, we mentioned that until we get the desired results, we keep iterating the training model by adding new variables or changing the parameters. In each iteration, we try to optimize for any one or two evaluation metrics. The following table summarizes the various types of metrics used for regression, classification, and recommender systems. Given the scope of this book, we will delve into more details on regression and classification algorithms:

Regression	Classification	Recommender System
• Mean Absolute Error (MAE) • Root Mean Squared Error (RMSE) • R-Squared and Adjusted R-Squared	• Recall • Precision • F1-Score • Accuracy • Area Under the Curve (AUC)	• Mean Reciprocal Rank • Root Mean Squared Error (RMSE)

Figure 3.14: Metrics for various types of machine learning algorithms.

Mean Absolute Error (MAE)

Absolute error is direction-agnostic, which means that it is does not matter whether the predicted value of the dependent variable by the model on the test dataset is less than or greater than the actual value. So, in our example of the Beijing PM2.5 dataset, MAE will give us the average absolute error (difference in the predicted and actual values of the dependent variable) in PM2.5 prediction indifferent to the direction of error (positive or negative):

$$MAE = \frac{1}{n}\sum_{i=1}^{n} | y_i - \hat{y}_i |$$

Here, y_i is the value of the ith observation of the dependent variable, and $\hat{y}_i$ is the predicted or expected value.

Root Mean Squared Error (RMSE)

Similar to MAE, root mean square error also computes the average prediction error. However, it is based on a quadratic scoring, where the square root of the average squared error is computed. Moreover, unlike MAE, which takes the absolute difference between the predicted and actual values, RMSE takes the square, which adds more weight to the high error values before taking the square root:

$$RMSE = \sqrt{\frac{1}{n}\sum_{i=1}^{n}(y_i - \hat{y}_i)^2}$$

Here, $(y_i - \hat{y}_i)$ represents the difference between the actual and estimated values of the dependent variable for the ith observation.

R-squared

R-squared measures the percentage (value between 0 and 1 or from 0% to 100%) of the variance in the response variable explained by the linear model. In other words, it measures the variance explained by the input features. 0% R-squared means the model's input feature explains nothing about the response variable. Closer to 100% means that the model is a good predictor of the response variable. For example, if we want to predict the price of a house in a locality, features such as the number of bedrooms, area in sq. ft, and proximity to a school and market decides the value of a property. However, R-squared alone cannot be used for assessing the goodness of the model. Various diagnostic checks on residual, normality, and heteroscedasticity are also required. We will discuss this in detail in *Chapter 4, Regression*.

$$SS_{res} = \sum_{i=1}^{n}(y_i - \hat{y}_i)^2$$

$$SS_{tot} = \sum_{i=1}^{n}(y_i - \bar{y})^2$$

Here, (SS_{res}) is the sum of the square difference between the actual and estimated values of the dependent variable, while SS_{tot} represents the sum of the square difference between the actual and mean of the dependent variable.

$$R^2 = 1 - \frac{SS_{res}}{SS_{tot}}$$

Adjusted R-square

When we add new variables in the regression model, the R-squared value of the model improves as the contribution of the newer variables in explaining the variation of the dependent variable increases. (A counter-argument arises if the newer variables are poorly designed and are not relevant for explaining the dependent variable.) So, for the evaluation metric to be agnostic to the number of variables, we penalize the R-squared value by incorporating n and q (number of observations and number of variables, respectively) in the calculation. This is called adjusted R-squared, adjusted for both the number of observations and variables. It is a good practice to look at the adjusted R-squared when dealing with multiple linear regression.

MSE (mean squared error):

$$MSE = \frac{SS_{res}}{n - q}$$

Here, n is the number of observations, and q is the number of coefficients in the model.

MST (mean squared total):

$$MST = \frac{SS_{tot}}{n - 1}$$

$$R^2_{adj} = 1 - \frac{MSE}{MST} = 1 - \left(\frac{(1 - R^2)(n - 1)}{n - q} \right)$$

Mean Reciprocal Rank (MRR)

MRR is popularly used to evaluate algorithms in search engines, recommender algorithms, and many other information retrieval algorithms in the digital space. MRR is easy to interpret. In general, it could be used to evaluate algorithms that produce a list of responses for an input. Examples are the search results you see in Google for your query and the product recommendations you see on Amazon. The following table shows an example of computing the reciprocal rank. MRR ranges from 0 to 1; a value closer to 1 indicates that the algorithm is giving relevant results at the top of the list.

$$MRR = \frac{1}{|Q|} \sum_{i=1}^{|Q|} \frac{1}{rank_i}$$

Query	Search Results	Correct Result	Rank	Reciprocal Rank
rain	mountain, wind, water	water	3	1/3
cyclone	mountain, lake, water, wind	wind	4	1/4
volcano	mountain, wind, water	mountain	1	1

Figure 3.15: Example of computing reciprocal rank.

Exercise 47: Finding Evaluation Metrics

In this exercise, we will find the MAE, RMSE, R-squared, Adjusted R-squared, and MRR.

Perform the following steps:

1. Import the required libraries and packages.

2. Create a variable named **y_predicted** and assign the value from the **multiple_PM25_linear_model**:

```
y_predicted <- predict(multiple_PM25_linear_model, data = PM25)
```

3. Use the following command to assign values from the **PM25** dataset:

```
y_actual <- PM25[!is.na(PM25$pm2.5),"pm2.5"]
```

4. Find the MAE using the mean function:

```
MAE <- mean(abs(y_actual - y_predicted))
```

The output is as follows:

```
## [1] 59.82112
```

5. Next, calculate the RMSE:

```
RMSE <- sqrt(mean((y_actual - y_predicted)^2))
```

The output is as follows:

```
## [1] 82.09164
```

6. Now, calculate the R-squared value using the following command:

```
model_summary <- summary(multiple_PM25_linear_model)
model_summary$r.squared
```

The output is as follows:

```
## [1] 0.216
```

7. Next, find the adjusted R-squared using the following command:

```
model_summary$adj.r.squared
```

The output is as follows:

```
## [1] 0.2159
```

8. Finally, use the following command to find the MRR:

```
Query_RR_Vector <- c(1/3,1/4,1)
MRR <- sum(Query_RR_Vector)/length(Query_RR_Vector)
```

The output is as follows:

```
## [1] 0.5277778
```

Observe that MAE gives a value of **59.82** and RMSE is **82.09,** which shows a high variance in the errors. In other words, the observations have a high error (which increases the variance of the frequency distribution of error magnitudes) in prediction; MAE fails to identify the error, whereas RMSE amplifies it well. If the MAE and RMSE are almost equal, we could infer that the variance in the frequency distribution of error magnitudes is low and that the model is doing well with all the observations.

Confusion Matrix-Based Metrics

Confusion matrix-based metrics are used in classification algorithms. There are a series of metrics one could derive from the confusion matrix (also called the **contingency table**). The following table computes the frequency of various cases as shown. The terms **Positive** and **Negative** are just conventions for calling out classes A and B. Otherwise, there is nothing negative or positive about the target variable. The contingency table could also be NxN, where N is the number of classes or categories in the response variable. For example, if we want to classify the 26 handwritten characters of the English alphabet in a given image, we need a 26x26 matrix:

S.No	Cases	Abbr.	Detail
1	Positive	(P)	The number of real positive cases in the data
2	Negative	(N)	The number of real negative cases in the data
3	True Positive	(TP)	Correct hits
4	True Negative	(TN)	Correct rejection
5	False Positive	(FP)	False alarm, Type I error
6	False Negative	(FN)	Miss classification, Type II error

Figure 3.16: Elements of the confusion matrix.

If we arrange the **TP**, **TN**, **FP**, and **FN** in a 2x2 contingency matrix, we obtain the confusion matrix, as shown in the following table:

Confusion Matrix		ACTUAL	
		Positive Case	Negative Case
PREDICTED	Predicted Positive	TP Power	FP Type 1 Error
	Predicted Negative	FN Type II Error	TN

Figure 3.17: Confusion matrix.

Accuracy

Accuracy measures the correct overall classifications by the model for both positive and negative examples. The sum of the diagonal elements in the matrix (TP and TN) divided by the total number of positive and negative observations gives the accuracy. Accuracy is not always a reliable metric in real-world scenarios. Consider that we would like to distinguish cancer CT scans from benign CT scans. Clearly, we may have many negative scans and few positive scans. This leads to what we call the **unbalanced dataset**. If the model mostly predicts benign scans accurately but produces a significant error in predicting cancer CT scans, the accuracy may still be high, but the model is not so useful.

$$ACC = \frac{TP + TN}{P + F}$$

Sensitivity

In order to tackle the issue we discussed with *accuracy*, we could use a combination of sensitivity, also known as recall, hit rate, or **true positive rate** (**TPR**), and specificity (discussed in the next section). Sensitivity gives the predictive power of the model with respect to the positive cases (detecting cancer in a CT scan). We obtain sensitivity from the ratio of all **true positive** (**TP**) cases to the number of **positive** (**P**) cases.

$$TPR = \frac{TP}{P}$$

Specificity

Specificity provides the quantitative assessment of correct predictions of negative examples (for example, detecting benign CT scans). We obtain sensitivity from the ratio of a number of true negative cases to the number of negative cases.

$$TNR = \frac{TN}{N}$$

High sensitivity and specificity values signify a superior model. In most cases, we try to balance the two metrics to get the best model.

F1 Score

F1 score combines precision and sensitivity by taking the harmonic mean (appropriate for taking averages of two or more rates) of both, as described by the following formulas. **Positive predictive value** (**PPV** or precision) measures the number of true predictions over the sum of a number of true and false positives, that is, how many of all the predictions of positive cases were correct.

$$PPV = \frac{TP}{TP + FP}$$

$$F_1 = 2 \times \frac{PPV.TPR}{PPV + TPR} = \frac{2TP}{2TP + FP + FN}$$

F1 score is more robust than accuracy but still suffers in the case of unbalanced classes.

There is no good or bad metric for evaluating the goodness of a classification model. Machine learning practitioners usually look at a combination of many metrics to conclude the goodness of a model. That is why it becomes important to know how to interpret each of the above discussed metrics.

Exercise 48: Working with Model Evaluation on Training Data

In this exercise, we will work with model evaluation on training data using the **confusionMatrix** function from the **caret** package. The function prints metrics such as accuracy, sensitivity, specificity, and many more.

Perform the following steps to complete the exercise:

1. Import the required libraries and packages into the system.

2. Create a variable name **predicated** and assign the value, as illustrated here:

   ```
   predicted <- ifelse(PM25_logit_model$fitted.values>0.5, 1,0)
   ```

3. Next, create another variable named **actual**, as illustrated here:

   ```
   actual <- PM25_for_class$pollution_level
   ```

4. Import the caret library:

   ```
   library(caret)
   ```

5. Finally, use the **confusionMatrix** method to describe the performance of the classification model:

   ```
   confusionMatrix(predicted, actual)
   ```

   The output is as follows:

   ```
   ## Confusion Matrix and Statistics
   ##
   ##           Reference
   ## Prediction    0    1
   ##          0 5437 2097
   ##          1 6232 27989
   ##
   ##
   ##                Accuracy : 0.8005
   ##                  95% CI : (0.7967, 0.8044)
   ##     No Information Rate : 0.7205
   ##     P-Value [Acc > NIR] : < 2.2e-16
   ##
   ##                   Kappa : 0.4444
   ##  Mcnemar's Test P-Value : < 2.2e-16
   ```

```
##
##              Sensitivity : 0.4659
##              Specificity : 0.9303
##           Pos Pred Value : 0.7217
##           Neg Pred Value : 0.8179
##               Prevalence : 0.2795
##           Detection Rate : 0.1302
##     Detection Prevalence : 0.1804
##        Balanced Accuracy : 0.6981
##
##         'Positive' Class : 0
```

Many of the metrics shown in the results of the `confusionMatric()` output are described in this section. However, here's a quick summary before you read the details. The accuracy of this logistic regression model is 80%, which is good as per the standard. This indicates that we can predict the normal and above normal PM2.5 values using other environmental factors with 80% accuracy. However, note that the accuracy is on the entire training dataset. We have not split the data into two parts for checking the overfitting scenarios, a condition in which the model performs really good when tested on training data but shows inferior results on testing (or unseen) data.

Sensitivity and specificity are 46% and 93%, respectively. This means the model is doing good for negative cases (1-Above normal PM2.5). Generally, there must be a tradeoff between these two metrics. However, in this case, the priority for the model is to be able to predict as many **Above Normal** states as possible. Hence, high specificity is desirable once we have the confusion matrix; it's possible to calculate all the metrics from it.

Receiver Operating Characteristic (ROC) Curve

In the context of classification models, the output of a prediction is obtained as a quantitative estimate, usually a probability measure. In a binary logistic regression, the usual choice of the threshold to classify one observation from the other (for example, spam versus non-spam) is 0.5. This means that if the probability is greater than 0.5, classify it as spam and if not, non-spam. Now, depending on the threshold, you will get different values of TP, TN, FP, and FN in the confusion matrix we discussed earlier. While it is a standard practice to look at the confusion matrix at a given threshold (usually 0.5), it might not give us the complete view of whether the model will perform well in the real world, which is why the choice of threshold is essential.

The ROC curve is an elegant visualization showing the variation between the true positive rate (often referenced by sensitivity) and the true negative rate (often referenced by specificity) at every possible threshold. It helps us identify the right threshold for classification. Also, the area under the ROC curve (referred to as AUC), which varies between 0 and 1, tells us how good the model is. Closer to 1 means that the model is successfully able to classify between positive and negative classes for most of the observation.

Using the ROCR package in R, we will obtain the ROC curve for the PM2.5 prediction using logistic regression. Also, we will observe the AUC in the next exercise.

Exercise 49: Creating an ROC Curve

In this exercise, we will use the ROCR package to obtain the ROC curve.

Perform the following steps:

1. Import the ROCR package into the system using the following command:

    ```
    library(ROCR)
    ```

2. Next, define the pred1 and pref1 objects:

    ```
    pred1 <- prediction(predict(PM25_logit_model), PM25_for_class$pollution_
    level)
    perf1 <- performance(pred1,"tpr","fpr")
    ```

3. Next, find the AUC using the following command:

    ```
    auc <- performance(pred1,"auc")
    as.numeric(auc@y.values)
    ```

    The output is as follows:

    ```
    ## [1] 0.8077673
    ```

4. Plot the graph using the plot command:

   ```
   plot(perf1)
   ```

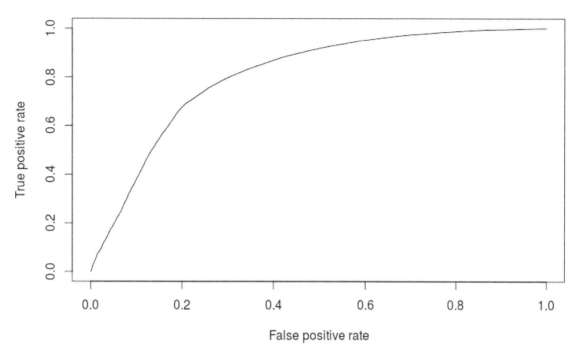

Figure 3.18: ROC curve between true positive rate (sensitivity) and false positive rate (specificity).

Summary

In this chapter, we started out with laying the process for building a machine learning workflow, starting from designing the problem and moving to deploying the model. We briefly discussed simple and multiple and logistic regressions along with all the evaluation metrics needed to interpret and judge the performance of the model. These two algorithms demonstrate the supervised learning for regression and classification problems, respectively.

Throughout the chapter, we used the Beijing PM2.5 dataset to build the models. In the process, we also converted a regression problem to a classification problem by simply re-engineering the dependent variable. Such re-engineering is often taken up on real-world problems to suit a particular use case.

In the next chapter, we will delve into the details of regression algorithms and will elaborate the various types of regression algorithms beyond linear regression and discuss when to use which one.

4

Regression

Learning Objectives

By the end of this chapter, you will be able to:

- Formulate regression problems
- Implement various types of regression approaches and its use cases
- Analyze and choose the right regression approach
- Connect statistics and machine learning through the lens of regression
- Deep dive into model diagnostics

In this chapter, we will focus on various type of regression and when to use which one along with demonstrations in R.

Introduction

In the previous chapter, we understood linear regression models and the linear relationship between an input variable (independent variable) and a target variable (dependent variable or explanatory variable). If one variable is used as an independent variable, it is defined as **simple linear regression**. If more than one explanatory (independent) variable is used, it's called **multiple linear regression**.

Regression algorithms and problems are based on predicting a numeric target variable (often called **dependent**), given all the input variables (often called **independent** variables), for example, predicting a house price based on location, area, proximity to a shopping mall, and many other factors. Many of the concepts of regression are derived from statistics.

The entire field of machine learning is now a right balance of mathematics, statistics, and computer science. In this chapter, we will use regression techniques to understand how to establish a relationship between input(s) and the target variable. We will also emphasize on model diagnostics as regression is full of assumptions, which needs to be checked before a model can be used in the real world.

Essentially, all models are wrong, but some are useful. – George Box

We have briefly touched upon simple and multiple linear regression in *Chapter 3, Introduction to Supervised Learning*. In this chapter, we will focus more on **model diagnostics** and other types of **regression algorithm**, and how it is different from linear regression.

Linear Regression

Let's revisit the multiple linear regression from *Chapter 3, Introduction to Supervised Learning*. The following equation is the mathematical representation of a linear equation, or linear predictor function, with **p** explanatory variables and **n** observations:

$$f(X) = \beta_0 + \sum_{j=1}^{p} \beta_j X_j$$

Where each X_j is a vector of column values (**explanatory variable**) and β_j is the **unknown parameters** or **coefficients**. $j = 1$, makes this equation suitable for simple linear regression. There are many algorithms to fit this function onto the data. The most popular one is **Ordinary Least Square (OLS)**.

Before understanding the details of OLS, first let's interpret the equation we got while trying to fit the Beijing PM2.5 data from the model building section of simple and multiple linear regression from *Chapter 3, Introduction to Supervised Learning*.

$$pm2.5 = \beta_0 + \beta_1 * DEWP + \beta_2 * TEMP + \beta_3 * Iws$$

If we substitute the values of regression coefficients, $\beta_0, \beta_1, \beta_2$ and β_3 from the output of the `lm()` function, we get:

$$pm2.5 = 161.151207 + 4.384196 * DEWP + -5.133511 * TEMP + -0.274337 * Iws$$

The preceding equation attempts to answer the question "Are the factors DEWP, TEMP, and Iws important for predicting the pm2.5 level?"

The model estimates how, on average, the DEWP, TEMP, and Iws values affect the pm2.5 level. For example, a unit increase in DEWP will increase the pm2.5 value by 4.384196. That is why we often call these coefficients **weights**. It is important to note that if the **R-squared value** is low, these estimated coefficients are not reliable.

Exercise 50: Print the Coefficient and Residual Values Using the multiple_PM_25_linear_model Object

In this exercise, we will print the coefficient and residual values using the `multiple_PM25_linear_model` object.

Perform the following steps to complete the exercise:

1. Extract the attribute coefficients using the `$` operator on the `multiple_PM25_linear_model` object:

    ```
    multiple_PM25_linear_model$coefficients
    ```

    The output is as follows:

    ```
    (Intercept)        DEWP        TEMP         Iws
    161.1512066    4.3841960  -5.1335111  -0.2743375
    ```

2. Extract the attribute residuals using the `$` operator on the `multiple_PM25_linear_model` object:

    ```
    multiple_PM25_linear_model$residuals
    ```

The output is as follows:

```
         25              26              27              28
   17.95294914     32.81291348     21.38677872     26.34105878
         29              30              31              32
```

Activity 7: Printing Various Attributes Using Model Object Without Using the Summary Function

In the *Multiple Linear Regression Model* section of *Chapter 3, Introduction to Supervised Learning*, we created a multiple linear regression model and stored it in the model object `multiple_PM25_linear_model` using the model object.

This activity will help in understanding how to extract some important model attributes once the model is built. In few cases, we will use the `$` operator, and in other cases, we will perform some simple calculation. Print the following model attributes using the `multiple_PM25_linear_model` object:

- Residuals
- Fitted values
- R-Ssquared value
- F-statistic
- Coefficient p-value

Let's print these values using the model object:

1. First, print the coefficient values. Make sure the output is like the output of the **summary** function using the **coefficients** option. The coefficients are fitted values from the model that uses the OLS algorithm:

   ```
   (Intercept)        DEWP         TEMP          Iws
   161.1512066   4.3841960   -5.1335111   -0.2743375
   ```

2. Find the residual value (difference) of the predicted and actual values of PM2.5, which should be as small as possible. Residual reflects how far the fitted values using the coefficients are from the actual value:

   ```
   25              26             27             28
      17.95294914   32.81291348   21.38677872   26.34105878
              29             30             31             32
   ```

3. Next, find the fitted values, which should be closer to the actual PM2.5 values for best model. Using the coefficients, we can compute the fitted values:

   ```
   25           26           27           28           29
   111.047051  115.187087  137.613221  154.658941  154.414781
           30           31           32           33           34
   ```

4. Find the R-Squared values. They should look the same as the ones you obtained in the output of the **summary** function next to the multiple R-squared text. R-square helps in evaluating the model performance. If the value is closer to 1, the better the model is:

    ```
    summary(multiple_PM25_linear_model)$r.squared
    ```

    The output is as follows:

    ```
    [1] 0.2159579
    ```

5. Find the F statistic values. Make sure the output looks the same as the one you obtained in the output of the **summary** function next to the text F statistics. This will tell you if your model fits better than just using the mean of the target variables. In many practical applications, F-Statistic is used along with p-values:

    ```
        value      numdf      dendf
     3833.506      3.000  41753.000
    ```

6. Finally, find the coefficient p-values and make sure the values look the same as the one you obtained in the output of the **summary** function under *coefficients* for each variable. It will be present under the column titled **Pr(>|t|):**. If the value is less than 0.05, the variable is statistically significant in predicting the target variable:

    ```
      (Intercept)           DEWP           TEMP             Iws
     0.000000e+00   0.000000e+00   0.000000e+00   4.279601e-224
    ```

> **Note**
>
> The solution for this activity can be found on page 449.

Ordinary Least Square (OLS)

In *Chapter 3, Introduction to Supervised Learning*, we saw sum of squared residuals (SS_{res}) (also called the **error sum of square** or **residual sum of squares**), which is a measure of the overall model fit, is given by the following equation:

$$S(\hat{\beta}) = \sum_{i=1}^{n} (y_i - x_i^T \hat{\beta})^2 = (y - X\hat{\beta})^T (y - X\hat{\beta})$$

Where T represents the matrix transpose, and the rows of X represent the values of all the input variables related to a specific value of the target variable are $X_i = x_i^T$. The value of $\hat{\beta}$ that minimizes $S(\hat{\beta})$ is called the **OLS estimator** for β. The OLS algorithm is designed to find the global minimum of $\hat{\beta}$ that will minimize $S(\hat{\beta})$.

From the previous chapter, you also learned that the R-squared value for `multiple_PM25_linear_model` on the Beijing PM2.5 dataset is quite low for this model to be useful in practical applications. One way of interpreting the poor results is to say the predictor variables `DEWP` and `TEMP` do not fully explain the variance in PM2.5, so they fall short of producing good results.

Before we could jump into the diagnostics of this model, let's see if we could explain some of the variances in PM2.5 using the variable `month` (of the readings). We will also use an interaction variable (more on this in the *Improving the Model* section) *DEWP*TEMP*month* in the `lm()` function that generates all possible combination of `DEWP`, `TEMP`, and `month`.

The reason for using `month` is justified by *Figure 3.3* in *Chapter 3, Introduction to Supervised Learning*, where we saw the seasonal effect in the values of `TEMP`, `DEWP`, and `PRES` (showing a nice sinusoidal pattern). The output of the following exercise shows all the interaction terms that got created to explain the PM2.5 dataset.

> **Note**
>
> The expression like `DEWP:TEMP` means multiplication and each value of `month` is a separate variable in `multiple_PM25_linear_model,` because we converted `month` into **factor** before running the model.

Exercise 51: Add the Interaction Term DEWP:TEMP:month in the lm() Function

In this exercise, we will add the interaction term to improve the model performance.

We will see how adding an additional interaction term helps in improving the model performance in terms of R-squared values. Perform the following steps to complete the exercise:

1. Read the Beijing PM2.5 dataset using the following command:

    ```
    PM25 <- read.csv("PRSA_data_2010.1.1-2014.12.31.csv")
    ```

2. Now, convert the `month` object into the `factor` variable as shown here:

    ```
    PM25$month <- as.factor(PM25$month)
    ```

3. Use the linear model with interaction terms of **DEWP**, **TEMP**, and **month**. Observe the term **DEWP*TEMP*month**, which will generate all the combinations of the variable **DEWP**, **TEMP**, and **month**:

```
multiple_PM25_linear_model <- lm(pm2.5 ~ Iws + DEWP*TEMP*month, data =
PM25)
```

4. Print the summary of the model to see the changes in coefficients and r-squared values because of the interaction term:

```
summary(multiple_PM25_linear_model)
```

The output is as follows:

```
## Call:
## lm(formula = pm2.5 ~ Iws + DEWP * TEMP * month, data = PM25)
##
## Residuals:
##      Min       1Q  Median       3Q      Max
## -298.41   -42.77   -9.35    30.91   967.39
##
## Coefficients:
##                        Estimate Std. Error t value Pr(>|t|)
...
## (Intercept)           2.917e+02  4.338e+00  67.257  < 2e-16 ***
## Signif. codes:  0 '***' 0.001 '**' 0.01 '*' 0.05 '.' 0.1 ' ' 1
##
## Residual standard error: 70.04 on 41708 degrees of freedom
##   (2067 observations deleted due to missingness)
## Multiple R-squared:  0.4217,  Adjusted R-squared:  0.4211
## F-statistic: 633.7 on 48 and 41708 DF,  p-value: < 2.2e-16
```

Notice the two-fold jump in the R-squared value from 0.216 to 0.4217. However, such a jump is at the cost of **model interpretability**. Though it is simple to explain the explanatory power of the model using individual variables, their multiplication creates an effect that is difficult to articulate.

In our example of Beijing PM2.5, it is more logical to think of the interaction **DEWP** and **TEMP** have with the **month** object of the **year** object, since both of these are environmental factors which vary with season.

However, we would also like to perform some diagnostics to fully understand how a linear regression model is studied end to end and not just look at the R-squared value.

Model Diagnostics

Often statistical models such as linear regression and logistic regressions come with many assumptions that need to be validated before accepting the final solution. A model violating the assumptions will result in erroneous prediction and results will be prone to misinterpretation.

The following code shows a method for obtaining the diagnostic plots from the output of the `lm()` method. The plot has four different plots looking at the residuals. Let's understand how to interpret each plot. All these plots are about how well the fit matches the regression assumptions. If there is a violation, it will be clearly shown in the plots of the following code:

```
par(mfrow = c(2,2))
plot(multiple_PM25_linear_model)
```

The output is as follows:

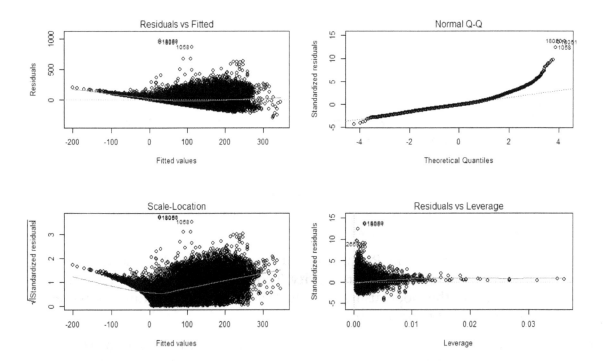

Figure 4.1: Diagnostics plot for the linear model fit on the Beijing PM2.5 dataset

In the next four sections, we will explore each of the plots with randomly generated data from a linear equation $(y_i = 5 + 12x_i - 3x_i + \epsilon_i)$ and a quadratic equation $(y_i = 5 + 12x_i - 3x_i^2 + \epsilon_i)$, and later come back to explain how the four plots in *Figure 4.1* fare in comparison with the ideal scenarios.

> **Note**
>
> In the quadratic equation, $(y_i = 5 + 12x_i - 3x_i^2 + \epsilon_i)$ ϵ_i is assumed to be normally distributed with mean 0 and variance 2.

In the following exercise, we will generate the plots using the linear and quadratic equations. Later, we will deep dive into understanding the various assumptions a linear model should follow using the model fit on the random data generated through the two equations.

Exercise 52: Generating and Fitting Models Using the Linear and Quadratic Equations

In this exercise, we will understand the linear and polynomial function and what happens when we fit a linear model on both.

Generate random numbers using a linear and a polynomial equation, and fit a linear model on both. Observe the difference between the two plots.

Perform the following steps to generate the required plots:

1. First, define the linear function using the following code:

    ```
    linear_function <- function(x){return (5+(12*x)-(3*x))}
    ```

2. Define the quadratic function as shown in the following command:

    ```
    quadratic_function <- function(x){return (5+(12*x)-(3*(x^2)))}
    ```

3. Now, generate the uniform random numbers (**x**), as shown here:

    ```
    uniform_random_x <- runif(50, min=0, max=15)
    ```

4. Generate the linear values (**y**) using (**x**), as shown here:

    ```
    linear_values_y <- linear_function(uniform_random_x) + rnorm(50,mean = 0,
    sd =sqrt(2))
    ```

5. Generate the quadratic values (**y**) using (**x**):

```
quadratic_values_y <- quadractic_function(uniform_random_x) +
rnorm(50,mean = 0, sd =sqrt(2))
df <- data.frame(linear_values_y, quadratic_values_y, uniform_random_x)
```

6. Fit a linear model for **linear_values_y** using **uniform_random_x**:

```
model_df_linear <- lm(linear_values_y ~ uniform_random_x, data = df)
```

7. Plot the diagnostic plot fora linear relationship:

```
par(mfrow = c(2,2))
plot(model_df_linear)
```

The plot is as follows:

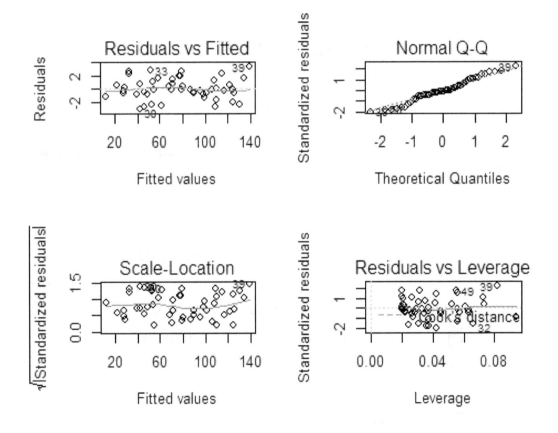

Figure 4.2: Plots using the linear regression

8. Fit a linear model for **quadratic_values_y** using **uniform_random_x**:

```
model_df_quad <- lm(quadratic_values_y ~ uniform_random_x, data = df)
```

9. Generate a diagnostic for non-linear relationships:

```
par(mfrow = c(2,2))
plot(model_df_quad)
```

The output is as follows:

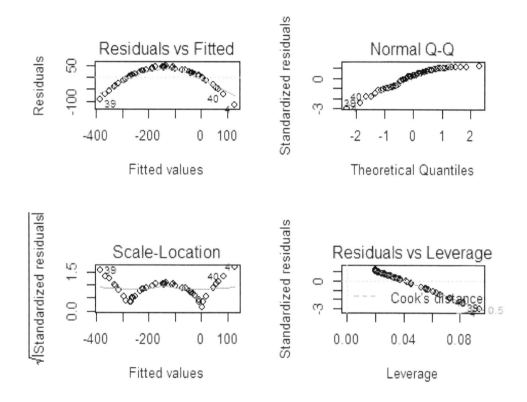

Figure 4.3: Plots using the quadratic regression

The difference between the plot in step 7 and 9 show the good and a poor fit of a linear relationship. A linear model can't fit a non-linear relationship between y and x. In the next sections, we will deep dive into understanding the four parts of the plots generated in step 7 and 9.

In *Chapter 3, Introduction to Supervised Learning, Figure 3.5* we discussed the various assumptions to consider while building a linear regression model. Through the four plots mentioned earlier in the chapter, we will examine if any of the assumptions are violated or not.

Residual versus Fitted Plot

This type of plot is between the fitted values and the residual (difference between **actual** and **fitted** values) from the `lm()` method. If the predictor and target variables have a non-linear relationship, the plot will help us identify.

In the following figure, the top plot shows the point scattered all around and the linear relationship between the predictor and target variable is clearly captured. In the bottom plot, the unexplained non-linear relationship is left out in the residuals, and hence the curve. The bottom plot clearly shows it is not the right fit for a linear regression model, a violation of the linear relationship between the predictor and target variable:

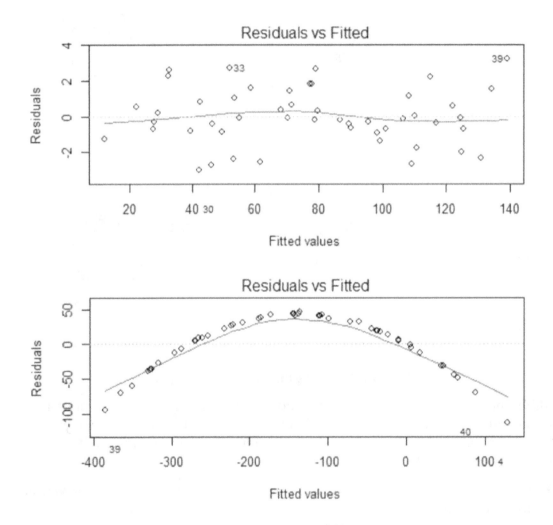

Figure 4.4: [Top] Residual versus fitted plot of the linear function. [Bottom] Residual versus fitted plot of the quadratic function

Normal Q-Q Plot

Q-Q plot, also called **Quantile-Quantile plot**, supports to check if the data plausibly comes from approximately theoretical distribution; in this instance, **Normal Distribution**. A Q-Q plot is a scatterplot shaped by plotting two sets of quantiles (points below which a certain proportion of the data falls) in contrast to one another. If both groups of quantiles came from a similar distribution, we must see the points creating a coarsely straight line. Provided a vector of data, the normal Q-Q plot plots the data in sorted order versus quantiles from a standard normal distribution.

The second assumption in linear regression was that all the predictor variables are normally distributed. If it is true, the residuals will also be normally distributed. Normal Q-Q is a plot between standardized residuals and theoretical quantiles. Visually, we can inspect whether the residuals follow the straight line, if it is normally distributed, or if there is any deviation that indicates violation.

In the following figure, the top part demonstrates the linear function, which shows an alignment with the straight diagonal line, with a few exceptions like observation number 39, 30, and 50. On the other hand, the bottom part of the figure shows the quadratic function, which surprisingly shows a fair alignment with the straight line, not exactly like the linear, as some divergence is seen in the top-right side of the plot:

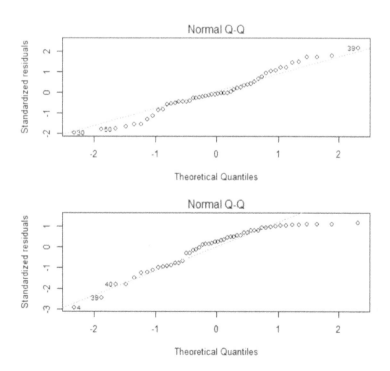

Figure 4.5: [Top] Normal Q-Q plot of the linear function. [Bottom] Normal Q-Q plot of the quadratic function

Scale-Location Plot

Scale-Location plot shows whether residuals are spread equally along the ranges of input variables (predictor). The assumption of equal variance (**homoscedasticity**) could also be checked with this plot. If we see a horizontal line with randomly spread points, it means that the model is good.

The plot is between fitted values and the square root of standardized residuals. In the following figure, the top plot shows the linear function, and the residuals are spread randomly along the horizontal lines, whereas in the bottom plot, there seems to be a pattern that is not random. Hence, the variance is not equal:

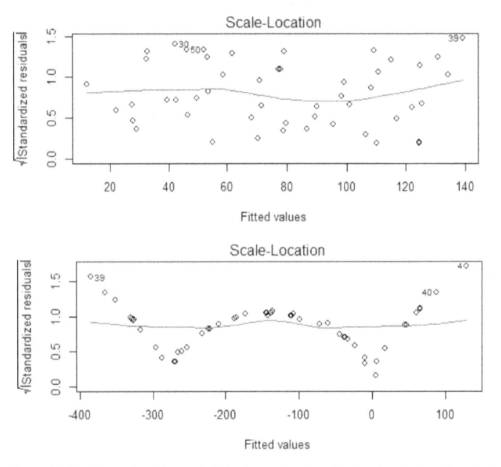

Figure 4.6: [Top] Scale-Location plot of the linear function. [Bottom] Scale-Location plot of the quadratic function

Residual versus Leverage

If there are any influential points in the data, the **Residual versus Leverage** plot helps in identifying it. It's common to think that all outlier points are influential, that is, it decides how the regression line comes out. However, not all outliers are influential points. Even if a point is within a reasonable range of values (not an outlier), it could still be an influential point.

In the next plot, we will look out for far off values at the top-right corner or at the bottom-right corner. Those regions are the spaces where observation can be *influential* in contrast to a regression line. In *Figure 4.7*, the observations of the red dashed line with high **Cook's distance** are influential for the regression results. The regression results will be changed if we remove those observations. In the following figure, the bottom plot shows that observation **40** and **39** outside of the dashed line (high Cook's distance). Note that these observations are consistently appearing in the other three plots as well, giving us a strong reason to eliminate these points, if we would like to see the linear relationship in the data. The plot on the top seems to have no red dashed line, ascertaining a good fit:

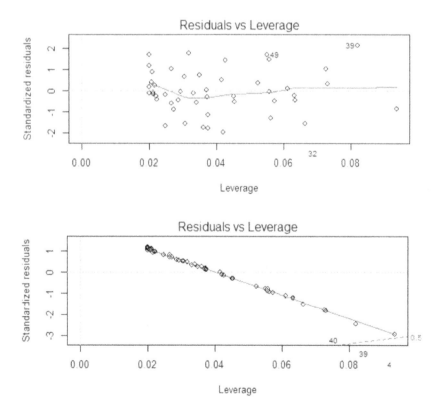

Figure 4.7: [Top] Residual versus Leverage plot of the linear function. [Bottom] Residual versus Leverage plot of the quadratic function

Now, if we revisit *Figure* 4.1, the diagnostics plot we obtained from the Beijing PM2.5 dataset; it seems like the model fit is *not the best* to be used for practical purposes. All the four plots show slight violation of linearity, normality and homoscedasticity assumptions.

In the next section, we have listed a few ways to improve the model, which may incrementally help increase the R-squared value and better fit the data. Also, similar to the visual inspection methods we just discussed, many statistical methods such as **Kolmogorov-Smirnov test** for testing normality, **Correlation** for testing multicollinearity, **Goldfeld–Quandt test** for testing homoscedasticity could be used.

Improving the Model

So far, we have seen the problems in the data, but you may ask whether you can fix or improve it. Let's discuss some ways to do that. In this section, you will learn some of the ways, such as variable transformation, dealing with outlier points, adding interaction effect and deciding to go with a non-linear model.

Transform the Predictor or Target Variable

The most common way to improve the model is to transform one or more variables (could also be the target variable) using a **log** function.

Log transformation corrects the skewed distribution. It gives the ability to handle the skewness in the data and at the same time the original value could be easily computed once the model is built. The most popular log transformation is natural *log*. A more detailed explanation for log transformation could be found in the section *Log Transformation* of *Chapter 6, Feature Selection and Dimensionality Reduction*.

The objective is to bring the normal distribution in the data by transforming. So, whichever function helps in attaining that is a good transformation. After log, square root is also widely used. Look at the distribution of the transformed variable to see if a symmetrical distribution (bell shaped) is obtained; if yes, then the transformation is going to be useful.

Choose a Non-Linear Model

It might be possible to get struck in a scenario where a linear model is not a right fit because there is a non-linear relationship between the predictor and the target variable and only a non-linear function could fit such data. See the section *Polynomial Regression* later in this chapter for more details on such a model.

Remove an Outlier or Influential Point

As we discussed in the *Residual versus Leverage* section's diagnostic plot, we may find an outlier or influential point playing a spoil spot in getting us the best model. If you have identified it properly, try seeing by removing the observation and see if things improve.

Adding the Interaction Effect

We might at times see the value(s) of two or more predictor (independent) variables in the dataset influencing the dependent variable in a multiplicative way. A linear regression equation with an interaction term might look like this:

$$\hat{y} = \beta_0 + \beta_1 x_1 + \beta_2 x_2 + \beta_3 x_1 x_2$$

One can go for the higher order of such an interaction (for example, using three variables); however, those are difficult to interpret and usually avoided.

Quantile Regression

When the data presents outliers, high skewness, and conditions leading to heteroscedasticity, we employ quantile regression for modelling. Also, one key question quantile regression answers, which linear regression cannot, is "Does DEWP, TEMP, and Iws influence PM2.5 levels differently for high PM2.5 than for average PM2.5?"

Quantile regression is quite similar to linear regression; however, the quantile regression parameter estimates the change in a certain quantile of the response variable produced by a unit change in the input predictor variable. In order to fully understand this statement, let's fit our Beijing data using quantile regression (without using the interaction terms).

We need to install the quantreg package to fit the quantile regression into the data. The package offers the method, rq() to fit the data using the argument tau, which is the model parameter specifying the value of quantile to be used for fitting the model into the data. Observe that the other parts of the arguments to the rq() method looks similar to lm().

Exercise 53: Fit a Quantile Regression on the Beijing PM2.5 Dataset

In this exercise, we will observe the difference in the quantile regression fit at various quantiles, particularly 25th, 50th, and 75th. The rq() function from quantreg will be used for building the model. In *Figure* 4.8, we will compare the coefficient values obtained through the lm() function versus the rq() function to compare the two types of regression.

Perform the following steps to complete the exercise:

1. Read the Beijing PM2.5 dataset using the following command:

```
PM25 <- read.csv("PRSA_data_2010.1.1-2014.12.31.csv")
```

2. Now, the next step is to install the required package. Use the following command to load the **quantreg** package:

```
library(quantreg)
```

3. Run the quantile regression tau values as 0.25, 0.5, and 0.75, which corresponds to the 25th, 50th, and 75th quantiles, respectively:

```
quantile_regression_PM25_all <- rq(pm2.5 ~ DEWP+TEMP+Iws, data = PM25, tau
= seq(0.25,0.99,by = 0.25))
```

4. Print the summary of the quantile regression model:

```
summary(quantile_regression_PM25_all)
```

The output is as follows:

```
## tau: [1] 0.25
##
## Coefficients:
##                 Value      Std. Error t value    Pr(>|t|)
## (Intercept)  63.62367   0.52894   120.28453   0.00000
## DEWP          2.08932   0.01859   112.39914   0.00000
## TEMP         -1.89485   0.02196   -86.27611   0.00000
## Iws          -0.09590   0.00179   -53.59211   0.00000
##
## tau: [1] 0.5
##
## Coefficients:
##                 Value      Std. Error t value    Pr(>|t|)
## (Intercept)  117.37344   0.73885   158.85921   0.00000
## DEWP          3.43276   0.02835   121.07849   0.00000
## TEMP         -3.37448   0.03225  -104.65011   0.00000
## Iws          -0.16659   0.00202   -82.56604   0.00000
##
## tau: [1] 0.75
##
## Coefficients:
##                 Value      Std. Error t value    Pr(>|t|)
## (Intercept)  201.16377   1.31859   152.55927   0.00000
```

```
## DEWP          5.12661    0.04901   104.59430    0.00000
## TEMP         -5.62333    0.05567  -101.01841    0.00000
## Iws          -0.25807    0.00510   -50.55327    0.00000
```

The following table summarizes the coefficient values of the linear regression that we obtained using lm() in the *Regression* section of *Chapter 3, Introduction to Supervised Learning* and the values we obtained using rq() in three quantiles.

According to the linear regression model, the mean PM2.5 level in the atmosphere increases by **4.384196** with one unit increase in DEWP. The quantile regression results in the following table, and it indicates that DEWP has a larger negative impact on the higher quantiles (observe the 75th quantile) of PM2.5:

Factors	Linear Regression	Quantile Regression		
		25th	50th	75th
Intercepts	161.151207	63.62367	117.37344	201.16377
DEWP	4.384196	2.08932	3.43276	5.12661
TEMP	-5.133511	-1.89485	-3.37448	-5.62333
Iws	-0.274337	-0.09590	-0.16659	-0.25807

Figure 4.8: Coefficient estimates for the 25th, 50th, 75th quantile regression and the linear regression coefficient estimates for the Beijing's PM2.5 estimation model

Exercise 54: Plotting Various Quantiles with More Granularity

In this exercise, instead of using the 25th, 50th and 75th quantiles, we will use the more granular values for tau in the **rq** function. The plot will help visualize the change in the coefficient values based on the quantile value. Use the **seq()** function from R that sets the quantile values starting from 0.05 to 0.95 with an increment of 0.05.

Perform the following steps to complete the exercise:

1. Create a **quantile_regression_PM25_granular** variable:

```
quantile_regression_PM25_granular <- rq(pm2.5 ~ DEWP + TEMP + Iws, data =
PM25, tau = seq(0.05,0.95,by = 0.05))
```

2. Now, store the value from the previously created variable using the **summary** function:

```
plot_granular <- summary(quantile_regression_PM25_granular)
```

3. Let's use the following command to plot the graph. Observe for the different values of tau, how the values of **Intercept**, **DEWP**, **TEMP**, and **Iws** change:

```
plot(plot_granular)
```

The output plot is as follows:

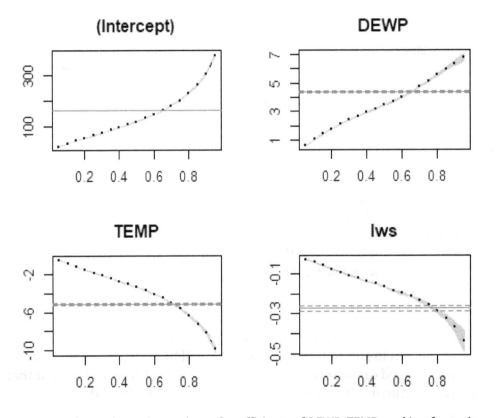

Figure 4.9: Shows the various values of coefficients of DEWP, TEMP, and Iws for various values of quantiles

In this exercise, we explored the granularity of the variable using more granular values for tau in the **rq** function. The previous figure shows the various values of the coefficients of DEWP, TEMP, and Iws. The X-axis in the plot shows the quantile. The single dotted line shows the estimation of the quantile regression, and the gray area is the confidence interval. The middle gray line is a representation of the OLS coefficient estimates, and the double dotted lines display the confidence intervals around the OLS coefficients. Observe that the red and the gray areas do not overlap, which justifies our use of quantile regression. If the two lines overlap, then there is no difference in the estimates using OLS and quantile regression.

> **Note**
>
> We are not claiming that quantile regression is giving better results than linear regression. The adjusted R-squared value is still low for this model and it works well in the real world. However, we claim that quantile regression can help in estimating the PM2.5 at different levels than just the average, which provides a robust interpretation for data with outliers, high skewness, and heteroscedasticity.

Polynomial Regression

Often in real-world data, the response variable and the predictor variable don't have a linear relationship, and we may need a **nonlinear polynomial function** to fit the data. Various scatterplot-like residual versus each predictor and residual versus fitted values reveal the violation of linearity if any, which could potentially help in identifying the need for introducing the quadratic or cubic term in the equation. The following function is a generic polynomial equation:

$$f(X) = \beta_0 + \beta_1 X + \beta_2 X^2 + \beta_3 X^3 + \beta_k X^k$$

Where k is the degree of the polynomial. For $k=2$, $f(X)$ is called **quadratic** and $h=4$ is called **cubic**. Note that polynomial regression is still considered linear regression since it is still linear in coefficient $\beta_1, \beta_2, \beta_3, ..., \beta_k$.

Before revisiting the Beijing PM2.5 example, let's understand how polynomial regression works using simulated data from the quadratic equation we introduced in the *Linear Regression* section.

Exercise 55: Performing Uniform Distribution Using the runif() Function

In this exercise, we will generate 50 random numbers from a uniform distribution using the function **runif()** in R and store the results in **uniform_random_x**. We have defined a function to generate values using the previous quadratic equation. Note that we will separately add ϵ_i to the values returned by the function; ϵ_i is generated from the normal distribution using the **rnorm()** function in R. The final value will then be stored in **quadratic_values_y**:

Perform these steps to perform the uniform distribution using the **runif()** function:

1. First, define the quadratic equation as illustrated in the following command:

    ```
    quadratic_function <- function(x){return (5+(12*x)-(3*(x^2)))}
    ```

2. Now, generate the uniform random number for **x**:

    ```
    uniform_random_x <- runif(50, min=0, max=15)
    ```

3. Add the error term to the quadratic equation, which is normally distributed with mean **0** and variance **2** (*standard deviation(sd) = square root of variance*):

    ```
    quadratic_values_y <- quadratic_function(uniform_random_x) + rnorm(50,mean
    = 0, sd =sqrt(2))
    ```

4. To store the data in data frame, let's use the following command:

    ```
    df <- data.frame(quadratic_values_y,uniform_random_x)
    ```

5. Now, plot the relationship between **x** and **y** based on the quadratic equation:

    ```
    library(ggplot2)
    ggplot(df, aes(x=uniform_random_x,y=quadratic_values_y))+
      geom_point()
    ```

The output is as follows:

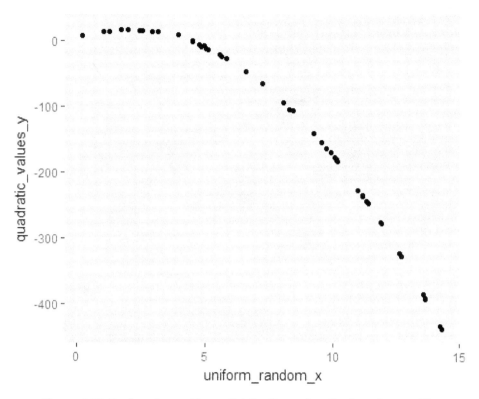

Figure 4.10: Performing uniform distribution using the function runif()

The following figure clearly shows the relationship between **uniform_random_x** and **quadratic_values_y** is not linear as expected. Now, if we try to fit a linear model, we expect to see some trouble in the diagnostics plot.

Residuals versus fitted value plots in *Figure* 4.12 display a curvature and they do not demonstrate uniform randomness as we have seen before. Also, **Normal Probability Plot** (**NPP**) seems to diverge from a straight line and curves down at the far away percentiles. These plots suggest that there is something incorrect with the model being used and indicate that a higher-order model may be needed.

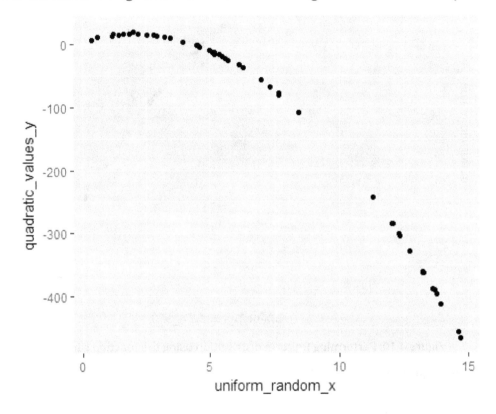

Figure 4.11: The plot shows the non-linear relationship between uniformly generated random number(x) and the value of x in the quadratic equation

6. Now, fit a linear regression model to the polynomial (quadratic) equation and display the diagnostic plot:

```
par(mfrow = c(2,2))
plot(lm(quadratic_values_y~uniform_random_x,data=df))
```

The output is as follows:

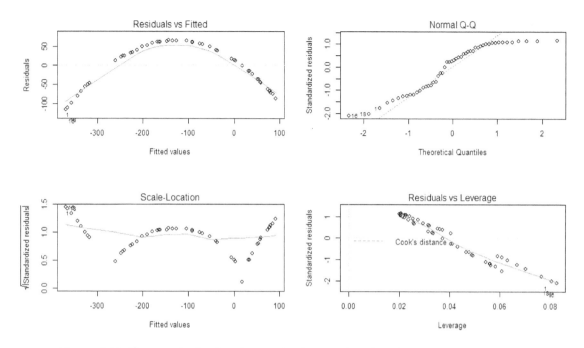

Figure 4.12: Diagnostic plot for the quadratic equation data fit using the lm() method

Now, let's see how polynomial regression fares on the Beijing PM2.5 dataset. We have introduced an additional quadratic term **DEWP^2**, which is simply **DEWP** raised to the power **2**. Refer to the scatterplot illustrated in *Figure 3.5* of *Chapter 3, Introduction to Supervised Learning* to justify the addition of such a higher order term.

7. Use polynomial regression on the Beijing PM2.5 dataset with the quadratic and cubic terms:

```
multiple_PM25_poly_model <- lm(pm2.5 ~ DEWP^2 + TEMP + Iws +
DEWP*TEMP*month, data = PM25)
```

8. To print the model summary, use the following command:

```
summary(multiple_PM25_poly_model)
```

The output is as follows:

```
## Residuals:
##       Min       1Q  Median       3Q      Max
## -298.41   -42.77   -9.35    30.91   967.39
##
## Coefficients:
##                           Estimate Std. Error t value Pr(>|t|)
## (Intercept)              2.917e+02  4.338e+00  67.257  < 2e-16 ***
## DEWP                     1.190e+01  2.539e-01  46.879  < 2e-16 ***
## TEMP                    -9.830e+00  8.806e-01 -11.164  < 2e-16 ***
## Iws                     -1.388e-01  7.707e-03 -18.009  < 2e-16 ***
## month2                  -2.388e+01  5.011e+00  -4.766 1.89e-06 ***
## month3                  -1.228e+02  5.165e+00 -23.780  < 2e-16 ***

## DEWP:TEMP:month9   4.455e-01  6.552e-02   6.800 1.06e-11 ***
## DEWP:TEMP:month10  5.066e-01  5.862e-02   8.642  < 2e-16 ***
## DEWP:TEMP:month11  5.111e-02  5.526e-02   0.925  0.35500
## DEWP:TEMP:month12  1.492e-01  6.599e-02   2.261  0.02375 *
## ---
## Signif. codes:  0 '***' 0.001 '**' 0.01 '*' 0.05 '.' 0.1 ' ' 1
##
## Residual standard error: 70.04 on 41708 degrees of freedom
##   (2067 observations deleted due to missingness)
## Multiple R-squared:  0.4217, Adjusted R-squared:  0.4211
## F-statistic: 633.7 on 48 and 41708 DF,  p-value: < 2.2e-16
```

Observe that in spite of an additional quadratic term, we are not attaining any better R-squared value than the linear model. At this juncture, we may conclude that the PM2.5 prediction needs a better independent variable, which could explain the variance in it to get the R-squared value to any higher level. The diagnostics plot seems to show similar interpretation.

9. Plot the diagnostics plot using the following command:

```
par(mfrow = c(2,2))
plot(multiple_PM25_poly_model)
```

The output is as follows:

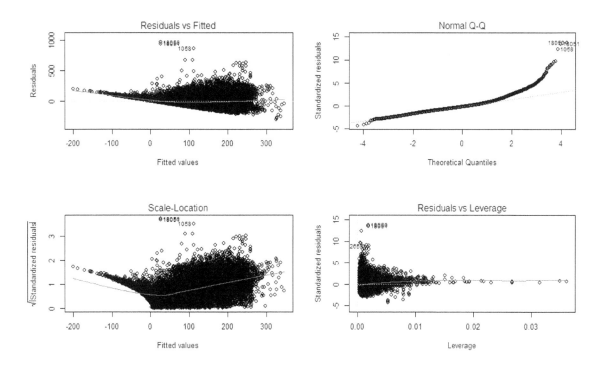

Figure 4.13: The diagnostics plot for polynomial regression model fit on the Beijing PM2.5 dataset

Ridge Regression

As we saw in linear regression, **Ordinary Least Square (OLS)** estimates the value of $\hat{\beta}$ in such a way that the sum of squares of residual $s(\hat{\beta})$ is minimized.

Since $\hat{\beta}$ is an estimate we compute from a given sample and it's not a *true population parameter*, we need to be careful of certain characteristics of an estimate. The two such primary characteristics are the bias and the variance.

If $\hat{f}(x_i)$ is the fit at the ith value of x, then the average (or expected) $s(\hat{\beta})$ on the test dataset could be decomposed into three quantities, the variance, the squared bias, and the variance of error terms as represented by the following equation:

$$E(y_0 - \hat{f}(x_i))^2 = Var\left(\hat{f}(x_i)\right) + [Bias\left(\hat{f}(x_i)\right)]^2 + Var(\varepsilon)$$

For the best estimate, a suitable algorithm such as OLS should simultaneously achieve low bias and low variance. We commonly call this the **Bias-Variance** trade off. The popular bull's eye picture shown in the following figure helps understand the various scenarios of the tradeoff:

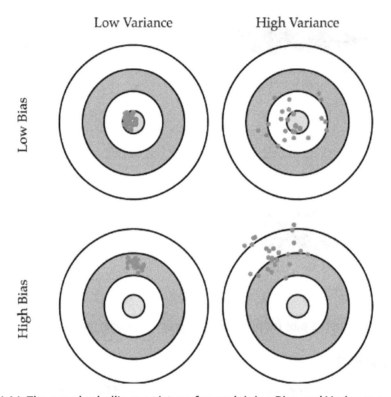

Figure 4.14: The popular bull's eye picture for explaining Bias and Variance scenarios

The bull's eye represents the true population value that OLS is trying to estimate, and the shots at it are the values of our estimates resulting from four different estimators. These are broadly classified into the following:

- Low Bias and Low Variance (most favorable)
- Low Bias and High Variance
- High Bias and Low Variance
- High Bias and High Variance (least favorable)

OLS method treats all variables as equally likely, thus having a low bias (results in **under-fitting** during training) and high variance (results in **prediction error** in testing data) as shown in the *Figure 4.11*. Such behavior is not ideal for obtaining the optimal model complexity. The general solution to this issue is to reduce variance at the cost of introducing some bias. This approach is called regularization. So, ridge regression could be thought of as an extension of linear regression with an additional regularization term.

The general form of multiple linear regression could be expressed as follows:

$$\operatorname*{argmin}_{\beta \in \mathbb{R}} \sum [y_i - \hat{y}_i] = \operatorname*{argmin}_{\beta \in \mathbb{R}} \left[y_i - (\beta_0 + \beta_1 x_1 + \beta_1 x_2 + \cdots + \beta_p x_p) \right]^2$$

Where, **argmin** means the minimum value of βs that make the function attain the minimum. In the context, it finds the βs that minimize the RSS. The βs are subject to the following constraints:

$$\beta_0^2 + \beta_1^2 + \cdots + \beta_p^2 \leq C^2$$

Regularization Term – L2 Norm

$$\|B\|_2 = \sqrt{\beta_0^2 + \beta_1^2 + \cdots + \beta_p^2}$$

$$\hat{\beta}^r = \operatorname*{argmin}_{\beta \in \mathbb{R}} \|y - XB\|_2^2 + \|B\|_2^2$$

The penalty term in the ridge beta increases if RSS increases. The following figure shows a plot between **Model Complexity** (number of predictors) and **Error**. It shows that when the number of predictors increase (model complexity increases), the **Variance** goes up and the **Bias** goes down.

The OLS estimate finds a place in the right side, away from the optimal trade-off point. This scenario necessitates the introduction of the regularization term and hence ridge regression becomes suitable choice of model:

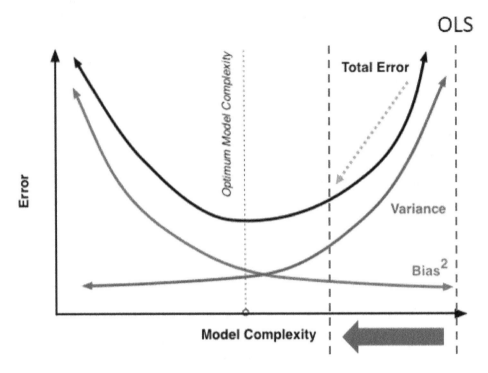

Figure 4.15: Bias versus variance

The OLS loss function for ridge regression could be represented by the following equation:

$$S_{ridge}(\hat{\beta}) = \sum_{i=1}^{n}(y_i - x_i^T\hat{\beta})^2 + \lambda\sum_{j=1}^{m}\hat{\beta}^2{}_j = \|y - X\hat{\beta}\|^2 + \lambda\|\hat{\beta}\|^2$$

Minimizing the $S_{ridge}(\hat{\beta})$ function with the regularization term that gives the ridge regression estimates. The interesting property of this loss function is that as λ becomes larger, the variance decreases and the bias increases.

Exercise 56: Ridge Regression on the Beijing PM2.5 dataset

This exercise fits the ridge regression on the Beijing PM2.5 dataset. We will use **glmnet** library's cross-validation function **cv.glmnet()** with the parameter **alpha = 0** and varying lambda values. The aim is to obtain an optimal value for lambda that will be returned in the **lambda.min** attribute of the function output.

Let's perform the following steps to complete the exercise:

1. Load the **glmnet** library and preprocess the PM25 DataFrame:

```
library(glmnet)
PM25 <- na.omit(PM25)
X <- as.matrix(PM25[,c("DEWP","TEMP","Iws")])
Y <- PM25$pm2.5
```

2. Now, let's use the following code to set up the **seed** to get similar results:

```
set.seed(100)
model_ridge = cv.glmnet(X,Y,alpha = 0,lambda = 10^seq(4,-1,-0.1))
```

3. To find the optimal value of lambda after cross validation, execute the following command:

```
optimal_lambda <- model_ridge$lambda.min
```

4. Coefficient values from the model fit:

```
ridge_coefficients <- predict(model_ridge, s = optimal_lambda, type =
"coefficients")
ridge_coefficients
```

The output is as follows:

```
## 4 x 1 sparse Matrix of class "dgCMatrix"
##                          1
## (Intercept) 160.7120263
## DEWP           4.3462480
## TEMP          -5.0902943
## Iws           -0.2756095
```

5. Use the **predict** function again and pass the matrix X to the **newx** parameter:

```
ridge_prediction <- predict(model_ridge, s = optimal_lambda, newx = X)
head(ridge_prediction)
```

The output is as follows:

```
             1
25 111.0399
26 115.1408
27 137.3708
28 154.2625
29 154.0172
30 158.8622
```

We see how ridge regression could be used to fit the Beijing PM2.5 dataset using the **glmnet** library.

LASSO Regression

Least Absolute Shrinkage and Selection Operator (**LASSO**) follows a similar structure to that of ridge regression, except for the penalty term, which in LASSO regression is L1 (sum of absolute values of the coefficient estimates) in contrast to ridge regression where it's L2 (sum of squared coefficients):

$$L_{lasso}(\hat{\beta}) = \sum_{i=1}^{n} (y_i - x_i^T \hat{\beta})^2 + \lambda \sum_{j=1}^{m} |\hat{\beta}_j|$$

LASSO regression turns some coefficients to zero, thus the effect of a particular variable is nullified. This makes it efficient in feature selection while fitting data.

Exercise 57: LASSO Regression

In this exercise, we will apply LASSO regression on the Beijing PM2.5 dataset. We will use the same **cv.glmnet()** function to find the optimal lambda value.

Perform the following steps to complete the exercise:

1. First, let's set up **seed** to get similar results using the following command:

   ```
   set.seed(100) #Setting the seed to get similar results.
   model_LASSO = cv.glmnet(X,Y,alpha = 1,lambda = 10^seq(4,-1,-0.1))
   ```

2. Now, use the following command to find the optimal value of lambda after cross validation:

   ```
   optimal_lambda_LASSO <- model_LASSO$lambda.min
   ```

3. Execute the following command to find the coefficient values from the model fit:

```
LASSO_coefficients <- predict(model_LASSO, s = optimal_lambda_LASSO, type =
"coefficients")

LASSO_coefficients
```

The output is as follows:

```
## 4 x 1 sparse Matrix of class "dgCMatrix"
##                       1
## (Intercept) 160.4765008
## DEWP          4.3324461
## TEMP         -5.0725046
## Iws          -0.2739729
```

4. Use the following command to find the prediction from the model:

```
LASSO_prediction <- predict(model_LASSO, s = optimal_lambda_LASSO, newx =
X)
head(LASSO_prediction)
```

The output is as follows:

```
          1
25 110.9570
26 115.0456
27 137.2040
28 154.0434
29 153.7996
30 158.6282
```

Observe the similarity in the predictions of ridge and LASSO regression. The Beijing PM2.5 dataset doesn't show any difference in these two approaches.

Elastic Net Regression

Elastic Net combines the penalty terms of ridge and LASSO regression to avoid the overdependence on data for variable selection (coefficient values tending to zero by which highly correlated variables are kept in check). Elastic Net minimizes the following loss function:

$$L_{enet}(\hat{\beta}) = \frac{\sum_{i=1}^{n}(y_i - x_i^T \hat{\beta})^2}{2n} + \lambda \left(\frac{1-\alpha}{2} \sum_{j=1}^{m} \hat{\beta}_j^2 + \alpha \sum_{j=1}^{m} |\hat{\beta}_j| \right)$$

Where the parameter α controls the right mix between ridge and LASSO.

In summary, if a model has many predictor variables or correlated variables, introducing the regularization term helps in reducing the variance and increase bias optimally, thus bringing the right balance of model complexity and error. *Figure 4.16* provides a flow diagram to help one choose between multiple, ridge, LASSO, and elastic net regression:

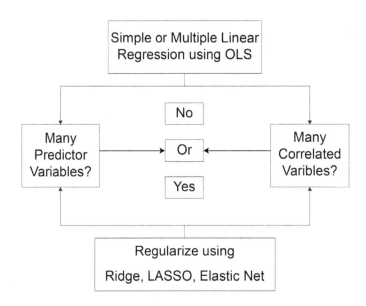

Figure 4.16: Selection criteria to choose between multiple, ridge, LASSO, and elastic net regression

Exercise 58: Elastic Net Regression

In this exercise, we will perform elastic net regression on the Beijing PM2.5 dataset.

Perform the following steps to complete the exercise:

1. Let's first set up **seed** to get similar results using the following command:

    ```
    set.seed(100)
    model_elanet = cv.glmnet(X,Y,alpha = 0.5,lambda = 10^seq(4,-1,-0.1))
    ```

2. Now, use the following command to find the optimal value of lambda after cross validation:

```
optimal_lambda_elanet <- model_LASSO$lambda.min
```

3. Next, execute the following command to find the coefficient values from the model fit:

```
elanet_coefficients <- predict(model_elanet, s = optimal_lambda_elanet,
type = "coefficients")
elanet_coefficients
```

The output is as follows:

```
## 4 x 1 sparse Matrix of class "dgCMatrix"
##                         1
## (Intercept) 160.5950551
## DEWP            4.3393969
## TEMP           -5.0814722
## Iws            -0.2747902
```

4. Use the following command to find the prediction from the model:

```
elanet_prediction <- predict(model_elanet, s = optimal_lambda_elanet, newx
= X)
```

The output is as follows:

```
25 110.9987
26 115.0936
27 137.2880
28 154.1538
29 153.9092
30 158.7461
```

Elastic Net Regression gives more or less the same predictions as of ridge and LASSO regression. In the next section, we compare all three together.

Comparison between Coefficients and Residual Standard Error

The following tables show the comparison of **Residual Standard Error (RSE)** and Coefficient values between linear, ridge, LASSO, and elastic net regression. With our Beijing PM2.5 dataset and three predictor variables (DEWP, TEMP, and Iws), there isn't much difference in the values, which suggests that ridge, LASSO, and elastic net regression with regularization terms are not any better than multiple linear regression approach. This also suggests that DEWP, TEMP, and Iws are independent variables with low or no correlations:

Number	Regression Type	RSE
1	Linear Regression	81.51
2	Ridge Regression	81.51059
3	LASSO Regression	81.51123
4	Elastic Net Regression	81.51087

Figure 4.17: Comparison of residual standard error between linear, ridge, LASSO, and elastic net regression

The following figure shows a comparison of the coefficient values of intercept and DEWP, TEMP and Iws variables using Linear, Ridge, LASSO and Elastic net regression:

No	Regression Type	Intercept	DEWP	TEMP	Iws
1	Linear Regression	161.1512066	4.3841960	-5.1335111	-0.2743375
2	Ridge Regression	160.7120263	4.3462480	-5.0902943	-0.2756095
3	LASSO Regression	160.4765008	4.3324461	-5.0725046	-0.2739729
4	Elastic Net Regression	160.5950551	4.3393969	-5.0814722	-0.2747902

Figure 4.18: Comparison of coefficient values between Linear, Ridge, LASSO, and Elastic Net regression

Exercise 59: Computing the RSE of Linear, Ridge, LASSO, and Elastic Net Regressions

In this exercise, we will compute the RSE of Linear, Ridge, LASSO, and Elastic Net regressions.

Perform the following steps to complete the exercise:

1. Use the following code to fit a linear model using the **Iws**, **DEWP**, and **TEMP** variables:

    ```
    multiple_PM25_linear_model <- lm(pm2.5 ~ Iws + DEWP + TEMP, data = PM25)
    ```

2. Now, use the following command for finding the **Residual Standard Error (RSE)** of linear regression:

    ```
    sqrt(sum(multiple_PM25_linear_model$residuals^2)/41753)
    ```

    The output is as follows:

    ```
    ## [1] 81.51
    ```

    Similarly, we will find the RSE of the remaining regression.

3. RSE of ridge regression:

    ```
    sqrt(sum((Y-ridge_prediction)^2)/41753)
    ```

    The output is as follows:

    ```
    ## [1] 81.51059
    ```

4. RSE of LASSO regression:

    ```
    sqrt(sum((Y-LASSO_prediction)^2)/41753)
    ```

    The output is as follows:

    ```
    ## [1] 81.51123
    ```

5. RSE of Elastic Net regression:

    ```
    sqrt(sum((Y-elanet_prediction)^2)/41753)
    ```

    The output is as follows:

    ```
    ## [1] 81.51087
    ```

This shows that the RSE for all three isn't significantly different.

Poisson Regression

In linear regression, we saw an equation of the form:

$$Y = f(X) = \beta_0 + \sum_{j=1}^{p} \beta_j X_j$$

In **Poisson Regression**, the response variable **Y** is a count or rate (**Y/t**) that has a **Poisson distribution** with expected (mean) count of y_i as $E(Y) = \mu$, which is equal to variance.

In case of logistic regression, we would probe for values that can maximize log-likelihood to get the **maximum likelihood estimators** (**MLEs**) for coefficients.

There are no closed-form solutions, hence the estimations of maximum likelihood would be obtained using iterative algorithms such as **Newton-Raphson** and **Iteratively re-weighted least squares** (**IRWLS**).

Poisson regression is suitable for the count-dependent variable, which must meet the following guidelines:

- It follows a Poisson distribution

- Counts are not negative

- Values are whole numbers (no fractions)

> **Note**
>
> The dataset used here to demonstrate Poisson regression comes from A. Colin Cameron and Per Johansson, "*Count Data Regression Using Series Expansion: With Applications*", Journal of Applied Econometrics, Vol. 12, No. 3, 1997, pp. 203-224.

The following table succinctly describes the variables:

No	Variable	Category	Description
1	NONDOCCO	Target variable	Number of consultations in the past four weeks with non-doctor health professionals (chemist, optician, physiotherapist, etc.)
2	SEX	Socio-economic variables	Gender of the patient (female=1)
3	AGE		Age of patient (in years)
4	INCOME		Patient's annual income (in hundreds of dollars)
5	LEVYPLUS	Health insurance status indicator variables	Dummy for private insurance coverage (=1)
6	FREEPOOR		Dummy for free government insurance coverage due to low income (=1)
7	FREEREPA		Dummy for free government insurance coverage due to old age, disability, or veteran status (=1)
8	ILLNESS	Recent health-status measures	Number of illnesses in the past two weeks
9	ACTDAYS		Number of days of reduced activity in the past two weeks due to illness or injury
10	HSCORE	Long-term health status measures	Health questionnaire score (high score=bad health)
11	CHCOND1		Dummy for a chronic condition not limiting activity (=1)
12	CHCOND2		Dummy for chronic condition limiting activity (=1)

Figure 4.19: Variables and its description from an Australian Health Survey dataset

Note

The blog http://www.econ.uiuc.edu/~econ508/Stata/e-ta16_Stata.html demonstrates the usage of the dataset.

Exercise 60: Performing Poisson Regression

In this exercise, we will perform Poisson regression on the dataset.

Perform the following steps to complete the exercise:

1. Carry out Poisson regression load the library **foreign** to read **dta** data:

```
library(foreign)
```

2. Using the **read.data** function from the **foreign** library to read the Australian health survey dataset:

```
df_health <- read.dta("health.dta")
```

3. Fit a generalized linear model using the **glm()** function with Poisson regression as the value in the family parameter:

```
poisson_regression_health <- glm(NONDOCCO ~ ., data = df_health,
family=poisson(link=log))
```

4. Print the summary of the model:

```
summary(poisson_regression_health)
```

The output is as follows:

```
## Coefficients:
##               Estimate Std. Error z value Pr(>|z|)
## (Intercept) -3.116128   0.137763 -22.620  < 2e-16 ***
## SEX          0.336123   0.069605   4.829 1.37e-06 ***
## AGE          0.782335   0.200369   3.904 9.44e-05 ***
## INCOME      -0.123275   0.107720  -1.144 0.252459
## LEVYPLUS     0.302185   0.097209   3.109 0.001880 **
## FREEPOOR     0.009547   0.210991   0.045 0.963910
## FREEREPA     0.446621   0.114681   3.894 9.84e-05 ***
## ILLNESS      0.058322   0.021474   2.716 0.006610 **
## ACTDAYS      0.098894   0.006095  16.226  < 2e-16 ***
## HSCORE       0.041925   0.011613   3.610 0.000306 ***
## CHCOND1      0.496751   0.086645   5.733 9.86e-09 ***
## CHCOND2      1.029310   0.097262  10.583  < 2e-16 ***
## ---
## Signif. codes:  0 '***' 0.001 '**' 0.01 '*' 0.05 '.' 0.1 ' ' 1
##
## (Dispersion parameter for poisson family taken to be 1)
##
##      Null deviance: 6127.9  on 5189  degrees of freedom
```

```
## Residual deviance: 5052.5  on 5178   degrees of freedom
## AIC: 6254.3
##
## Number of Fisher Scoring iterations: 7
```

5. Load the **ggplot2** library:

   ```
   library(ggplot2)
   ```

6. Combine the actual values of **NONDOCCO** and Poisson regression-fitted values of **NONDOCCO**:

   ```
   df_pred_actual <- data.frame(cbind(df_health$NONDOCCO,poisson_regression_
   health$fitted.values))
   ```

7. Name the columns:

   ```
   colnames(df_pred_actual) <- c("actual_NONDOCCO","predicted_NONDOCCO")
   ```

8. Plot the actual versus predicted values of the **NONDOCCO** target variable:

   ```
   ggplot(df_pred_actual, aes(x=actual_NONDOCCO, y =predicted_NONDOCCO))+
       geom_point()
   ```

The output plot is as follows:

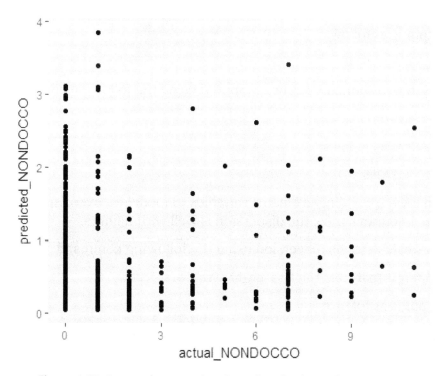

Figure 4.20: Comparing actual and predicted values of NONDOCCO

Given the value of the residual deviance statistic of 5052.5 with 5178 degree of freedom, the p-value is zero and the 5052.5/5178 = 0.975 is less than 1, so the model does to a certain level. We can also check overdispersion (presence of greater variability in a dataset than would be expected based on a given statistical model). Overdispersion is computed by dividing **sample_variance** with **sample_mean**. Let's examine the following exercise.

Exercise 61: Computing Overdispersion

In this exercise, we will perform computing overdispersion on the dataset.

Perform the following steps to complete the exercise:

1. First, let's find the sample mean using the following command:

    ```
    s_mean <- mean(df_health$NONDOCCO)
    s_mean
    ```

    The output is as follows:

    ```
    ## [1] 0.2146435
    ```

2. Now, use the following command for finding the sample variance:

    ```
    s_variance <- var(df_health$NONDOCCO)
    s_variance
    ```

    The output is as follows:

    ```
    ## [1] 0.931757
    ```

3. Similarly, overdispersion can be computed using the following command:

    ```
    s_variance/s_mean
    ```

    The output is as follows:

    ```
    ## [1] 4.34095
    ```

    So, even if we try adding predictor variables to model fit, overdispersion starts to go down. In our example, the dispersion is well within limits.

4. Now, let's calculate the dispersion using the following command:

    ```
    summary.glm(poisson_regression_health)$dispersion
    ```

    The output is as follows:

    ```
    ## [1] 1
    ```

However, in cases where dispersion is over the limit, a higher order Poisson regression is a suitable solution. Keeping the scope of this book in mind, we will not delve into such model in detail here. Interested readers could read more on Baseline Density Poisson (**Poisson Polynomial of order p** (**PPp**) models).

Cox Proportional-Hazards Regression Model

The basis for the Cox regression models comes from the survival analysis, a set of statistical methods helpful in investigating the time it takes for an event to occur. Some examples are as follows:

- Time until a lead is converted to sales

- Time until a product failure from the start of usage

- Time after the start of the insurance policy until death

- Time after diagnosing until death

- Time until a warranty is claimed for a product

- Time from customer registration

All these examples are some of the use cases of survival analysis. In most of the survival analysis, there are three wide-spread methods used for carrying out such time-to-event analysis:

- Kaplan-Meier survival curves for analysis of different groups
- The logrank test for comparing two or more survival curves
- Cox proportional hazards regression to describe the effect of variables on survival

Keeping in mind the scope of this chapter and book, we will focus only on the Cox proportional hazards regression. The fundamental idea is that the first two methods only help in performing univariate analysis, in other words, you can understand the effect of only one factor on the time-to-event, whereas Cox regression helps in assessing the effect of multiple factors on the survival time. Also, Cox regression works equally good with both categorical and numeric factors, while the first two methods only work with categorical factors.

The Cox model is expressed by the hazard function denoted by **h(t)**, which represents in the medical research, where its predominately used, the risk of dying at time **t**:

$$h(t) = h_0(t) \times e^{(b_1 x_1 + b_2 x_2 + \cdots + b_p x_p)}$$

Some observations from this equation are as follows:

- **t** denotes the survival time.

- **h(t)** represents the hazard function determined by the **p** covariates $(x_1, x_2, \dots, x_p)$. Covariates is the term used for describing predictor variables in survival analysis.

- The coefficients $(b_1, b_2, \dots, b_p)$ suggest the impact of covariates.

- The term $h_0(t)$ is called the baseline hazard at time t. If all the coefficients are zero $(e^0 = 1)$, $h_0(t)$ becomes the value of the hazard function.

This function looks somewhat relatable to logistic regression (uses an exponential term), which will be discussed in detail in *Chapter 5, Classification*. We have logically split all the supervised learning algorithms discussed in this book into **Regression** and **Classification**. Though logistic regression predicts numeric values in the form of probabilities, it is used widely as a **Classification algorithm**. However, in the context of this section, it suffices to note that logistic regression uses a binary dependent variable (**yes/no, 1/0**) but disregards the timing of events.

As you may have observed from the hazard function, survival models comprise of:

- A continuous variable demonstrative of the time to event

- A binary variable illustrative of the status whether event happened or not

NCCTG Lung Cancer Data

NCCTG Lung Cancer Data from survival in patients with advanced lung cancer is from the *North Central Cancer Treatment Group*. The data is a collection of few metadata, such as which institution collected it, age of the patient, sex, and so on. The performance scores in this dataset rates how well the patient can perform the daily activities. The most important variable in any survival analysis dataset is the *knowledge* about the **time-to-event**, for example, time until death.

Survival analysis is usually defined as a set of methods for examining data where the outcome variable is the time till the incidence of an event of interest.

No	Variable	Description
1	inst:	Institution code
2	time:	Survival time in days
3	status:	censoring status 1=censored, 2=dead
4	age:	Age in years
5	sex:	Male=1 Female=2
6	ph.ecog:	ECOG performance score (0=good 5=dead)
7	ph.karno:	Karnofsky performance score (bad=0-good=100) rated by the physician
8	pat.karno:	Karnofsky performance score as rated by the patient
9	meal.cal:	Calories consumed at meals
10	wt.loss:	Weight loss in the last six months

Figure 4.21: Variables and its descriptions of North Central Cancer Treatment Group

In the next exercise, we will learn how to create the survival object using the method Surv from the **survival** package. Note that in the summary of the dataset after adding the survival object, two additional variables SurvObject.time and SurvObject.status are created, which stores the information about time-to-event (time until death), which then becomes the dependent variable for the **Cox Proportional-Hazards Regression Model**.

Observations are **censored** when there is a scarce number of indications around a patient's survival time. Popularly, the most prevalent form is right censoring. Let's assume that we are following a study for 20 weeks. A patient not going through the event of interest during the study can be called as right censored. The person's survival time is at least the duration of the study; in this case, 20 weeks.

Exercise 62: Exploring the NCCTG Lung Cancer Data Using Cox-Regression

In this exercise, we will explore the NCCTG Lung Cancer Data using Cox-Regression.

Perform the following steps to complete the exercise:

1. Import the **survival** library:

    ```
    library(survival)
    ```

2. Import the Lung Cancer Data:

    ```
    df_lung_cancer <- lung
    ```

3. Print the dataset using the **head** function:

    ```
    head(df_lung_cancer)
    ```

    The output is as follows:

    ```
    ##   inst time status age sex ph.ecog ph.karno pat.karno meal.cal wt.loss
    ## 1    3  306      2  74   1       1       90       100     1175      NA
    ## 2    3  455      2  68   1       0       90        90     1225      15
    ## 3    3 1010      1  56   1       0       90        90       NA      15
    ## 4    5  210      2  57   1       1       90        60     1150      11
    ## 5    1  883      2  60   1       0      100        90       NA       0
    ## 6   12 1022      1  74   1       1       50        80      513       0
    ```

4. Lung Cancer Data where **status == 2** represents death:

    ```
    df_lung_cancer$SurvObject <- with(df_lung_cancer, Surv(time, status == 2))
    ```

5. Find the Cox Proportional Hazards Regression model:

    ```
    cox_regression <- coxph(SurvObject ~ age + sex + ph.karno + wt.loss, data
    = df_lung_cancer)
    cox_regression
    ```

    The output is as follows:

    ```
    ## Call:
    ## coxph(formula = SurvObject ~ age + sex + ph.karno + wt.loss,
    ##       data = df_lung_cancer)
    ##
    ##
    ##               coef exp(coef) se(coef)     z      p
    ## age        0.01514   1.01525  0.00984  1.54 0.1238
    ## sex       -0.51396   0.59813  0.17441 -2.95 0.0032
    ## ph.karno  -0.01287   0.98721  0.00618 -2.08 0.0374
    ## wt.loss   -0.00225   0.99776  0.00636 -0.35 0.7239
    ```

```
##
## Likelihood ratio test=18.8  on 4 df, p=0.000844
## n= 214, number of events= 152
##    (14 observations deleted due to missingness)
```

This exercise demonstrates the Cox proportional hazards regression model using the survival library.

Summary

In this chapter, we discussed linear regression in more detail after a brief introduction in the previous chapter. Certainly, the discussion on linear regression led to a series of diagnostics that gave directions to discussing other type of regression algorithms. Quantile, polynomial, ridge, LASSO, and elastic net, all of these are derived from linear regression, with the differences coming from the fact that there are some limitations in linear regression that each of these algorithms helped overcome. Poisson and Cox proportional hazards regression model came out as a special case of regression algorithms that work with count and time-to-event dependent variables, respectively, unlike the others that work with any quantitative dependent variable.

In the next chapter, we will explore the second most commonly applied machine learning algorithm and solve problems associated with it. You will also learn more about classification in detail. *Chapter 5, Classification*, similar to this chapter, is designed to cover classification algorithms ranging from **Decision Trees** to **Deep Neural Network** in detail.

5

Classification

Learning Objectives

By the end of this chapter, you will be able to:

- Define binary classification in supervised machine learning

- Perform binary classification using white-box models: logistic regression and decision trees

- Evaluate the performance of supervised classification models

- Perform binary classification using black-box ensemble models – Random Forest and XGBoost

- Design and develop deep neural networks for classification

- Select the best model for a given classification use case

In this chapter, we will focus on solving classification use cases for supervised learning. We will use a dataset designed for a classification use case, frame a business problem around it, and explore a few popular techniques to solve the problem.

Introduction

Let's quickly brush up on the topics we learned in *Chapter 3, Introduction to Supervised Learning*. Supervised learning, as you already know by now, is the branch of machine learning and artificial intelligence that helps machines learn without explicit programming. A more simplified way of describing supervised learning would be developing algorithms that learn from labeled data. The broad categories in supervised learning are classification and regression, differentiated fundamentally by the type of label, that is, **continuous** or **categorical**. Algorithms that deal with continuous variables are known as **regression algorithms**, and those with categorical variables are called **classification algorithms**.

In classification algorithms, our target, dependent, or criterion variable is a **categorical variable**. Based on the number of classes, we can further divide them into the following groups:

- Binary classification

- Multinomial classification

- Multi-label classification

In this chapter, we will focus on **binary classification**. Discussing the specifics and practical examples of multinomial and multi-class classification is beyond the scope of this chapter; however, a few additional reading references for advanced topics will be listed before wrapping up the chapter.

Binary classification algorithms are the most popular class of algorithms within machine learning and have numerous applications in business, research, and academia. Simple models that classify a student's chances of passing a future exam based on their past performance as pass or fail, predict whether it will rain or not, predict whether a customer will default on a loan or not, predict whether a patient has cancer or not, and so on are all common use cases that are solved by classification algorithms.

Before diving deeper into algorithms, we will first get started with a use case that will help us solve a supervised learning classification problem with hands-on exercises.

Getting Started with the Use Case

In this chapter, we will refer to the **rainfall prediction problem** using the `weather` dataset, obtained from the Australian Commonwealth Bureau of Meteorology and made available through R. The dataset has two target variables, `RainTomorrow`, a flag indicating whether it will rain tomorrow, and `RISK_MM`, which measures the amount of rainfall for the following day.

In a nutshell, we can use this dataset for **regression** as well as **classification**, since we have two target variables. However, we will drop the continuous target variable and only consider the categorical target variable, `RainTomorrow`, for our classification exercise. The metadata and additional details about the dataset are available to explore at https://www.rdocumentation.org/packages/rattle/versions/5.2.0/topics/weather. Since the dataset is readily available through R, we don't need to separately download it; instead, we can directly use the R function within the `rattle` library to load the data into system memory.

Some Background on the Use Case

Several weather parameters, such as temperature, direction, pressure, cloud cover, humidity, and sunshine, were recorded daily for one year. The rainfall for the next day is already engineered in the dataset as the target variable, `RainTomorrow`. We can leverage this data to define a machine learning model that learns from the present day's weather parameters and predicts the chances of rain for the next day.

Rainfall prediction is of paramount importance to many industries. Long-haul journeys by train and buses usually look at changing weather patterns, primarily rainfall, to estimate the arrival time and journey length. Similarly, most brick and mortar stores, small restaurants and food joints, and others are all heavily impacted by rainfall. Gaining visibility of the weather conditions for the next day can help businesses better prepare in several ways, to combat business losses and, in some cases, maximize business outcomes.

To build nice intuition around the problem-solving exercise, let's frame a business problem using the dataset and develop the problem statement for the use case. Since the data is about rainfall prediction, we will choose a popular business problem faced by today's hyper-local food-delivery services. Start-ups such as DoorDash, Skip the Dishes, FoodPanda, Swiggy, Foodora, and many others offer hyper-local food delivery services to customers in different countries. A common trend observed in most countries is the rise in food delivery orders with the onset of rain. In general, most delivery companies expect around a 30%-40% increase in the total number of deliveries on a given day. Given the limited number of delivery agents, the delivery time is impacted immensely due to increased orders on rainy days. To keep costs optimal, it is not viable for these companies to increase the number of full-time agents; therefore, a common strategy is to dynamically hire more agents for days when demand for the service is expected to be high. To plan better, visibility of rainfall predictions for the next day is of paramount importance.

Defining the Problem Statement

With the context of the problem set up, let's try to define our problem statement for a hyper-local food-delivery service company to predict the rainfall for the next day. To keep things simple and consistent, let's frame the problem statement using the frameworks we studied previously, in *Chapter 2, Exploratory Analysis of Data*. This will help us distill the end goal we want to solve in a business-first approach while keeping the machine learning perspective at the forefront.

The following figure creates a simple visual for the **Situation** - **Complication** - **Question** (**SCQ**) framework for the previously defined use case:

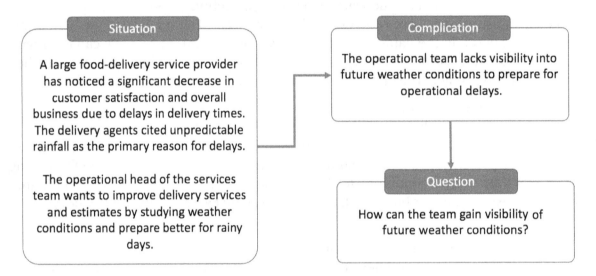

Figure 5.1: SCQ for the classification use case

We can clearly answer the question from the SCQ: we would need a predictive model to predict the chances of rain for the next day as a solution to the problem. Let's move on to the next step – gathering data to build a predictive model that will help us solve the business problem.

Data Gathering

The **rattle.data** package provides us with the data for the use case, which can be accessed using the internal dataset methods of R. In case you have not already installed the packages, you can easily install them using the **install.packages("rattle.data")** command.

Exercise 63: Exploring Data for the Use Case

In this exercise, we will perform the initial exploration of the dataset we have gathered for the use case. We will explore the shape of the data, that is, the number of rows and columns, and study the content within each column.

To explore the shape (rows x columns) and content of the data, perform the following steps:

1. First, load the **rattle** package using the following command:

    ```
    library(rattle.data)
    ```

2. Load the data for our use case, which is available from the **rattle** package:

    ```
    data(weatherAUS)
    ```

    > **Note**
    >
    > The **weatherAUS** dataset is a DataFrame containing more than 1,40,000 daily observations from over 45 Australian weather stations.

3. Now, load the weather data directly into a DataFrame called **df**:

    ```
    df <- weatherAUS
    ```

4. Explore the DataFrame's content using the **str** command:

    ```
    str(df)
    ```

The output is as follows:

```
'data.frame':   145460 obs. of  24 variables:
 $ Date         : Date, format: "2008-12-01" "2008-12-02" ...
 $ Location     : Factor w/ 49 levels "Adelaide","Albany",..: 3 3 3 3 3 3 3 3 3 3 ...
 $ MinTemp      : num  13.4 7.4 12.9 9.2 17.5 14.6 14.3 7.7 9.7 13.1 ...
 $ MaxTemp      : num  22.9 25.1 25.7 28 32.3 29.7 25 26.7 31.9 30.1 ...
 $ Rainfall     : num  0.6 0 0 0 1 0.2 0 0 0 1.4 ...
 $ Evaporation  : num  NA NA NA NA NA NA NA NA NA NA ...
 $ Sunshine     : num  NA NA NA NA NA NA NA NA NA NA ...
 $ WindGustDir  : Ord.factor w/ 16 levels "N"<"NNE"<"NE"<..: 13 14 12 3 13 14 13 13 16 13 ...
 $ WindGustSpeed: num  44 44 46 24 41 56 50 35 80 28 ...
 $ WindDir9am   : Ord.factor w/ 16 levels "N"<"NNE"<"NE"<..: 13 16 13 7 4 13 11 8 7 9 ...
 $ WindDir3pm   : Ord.factor w/ 16 levels "N"<"NNE"<"NE"<..: 14 12 12 5 15 13 13 13 15 8 ...
 $ WindSpeed9am : num  20 4 19 11 7 19 20 6 7 15 ...
 $ WindSpeed3pm : num  24 22 26 9 20 24 24 17 28 11 ...
 $ Humidity9am  : int  71 44 38 45 82 55 49 48 42 58 ...
 $ Humidity3pm  : int  22 25 30 16 33 23 19 19 9 27 ...
 $ Pressure9am  : num  1008 1011 1008 1018 1011 ...
 $ Pressure3pm  : num  1007 1008 1009 1013 1006 ...
 $ Cloud9am     : int  8 NA NA NA 7 NA 1 NA NA NA ...
 $ Cloud3pm     : int  NA NA 2 NA 8 NA NA NA NA NA ...
 $ Temp9am      : num  16.9 17.2 21 18.1 17.8 20.6 18.1 16.3 18.3 20.1 ...
 $ Temp3pm      : num  21.8 24.3 23.2 26.5 29.7 28.9 24.6 25.5 30.2 28.2 ...
 $ RainToday    : Factor w/ 2 levels "No","Yes": 1 1 1 1 1 1 1 1 1 2 ...
 $ RISK_MM      : num  0 0 0 1 0.2 0 0 0 1.4 0 ...
 $ RainTomorrow : Factor w/ 2 levels "No","Yes": 1 1 1 1 1 1 1 1 2 1 ...
```

Figure 5.2: Final output

We have almost 1,50,000 rows of data and 24 variables. We would need to drop the **RISK_MM** variable, as it will be the target variable for the regression use case (that is, predicting how much it will rain the next day). Therefore, we are left with 22 independent variables and 1 dependent variable, **RainTomorrow**, for our use case. We can also see a good mix of continuous and categorical variables. The **Location**, **WindDir**, **RainToday**, and many more variables are categorical, and the remainder are continuous.

> **Note**
>
> You can find the complete code on GitHub: http://bit.ly/2Vwgu8Q.

In the next exercise, we will calculate the total percentage of the null values in each column.

Exercise 64: Calculating the Null Value Percentage in All Columns

The dataset we explored in *Exercise 1, Exploring Data for the Use Case* has quite a few null values. In this exercise, we will write a script to calculate the percentage of null values within each column.

We can see the presence of null values in a few variables. Let's check the percentage of null values in each column within the **df** dataset.

Perform the following steps to calculate the percentage of null values in each column of the dataset:

1. First, remove the column named **RISK_MM**, since it is supposed to be used as a target variable for regression use. (Adding this to our model will result in data leakage.):

   ```
   df$RISK_MM <- NULL
   ```

2. Create a **temp_df** DataFrame object and store the value in it:

   ```
   temp_df<-as.data.frame(
     sort(
     round(
     sapply(df, function(y) sum(length(which(is.na(y)))))/dim(df)[1],2)
     )
   )
   colnames(temp_df) <- "NullPerc"
   ```

3. Now, use the **print** function to display the percentage null values in each column using the following command:

   ```
   print(temp_df)
   ```

   The output is as follows:

   ```
                 NullPerc
   Date             0.00
   Location         0.00
   MinTemp          0.01
   MaxTemp          0.01
   WindSpeed9am     0.01
   Temp9am          0.01
   Rainfall         0.02
   WindSpeed3pm     0.02
   Humidity9am      0.02
   Temp3pm          0.02
   RainToday        0.02
   ```

```
RainTomorrow      0.02
WindDir3pm        0.03
Humidity3pm       0.03
WindGustDir       0.07
WindGustSpeed     0.07
WindDir9am        0.07
Pressure9am       0.10
Pressure3pm       0.10
Cloud9am          0.38
Cloud3pm          0.41
Evaporation       0.43
Sunshine          0.48
```

We can see that the last four variables have more than 30% missing or null values. This is a significantly huge drop. It would be best to drop these variables from our analysis. Also, we can see that there are a few other variables that have roughly 1%-2%, and in some cases, up to 10% missing or null values. We can treat these variables using various missing value treatment techniques, such as replacing them with mean or mode. In some important cases, we can also use additional techniques, such as clustering-based mean and mode replacement, for improved treatment. Additionally, in very critical scenarios, we can use a regression model to estimate the remainder of the missing values by defining a model where the column with the required missing value is treated as a function of the remaining variables.

> **Note**
>
> You can find the complete code on GitHub: http://bit.ly/2ViZEp1.

In the following exercise, we will remove null values. We will revisit data if we do not have a good model in place.

Exercise 65: Removing Null Values from the Dataset

John is working on the newly created dataset, and while doing analysis, he has found out that the dataset contains significant null values. To make the dataset useful for further analysis, he must remove the null values from it.

Perform the following steps to remove the null values from the **df** dataset:

1. First, select the last four columns to drop that have more than 30% null values using the following command:

    ```
    cols_to_drop <-tail(rownames(temp_df),4)
    ```

2. Remove all the rows from the DataFrame that will have one or more columns with null values using the **na.omit** command, which removes all of the null rows from the DataFrame:

    ```
    df_new<- na.omit(df[,!names(df) %in% cols_to_drop])
    ```

3. Now, print the newly formatted data using the following **print** commands:

    ```
    print("Shape of data after dropping columns:")
    print(dim(df_new))
    ```

    The output is as follows:

    ```
    Shape of data after dropping columns:
    112925    19
    ```

4. Using the following command, verify whether the newly created dataset contains null values or not:

    ```
    temp_df<-as.data.frame(sort(round(sapply(df_new,
    function(y) sum(length(which(is.na(y)))))/dim(df)[1],2)))
    colnames(temp_df) <- "NullPerc"
    ```

5. Now, print the dataset using the following **print** command:

    ```
    print(temp_df)
    ```

    The output is as follows:

    ```
                  NullPerc
    Date                 0
    Location             0
    MinTemp              0
    MaxTemp              0
    Rainfall             0
    WindGustDir          0
    WindGustSpeed        0
    ```

```
WindDir9am         0
WindDir3pm         0
WindSpeed9am       0
WindSpeed3pm       0
Humidity9am        0
Humidity3pm        0
Pressure9am        0
Pressure3pm        0
Temp9am            0
Temp3pm            0
RainToday          0
RainTomorrow       0
```

We can now double check and see that the new dataset has no more missing values and the overall number of rows in the dataset also reduced to 112,000, which is around a 20% loss of training data. We should use missing value treatment techniques such as replacing missing values with the mean, mode, or median to combat such high losses due to the omission of missing values. A rule of thumb would be to safely ignore anything less than a 5% loss. Since, we have more than 1,00,000 records (a reasonably high number of records for a simple use case), we are ignoring this rule of thumb.

> **Note**
>
> You can find the complete code on GitHub: http://bit.ly/2Q3HIgT.

Additionally, we can also engineer date- and time-related features using the **Date** column. The following exercise creates numeric features such as day, month, day of the week, and quarter of the year as additional time-related features and drops the original **Date** variable.

We will use the **lubridate** library in R to work with date and time-related features. It provides us with extremely easy-to-use functions to perform date and time operations. If you have not already installed the package, please install the library using the **install.packages('lubridate')** command.

Exercise 66: Engineer Time-Based Features from the Date Variable

Time- and date-related attributes cannot be directly used in a supervised classification model. To extract meaningful properties from date- and time-related variables, it is a common practice to create month, year, week, and quarter from the date as features.

Perform the following steps to work with the data and time function in R:

1. Import the **lubridate** library into RStudio using the following command:

   ```
   library(lubridate)
   ```

   > **Note**
   >
   > The **lubridate** library provides handy date- and time-related functions.

2. Extract **day**, **month**, **dayofweek**, and **quarter** as new features from the **Date** variable using the **lubridate** function:

   ```
   df_new$day <- day(df_new$Date)
   df_new$month <- month(df_new$Date)
   df_new$dayofweek <- wday(df_new$Date)
   df_new$quarter <- quarter(df_new$Date)
   ```

3. Examine the newly created variables:

   ```
   str(df_new[,c("day","month","dayofweek","quarter")])
   ```

4. Now that we have created all of the date- and time-related features, we won't need the actual **Date** variable. Therefore, delete the previous **Date** column:

   ```
   df_new$Date <- NULL
   ```

   The output is as follows:

   ```
   'data.frame':       112925 obs. of  4 variables:
    $ day       : int  1 2 3 4 5 6 7 8 9 10 ...
    $ month     : num  12 12 12 12 12 12 12 12 12 12 ...
    $ dayofweek: num  2 3 4 5 6 7 1 2 3 4 ...
    $ quarter   : int  4 4 4 4 4 4 4 4 4 4 ...
   ```

In this exercise, we have extracted meaningful features from date- and time-related attributes from the data and removed the actual date-related columns.

> **Note**
>
> You can find the complete code on GitHub: http://bit.ly/2E4hOEU.

Next, we need to process or clean another feature within the DataFrame: **location**.

Exercise 67: Exploring the Location Frequency

The **Location** variable defines the actual location where the weather data was captured for the specified time. Let's do a quick check on the number of distinct values that are captured within this variable and see whether there are any interesting patterns that might be of importance.

In the following exercise, we will be using the **Location** variable to define the actual location where the weather data was captured for the specified time.

Perform the following steps:

1. Calculate the frequency of rain across each location using the grouping functions from the **dplyr** package:

```
location_dist <- df_new %>%
    group_by(Location) %>%
    summarise(Rain  = sum(ifelse(RainTomorrow =="Yes",1,0)), cnt=n()) %>%
    mutate(pct = Rain/cnt) %>%
    arrange(desc(pct))
```

2. Examine the number of distinct locations for sanity:

```
print(paste("#Distinct locations:",dim(location_dist)[1]))
```

The output is as follows:

```
"#Distinct locations: 44"
```

3. Print **summary** to examine the aggregation performed:

```
print(summary(location_dist))
```

The output is as follows:

```
      Location          Rain               cnt             pct
   Adelaide    : 1   Min.   : 102.0   Min.   : 670    Min.   :0.06687
   Albury      : 1   1st Qu.: 427.8   1st Qu.:2330    1st Qu.:0.18380
   AliceSprings: 1   Median : 563.5   Median :2742    Median :0.21833
   BadgerysCreek: 1  Mean   : 568.6   Mean   :2566    Mean   :0.21896
   Ballarat    : 1   3rd Qu.: 740.5   3rd Qu.:2884    3rd Qu.:0.26107
   Bendigo     : 1   Max.   :1031.0   Max.   :3117    Max.   :0.36560
   (Other)     :38
```

We can see that there are 44 distinct locations in the data. The **cnt** variable, which defines the number of records (in the previous transformed data) for each location, has an average 2,566 records. The similar number distribution between the first quartile, median, and third quartile denote that the locations are evenly distributed in the data. However, if we investigate the percentage of records where rain was recorded (**pct**), we see an interesting trend. Here, we have locations with around a 6% chance of rain and some with around a 36% chance of rain. There is a huge difference in the possibility of rain, based on the location.

> **Note**
>
> You can find the complete code on GitHub: http://bit.ly/30aKUMx.

Since we have around 44 distinct locations, it is difficult to utilize this variable directly as a categorical feature. In R, most supervised learning algorithms internally convert the categorical column into a numerical form that can be interpreted by the model. However, with an increased number of classes within the categorical variable, the complexity of the model increases with no additional value. To keep things simple, we can transform the **Location** variable as a new variable with a reduced number of levels. We will select the top five and the bottom five locations with chances of rain and tag all other locations as **Others**. This will reduce the number of distinct levels in the variable as 10+1 and will be more suitable for the model.

Exercise 68: Engineering the New Location with Reduced Levels

The **location** variable has too many distinct values (44 locations), and machine learning models in general do not perform well with categorical variables with a high frequency of distinct classes. We therefore need to prune the variable by reducing the number of distinct classes within it. We will select the top five and the bottom five locations with chances of rain and tag all other locations as **Others**. This will reduce the number of distinct levels in the variable as 10+1 and will be more suitable for the model.

Perform the following steps to engineer a new variable for location with a reduced number of distinct levels:

1. Convert the **location** variable from a factor into a character:

```
location_dist$Location <- as.character(location_dist$Location)
```

2. Create a list with the top five and the bottom five locations with respect to the chances of rain. We can do this by using the **head** command for the top five and the **tail** command for the bottom five locations after ordering the DataFrame in ascending order:

```
location_list <- c(head(location_dist$Location,5),tail(location_
dist$Location,5))
```

3. Print the list to double-check that we have the locations correctly stored:

```
print("Final list of locations - ")
print(location_list)
```

The output is as follows:

```
[1] "Final list of locations - "
 [1] "Portland"      "Walpole"       "Dartmoor"      "Cairns"
 [5] "NorfolkIsland" "Moree"         "Mildura"       "AliceSprings"
 [9] "Uluru"         "Woomera"
```

4. Convert the **Location** variable in the main **df_new** DataFrame into a **character**:

```
df_new$Location <- as.character(df_new$Location)
```

5. Reduce the number of distinct locations in the variable. This can be done by tagging all the locations that are not a part of the **location_list** list as **Others**:

```
df_new$new_location <- factor(ifelse(df_new$Location %in% location_
list,df_new$Location,"Others"))
```

6. Delete the old **Location** variable using the following command:

```
df_new$Location <- NULL
```

7. To ensure that the fifth step was correctly performed, we can create a temporary DataFrame and summarize the frequency of records against the new **location** variable we created:

```
temp <- df_new %>% mutate(loc = as.character(new_location)) %>%
    group_by(as.character(loc)) %>%
    summarise(Rain  = sum(ifelse(RainTomorrow =="Yes",1,0)), cnt=n()) %>%
    mutate(pct = Rain/cnt) %>%
    arrange(desc(pct))
```

8. Print the temporary test DataFrame and observe the results. We should see only 11 distinct location values:

```
print(temp)
```

The output is as follows:

```
# A tibble: 11 x 4
   `as.character(loc)`  Rain   cnt    pct
   <chr>               <dbl> <int>  <dbl>
   Portland             1031  2820 0.366
   Walpole               864  2502 0.345
   Dartmoor              770  2294 0.336
   Cairns                910  2899 0.314
   NorfolkIsland         883  2864 0.308
   Others              19380 86944 0.223
   Moree                 336  2629 0.128
   Mildura               315  2897 0.109
   AliceSprings          227  2744 0.0827
   Uluru                 110  1446 0.0761
   Woomera               193  2886 0.0669
```

We first convert the **Location** variable from a factor to a character to ease the string operation's tasks. The DataFrame is sorted in descending order according to the percentage chance of rain. The **head** and the **tail** commands are used to extract the top and bottom five locations in a list. This list is then used as a reference check to reduce the number of levels in the new feature. Finally, after engineering the new feature with the reduced levels, we do a simple check to ensure that our feature has been engineered in the way we expect.

> **Note**
>
> You can find the complete code on GitHub: http://bit.ly/30fnR31.

Let's now get into the most interesting topic of the chapter and explore classification techniques for supervised learning.

Classification Techniques for Supervised Learning

To approach a **supervised classification algorithm**, we first need to understand the basic functioning of the algorithm, explore a bit of the math in an abstract way, and then develop the algorithm using readily available packages in R. We will cover a few basic algorithms, such as white-box algorithms such as Logistic Regression and Decision Trees, and then we will move on to advanced modeling techniques, such as black-box models such as Random Forest, XGBoost, and neural networks. The list of algorithms we plan to cover is not exhaustive, but these five algorithms will help you gain a broad understanding of the topic.

Logistic Regression

Logistic regression is the most favorable white-box model used for binary classification. White-box models are defined as models where we have visibility of the entire reasoning used for the prediction. For each prediction made, we can leverage the model's mathematical equation and decode the reasons for the prediction made. There are also a set of classification models that are completely black-box, that is, by no means can we understand the reasoning for the prediction leveraged by the model. In situations where we want to focus on only the end outcome, we should prefer black-box models, as they are more powerful.

Though the name ends with *regression*, logistic regression is a technique used to predict binary categorical outcomes. We would need a different approach to model for a categorical outcome. This can be done by transforming the outcome into a log of odds ratio or the probability of the event happening.

Let's distill this approach into simpler constructs. Assume the probability of success for an event is 0.8. Then, the probability of failure for the same event would be defined as (1-0.8) = 0.2. The odds of success are defined as the ratio of the probability of success over the probability of failure.

In the following example, the odds of success would be (0.8/0.2) = 4. That is, the odds of success are four to one. If the probability of success is 0.5, that is, a 50-50 percent chance, then the odds of success are 0.5 to 1. The logistic regression model can be mathematically represented as follows:

$$Ln\left(\frac{p}{1-p}\right) = \beta_0 + \beta_1 X_1 + \beta_2 X_2 + \ldots + \beta_n X_n$$

Where, $Ln\left(\frac{p}{1-p}\right)$ is the log of odds ratio.

Solving the math further, we can deduce the probability of the outcome as follows:

$$p = \left(\frac{e^{(\beta 0 + \beta 1X1 + \beta 2X2 + \dots + \beta nXn)}}{1 + e^{(\beta 0 + \beta 1X1 + \beta 2X2 + \dots + \beta nXn)}} \right)$$

Discussing the mathematical background and derivation of the equations is beyond the scope of the chapter. To summarize, the `logit` function, that is, the link function, helps logistic regression reframe the problem (predicted outcome) intuitively as the log of odds ratio. When solved, it helps us predict the probability of a binary dependent variable.

How Does Logistic Regression Work?

Just like linear regression, where the beta coefficients for the variables are estimated using the **Ordinary Least Squares (OLS)** method, a logistic regression model leverages the **maximum-likelihood estimation (MLE)**. The MLE function estimates the best set of values of the model parameters or beta coefficients such that it maximizes the likelihood function, that is, the probability estimates, which can be also defined as the *agreement* of the selected model with the observed data. When the best set of parameter values are estimated, plugging these values or beta coefficients into the model equation as previously defined would help in estimating the probability of the outcome for a given sample. Akin to OLS, MLE is also an iterative process.

Let's see a logistic regression model in action on our dataset. To get started, we will use only a small subset of variables for the model. Ideally, it is recommended to start with the most important variables based on the EDA exercise and then incrementally add remainder variables. For now, we will start with a temperature-related variable for the maximum and minimum values, a wind speed-related variable, pressure and humidity at 3 P.M., and the rainfall for the current day.

We will divide the entire dataset into train (70%) and test (30%). While fitting the data to the model, we will only use the train dataset and will later evaluate the performance of the model on the train, as well as the unseen test data. This approach will help us understand whether our model is overfitting and provide a more realistic model performance on unseen data.

Exercise 69: Build a Logistic Regression Model

We will build a binary classification model using logistic regression and the dataset we explored in the Exercises 1-6. We will divide the data into train and test (70% and 30%, respectively) and leverage the training data to fit the model and the test data to evaluate the model's performance on unseen data.

Perform the following steps to complete the exercise:

1. First, set **seed** for reproducibility using the following command:

   ```
   set.seed(2019)
   ```

2. Next, create a list of indexes for the training dataset (70%):

   ```
   train_index <- sample(seq_len(nrow(df_new)),floor(0.7 * nrow(df_new)))
   ```

3. Now, split the data into test and train datasets using the following commands:

   ```
   train <- df_new[train_index,]
   test <- df_new[-train_index,]
   ```

4. Build the logistic regression model with **RainTomorrow** as the dependent variable and a few independent variables (we selected **MinTemp, Rainfall, WindGustSpeed, WindSpeed3pm, Humidity3pm. Pressure3pm, RainToday, Temp3pm**, and **Temp9am**). We can add all the available independent variables in the DataFrame too:

   ```
   model <- glm(RainTomorrow ~ MinTemp + Rainfall + WindGustSpeed +
           WindSpeed3pm +Humidity3pm + Pressure3pm +
           RainToday +  Temp3pm + Temp9am,
           data=train,
           family=binomial(link='logit'))
   ```

5. Print the summary of the dataset using the **summary** function:

   ```
   summary(model)
   ```

   The output is as follows:

   ```
   Call:
   glm(formula = RainTomorrow ~ MinTemp + Rainfall + WindGustSpeed +
       WindSpeed3pm + Humidity3pm + Pressure3pm + RainToday + Temp3pm +
       Temp9am, family = binomial(link = "logit"), data = train)

   Deviance Residuals:
       Min        1Q    Median        3Q       Max
   -2.9323   -0.5528   -0.3235   -0.1412    3.2047
   ```

```
Coefficients:
                Estimate Std. Error z value Pr(>|z|)
(Intercept)     6.543e+01  1.876e+00  34.878  < 2e-16 ***
MinTemp         9.369e-05  5.056e-03   0.019    0.985
Rainfall        7.496e-03  1.404e-03   5.337 9.44e-08 ***
WindGustSpeed   5.817e-02  1.153e-03  50.434  < 2e-16 ***
WindSpeed3pm   -4.331e-02  1.651e-03 -26.234  < 2e-16 ***
Humidity3pm     7.363e-02  9.868e-04  74.614  < 2e-16 ***
Pressure3pm    -7.162e-02  1.821e-03 -39.321  < 2e-16 ***
RainTodayYes    4.243e-01  2.751e-02  15.425  < 2e-16 ***
Temp3pm         3.930e-02  5.171e-03   7.599 2.98e-14 ***
Temp9am        -4.605e-02  6.270e-03  -7.344 2.07e-13 ***
---
Signif. codes:  0 '***' 0.001 '**' 0.01 '*' 0.05 '.' 0.1 ' ' 1

(Dispersion parameter for binomial family taken to be 1)

    Null deviance: 83718 on 79046 degrees of freedom
Residual deviance: 56557 on 79037 degrees of freedom

AIC: 56577

Number of Fisher Scoring iterations: 5
```

The **set.seed** command ensures that the random selections used for the train and test data split can be reproduced. We divide the data into 70% train and 30% test. The set seed function ensures that, for the same seed, we get the same split every time. The **glm** function is used in R to build generalized linear models. Logistic regression is defined in the model using the **family** parameter value set to **binomial(link ='logit')**. The **glm** function can be used to build several other models too (such as gamma, Poisson, and binomial). The formula defines the dependent, as well as the set of independent, variables. It takes the general form *Var1 ~ Var2 + Var3 + ...*, which denotes **Var1** as the dependent or target variable and the remainder as the independent variables. If we want to use all of the variables in the DataFrame as independent variables, we can instead use **formula = Var1 ~ .**, which would indicate that **Var1** is the dependent variable and the rest are all independent variables.

> **Note**
>
> You can find the complete code on GitHub: http://bit.ly/2HwwUUX.

Interpreting the Results of Logistic Regression

We previously had a glimpse of logistic regression in *Chapter 2, Exploratory Analysis of Data*, but we didn't get into the specifics of the model results. The results demonstrated in the previous output snippet will look like what you observed in linear regression, but with some differences. Let's explore and interpret the results part by part.

Firstly, we have the **Deviance Residuals** displayed right after the formula. Like linear regression, a deviance residual is a measure of goodness of fit. The `glm` function calculates two types of residuals, that is, **Null Deviance** and **Residual Deviance**. The difference between the two is that one reports the goodness of fit when only the intercept (that is, no dependent variables) is used and the other reports when all the provided independent variables are used. The reduction in deviance between null and residual deviance helps us understand the quantified value added by the independent variables in defining the variance or the predictive correctness. The distribution of deviance residuals is reported right after the formula.

Next, we have the **beta coefficients** and the associated **standard error**, the *z-value* and the *p-value*, which is the probability of significance. For each variable provided, R internally calculates the coefficients and, along with the parameter value, it also reports additional test results to help us interpret how effective these coefficients are. The absolute value of the coefficient is a simple way to understand how important that variable is to the final predictive power, that is, how impactful the variable is in determining the end outcome of the prediction. We can see that all variables have a low value for the coefficient.

Next, the standard error helps us quantify how stable the value will be. A lower value for the standard error would indicate more consistent or stable values for the beta coefficients. The standard errors for all the variables in our exercise are low. The *z-value* and the probability of significance together help us take a call as to whether the results are statistically significant or just appear as they are due to random chance. This idea follows on from the same principle we learned about the null and alternate hypothesis in *Chapter 2, Exploratory Analysis of Data*, and is akin to linear regression parameter significance, which we learned about in *Chapter 4, Regression*.

The easiest way to interpret the significance would be to study the *asterix* besides each independent variable, that is, *. The number of * is defined by the actual probability value, as defined below the parameter values. In our exercise, notice that the `MinTemp` variable is not statistically significant, that is, $p\text{-}value > 0.05$. The rest are all statistically significant variables.

The **Akaike Information Criterion** (**AIC**) is again a metric reported by R to assess the goodness of fit of the model or the quality of the model. This number comes in handy to compare different models for the same use case. Say you fit several models using a combination of independent variables but the same dependent variable, the AIC can be used to study the best model by way of a simple comparison of the value in all models. The calculation of the metric is derived from the deviance between the model's prediction and the actual labels, but factors in the presence of variables that are not adding any value. Therefore, akin to **R Squared** and **adjusted R Squared** in linear regression, the AIC helps us to avoid building complicated models. To select the best model from a list of candidate models, we should select the model with the lowest AIC.

Toward the end of the previous output, we can see the results from **Fisher's Scoring** algorithm, which is a derivative of Newton's method for solving maximum likelihood problems numerically. We see that it required five iterations to fit the data to the model, but beyond that, this information is not of much value to us. It is a simple indication for us to conclude that the model did converge.

We now understand how logistic regression works and have interpreted the results reported by the model in R. However, we still need to evaluate the model results using our train and test dataset and ensure that the model performs well on unseen data. To study the performance of a classification model, we would need to leverage various metrics, such as accuracy, precision, and recall. Though we already explored them in *Chapter 4, Regression*, let's now study them in more detail.

Evaluating Classification Models

Classification models require a bunch of different metrics to be thoroughly evaluated, unlike regression models. Here, we don't have something as intuitive as **R Squared**. Moreover, the performance requirements completely change based on a specific use case. Let's take a brief look at the various metrics that we already studied in *Chapter 3, Introduction to Supervised Learning*, for classification.

Confusion Matrix and Its Derived Metrics

The first basis for studying model performance for classification algorithms starts with a **confusion matrix**. A confusion matrix is a simple representation of the distribution of predictions of each class across the actuals of each class:

		Predicted	
		No	Yes
Actual	No	True Negative	False Positive
	Yes	False Negative	True Positive

Figure 5.3: Confusion matrix

The previous table is a simple representation of a confusion matrix. Here, we assume that the **Yes** class is labelled **Positive**. When the actual value of a given sample is **Yes** and it is correctly predicted as **Positive**, we define it as **True Positive**, whereas, if the actual value is **Yes**, but was predicted by the model as **No**, then we define it as **False Positive**. The same story holds true for **True Negative** and **False Negative**. Here's a simple rule: to avoid confusion in interpreting the names, consider the value of the label **Positive** for (1) and **Negative** for (0); when the result is correctly predicted, then we assign **True** to the label, otherwise **False**. Therefore, **True Positive** would be indicative of value 1 correctly predicted as 1 and so on for the remaining outcomes.

Based on the confusion matrix and the values defined from it, we can further define a couple of metrics that will help us better understand the model's performance. We will now use the abbreviations **TP** for **True Positive**, **FP** for **False Positive**, **TN** for **True Negative**, and **FN** for **False Negative** going forward:

- **Overall accuracy**: Overall accuracy is defined as the ratio of total correct predictions to the total number of predictions in the entire test sample. So, this would be simply the sum of **True Positives** and **True Negatives** divided by all the metrics in the confusion matrix:

$$\text{Overall Accuracy} = \frac{TP+TN}{TP+TN+FP+FN}$$

- **Precision** or <u>**Positive Predictive Value**</u> (<u>**PPV**</u>): Precision is defined as the ratio of correctly predicted positive labels to the total number of positively predicted labels:

$$\text{Precision (PPV)} = \frac{TP}{TP+FP}$$

- **Recall** or **Sensitivity**: Recall measures how sensitive your model is by representing the ratio of the number of correctly predicted positive labels to the total number of actual positive labels:

$$\text{Recall (Sensitivity)} = \frac{TP}{TP+FN}$$

- **Specificity** or **True Negative Rate** (**TNR**): Specificity defines the ratio of correctly predicted negative labels to the total number of actual negative labels:

$$\text{Specificity (TNR)} = \frac{TN}{TN+FP}$$

- **F1 Score**: The F1 score is the harmonic mean between precision and recall. It is a better metric to consider than overall accuracy for most cases:

$$\text{F1 Score} = 2 \times \frac{Precision * Recall}{Precision+Recall}$$

What Metric Should You Choose?

Another important aspect to consider on a serious note, is which metric we should consider while evaluating a model. There is no straightforward answer, as the best combination of metrics completely depend on the type of classification use case we are dealing with. One situation that commonly arises in classification use cases is imbalanced classes. It is not necessary for us to always have an equal distribution of positive and negative labels in data. In fact, in most cases, we would be dealing with a scenario where the positive class would be less than 30% of the data. In such cases, the overall accuracy would not be the ideal metric to consider.

Let's take a simple example to understand this better. Consider the example of predicting fraud in credit card transactions. In a realistic scenario, for every 100 transactions there may be just one or two fraud transactions. Now, if we use overall accuracy as the only metric to evaluate a model, even if we predict all the labels as **No**, that is, **Not Fraud**, we would have approximately 99% accuracy, 0% precision, and 0% recall. The 99% accuracy might seem a great number for model performance; however, in this case, it would not be the ideal metric to evaluate.

To deal with such a situation, there is often additional business context required to make a tangible call, but in most cases (for this type of a scenario), the business would want a higher recall with a bit of compromise on the overall accuracy and precision. The rationale to use high recall as the metric for model evaluation is that it would still be fine to predict a transaction as fraud even if it is authentic; however, it would be a mistake to predict a fraud transaction as authentic; the business losses would be colossal.

Often, the evaluation of a model is taken with a combination of metrics based on business demands. The biggest decision maker would be the trade-off between precision and recall. As indicated by the confusion matrix, whenever we try to improve precision, it hurts recall and vice versa.

Here are some business situations in which we prioritize different metrics:

- **Predicting a rare event with catastrophic consequences**: When predicting whether a patient has cancer or not, whether a transaction is fraud, and so on, it is OK to predict a person without cancer as having cancer, but the other way around would result in the loss of life. Such scenarios demand high recall by compromising *precision* and *overall accuracy*.

- **Predicting a rare event with not such catastrophic consequences**: When predicting whether a customer will churn or whether a customer will positively respond to a marketing campaign, the business outcome is not jeopardized by an incorrect prediction, but would be the campaign. In such cases, based on the situation, it would make sense to have high precision with a bit of compromise on recall.

- **Predicting a regular (non-rare) event with not such catastrophic consequences**: This would deal with most classification use cases, where the cost of correctly predicting a class is almost equal to the cost of incorrectly predicting the class. In such cases, we can use the F1 score, which represents a harmonic mean between precision and recall. It would be ideal to use overall accuracy in conjunction with the F1 score, as accuracy is more easily interpretable.

Evaluating Logistic Regression

Let's now evaluate the logistic regression model that we built previously.

Exercise 70: Evaluate a Logistic Regression Model

Machine learning models fitted on a training dataset cannot be evaluated using the same dataset. We would need to leverage a separate test dataset and compare the model's performance on a train as well as a test dataset. The **caret** package has some handy functions to compute the model evaluation metrics previously discussed.

Perform the following steps to evaluate the logistic regression model we built in *Exercise 7, Build a Logistic Regression Model*:

1. Compute the distribution of records for the **RainTomorrow** target variable in the **df_new** DataFrame:

    ```
    print("Distribution of labels in the data-")
    print(table(df_new$RainTomorrow)/dim(df_new)[1])
    ```

    The output is as follows:

    ```
    "Distribution of labels in the data-"
            No       Yes
    0.7784459 0.2215541
    ```

2. Predict the **RainTomorrow** target variable on the train data using the **predict** function and cast observations with values (probability >0.5) as **Yes**, else **No**:

    ```
    print("Training data results -")
    pred_train <-factor(ifelse(predict(model,
                            newdata=train, type="response")>
    0.5,"Yes","No"))
    ```

3. Create the confusion matrix and print the results for the train data:

    ```
    train_metrics <- confusionMatrix(pred_train,
                                    train$RainTomorrow,positive="Yes")
    print(train_metrics)
    ```

    The output is as follows:

    ```
    [1] "Training data results -"
    Confusion Matrix and Statistics

              Reference
    Prediction    No   Yes
           No  58233  8850
           Yes  3258  8706

                   Accuracy : 0.8468
                     95% CI : (0.8443, 0.8493)
        No Information Rate : 0.7779
        P-Value [Acc > NIR] : < 2.2e-16

                      Kappa : 0.4998
     Mcnemar's Test P-Value : < 2.2e-16
    ```

```
         Sensitivity : 0.4959
         Specificity : 0.9470
      Pos Pred Value : 0.7277
      Neg Pred Value : 0.8681
          Prevalence : 0.2221
      Detection Rate : 0.1101
Detection Prevalence : 0.1514
   Balanced Accuracy : 0.7215

    'Positive' Class : Yes
```

4. Predict the results on the test data, similar to the second step:

```
print("Test data results -")
pred_test <-factor(ifelse(predict(model,newdata=test,type = "response") >
0.5,"Yes","No"))
```

5. Create a confusion matrix for the test data predictions and print the results:

```
test_metrics <- confusionMatrix(pred_test,
                              test$RainTomorrow,positive="Yes")
print(test_metrics)
```

The output is as follows:

```
[1] "Test data results -"
Confusion Matrix and Statistics

          Reference
Prediction    No    Yes
       No   25066  3754
      Yes    1349  3709

               Accuracy : 0.8494
                 95% CI : (0.8455, 0.8532)
    No Information Rate : 0.7797
    P-Value [Acc > NIR] : < 2.2e-16

                  Kappa : 0.5042
 Mcnemar's Test P-Value : < 2.2e-16

            Sensitivity : 0.4970
            Specificity : 0.9489
         Pos Pred Value : 0.7333
         Neg Pred Value : 0.8697
```

```
          Prevalence : 0.2203
      Detection Rate : 0.1095
Detection Prevalence : 0.1493
   Balanced Accuracy : 0.7230


     'Positive' Class : Yes
```

We first load the necessary **caret** library, which will provide the functions to compute the desired metrics, as discussed. We then use the **predict** function in R to predict the results using the previously fitted model on the train as well as the test data (separately). The **predict** function for logistic regression returns the value of the **link** function, by default. Using the **type= 'response'** parameter, we can override the function to return probabilities for the target. For simplicity, we use **0.5** as a threshold on the predictions. Therefore, anything above 0.5 would be **Yes**, else **No**. The **confusionMatrix** function from the **caret** library provides us with a simple way to construct the confusion matrix and calculate an exhaustive list of metrics. We would need to pass the actual, as well the predicted labels, to the function.

> **Note**
>
> You can find the complete code on GitHub: http://bit.ly/2Q6mYW0.

The distribution of the target label is imbalanced: 77% no and 23% yes. In such a scenario, we cannot rely only on the overall accuracy as a metric to evaluate the model's performance. Also, the confusion matrix, as shown in the output for steps 3 and 5, is inverted when compared to the illustration shown in the previous section, *Confusion Matrix and Its Derived Metrics*. We have the predictions as rows and actual values as columns. However, the interpretation and results will remain the same. The next set of output reports the metrics of interest, along with a few others we have not explored. We have covered the most important ones (sensitivity and precision, that is, positive predictive value); however, it is recommended to explore the remaining metrics, such as negative predicted value, prevalence and detection rate. We can see that we are getting precision of around 73% and 50% recall and overall accuracy of 85%. The results are similar on the train and test datasets; therefore, we can conclude that the model doesn't overfit.

> **Note**
>
> The results are not bad overall. Please don't be surprised to see the low recall rate; in scenarios where we have imbalanced datasets, the metrics that are used to assess model performance are business-driven.

We can conclude that we would correctly predict at least half of the time whenever there is a possibility of rain, and whenever we predict, we are 73% correct. From a business perspective, if we try to contemplate whether we should strive for high recall or precision, we would need to estimate the cost of misclassification.

In our use case, whenever we predict that there is rainfall predicted for the next day, the operations management team would prepare the team with a higher number of agents to deliver faster. Since there isn't a pre-existing technique to combat rainfall-related problems, we have an opportunity to cover even if we recall only 50% of the times when there is rain. In this problem, since the cost of incorrectly predicting rain will be more expensive for the business, that is, if the chances of rainfall are predicted, the team would invest in pooling more agents for delivery, which comes at an additional cost. Therefore, we would want higher precision, while we are OK to compromise on recall.

> **Note**
>
> The ideal scenario is to have high precision and high recall. However, there is always a trade-off in achieving one over the other. In most real-life machine learning use cases, a business-driven decision finalizes the priority to choose either precision or recall.

The previous model developed in *Exercise 8, Evaluate a Logistic Regression Model*, was developed only using a few variables that were available in the **df_new** dataset. Let's build an improved model with all the available variables in the dataset and check the performance on the test dataset.

The best way to iterate for model improvements would be with feature selection and hyperparameter tuning. Feature selection involves selecting the best set of features from the available list through various validation approaches and finalizing a model with the best performance and the least number of features. Hyperparameter tuning deals with building generalized models that will not overfit, that is, a model that performs well on training as well as unseen test data. These topics will be covered in detail in *Chapter 6, Feature Selection and Dimensionality Reduction*, and *Chapter 7, Model Improvements*. For now, the scope of the chapter will be restricted to demonstrate model evaluation only. We will touch on the same use case for hyperparameter tuning and feature selection in upcoming chapters.

Exercise 71: Develop a Logistic Regression Model with All of the Independent Variables Available in Our Use Case

In the previous exercise, we limited the number of independent variables to only a few. In this example, we will use all the available independent variables in our **df_new** dataset and create an improved model. We will again use the train dataset to fit the model and test to evaluate the model's performance.

Perform the following steps to build a logistic regression model with all of the independent variables available within the use case:

1. Fit the logistic regression model with all the available independent variables:

    ```
    model <- glm(RainTomorrow~., data=train ,family=binomial(link='logit'))
    ```

2. Predict on the train dataset:

    ```
    print("Training data results-")
    pred_train <-factor(ifelse(predict(model,newdata=train,type = "response")
    >= 0.5,"Yes","No"))
    ```

3. Create the confusion matrix:

    ```
    train_metrics <- confusionMatrix(pred_train,
    train$RainTomorrow,positive="Yes")
    print(train_metrics)
    ```

    The output is as follows:

    ```
    "Training data results -"
    Confusion Matrix and Statistics

              Reference
    Prediction    No    Yes
           No  58189   8623
           Yes  3302   8933

                   Accuracy : 0.8491
                     95% CI : (0.8466, 0.8516)
        No Information Rate : 0.7779
        P-Value [Acc > NIR] : < 2.2e-16

                      Kappa : 0.5104
     Mcnemar's Test P-Value : < 2.2e-16

                Sensitivity : 0.5088
    ```

```
            Specificity : 0.9463
       Pos Pred Value : 0.7301
       Neg Pred Value : 0.8709
           Prevalence : 0.2221
       Detection Rate : 0.1130
 Detection Prevalence : 0.1548
    Balanced Accuracy : 0.7276

      'Positive' Class : Yes
```

4. Predict the results on the test data:

```
print("Test data results -")
pred_test <-factor(ifelse(predict(model,newdata=test,type = "response") >
0.5,"Yes","No"))
```

5. Create the confusion matrix:

```
test_metrics <- confusionMatrix(pred_test,
test$RainTomorrow,positive="Yes")
print(test_metrics)
```

The output is as follows:

```
"Test data results -"
Confusion Matrix and Statistics

          Reference
Prediction    No    Yes
       No   25057  3640
      Yes    1358  3823

               Accuracy : 0.8525
                 95% CI : (0.8486, 0.8562)
    No Information Rate : 0.7797
    P-Value [Acc > NIR] : < 2.2e-16

                  Kappa : 0.5176
 Mcnemar's Test P-Value : < 2.2e-16

            Sensitivity : 0.5123
            Specificity : 0.9486
         Pos Pred Value : 0.7379
         Neg Pred Value : 0.8732
             Prevalence : 0.2203
```

```
        Detection Rate : 0.1128
  Detection Prevalence : 0.1529
     Balanced Accuracy : 0.7304

      'Positive' Class : Yes
```

We leverage all the variables within the dataset to create a logistic regression model using the **glm** function. We then use the **fitted** model to predict the outcomes for the train and the test datasets; akin to the previous exercise.

> **Note**
>
> You can find the complete code on GitHub: http://bit.ly/2HgwjaU.

Notice how the overall accuracy, precision, and recall has improved a bit (though marginally). The results are fair and we can iterate with logistic regression to improving them further. For now, let's explore a few other classification techniques and study the performance of the model.

> **Note**
>
> In this exercise, we have not printed the model's summary statistics, akin to the first model, with a few variables. If printed, the results would consume less than two pages of the chapter. For now, we will ignore that since we are not exploring the model characteristics that are reported by R; instead, we are evaluating a model purely from the accuracy, precision, and recall metrics on the train and test dataset.
>
> The ideal way to get the best model would be to eliminate all statistically insignificant variables, remove multicollinearity, and treat the data for outliers, and so on. All these steps have been ignored for now, given the scope of the chapter.

Activity 8: Building a Logistic Regression Model with Additional Features

We built a simple model with few features in *Exercise 8, Evaluate a Logistic Regression Model*, and then with all the features in *Exercise 9, Develop a Logistic Regression Model with All of the Independent Variables Available in Our Use Case*. In this activity, we will build a logistic regression model with additional features that we can generate using simple mathematical transformations. It is good practice to add additional transformations of numeric features with log transformations, square and cube power transformations, square root transformations, and so on.

Perform the following steps to develop a logistic regression model with additional features engineered:

1. Create a copy of the **df_new** dataset in **df_copy** for the activity and select any three numeric features (for example, **MaxTemp**, **Rainfall** and **Humidity3pm**).

2. Engineer new features with square and cube power and square root transformations for each of the selected features.

3. Divide the **df_copy** dataset into train and test in a 70:30 ratio.

4. Fit the model with the new train data, evaluate it on test data, and finally, compare the results.

   The output is as follows:

```
"Test data results -"
Confusion Matrix and Statistics

          Reference
Prediction   No    Yes
       No  25057  3640
      Yes   1358  3823

               Accuracy : 0.8525
                 95% CI : (0.8486, 0.8562)
    No Information Rate : 0.7797
    P-Value [Acc > NIR] : < 2.2e-16

                  Kappa : 0.5176
 Mcnemar's Test P-Value : < 2.2e-16

            Sensitivity : 0.5123
            Specificity : 0.9486
         Pos Pred Value : 0.7379
         Neg Pred Value : 0.8732
```

```
          Prevalence : 0.2203
      Detection Rate : 0.1128
Detection Prevalence : 0.1529
   Balanced Accuracy : 0.7304

      'Positive' Class : Yes
```

> **Note**
>
> You can find the solution for this activity on page 451.

Decision Trees

Like logistic regression, there is another popular classification technique that is very popular due to its simplicity and white-box nature. A decision tree is a simple flowchart that is represented in the form of a tree (an inverted tree). It starts with a root node and branches into several nodes, which can be traversed based on a decision, and ends with a leaf node where the *final outcome* is determined. Decision trees can be used for regression, as well as classification use cases. There are several variations of decision trees implemented in machine learning. A few popular choices are listed here:

- **Iterative Dichotomiser 3 (ID3)**

- **Successor to ID3 (C4.5)**

- **Classification and Regression Tree (CART)**

- **CHi-squared Automatic Interaction Detector (CHAID)**

- **Conditional Inference Trees (C Trees)**

The preceding list is not exhaustive. There are other alternatives, and each of them has small variations in how they approach the tree creation process. In this chapter, we will limit our exploration to **CART Decision Trees**, which are the most widely used. R provides a few packages that house the implementation of the CART algorithm. Before we delve into the implementation, let's explore a few important aspects of decision trees in the following sections.

How Do Decision Trees Work?

Each variation of decision trees has a slightly different approach. Overall, if we try to simplify the pseudocode for a generic decision tree, it can be summarized as follows:

1. Select the root node (the node corresponds to a variable).

2. Partition the data into groups.

3. For each group from the previous step:

   Create a decision node or leaf node (based on the splitting criteria).

   Repeat until node size <= threshold or features = empty.

Variations between different forms of tree implementations include the way categorical and numerical variables are handled, the approach used to select the root node and consecutive nodes in the tree, the rules to branch each decision node, and so on.

The following visual is a sample decision tree. The root node and the decision nodes are the independent variables we provide to the algorithm. The leaf nodes denote the final outcome, whereas the root node and the intermediate decision nodes help in traversing the data to the leaf node. The simplicity of a decision tree is what makes it so effective and easy to interpret. This helps in easily identifying rules for a prediction task. Often, many research and business initiatives leverage decision trees to design a set of rules for a simple classification system:

Decision Tree

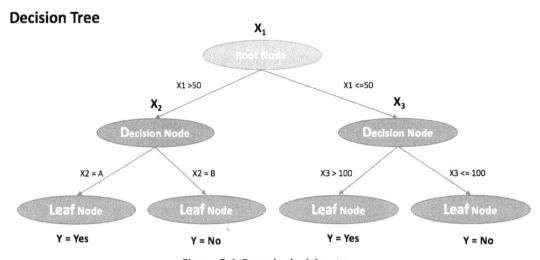

Figure 5.4: Sample decision tree

In a general sense, given a combination of dependent and several independent variables, the decision tree algorithm calculates a metric that represents the goodness of fit between the dependent target variable and all independent variables. For classification use cases, entropy and information gain are commonly used metrics in CART decision trees. The variable with the best fit for the metric is chosen as the root node and the next best is used as the decision nodes in the descending order of fit. The nodes are terminated into leaf nodes based on a defined threshold. The tree keeps growing till it exhausts the number of variables for decision nodes or when a predefined threshold for the number of nodes is reached.

To improve tree performance and reduce overfitting, a few strategies, such as restricting the depth or breadth of the tree or additional rules for leaf nodes or decision nodes help in generalizing a tree for prediction.

Let's implement the same use case using CART decision trees in R. The CART model is available through the **rpart** package in R. This algorithm was developed by Leo Breiman, Jerome Friedman, Richard Olshen, and Charles Stone in 1984 and has been widely adopted in the industry.

Exercise 72: Create a Decision Tree Model in R

In this exercise, we will create a decision tree model in R using the same data and the use case we leveraged in *Exercise 9, Develop a Logistic Regression Model with All of the Independent Variables Available in Our Use Case*. We will try to study whether there are any differences in the performance of a decision tree model over a logistic regression model.

Perform the following steps to create a decision tree model in R:

1. Import the **rpart** and **rpart.plot** packages using the following command:

    ```
    library(rpart)
    library(rpart.plot)
    ```

2. Build the CART model with all of the variables:

    ```
    tree_model <- rpart(RainTomorrow~.,data=train)
    ```

3. Plot the cost parameter:

    ```
    plotcp(tree_model)
    ```

The output is as follows:

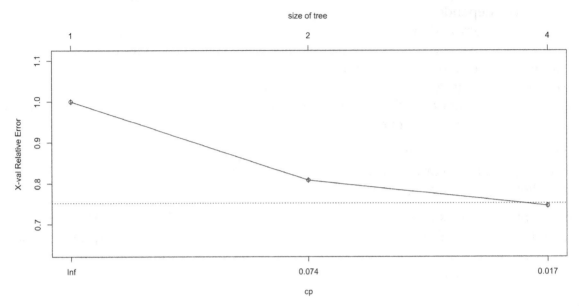

Figure 5.5: Decision tree model

4. Plot the tree using the following command:

```
rpart.plot(tree_model,uniform=TRUE, main="Predicting RainFall")
```

The output is as follows:

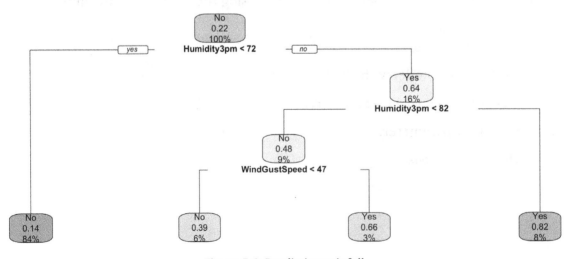

Figure 5.6: Predicting rainfall

5. Make predictions on the train data:

```
print("Training data results -")
pred_train <- predict(tree_model,newdata = train,type = "class")
confusionMatrix(pred_train, train$RainTomorrow,positive="Yes")
```

The output is as follows:

```
"Training data results -"
Confusion Matrix and Statistics

          Reference
Prediction    No    Yes
       No  59667  11215
       Yes  1824   6341

               Accuracy : 0.835
                 95% CI : (0.8324, 0.8376)
    No Information Rate : 0.7779
    P-Value [Acc > NIR] : < 2.2e-16

                  Kappa : 0.4098
 Mcnemar's Test P-Value : < 2.2e-16

            Sensitivity : 0.36119
            Specificity : 0.97034
         Pos Pred Value : 0.77661
         Neg Pred Value : 0.84178
             Prevalence : 0.22210
         Detection Rate : 0.08022
   Detection Prevalence : 0.10329
      Balanced Accuracy : 0.66576

       'Positive' Class : Yes
```

6. Make predictions on the test data:

```
print("Test data results -")
pred_test <- predict(tree_model,newdata = test,type = "class")
confusionMatrix(pred_test, test$RainTomorrow,positive="Yes")
```

The output is as follows:

```
[1] "Test data results -"
Confusion Matrix and Statistics

              Reference
Prediction    No    Yes
        No  25634   4787
        Yes   781   2676


                Accuracy : 0.8356
                  95% CI : (0.8317, 0.8396)
     No Information Rate : 0.7797
     P-Value [Acc > NIR] : < 2.2e-16

                   Kappa : 0.4075
  Mcnemar's Test P-Value : < 2.2e-16

             Sensitivity : 0.35857
             Specificity : 0.97043
          Pos Pred Value : 0.77408
          Neg Pred Value : 0.84264
              Prevalence : 0.22029
          Detection Rate : 0.07899
    Detection Prevalence : 0.10204
       Balanced Accuracy : 0.66450

        'Positive' Class : Yes
```

The **rpart** library provides us with the CART implementation of decision trees. There are additional libraries that help us visualize the decision tree in R. We have used **rpart. plot** here. If the package is not already installed, please install it using the **install. packages** command. We use the **rpart** function to create the tree model and we use all the available independent variables. We then use the **plotcp** function to visualize the complexity parameter's corresponding validation error on different iterations. We also use the **plot.rpart** function to plot the decision tree.

Finally, we make predictions on the train as well as the test data and build the confusion matrix and calculate the metrics of interest using the **confusionMatrix** function for the train and test datasets individually.

> **Note**
>
> You can find the complete code on GitHub: http://bit.ly/2WECLgZ.

The CART decision tree implemented in R has several optimizations already in place. The function, by default, sets a ton of parameters for optimum results. In a decision tree, there are several parameters that we can manually set to tune the performance based on our requirements. However, the R implementation does a great job of setting a wide number of parameters with a relatively good value by default. These additional settings can be added to the **rpart** tree with the **control** parameter.

We can add the following parameter to the tree model:

```
control = rpart.control(
    minsplit = 20,
    minbucket = round(minsplit/3),
    cp = 0.01,
    maxcompete = 4,
    maxsurrogate = 5,
    usesurrogate = 2, xval = 10,
    surrogatestyle = 0,
    maxdepth = 30
)
```

One parameter of interest would be the **complexity parameter**. The complexity parameter restricts a split in the decision node if it does not decrease the overall lack of fit by the factor of the defined value. The default value is set to **0.01**. We can further change this to a lower number that would make the tree grow deeper and become more complicated. The **plotcp** function visualizes the relative validation error for different values of **cp**, that is, the complexity parameter. The most ideal value for **cp** is the leftmost value below the dotted line in the plot in *Figure* 5.4. In this case (as shown in the plot), the best value is 0.017. Since this value is not very different from the default value, we don't change it further.

The next plot in *Figure 5.5* helps us visualize the actual decision tree constructed by the algorithm. We can see the simple set of rules being constructed using the available data. As you can see, only two independent variables, that is, `Humidity3pm` and `WindGustSpeed`, have been selected for the tree. If we change the complexity parameter to 0.001 instead of 0.01, we can see a much deeper tree (which could overfit the model) would have been constructed. Finally, we can see the results from the confusion matrix (step 6) along with additional metrics of interest for the train and test dataset.

We can see that the results are similar for the train and test dataset. We can therefore conclude that the model doesn't overfit. However, there is a significant drop in accuracy (83%) and recall (35%), while the precision has increased to a slightly higher value (77%).

We have now worked with a few white-box modeling techniques. Given the simplicity and ease of interpretation of white-box models, they are the most preferred technique for classification use cases in business, where reasoning and driver analysis is of paramount importance. However, there are a few scenarios where a business might be more interested in the *net outcome* of the model rather than the entire interpretation of the outcome. In such cases, the end model performance is of more interest. In our use case, we want to achieve high precision. Let's explore a few black-box models that are superior (in most cases) to white-box models in terms of model performance and that can be achieved with far less effort and more training data.

Activity 9: Create a Decision Tree Model with Additional Control Parameters

The decision tree model we created in *Exercise 10, Create a Decision Tree Model in R*, used the default control parameters for the tree. In this activity, we will override a few control parameters and study its impact on the overall tree-fitting process.

Perform the following steps to create a decision tree model with additional control parameters:

1. Load the **rpart** library.

2. Create the control object for the decision tree with new values: `minsplit` =15 and `cp = 0.00`.

3. Fit the tree model with the train data and pass the control object to the **rpart** function.

4. Plot the complexity parameter plot to see how the tree performs at different values of `CP`.

5. Use the fitted model to make predictions on the train data and create the confusion matrix.

6. Use the fitted model to make predictions on the test data and create the confusion matrix.

The output is as follows:

```
"Test data results -"
Confusion Matrix and Statistics

          Reference
Prediction    No    Yes
       No  25068   3926
       Yes  1347   3537

                Accuracy : 0.8444
                  95% CI : (0.8404, 0.8482)
     No Information Rate : 0.7797
     P-Value [Acc > NIR] : < 2.2e-16

                   Kappa : 0.4828
 Mcnemar's Test P-Value : < 2.2e-16

             Sensitivity : 0.4739
             Specificity : 0.9490
          Pos Pred Value : 0.7242
          Neg Pred Value : 0.8646
              Prevalence : 0.2203
          Detection Rate : 0.1044
    Detection Prevalence : 0.1442
       Balanced Accuracy : 0.7115

        'Positive' Class : Yes
```

Note

You can find the solution for this activity on page 454.

Ensemble Modelling

Ensemble modeling is one of the most popular approaches used in classification and regression modeling techniques when there is a need for improved performance with a larger training sample. In simple words, ensemble modeling can be defined by breaking down the name into individual terms: **ensemble** and **modeling**. We have already studied modeling in this book; an ensemble in simple terms is a **group**. Therefore, the process of building several models for the same task instead of just one model and then combining the results into a single outcome through any means, such as averaging or voting, and many others, is called **ensemble modeling**.

We can build ensembles of any models, such as linear models or tree models, and in fact can even build an ensemble of ensemble models. However, the most popular approach is using tree models as the base for ensembles. There are two broad types of ensemble models:

- **Bagging**: Here, each model is built in parallel with some randomization introduced within each model, and the results of all models are combined using a simple voting mechanism. Say we built 100 tree models and 60 models predicted the outcome as Yes and 40 predicted it as No. The end result would be a Yes.

- **Boosting**: Here, models are built sequentially and the results of the first model are used to tune the next model. Each model iteratively learns from errors made by the previous model and tries to improve with successive iterations. The result is usually a weighted average of all the individual outcomes.

There are several implementations available in bagging as well as boosting. **Bagging** itself is an ensemble model available in R. By far the most popular bagging technique used is random forest. Another bagging technique along similar lines as random forest is **extra trees**. Similarly, a few examples of boosting techniques are AdaBoost, Stochastic Gradient Boosting, BrownBoost, and many others. However, the most popular boosting technique is **XGBoost**, which is derived from the name **EXtreme Gradient Boosting**. In most cases, for classification as well as regression use cases, data scientists prefer using random forests or XGBoost models. A recent survey on Kaggle (an online data science community) revealed the most popular technique used for most machine learning competitions were always random forest and XGBoost. In this chapter, we will take a closer look at both models.

Random Forest

Random forest is the most popular bagging technique used in machine learning. It was developed by Leo Brieman, the author of CART. This simple technique is so effective that it is almost always the first choice of algorithm for a data scientist given a supervised use case. Random forest is a good choice for classification as well as regression use cases. It is a highly effective method for reducing overfitting with a bare minimum amount of effort. Let's have a deeper understanding of how random forests work.

As we already know, random forest is an ensemble modeling technique, where we build several models and combine their results using a simple voting technique. In random forests, we use decision trees as the base model. The inner workings of the algorithm can be fairly guessed from the name itself, that is, random (since it induces a layer of randomization in every model that is built) and forest (since there are several *tree* models we build). Before we get into the actual workings of the algorithm, we first need to understand the story of its predecessor, **bagging**, and study why we need ensembles.

Why Are Ensemble Models Used?

The first question that would have surfaced in your thoughts may be, why do we need to build several models for the same task in the first place? Is it necessary? Well, yes! When we build ensembles, we don't build the exact same model several times; instead, every model we build will be different from the others in some way. The intuition behind this can be understood using a simple example from our day-to-day lives. It is built on the principle that several weak learners combined together build a stronger and more robust model.

Let's understand this idea using a simple example. Say you reach a new city and want to know the chances of there being rain in the city the next day. Assuming technology is not an available option, the easiest way you could find this out would be to ask someone in the neighborhood who has been a dweller of the place for a while. Maybe the answer would not always be correct; if someone said that there was a very high chance of rain the next day, it doesn't necessarily mean that it would certainly rain. Therefore, to make an improved guess, you ask several people in the neighborhood. Now, if 7 out of the 10 people you asked mentioned that there was a high chance of rain the next day, then it almost certainly would rain the very next day. The reason this works effectively is because every person you reached out to would have some understanding about rain patterns and also every person's understanding about those patterns would be a bit different. Though the differences are not miles apart, some level of randomness among the people's understanding when aggregated for a collective answer would yield a better answer.

Bagging – Predecessor to Random Forest

Ensemble modeling works on the same principle. Here, in each model, we induce some level of randomness. The bagging algorithm brings in this randomness for each model on the training data. The name bagging is derived from **Bootstrap Aggregation**; a process where we sample two-thirds of the available data with replacement data for training and the remainder for testing and validation. Here, each model, that is, a decision tree model, trains on a slightly different dataset and therefore might have a slightly different outcome for the same test sample. Bagging, in a way, mimics the real-world example that we discussed and therefore combines several weak learners (decision tree models) into a strong learner.

How Does Random Forest Work?

Random forest is basically a successor to bagging. Here, apart from the randomness in the training data, random forest adds an additional layer of randomness with the feature set. Therefore, each decision tree not only has bootstrap aggregation, that is, two thirds of the training data with replacement, but also a subset of features randomly selected from the available list. Thus, each individual decision tree in the ensemble has a slightly different training dataset and a slightly different set of features to train. This additional layer of randomness works effectively in generalizing the model and reduces variance.

Exercise 73: Building a Random Forest Model in R

In this exercise, we will build a random forest model on the same dataset we leveraged in Exercises 8, 9, and 10. We will leverage ensemble modelling and test whether the overall model performance improves compared to decision trees and logistic regression.

> ### Note
>
> To get started, we can quickly build a random forest model using the same dataset we used earlier. The **randomForest** package in R provides the implementation for the model, along with a few additional functions to optimize the model.

Let's look at a basic random forest model. Perform the following steps:

1. First, import the **randomForest** library using the following command:

    ```
    library(randomForest)
    ```

2. Build a random forest model with all of the independent features available:

    ```
    rf_model <- randomForest(RainTomorrow ~ . , data = train, ntree = 100,
                                                    importance = TRUE,
                                                    maxnodes=60)
    ```

3. Evaluate on the training data:

    ```
    print("Training data results -")
    pred_train <- predict(rf_model,newdata = train,type = "class")
    confusionMatrix(pred_train, train$RainTomorrow,positive="Yes")
    ```

4. Evaluate on the test data:

    ```
    print("Test data results -")
    pred_test <- predict(rf_model,newdata = test,type = "class")
    confusionMatrix(pred_test, test$RainTomorrow,positive="Yes")
    ```

5. Plot the feature importance:

    ```
    varImpPlot(rf_model)
    ```

    The output is as follows:

    ```
    [1] "Training data results -"
    Confusion Matrix and Statistics

              Reference
    Prediction    No    Yes
           No  59630  10133
          Yes   1861   7423

                   Accuracy : 0.8483
                     95% CI : (0.8457, 0.8508)
        No Information Rate : 0.7779
        P-Value [Acc > NIR] : < 2.2e-16

                      Kappa : 0.472
     Mcnemar's Test P-Value : < 2.2e-16
    ```

```
            Sensitivity : 0.42282
            Specificity : 0.96974
         Pos Pred Value : 0.79955
         Neg Pred Value : 0.85475
             Prevalence : 0.22210
         Detection Rate : 0.09391
   Detection Prevalence : 0.11745
      Balanced Accuracy : 0.69628

       'Positive' Class : Yes
```

```
[1] "Test data results -"
Confusion Matrix and Statistics

          Reference
Prediction    No   Yes
       No  25602  4369
       Yes   813  3094

               Accuracy : 0.847
                 95% CI : (0.8432, 0.8509)
    No Information Rate : 0.7797
    P-Value [Acc > NIR] : < 2.2e-16

                  Kappa : 0.4629
 Mcnemar's Test P-Value : < 2.2e-16

            Sensitivity : 0.41458
            Specificity : 0.96922
         Pos Pred Value : 0.79191
         Neg Pred Value : 0.85423
             Prevalence : 0.22029
         Detection Rate : 0.09133
   Detection Prevalence : 0.11533
      Balanced Accuracy : 0.69190

       'Positive' Class : Yes
```

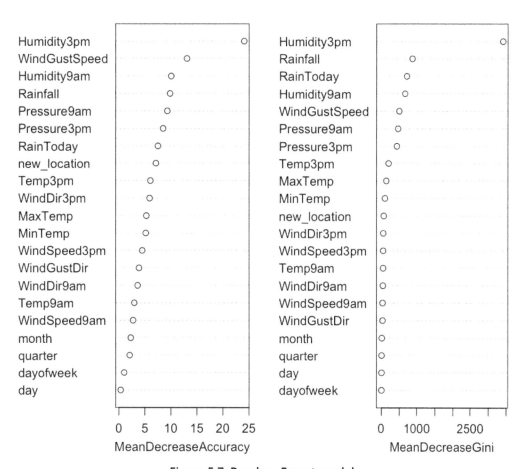

Figure 5.7: Random Forest model

Note

You can find the complete code on GitHub: http://bit.ly/2Q2xKwd.

Activity 10: Build a Random Forest Model with a Greater Number of Trees

In *Exercise 11, Building a Random Forest Model in R*, we created a random forest model with just 100 trees; we can build a more robust model with a higher number of trees. In this activity, we will create a random forest model with 500 trees and study the impact of the model having only 100 trees. In general, we expect the model's performance to improve (at least marginally with an increased number of trees). This comes with higher computational time for the model to converge.

Perform the following steps to build a random forest model with 500 trees:

1. Develop a random forest model with a higher number of trees; say, 500. Readers are encouraged to try higher numbers such as 1,000, 2,000, and so on, and study the incremental improvements in each version.

2. Leverage the fitted model to predict estimates on the train-and-test data and study whether there was any improvement compared to the model with 100 trees.

> **Note**
>
> You can find the solution for this activity on page 457.

XGBoost

XGBoost is the most popular boosting technique in recent times. Although there have been various new versions that have been developed by large corporations, XGBoost still remains the undisputed king. Let's look at a brief history of boosting.

How Does the Boosting Process Work?

Boosting differs from bagging in its core principles; the learning process is, in fact, sequential. Every model built in an ensemble is ideally an improved version of the previous model. To understand boosting in simple terms, imagine you are playing a game where you must remember all the objects placed on the table that you are shown just once for 30 seconds. The moderator of the game arranges around 50-100 different objects on a table, such as a bat, ball, clock, die, coins, and so on, and covers them with a large piece of cloth. When the game begins, he withdraws the cloth from the table and gives you exactly 30 seconds to see them and puts the curtain back. You now must recollect all the objects you can remember. The participant who can recollect the most, aces the game.

In this game, let's add one new dimension. Assume you are a team and the players take turns one by one to announce all the objects they can recollect, while the others listen to them. Say there are 10 participants; each participant steps forward and announces out loud the objects they can recollect from the table. By the time the second player steps forward, they have heard all the objects called out by the first player. They would have mentioned a few objects that the second player might not have recollected. To improve on the first player, the second player learns a few new objects from the first player, adds them to his list, and then announces them out loud. By the time the last player steps forward, they have already learned several objects that other players recollected, which they failed to recollect themselves.

Putting those together, that player creates the most exhaustive list and aces the competition. The fact that each player announces the list sequentially helps the next player learn from their mistakes and improvise on it.

Boosting works in the same way. Each model trained sequentially is imparted with additional knowledge, such that the errors of the first model are learned better in the second model. Say the first model learns to classify well for most cases of a specific independent variable; however, it fails to correctly predict for just one specific category. The next model is imparted with a different training sample, such that the model learns better for the category where the previous model fails. A simple example would be oversampling based on the variable or category of interest. Boosting effectively reduces bias and therefore improves the model's performance.

What Are Some Popular Boosting Techniques?

The boosting techniques introduced earlier were not very popular, because they were easily overfit and often required, relatively, a lot of effort in tuning to achieve great performance. AdaBoost, BrownBoost, Gradient Boosting, and Stochastic Gradient Boosting are all boosting techniques that were popular for a long time. However, in 2014, when T Chen and others introduced XGBoost (**Extreme Gradient Boosting**), it ushered in a new height in the boosting performance.

How Does XGBoost Work?

XGBoost natively introduced regularization, which helps models combat overfitting and thus delivered high performance. Compared to other available boosting techniques at the time, XGBoost reduced the overfitting problem significantly and with the least amount of effort. With current implementations of the model in R or any other language, XGBoost almost always performs great with the default parameter setting. (Though, this is not always true; in many cases, random forest outperforms XGBoost). XGBoost has been among the most popular choice of algorithms used in data science hackathons and enterprise projects.

In a nutshell, XGBoost has regularization introduced in the objective function, which penalizes the model when it gets more complicated in a training iteration. Discussing the depth of mathematical constructs that goes into XGBoosting is beyond the scope of this chapter. You can refer to T Chen's paper here (https://arxiv.org/abs/1603.02754) for further notes. Also, this blog will help you to understand the mathematical differences between GBM and XGBoost in a simple way: https://towardsdatascience.com/boosting-algorithm-xgboost-4d9ec0207d.

Implementing XGBoost in R

We can leverage the XGBoost package, which provides a neat implementation of the algorithm. There are a few differences in the implementation approach that we will need to take care of before getting started. Unlike other implementations of algorithms in R, XGBoost does not handle categorical data (others take care of converting it into numeric data internally). The internal functioning of XGBoost in R doesn't handle the automatic conversion of categorical columns into numeric columns. Therefore, we manually convert categorical columns into numeric or one-hot encoded form.

A one-hot encoded form basically represents a single categorical column as a binary encoded form. Say we have a categorical column with values such as **Yes/No/Maybe**; then, we transform this single variable, where we have an individual variable for each value of the categorical variable indicating its value as **0** or **1**. So, the values for the columns **Yes**, **No**, and **Maybe** will take **0** and **1** based on the original value.

One-hot encoding is demonstrated in the following table:

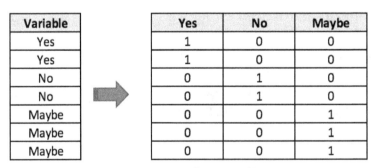

Variable		Yes	No	Maybe
Yes		1	0	0
Yes		1	0	0
No		0	1	0
No		0	1	0
Maybe		0	0	1
Maybe		0	0	1
Maybe		0	0	1

Figure 5.8: One-hot encoding

Let's transform the data into the required form and build an XGBoost model on the dataset.

Exercise 74: Building an XGBoost Model in R

Just as we did in *Exercise 11, Building a Random Forest Model in R*, we will try to improve the performance of the classification model by building an XGBoost model for the same use case and dataset as in *Exercise 11, Building a Random Forest Model in R*.

Perform the following steps to build an XGBoost model in R.

1. Create list placeholders for the target, categorical, and numeric variables:

   ```
   target<- "RainTomorrow"
   categorical_columns <- c("RainToday","WindGustDir","WindDir9am",
   "WindDir3pm", "new_location")
   numeric_columns <- setdiff(colnames(train),c(categorical_columns,target))
   ```

2. Convert the categorical factor variables into character. This will be useful for converting them into one-hot-encoded forms:

   ```
   df_new <- df_new %>% mutate_if(is.factor, as.character)
   ```

3. Convert the categorical variables into one-hot encoded forms using the **dummyVars** function from the **caret** package:

   ```
   dummies <- dummyVars(~ RainToday + WindGustDir + WindDir9am +
                        WindDir3pm + new_location, data = df_new)
   df_all_ohe <- as.data.frame(predict(dummies, newdata = df_new))
   ```

4. Combine numeric variables and the one-hot encoded variables from the third step into a single DataFrame named **df_final**:

   ```
   df_final <- cbind(df_new[,numeric_columns],df_all_ohe)
   ```

5. Convert the target variable into numeric form, as the XGBoost implementation in R doesn't accept factor or character forms:

   ```
   y <- ifelse(df_new[,target] == "Yes",1,0)
   ```

6. Split the **df_final** dataset into train (70%) and test (30%) datasets:

   ```
   set.seed(2019)
   train_index <- sample(seq_len(nrow(df_final)),floor(0.7 * nrow(df_final)))
   xgb.train <- df_final[train_index,]
   y_train<- y[train_index]
   xgb.test <- df_final[-train_index,]
   y_test <- y[-train_index]
   ```

7. Build an XGBoost model using the **xgboost** function. Pass the train data and **y_train** target variable and define the **eta = 0.01**, **max_depth = 6**, **nrounds = 200**, and **colsample_bytree = 1** hyperparameters, define the evaluation metric as **logloss**, and the **objective** function as **binary:logistic**, since we are dealing with binary classification:

```
xgb <- xgboost(data = data.matrix(xgb.train),
                label = y_train,
                eta = 0.01,
                max_depth = 6,
                nround=200,
                subsample = 1,
                colsample_bytree = 1,
                seed = 1,
                eval_metric = "logloss",
                objective = "binary:logistic",
                nthread = 4
)
```

8. Make a prediction using the fitted model on the train dataset and create the confusion matrix to evaluate the model's performance on the train data:

```
print("Training data results -")
pred_train <- factor(ifelse(predict(xgb,data.matrix(xgb.
train),type="class")>0.5,1,0))
confusionMatrix(pred_train,factor(y_train),positive='1')
```

The output is as follows:

```
"Training data results -"

Confusion Matrix and Statistics

          Reference
Prediction     0     1
         0 58967  8886
         1  2524  8670

               Accuracy : 0.8557
                 95% CI : (0.8532, 0.8581)
    No Information Rate : 0.7779
    P-Value [Acc > NIR] : < 2.2e-16

                  Kappa : 0.5201
```

```
Mcnemar's Test P-Value : < 2.2e-16

            Sensitivity : 0.4938
            Specificity : 0.9590
         Pos Pred Value : 0.7745
         Neg Pred Value : 0.8690
             Prevalence : 0.2221
         Detection Rate : 0.1097
   Detection Prevalence : 0.1416
      Balanced Accuracy : 0.7264

       'Positive' Class : 1
```

9. Now, as in the previous step, make predictions using the fitted model on the test dataset and create the confusion matrix to evaluate the model's performance on the test data:

```
print("Test data results -")
pred_test <- factor(ifelse(predict(xgb,data.matrix(xgb.test),
type="class")>0.5,1,0))
confusionMatrix(pred_test,factor(y_test),positive='1')
```

The output is as follows:

```
[1] "Test data results -"
Confusion Matrix and Statistics

            Reference
Prediction     0     1
         0 25261  3884
         1  1154  3579

                Accuracy : 0.8513
                  95% CI : (0.8475, 0.8551)
     No Information Rate : 0.7797
     P-Value [Acc > NIR] : < 2.2e-16

                   Kappa : 0.5017
  Mcnemar's Test P-Value : < 2.2e-16

             Sensitivity : 0.4796
             Specificity : 0.9563
          Pos Pred Value : 0.7562
          Neg Pred Value : 0.8667
```

```
             Prevalence : 0.2203
         Detection Rate : 0.1056
   Detection Prevalence : 0.1397
      Balanced Accuracy : 0.7179

        'Positive' Class : 1
```

If we take a closer look at the results from the model, we can see a slight improvement in the performance compared to random forest model results. The **recall** is around 48% on the test dataset and **Precision** is around 76%. We can see that the recall for the XGBoost model has improved from 41% but the precision has decreased from 79% to 76%. If we tweak the model predictions (as mentioned earlier) by shifting the probability cut-off threshold a notch higher, say `0.54` instead of `0.5`, we can increase the precision (to match random forest) while still having slightly higher recall than random forest. The increase in recall for XGBoost is significantly higher than the decrease in precision. The threshold value for the probability cutoff is not a defined, hard cutoff. We can tweak the threshold based on our use case. The best number can be studied with empirical experiments or by studying the sensitivity, specificity distribution.

> **Note**
>
> You can find the complete code on GitHub: http://bit.ly/30gzSW0.

The following exercise uses 0.54 instead of 0.5 as the probability cutoff to study the improvement in precision at the cost of recall.

Exercise 75: Improving the XGBoost Model's Performance

We can tweak the model performance of binary classification models by adjusting the threshold value of the output. By default, we select 0.5 as the default probability cutoff. So, all responses above 0.5 are tagged as **Yes**, else **No**. Adjusting the threshold can help us achieve more sensitive or more precise models.

Perform the following steps to improve the XGBoost model's performance by adjusting the threshold for the probability cutoff:

1. Increase the probability cutoff for the prediction on the train dataset from 0.5 to 0.53 and print the results:

    ```
    print("Training data results -")
    pred_train <- factor(ifelse(predict(xgb,data.matrix(xgb.train),
    type="class")>0.53,1,0))
    confusionMatrix(pred_train,factor(y_train),positive='1')
    ```

The output is as follows:

```
[1] "Training data results -"
Confusion Matrix and Statistics

          Reference
Prediction     0     1
         0 59626  9635
         1  1865  7921

              Accuracy : 0.8545
                95% CI : (0.852, 0.857)
   No Information Rate : 0.7779
   P-Value [Acc > NIR] : < 2.2e-16

                 Kappa : 0.4999
 Mcnemar's Test P-Value : < 2.2e-16

           Sensitivity : 0.4512
           Specificity : 0.9697
        Pos Pred Value : 0.8094
        Neg Pred Value : 0.8609
            Prevalence : 0.2221
        Detection Rate : 0.1002
  Detection Prevalence : 0.1238
     Balanced Accuracy : 0.7104

      'Positive' Class : 1
```

2. Increase the probability cutoff for the prediction on the test dataset from 0.5 to 0.53 and print the results:

```
print("Test data results -")
pred_test <- factor(ifelse(predict(xgb,data.matrix(xgb.test),
type="class")>0.53,1,0))
confusionMatrix(pred_test,factor(y_test),positive='1')
```

The output is as follows:

```
1] "Test data results -"
Confusion Matrix and Statistics

          Reference
Prediction     0     1
```

```
0 25551  4210
1   864  3253
```

```
               Accuracy : 0.8502
                 95% CI : (0.8464, 0.854)
    No Information Rate : 0.7797
    P-Value [Acc > NIR] : < 2.2e-16

                  Kappa : 0.4804
 Mcnemar's Test P-Value : < 2.2e-16

            Sensitivity : 0.43588
            Specificity : 0.96729
         Pos Pred Value : 0.79014
         Neg Pred Value : 0.85854
             Prevalence : 0.22029
         Detection Rate : 0.09602
   Detection Prevalence : 0.12152
      Balanced Accuracy : 0.70159

       'Positive' Class : 1
```

We see that, at 44% recall, we have 80% precision on the test dataset, and the difference in performance between the train and test datasets is also negligible. We can therefore conclude that the model performance of XGBoost is a bit better than random forest, though only a bit.

> **Note**
>
> You can find the complete code on GitHub: http://bit.ly/30c5DQ9.

Before wrapping up our chapter, let's experiment with the last supervised technique for classification, that is, deep neural networks.

Deep Neural Networks

The last type of technique that we will be discussing before wrapping up our chapter is deep neural networks or deep learning. This is a long and complicated topic, which by no means will we be able to do justice in a short section of this chapter. A complete book may not even suffice to cover the surface of the topic! We will explore the topic from 100 feet and quickly study an easy implementation in R.

Deep neural networks, which are primarily used in the field of computer vision and natural language processing, have also found significance in machine learning use cases for regression and classification on tabular cross-sectional data. With large amounts of data, deep neural networks have been proved to be very effective at learning latent patterns and thus training models with better performance.

A Deeper Look into Deep Neural Networks

Deep neural networks were inspired by the neural structure of the human brain. The field of deep learning became popular for solving computer vision problems, that is, the area of problems that were easily solved by humans, but computers struggled with for a long time. The motivation for designing deep neural networks akin to a miniature and highly simplified human brain was to solve problems that were specifically easy for humans. Later, with the success of deep learning in the field of computer vision, it was embraced in several other fields, including traditional machine learning supervised use cases.

A neural network is organized as a hierarchy of neurons, just like the neurons in the human brain. Each neuron is connected to other neurons, which enables communication between them that traverses as a signal to other neurons and results in a large complex network that can learn with a feedback mechanism.

The following figure demonstrates a simple neural network:

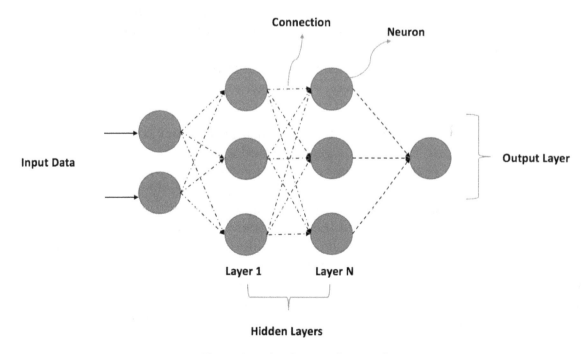

Figure 5.9: Simple neural network

The input data forms the 0th layer in the network. This layer then connects to the neurons within the next layer, which is hidden. It is called **hidden** as the network can be perceived as a black box where we provide input to the network and directly see the output. The intermediate layers are hidden. In a neural network, a layer can have any number of neurons and each network can have any number of layers. The larger the number of layers, the 'deeper' the network will be. Hence the name deep learning and deep neural networks. Every neuron in each hidden layer computes a mathematical function, which is called the activation function in deep learning. This function helps in mimicking the signal between two neurons. If the function (activation) computes a value greater than a threshold, it sends a signal to the immediate connected neuron in the next layer. The connection between these two neurons is moderated by a weight. The weight decides how important the incoming neuron's signal is for the receiving neuron. The learning method in the deep learning model updates the weights between neurons such that the end prediction, akin to machine learning models, is the most accurate one.

How Does the Deep Learning Model Work?

To understand how a neural network works and learns to make predictions on data, let's consider a simple task that is, relatively, very easy for humans. Consider the task of learning to identify different people by their faces. Most of us meet a few different people every day; say, at work, school, or on the street. Every person we meet is different from each other in some dimension. Though everyone would have a ton of similar features, such as two eyes, two ears, lips, two hands, and so on, our brain easily distinguishes between two individuals. The second time we meet a person, we would most probably recognize them and distinguish them as someone we met previously. Given the scale at which this happens and the fact that our brain effectively works to solve this mammoth problem with ease, it makes us wonder how exactly this happens.

To understand this and appreciate the beauty of our brain, we need to understand how the brain fundamentally learns. The brain is a large, complex structure of interconnected neurons. Each neuron gets activated when it senses something essential and passes a message or signal to other neurons it is connected to. The connection between neurons is strengthened by constant learning from the feedback they receive. Here, when we see a new face, rather than learning the structure of the face to identify people, the brain learns how different the given face is from a generic baseline face. This can be further simplified as calculating the difference between important facial features, such as eye shape, nose, lips, ears, and lip structure, color deviations of the skin and hair, and other attributes. These differences, which are quantified by different neurons, are then orchestrated in a systematic fashion for the brain to distinguish one face from another and recall a face from memory. This entire computation happens subconsciously, and we barely realize this as the results are instant for us to notice anything specific.

A neural network essentially tries to mimic the learning functionality of the brain in an extremely simplified form. Neurons are connected to each other in a layer-wise fashion and initialized with random weights. A mathematical calculation across the network combines the inputs from all neurons layer-wise and finally reaches the end outcome. The deviation of the end outcome (the predicted value) is then quantified as an error and is given as feedback to the network. Based on the error, the network tries updating the weights of the connections and tries to reduce the error in the prediction iteratively. With several iterations, the network updates its weights in an ordered fashion and thus learns to recognize patterns to make a correct prediction.

What Framework Do We Use for Deep Learning Models?

For now, we will experiment with deep neural networks for our classification use case, using Keras for R. For deep learning model development, we would need to write a ton of code, which would render the building blocks for the network. To speed up our process, we can leverage Keras, a deep learning framework that provides neat abstraction for deep learning components. Keras has an R interface and works on top of a low-level deep learning framework.

The deep learning frameworks available in today's AI community are either low-level or high-level. Frameworks such as TensorFlow, Theano, PyTorch, PaddlePaddle, and mxnet are low-level frameworks that provide the basic building blocks for deep learning models. Using low-level frameworks offers a ton of flexibility and customization to the end network design. However, we would still need to write quite a lot of code to get a relatively large network working. To simplify this further, there are a few high-level frameworks available that work on top of the low-level frameworks and provide a second layer of abstraction in the process of building deep learning models. Keras, Gluon, and Lasagne are a few frameworks that leverage the aforementioned low-level framework as a backend and provide a new API that makes the overall development process far easier. This reduces the flexibility when compared to directly using a low-level framework such as TensorFlow, and offers a robust solution for most networks. For our use case, we can directly leverage Keras with the R interface.

Using the `install.packages('keras')` command would install the R interface to Keras and would also automatically install TensorFlow as the low-level backend for Keras.

Building a Deep Neural Network in Keras

To leverage Keras in R, we would need additional data augmentations to our existing training dataset. In most machine learning functions available under R, we can pass the categorical column directly coded as a factor. However, we saw that XGBoost had a mandate that the data needs to be rendered into one-hot encoded form, as it does not internally transform the data into the required format. We therefore used the `dummyVars` function in R to transform the training and test dataset into a one-hot encoded version, such that we have only numerical data in the dataset. In Keras, we would need to feed a matrix instead of a DataFrame as the training dataset. Therefore, in addition to transforming the data into a one-hot encoded form, we would also need to convert the dataset into a matrix.

Moreover, it is also recommended that we standardize, normalize, or scale all our input dimensions. The process of normalization rescales data values into the range 0 to 1. Similarly, standardization rescales data to have a mean (μ) of 0 and standard deviation (σ) of 1 (unit variance). This transformation is a good feature to have in machine learning, as some algorithms tend to benefit and learn better. However, in deep learning, this transformation becomes crucial, as the model learning process suffers if we provide an input training dataset such that all dimensions are in a different range or scale. The reason behind this issue is the type of activation function used in neurons.

The following code snippet implements a basic neural network in Keras. Here, we use an architecture that has three layers with 250 neurons each. Finding the right architecture is an empirical process and does not have a definitive guide. The deeper network is designed, the more computation it will need to fit the data. The dataset used in the following snippet is the same as was used for XGBoost and already has the one-hot encoded forms.

Exercise 76: Build a Deep Neural Network in R using R Keras

In this exercise, we will leverage deep neural networks to build a classification model for the same use case as *Exercise 13, Improving XGBoost Model Performance*, and try to improve the performance. Deep neural networks will not always perform better than ensemble models. They are usually a preferred choice when we have a very high number of training samples, say 10 million. However, we will experiment and check whether we can achieve any better performance than the models we built in exercises 10-13.

Perform the following steps to build a deep neural network in R.

1. Scale the input dataset in the range 0 to 1. We would first need to initiate a **preProcess** object on the training data. This will be later used to scale the train as well as the test data. Neural networks perform better with scaled data. The train data alone is used for creating the object to scale:

```
standardizer <- preProcess(x_train, method='range',rangeBounds=c(0,1))
```

2. Use the **standardizer** object created in the previous step to scale the train and test data:

```
x_train_scaled <- predict(standardizer, newdata=x_train)
x_test_scaled <- predict(standardizer, newdata=x_test)
```

3. Store the number of predictor variables in a variable called **predictors**. We will use this information to construct the network:

```
predictors <-  dim(x_train_scaled)[2]
```

4. Define the structure for a deep neural network. We will use the **keras_model_sequential** method. We will create a network with three hidden layers, having 250 neurons each and **relu** as the activation function. The output layer will have one neuron with the **sigmoid** activation function (since we are developing a binary classification mode):

```
dl_model <-  keras_model_sequential()  %>%
  layer_dense(units = 250, activation = 'relu',
input_shape =c(predictors)) %>%
  layer_dense(units = 250, activation = 'relu' ) %>%
  layer_dense(units = 250, activation = 'relu') %>%
  layer_dense(units = 1, activation = 'sigmoid')
```

5. Define the model optimizer as **adam**, loss function, and the metrics to capture for the model's training iteration:

```
dl_model %>% compile(
  loss = 'binary_crossentropy',
  optimizer = optimizer_adam(),
  metrics = c('accuracy')
)
summary(dl_model)
```

The output is as follows:

```
----------------------------------------------------------
Layer (type)                 Output Shape              Param #
==========================================================
dense_34 (Dense)             (None, 250)               16750
----------------------------------------------------------
dense_35 (Dense)             (None, 250)               62750
----------------------------------------------------------
dense_36 (Dense)             (None, 250)               62750
----------------------------------------------------------
dense_37 (Dense)             (None, 1)                 251
==========================================================
Total params: 142,501
Trainable params: 142,501
Non-trainable params: 0
```

6. Fit the model structure we created in steps 4-5 with the training and test data from steps 1-2:

```
history <- dl_model %>% fit(
  as.matrix(x_train_scaled), as.matrix(y_train),
  epochs = 10, batch_size = 32,
  validation_split = 0.2
)
```

The output is as follows:

```
Train on 63237 samples, validate on 15810 samples
Epoch 1/10
63237/63237 [==============================] - 7s 104us/step -
loss: 0.3723 - acc: 0.8388 - val_loss: 0.3639 - val_acc: 0.8426
Epoch 2/10
63237/63237 [==============================] - 6s 102us/step -
loss: 0.3498 - acc: 0.8492 - val_loss: 0.3695 - val_acc: 0.8380
Epoch 3/10
63237/63237 [==============================] - 6s 97us/step -
loss: 0.3434 - acc: 0.8518 - val_loss: 0.3660 - val_acc: 0.8438
Epoch 4/10
63237/63237 [==============================] - 6s 99us/step -
loss: 0.3390 - acc: 0.8527 - val_loss: 0.3628 - val_acc: 0.8395
Epoch 5/10
63237/63237 [==============================] - 6s 97us/step -
loss: 0.3340 - acc: 0.8551 - val_loss: 0.3556 - val_acc: 0.8440
```

```
Epoch 6/10
63237/63237 [==============================] - 7s 119us/step -
loss: 0.3311 - acc: 0.8574 - val_loss: 0.3612 - val_acc: 0.8414
Epoch 7/10
63237/63237 [==============================] - 7s 107us/step -
loss: 0.3266 - acc: 0.8573 - val_loss: 0.3536 - val_acc: 0.8469
Epoch 8/10
63237/63237 [==============================] - 7s 105us/step -
loss: 0.3224 - acc: 0.8593 - val_loss: 0.3575 - val_acc: 0.8471
Epoch 9/10
63237/63237 [==============================] - 7s 105us/step -
loss: 0.3181 - acc: 0.8607 - val_loss: 0.3755 - val_acc: 0.8444
Epoch 10/10
63237/63237 [==============================] - 7s 104us/step -
loss: 0.3133 - acc: 0.8631 - val_loss: 0.3601 - val_acc: 0.8468
```

7. Predict the responses using the fitted model on the train dataset:

```
print("Training data results - ")
pred_train <- factor(ifelse(predict(dl_model,
as.matrix(x_train_scaled))>0.5,1,0))
confusionMatrix(pred_train,factor(y_train),positive='1')
```

The output is as follows:

```
"Training data results - "
Confusion Matrix and Statistics
          Reference
Prediction     0     1
         0 59281  8415
         1  2351  9000

               Accuracy : 0.8638
                 95% CI : (0.8614, 0.8662)
    No Information Rate : 0.7797
    P-Value [Acc > NIR] : < 2.2e-16

                  Kappa : 0.547
 Mcnemar's Test P-Value : < 2.2e-16

            Sensitivity : 0.5168
            Specificity : 0.9619
         Pos Pred Value : 0.7929
         Neg Pred Value : 0.8757
```

```
            Prevalence : 0.2203
        Detection Rate : 0.1139
  Detection Prevalence : 0.1436
     Balanced Accuracy : 0.7393


      'Positive' Class : 1
```

8. Predict the responses using the fitted model on the test dataset:

```
#Predict on Test Data
pred_test <- factor(ifelse(predict(dl_model,
                        as.matrix(x_test_scaled))>0.5,1,0))
confusionMatrix(pred_test,factor(y_test),positive='1')
```

The output is as follows:

```
"Test data results - "
Confusion Matrix and Statistics

           Reference
Prediction    0     1
         0 25028  3944
         1  1246  3660


               Accuracy : 0.8468
                 95% CI : (0.8429, 0.8506)
    No Information Rate : 0.7755
    P-Value [Acc > NIR] : < 2.2e-16

                  Kappa : 0.4965
 Mcnemar's Test P-Value : < 2.2e-16

            Sensitivity : 0.4813
            Specificity : 0.9526
         Pos Pred Value : 0.7460
         Neg Pred Value : 0.8639
             Prevalence : 0.2245
         Detection Rate : 0.1080
```

```
Detection Prevalence : 0.1448
   Balanced Accuracy : 0.7170
     'Positive' Class : 1
```

> **Note**
>
> You can find the complete code on GitHub: http://bit.ly/2Vz8Omb.

The preprocessor function helps to transform the data into the required scale or range. Here, we scale the data to a 0 to 1 scale. We should only consider using the train data as the input to the function generator and use the fitted method to scale the test data. This is essential, as we won't have access to the test data in a real-time scenario. Once the **preProcess** method is fit, we use it to transform the train and test data. We then define the architecture for the deep neural network model. R provides the easy to extend pipe operator with **%>%**, which enables the easy concatenation of the operators. We design a network with three layers and 250 neurons each. The input data will form the 0th layer and the last layer will be the predicted outcome. The activation function used in the network for the hidden layers is **relu**, the most recommended activation function for any deep learning use case. The final layer has the **sigmoid** activation function, as we have a binary classification use case. There are a ton of activation functions to choose from in Keras, such as **prelu**, **tanh**, **swish**, and so on. Once, the model architecture is defined, we define the loss function, **binary_crossentropy**, which is analogous to binary **logloss** (akin to XGBoost), the optimizer, that is, technique, used by the model to learn and backpropagate. The errors in the prediction are backpropagated to the network so that it can adjust the weights in the right direction and iteratively reduce the error.

The mathematical intuitiveness of this functionality can take various approaches. Adam optimization, which is based on adaptive estimates of lower-order moments, is the most popular choice, which we can almost blindly experiment with for most use cases in deep learning. Some of the other options are **rmsprop**, stochastic gradient descent, and **Adagrad**. We also define the metrics to calculate on the validation dataset after each epoch, that is, one complete presentation of training samples to the network. The **summary** function displays the resultant architecture we defined in the preceding section using the Keras constructs. The **summary** function gives us a brief idea of the number of parameters in each layer and additionally represents the network in a hierarchical structure to help us visualize the model architecture. Lastly, we use the **fit** function which trains or 'fits' the data to the network. We also define the number of epochs the model should iterate; the higher the number of epochs, the longer the training process will take to compute.

The batch size indicates the number of training samples the network consumes in one single pass before updating the weights of the network; a lower number for the batch indicates more frequent weight updates and helps the RAM memory to be effectively utilized. The validation split defines the percentage of training samples to be used for validation at the end of each epoch. Finally, we validate the model's performance on the train and test data.

> **Note**
>
> This explanation in the code snippet will by no means be a justification for the topic. A deep neural network is an extremely vast and complex topic that might need a complete book for a basic introduction. We have wrapped the context into a short paragraph for you to understand the constructs used in the model development process. Exploring the depth of the topic would be beyond the scope of this book.

Looking at the results, we can see similar results as for the previous models. The results are almost comparable with the XGBoost model we developed previously. We have around 48% recall and 75% precision on the test dataset. The results can be further tweaked to reduce recall and enhance precision (if necessary).

We can therefore conclude that we got fairly good results from our simple logistic regression model, XGBoost, and the deep neural network model. The differences between all three models were relatively slight. This might bring important questions into your mind: Is it worth iterating for various models on the same use case? Which model will ideally give the best results? Though there are no straightforward answers to these questions, we can say that, overall, simple models always do great; ensemble models perform better with lots of data; and deep learning models perform better with a ton of data. In the use case that we experimented with in this chapter, we will get improved results from all the models with hyperparameter tuning and; most importantly; feature engineering. We will explore hyperparameter tuning in *Chapter 7, Model Improvements*, and feature engineering on a light node in *Chapter 6, Feature Selection and Dimensionality Reduction*. The process of feature engineering is very domain-specific and can only be generalized to a certain extent. We will have a look at this in more detail in the next chapter. The primary agenda for this chapter was to introduce the range of modeling techniques that cover a substantial area in the field and can help you build the foundations for any machine learning technique to be developed for a classification use case.

Choosing the Right Model for Your Use Case

So far, we have explored a set of white-box models and a couple of black-box machine learning models for the same classification use case. We also extended the same use case with a deep neural network in Keras and studied its performance. With the results from several models and various iterations, we need to decide which model would be the best for a classification use case. There isn't a simple and straightforward answer to this. In a more general sense, we can say that the best model would be a Random Forest or XGBoost for most use cases. However, this is not true for all types of data. There will be numerous scenarios where ensemble modeling may not be the right fit and a linear model would outperform it and vice versa. In most experiments conducted by data scientists for classification use cases, the approach would be an exploratory and iterative one. There is no one-size-fits-all model in machine learning. The process of designing and training a machine learning model is arduous and extremely iterative and will always depend on the type of data used to train it.

The best approach to proceed, given the task of building a supervised machine learning model, would be as follows:

- **Step 0**: **EDA, Data Treatment and Feature Engineering**: Study the data extensively using a combination of visualization techniques and then treat the data for missing values, remove outliers, engineer new features, and build the train and test datasets. (If necessary, create a validation dataset too.)

- **Step 1**: **Start with a simple white-box model such as logistic regression**: The best starting point in the modeling iterations is a simple white-box model that helps us study the impact of each predictor on the dependent variable in an easy-to-quantify way. A couple of model iterations will help with feature selection and getting a clear understanding of the best predictors and a model benchmark.

- **Step 2**: **Repeat the modeling experiments with a decision tree model**: Leveraging decision tree models will always help us get a new perspective on the model and feature patterns. It might give us simple rules and thereby new ideas to engineer features for an improved model.

- **Step 3**: If there is enough data, experiment with ensemble modeling; otherwise, try alternative approaches, such as support vector machines.

  Ensemble modeling with Random Forest and XGBoost is almost always a safe option to experiment with. But in cases where there is a scarcity of data to train, ensemble modeling might not be an effective approach to proceed. In such cases, a black box kernel-based model would be more effective at learning data patterns and, thus, would improve model performance. We have not covered **Support Vector Machines** (**SVM**) in this chapter, given the scope. However, with the wide range of topics covered in the chapter, getting started with SVMs would be a straightforward task for you. This blog provides a simple and easy to understand guide to SVMs: https://eight2late.wordpress.com/2017/02/07/a-gentle-introduction-to-support-vector-machines-using-r/.

  Additionally, to understand whether the number of training samples is less or more, you can use a simple rule of thumb. If there are at least 100 rows of training samples for every feature in the dataset, then there is enough data for ensemble models; if the number of samples is lower than that, then ensemble models might not always be effective. It is still worth a try, though. For example, if there are 15 features (independent variables) and 1 dependent variable, and then if we have 15 x 100 = 1500 training samples, ensemble models might have better performance on a white-box model.

- **Step 4**: If there is more than enough data, try deep neural networks. If there are at least 10,000 samples for every feature in the dataset, experimenting with deep neural networks might be a good idea. The problem with neural networks is mainly the huge training data and large number of iterations required to get good performance. In most generic cases for classification using tabular cross-sectional data (the type of use case we solved in this book), deep neural networks are just as effective as ensemble models but require significantly more effort in training and tuning to achieve the same results. They do outperform ensemble models when there is a significantly large number of samples to train. Investing the effort in deep neural networks only returns favorable results when there is a significantly higher number of training samples.

Summary

In this chapter, we explored different types of classification algorithms for supervised machine learning. We leveraged the Australian weather data, designed a business problem around it, and explored various machine learning techniques on the same use case. We studied how to develop these models in R and studied the functioning of these algorithms in depth with mathematical abstractions. We summarized the results from each technique and studied a generalized approach to tackle common classification use cases.

In the next chapter, we will study feature selection, dimensionality reduction, and feature engineering for machine learning models.

Feature Selection and Dimensionality Reduction

Learning Objectives

By the end of this chapter, you will be able to:

- Implement feature engineering techniques such as discretization, one-hot encoding, and transformation

- Execute feature selection methods on a real-world dataset using univariate feature selection, correlation matrix, and model-based feature importance ranking

- Apply feature reduction using principal component analysis (PCA) for dimensionality reduction, variable reduction with clustering, and linear discriminant analysis (LDA)

- Implement PCA and LDA and observe the differences between them

In this chapter, we will explore the feature selection and dimensionality reduction methods to build an effective feature set and hence improve the model performance.

Introduction

In the last two chapters (on regression and classification), we focused on understanding and implementing the various machine learning algorithms in the supervised learning category on a given dataset pertaining to a problem.

In this chapter, we will focus more on effectively using the features of the dataset to build the best performing model. Often in many datasets, the feature space is quite large (with many features). The model performance takes a hit as the patterns are hard to find and often much noise is present in the data. Feature selections are specific methods that are used to identify the importance of each feature and assign a score to each. We can then select the top 10 or 15 features (or even more) based on the score for building our model.

Another possibility is to create new variables using a linear combination of all the input variables. This helps in keeping the representation of all variables and reducing the dimensionality of feature space. However, such a reduction often reduces the explainable variance. In this chapter, we will focus on the three major actions we perform on the dataset for improving model performance:

- **Feature engineering:** Essentially transforms the features so the machine learning algorithms will work

- **Selection:** Selects the features with high importance to bring out the best performance of the model

- **Reduction:** Reduces the feature dimensionality by representing a higher order dataset into a lower dimension

All three are closely related yet different in how they function.

In this chapter, in addition to the Beijing PM2.5 dataset, we will use the Los Angeles ozone pollution data, 1976, provided in the **mlbench** library of R. It is a data frame with 366 observations on 13 variables, where each observation is of one day.

No	Details
1	Month: 1 = January, ..., 12 = December
2	Day of month
3	Day of week: 1 = Monday, ..., 7 = Sunday
4	Daily maximum one-hour-average ozone reading
5	500 millibar pressure height (m) measured at Vandenberg AFB
6	Wind speed (mph) at Los Angeles International Airport (LAX)
7	Humidity (%) at LAX
8	Temperature (degrees F) measured at Sandburg, CA
9	Temperature (degrees F) measured at El Monte, CA
10	Inversion base height (feet) at LAX
11	Pressure gradient (mm Hg) from LAX to Daggett, CA
12	Inversion base temperature (degrees F) at LAX
13	Visibility (miles) measured at LAX

Figure 6.1: List of variables in Los Angeles ozone pollution data, 1976

Originally, the dataset was provided for the problem of predicting the daily maximum one-hour-average ozone readings (the fourth variable in the table). Both Beijing PM2.5 and Los Angeles ozone datasets resonate with the effects of pollutants on our environment.

Feature Engineering

The algorithms we use in machine learning will perform based on the quality and goodness of the data; they do not have any intelligence of their own. The better and innovative you become in designing features, the better the model performance. **Feature engineering** in many ways helps in bringing the best out of data. The term feature engineering essentially refers to the process of the **derivation** and **transformation** of given features, thus better characterizing the meaning of the features and representing the underlying problem of the predictive model. By this process, we anticipate the improvement in the model's **predictability power** and **accuracy**.

Discretization

In *Chapter 3*, *Introduction to Supervised Learning*, we converted the numeric values of a 3-hour rolling average of PM2.5 in the Beijing dataset to the binary values 1 and 0 for logistic regression, based on the threshold of 35, where 1 means **normal** and 0 means **above normal**. The process is called **discretization**, also commonly referred to as **binning, or** in our case, **binary discretization**. More broadly, in applied mathematics, discretization is the process of transferring continuous functions, models, variables, and equations into discrete counterparts. Now, let's perform the process on a variable.

Exercise 77: Performing Binary Discretization

In this exercise, we will create a binary variable using the pm2.5 variable of the Beijing PM2.5 dataset. Binary discretization of the pm2.5 variable will create a column that will be 1 if the PM2.5 level is greater than 35, else it will be 0. This process will help us create a discrete categorical variable (to be called **pollution_level**) from a continuous numeric variable.

Perform the following steps to complete the exercise:

1. Start with reading the Beijing PM2.5 dataset using the following command:

    ```
    PM25 <- read.csv("PRSA_data_2010.1.1-2014.12.31.csv")
    ```

2. Load the following libraries:

    ```
    library(dplyr)
    library(lubridate)
    library(tidyr)
    library(ggplot2)
    library(grid)
    library(zoo)
    ```

3. Combine year, month, day, and hour into a **datetime** variable using the with function from the lubridate package:

    ```
    PM25$datetime <- with(PM25, ymd_h(sprintf('%04d%02d%02d%02d', year, month,
    day,hour)))
    ```

4. Now, remove any row with an NA in the column:

    ```
    PM25_subset <- na.omit(PM25[,c("datetime","pm2.5")])
    ```

5. Using the zoo structure, compute the moving average every **3** hours:

    ```
    PM25_three_hour_pm25_avg <- rollapply(zoo(PM25_subset$pm2.5,PM25_
    subset$datetime), 3, mean)
    ```

6. Next, convert the output of the moving average into a DataFrame:

```
PM25_three_hour_pm25_avg <- as.data.frame(PM25_three_hour_pm25_avg)
```

7. Now, put the timestamp in the row names into the main columns:

```
PM25_three_hour_pm25_avg$timestamp <- row.names(PM25_three_hour_pm25_avg)
```

8. Get rid of the row names (optional):

```
row.names(PM25_three_hour_pm25_avg) <- NULL
```

9. Rename the columns:

```
colnames(PM25_three_hour_pm25_avg) <- c("avg_pm25","timestamp")
```

10. Create two levels based on the PM2.5 average. 0 implies **normal** and 1 implies **above the normal**:

```
PM25_three_hour_pm25_avg$pollution_level <- ifelse(PM25_three_hour_pm25_avg$avg_pm25 <= 35, 0,1)
```

11. Randomly select 10 rows using the following command:

```
r_index <- sample(nrow(PM25_three_hour_pm25_avg),10)
```

12. Print the output using the following command:

```
PM25_three_hour_pm25_avg[r_index,]
##          avg_pm25               timestamp pollution_level
## 405    399.33333 2010-01-18 21:00:00                    1
## 3694   142.33333 2010-06-14 23:00:00                    1
## 8072    14.33333 2010-12-31 05:00:00                    0
## 3502   107.00000 2010-06-01 14:00:00                    1
## 20828   80.33333 2012-07-21 16:00:00                    1
## 32010   95.66667 2013-11-15 20:00:00                    1
## 3637   103.33333 2010-06-12 14:00:00                    1
## 4736   192.66667 2010-07-29 11:00:00                    1
## 22053   37.33333 2012-09-17 19:00:00                    1
## 7135    32.33333 2010-11-22 02:00:00                    0
```

Observe that the variable **pollution_level** is now a binary categorical variable, which we created in Step 11. The dataset with **pollution_level** as an output variable could be used with any classification algorithm.

Multi-Category Discretization

A more general form of discretization is to divide the range of values of a continuous variable into many smaller ranges of values using appropriate cut-points. One way of identifying the appropriate cut-point is to analyze the distribution of the variable.

Using the following code, plot a histogram of **avg_pm25** with **binwidth** of **30** (meaning the range of values will be divided into ranges of size **30**):

```
ggplot(PM25_three_hour_pm25_avg, aes(x=avg_pm25)) +
  geom_histogram(binwidth = 30,color="darkblue", fill="lightblue")
```

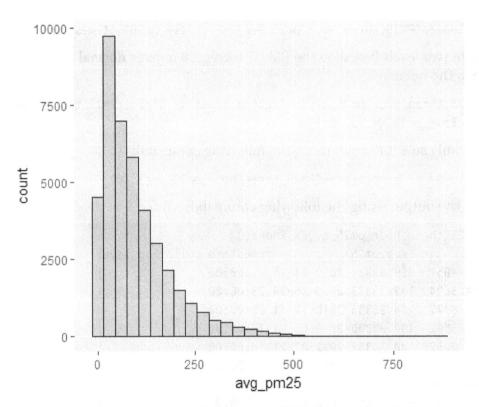

Figure 6.2: Histogram of 3-hour rolling average of PM2.5 values from Beijing dataset

The plot in *Figure* 6.2 shows the right skewness in the variable, which means the majority of values are on the left of the range of values, mostly concentrated between 0 and 250. Such skewness inhibits the model from generalizing, hence it has a lower predictive power. Now, let's explore how we can utilize multi-category discretization to improve this scenario.

Exercise 78: Demonstrating the Use of Quantile Function

In this exercise, we will demonstrate the use of the **quantile function**, which gives cut-points corresponding to the 0th, 25th, 50th, 75th, and 100th percentile points from the values of **avg_pm25**.

Perform the following steps to complete the exercise:

1. Import the required libraries and packages.

2. Find the quantiles on **avg_pm25**:

    ```
    avg_pm25 <- PM25_three_hour_pm25_avg$avg_pm25
    quartiles = quantile(round(avg_pm25), seq(0,1, .25), include.lowest=T)
    ```

3. Next, calculate the vertical lines on the quantile points:

    ```
    ggplot(PM25_three_hour_pm25_avg, aes(x=avg_pm25))+
      geom_histogram(binwidth = 30,color="darkblue", fill="lightblue")+
        geom_vline(xintercept=quartiles,
              color="blue", linetype="dashed", size=1)
    ```

    The plot is as follows:

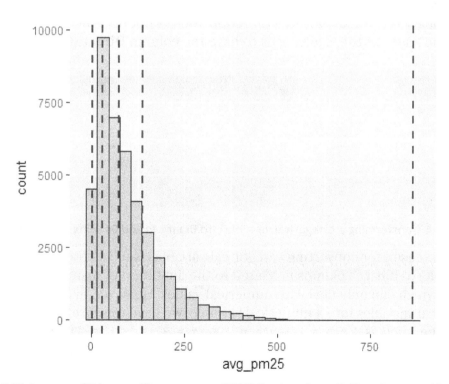

Figure 6.3 Histogram of 3-hour rolling average of PM2.5 values from Beijing dataset with cut-lines corresponding to 0th, 25th, 50th, 75th, and 100th percentile points

The following code snippet creates the variable **avg_pm25_quartiles** in the dataset, which represents the five percentile points on the values of **avg_pm25**. This new variable could be used in modeling after **one-hot encoding**, which we will discuss in the next section.

4. Let's use the following code to add a new variable **avg_pm25_quartiles** in the dataset:

```
PM25_three_hour_pm25_avg$avg_pm25_quartiles <- as.integer(cut(avg_
pm25,breaks=quantile(round(avg_pm25), seq(0,1, .25), include.lowest=T)))
```

We have just seen how discretization helps to remove any data skewness before modelling.

One-Hot Encoding

One-hot encoding is a process of binarizing the categorical variable. This is done by transforming a categorical variable with n unique values into n unique columns in the datasets while keeping the number of rows the same. The following table shows how the wind direction column is transformed into five binary columns. For example, the row number **1** has the value **North**, so we get a **1** in the corresponding column named **Direction_N** and **0** in the remaining columns. So on for the other rows. Note that out of these sample five rows of data, the direction **West** is not present. However, the larger dataset would have got the value for us to have the column **Direction_W**.

Row Number	Direction
1	North
2	North-West
3	South
4	East
5	North-West

Row Number	Direction_N	Direction_S	Direction_W	Direction_E	Direction_NW
1	1	0	0	0	0
2	0	0	0	0	1
3	0	1	0	0	0
4	0	0	0	1	0
5	0	0	0	0	1

Figure 6.4 Transforming a categorical variable into Binary 1s and 0s using one-hot encoding

One primary reason for converting categorical variables (such as the one shown in the previous table) to binary columns is related to the limitation of many machine learning algorithms, which can only deal with numerical values. However, in order to convert the categorical variables into a numerical variable, we have to represent it with some mapping value, such as **North = 1**, **South = 2**, **West = 3**, and so on. The problem with such encoding is that the values **1**, **2**, and **3** are integers, where **3>2>1**; however, this is not the case with wind direction.

The interpretation is entirely wrong. Binary one-hot encoding overcomes this challenge by creating one column for each value in the categorical variable, thus giving us a more elegant representation. We can now use any algorithm from machine learning on such data as long as it satisfies the type of problem.

Exercise 79: Using One-Hot Encoding

In this exercise, we will use the one-hot encoding for creating one column for each value in the categorical variable.

Perform the following steps to complete the exercise:

1. Import the required libraries and packages.

2. Create the **OzoneData** variable and store the value of **ozone1.csv** using the **read.csv** function:

   ```
   OzoneData <- read.csv("ozone1.csv", stringsAsFactors=F)
   ```

3. Import the required **caret** packages into the system:

   ```
   library(caret)
   ```

4. Create input datasets:

   ```
   OzoneData$Day_of_week <- as.factor(OzoneData$Day_of_week)
   OzoneData_OneHot <- dummyVars(" ~ .", data = OzoneData)
   ```

5. Create the response DataFrame:

   ```
   OzoneData_OneHot <- data.frame(predict(OzoneData_OneHot, newdata =
   OzoneData))
   ```

6. Plot the data using the **head()** function:

   ```
   head(OzoneData_OneHot)
   ```

   The output is as follows:

   ```
   ##    Month Day_of_month Day_of_week.1 Day_of_week.2 Day_of_week.3
   ## 1      1            1             0             0             0
   ## 2      1            2             0             0             0
   ## 3      1            3             0             0             0
   ## 4      1            4             0             0             0
   ## 5      1            5             1             0             0
   ## 6      1            6             0             1             0
   ##    Day_of_week.4 Day_of_week.5 Day_of_week.6 Day_of_week.7 ozone_reading
   ## 1              1             0             0             0             3
   ## 2              0             1             0             0             3
   ```

```
## 3                 0               0              1                    0            3
## 4                 0               0              0                    1            5
## 5                 0               0              0                    0            5
## 6                 0               0              0                    0            6
##    pressure_height Wind_speed Humidity Temperature_Sandburg
## 1             5480          8 20.00000              40.53473
## 2             5660          6 40.96306              38.00000
## 3             5710          4 28.00000              40.00000
## 4             5700          3 37.00000              45.00000
## 5             5760          3 51.00000              54.00000
## 6             5720          4 69.00000              35.00000
##    Temperature_ElMonte Inversion_base_height Pressure_gradient
## 1            39.77461              5000.000               -15
## 2            46.74935              4108.904               -14
## 3            49.49278              2693.000               -25
## 4            52.29403               590.000               -24
## 5            45.32000              1450.000                25
## 6            49.64000              1568.000                15
##    Inversion_temperature Visibility
## 1             30.56000          200
## 2             48.02557          300
## 3             47.66000          250
## 4             55.04000          100
## 5             57.02000           60
## 6             53.78000           60
```

Observe the **OneHot** variable we have created in the **OzoneData** DataFrame. After one-hot encoding, each value (1 to 7) in **Day_of_week** is represented as a separate column.

Activity 11: Converting the CBWD Feature of the Beijing PM2.5 Dataset into One-Hot Encoded Columns

In this activity, we will learn how to convert any categorical variable into a one-hot encoded vector. Particularly, we will convert the CBWD feature of the Beijing PM2.5 dataset into one-hot encoded columns. Many machine learning algorithms work only on numerical features; in such cases, it becomes imperative to use one-hot encoding.

Perform the following steps to complete the activity:

1. Read the Beijing PM2.5 dataset.

2. Create a variable **cbwd_one_hot** for storing the result of the **dummyVars** function with **~ cbwd** as its first argument.

3. Use the output of the **predict()** function on **cbwd_one_hot**.

4. Remove the original **cbwd** variable from the **PM25** DataFrame.

5. Using the **cbind()** function, add **cbwd_one_hot** to the **PM25** DataFrame.

6. Print the top six rows of **PM25**.

   The output is as follows:

```
##    No year month day hour pm2.5 DEWP TEMP PRES   Iws Is Ir cbwd.cv cbwd.
NE
## 1  1 2010     1   1    0    NA  -21  -11 1021  1.79 0  0          0
0
## 2  2 2010     1   1    1    NA  -21  -12 1020  4.92 0  0          0
0
## 3  3 2010     1   1    2    NA  -21  -11 1019  6.71 0  0          0
0
## 4  4 2010     1   1    3    NA  -21  -14 1019  9.84 0  0          0
0
## 5  5 2010     1   1    4    NA  -20  -12 1018 12.97 0  0          0
0
## 6  6 2010     1   1    5    NA  -19  -10 1017 16.10 0  0          0
0
##    cbwd.NW cbwd.SE
## 1        1       0
## 2        1       0
## 3        1       0
## 4        1       0
## 5        1       0
## 6        1       0
```

> **Note**
>
> The solution for this activity can be found on page 459.

Log Transformation

The most common technique to correct for skewed distribution is to find an appropriate mathematical function that has an inverse. One such function is a log, represented as follows:

$$y = log_b(x)$$

In other words, y is the log of x to the base b. The inverse, to find the x, can be computed as follows:

$$x = b^y$$

This transformation gives the ability to handle the skewness in the data; at the same time, the original value can be easily computed once the model is built. The most popular log transformation is the natural log, where b is the mathematical constant e, which equals roughly **2.71828**.

One useful property of the log function is that it handles the data skewness elegantly. For example, the following code demonstrates the difference between **log(10000)** and **log(1000000)** as just **4.60517**. The number 10^6 is 100 times bigger than 10^4. This reduces the skewness that we otherwise let the model handle, which it might not do sufficiently.

```
#Natural Log
log(10000)
## [1] 9.21034


# 10 times bigger value
log(100000)
## [1] 11.51293


# 100 times bigger value
log(1000000)
## [1] 13.81551
```

Let's see the result of applying the natural log on the 3-hour rolling average of the PM2.5 values.

Exercise 80: Performing Log Transformation

In this exercise, we will draw a histogram of the **avg_pm25** variable with log transformation and compare it with the skewed distribution of the original values.

Perform the following steps to complete the exercise:

1. Import the required libraries and packages.

2. Create a histogram of **avg_pm25**:

    ```
    ggplot(PM25_three_hour_pm25_avg, aes(x=avg_pm25))+
      geom_histogram(color="darkblue", fill="lightblue")
    ```

    The output is as follows:

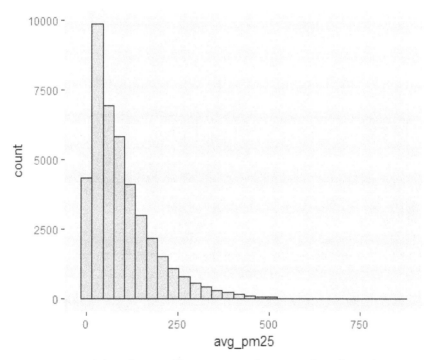

Figure 6.5 Histogram of the 3-hour rolling average of PM2.5 values from the Beijing dataset

3. Create a histogram of **log_avg_pm25**:

```
ggplot(PM25_three_hour_pm25_avg, aes(x=log_avg_pm25))+
  geom_histogram(color="darkblue", fill="lightblue")
```

The output is as follows:

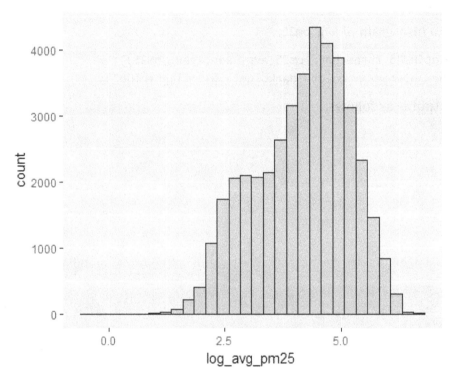

Figure 6.6 Histogram of the natural log of the 3-hour rolling average of PM2.5 values from the Beijing dataset

In this exercise, we drew a plot to show the 3-hour rolling average of the PM2.5 values from the Beijing dataset and contrasted it with the histogram of the natural log of the 3-hour rolling average of the PM2.5 values from the Beijing dataset. Taking the log made the histogram look more symmetrical around the mean and the skewness.

Feature Selection

While **feature engineering** ensures that the quality and data issues are rectified, **feature selection** helps with determining the right set of features for improving the performance of the model. Feature selection techniques identify the features that contribute the most in the prediction ability of the model. Features with less importance inhibit the model's ability to learn from the independent variable.

Feature selection offers benefits such as:

- Reducing overfitting

- Improving accuracy

- Reducing the time to train the model

Univariate Feature Selection

A statistical test such as the **chi-squared** (X^2) test is a popular method to select features with a strong relationship to the dependent or target variable. It mainly works on categorical features in a classification problem. So, for this to work on a numerical variable, one needs to make the feature into categorical using discretization.

In the most general form, chi-squared statistics could be computed as follows:

$$X^2 = \frac{(observed\_frequency - expected\_frequency)^2}{expected\_frequency}$$

This tests whether or not there is a significant difference between observed frequency and expected frequency. A higher chi-squared value establishes a stronger dependence of the target variable and the particular feature. More formally:

$$X^2 = \sum_{i=1}^{k} \frac{(x_i - m_i)^2}{m_i}$$

Where:

n = number of observations in a random sample from the dataset

k = number of mutually exclusive classes (for example, male and female in the Gender feature)

x_i = frequency of occurrence in class i

m_i = expected frequency of occurrence in class i, which equals np_i

p_i = probability that an observation falls in class i

Exercise 81: Exploring Chi-Squared

In this exercise, we will compute the chi-squared statistic for all the variables in the **Ozone** dataset. The top five variables with the highest chi-squared value will be our best feature for modelling.

Perform the following steps to complete the exercise:

1. Import the required libraries and packages.

2. Create a variable named **OzoneData** and assign the value from the **read.csv** function:

    ```
    OzoneData <- read.csv("ozone1.csv", stringsAsFactors=F)
    ```

3. Now, set the **path** as illustrated here:

    ```
    path="C:\\Program Files\\Java\\jdk1.8.0_92"
    ```

4. Next, use the Sys.getenv function to obtain the values of the environment variables:

    ```
    if (Sys.getenv("JAVA_HOME")!="")
      Sys.setenv(JAVA_HOME=path)
    ```

5. Install the required packages using the following command:

    ```
    install.packages("rJava")
    install.packages("FSelector")
    ```

6. Import the **rJava** package:

    ```
    library(rJava)
    ## Warning: package 'rJava' was built under R version 3.2.5
    library(FSelector)#For method
    library(mlbench)# For data
    ```

7. Calculate the chi-squared statistics:

    ```
    weights<- chi.squared(ozone_reading~., OzoneData)
    ```

8. Print the results:

    ```
    print(weights)
    ```

    The output is as follows:

    ```
    ##                      attr_importance
    ## Month                      0.4240813
    ## Day_of_month               0.0000000
    ## Day_of_week                0.0000000
    ```

```
## pressure_height            0.4315521
## Wind_speed                 0.0000000
## Humidity                   0.3923034
## Temperature_Sandburg       0.5191951
## Temperature_ElMonte        0.5232244
## Inversion_base_height      0.6160403
## Pressure_gradient          0.4120630
## Inversion_temperature      0.5283836
## Visibility                 0.4377749
```

9. Select the top five variables:

    ```
    subset<- cutoff.k(weights, 5)
    ```

10. Print the final formula that can be used for classification:

    ```
    f<- as.simple.formula(subset, "Class")
    print(f)
    ```

    The output is as follows:

    ```
    ## Class ~ Inversion_base_height + Inversion_temperature + Temperature_
    ElMonte +
    ##       Temperature_Sandburg + Visibility
    ## <environment: 0x000000001a796d18>
    ```

We used the chi.squared() function to compute the chi-squared values for each feature in our Ozone dataset. The function outputs the attribute importance based on the chi-squared value. The formula in Step 10 that uses the top five features from the chi-squared statistic could be used for building a supervised learning model.

Highly Correlated Variables

Generally, two highly correlated variables likely contribute to the prediction ability of the model, which makes one redundant. For example, if we have a dataset with **age**, **height**, and **BMI** as variables, we know that **BMI** is a function of **age** and **height** and it will always be highly correlated with the other two. If it's not, then something is wrong with the BMI calculation. In such cases, one might decide to remove the other two. However, it is always not this straight. In certain cases, a pair of variables might be highly correlated, but it is not easy to interpret why that is the case. In such cases, one can randomly drop one of the two.

Exercise 82: Plotting a Correlated Matrix

In this exercise, we will compute the correlation between a pair of variables and draw a correlation plot using the **corrplot** package.

Perform the following steps to complete the exercise:

1. Import the required libraries using the following command:

```
library(mlbench)
library(caret)
```

The output is as follows:

```
## Warning: package 'caret' was built under R version 3.2.5
## Loading required package: lattice
```

2. Now, load the data and calculate the correlation matrix:

```
correlationMatrix <- cor(OzoneData)
```

3. Summarize the correlation matrix:

```
print(correlationMatrix)
```

The output is as follows:

```
##                         Month Day_of_month  Day_of_week ozone_
reading
## Month              1.000000000   0.00644330 -0.007345951
0.054521859
## Day_of_month       0.006443300   1.00000000  0.002679760
0.079493243
## Day_of_week       -0.007345951   0.00267976  1.000000000
-0.042135770
## ozone_reading       0.054521859   0.07949324 -0.042135770
1.000000000
```

4. Find attributes that are highly correlated (ideally >0.75):

```
highlyCorrelated <- findCorrelation(correlationMatrix, cutoff=0.5)
```

5. Print the indexes of the highly correlated attributes:

```
print(highlyCorrelated)
```

The output is as follows:

```
## [1] 12  9  8  5  4  7
```

6. Import the **corrplot** library:

```
library(corrplot)
```

7. Plot the correlation matrix:

```
corrplot(correlationMatrix)
```

The output is as follows:

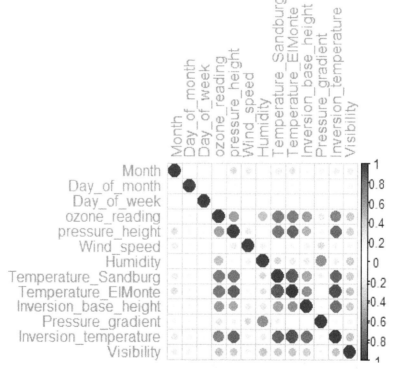

Figure 6.7: Plotting correlated matrix

Observe in *Figure* 6.7 that the dark blue circles represent high positive correlation and the dark red circles represent high negative correlation. The range of correlation values is between –1 and 1. Visually inspecting, we can see the variable `Inversion_temperature` has high positive correlation with `pressure_height` and high negative correlation with `Inversion_base_height`. For example, if `Inversion_temperature` increases, `pressure_height` will also increase and vice versa.

> **Note**
>
> Figure 6.7 can be found on GitHub: https://github.com/TrainingByPackt/Applied-Supervised-Learning-with-R/blob/master/Lesson06/C12624_06_07.png.

Model-Based Feature Importance Ranking

A model such as random forest, an ensemble modeling technique where we build several models and combine their results using a simple voting technique (as described in *Chapter* 5, *Classification*), has a useful technique to utilize all the variables in a dataset and at the same time not compromise the model performance. The simple idea behind the random forest model is that it randomly selects a subset of data and variables to build many decision trees. The final model prediction happens through not one decision tree but collectively using many decision trees. Majority voting is a commonly used technique for final prediction; in other words, what the majority of the decision tree predicts is the final prediction.

The technique naturally gives a combination of variables that result in highest accuracy. (Other model evaluation metrics could also be used.)

> **Note**
>
> For certain research work in genomics and computational biology*, where potential predictor variables vary in their scale of measurement (input features including both sequence and categorical variables such as folding energy) and their number of categories (for example, when amino acid sequence data show different numbers of categories), random forest importance measures are not reliable.
>
> * Bias in random forest variable importance measures: Illustrations, sources and a solution: https://link.springer.com/article/10.1186/1471-2105-8-25.

Exercise 83: Exploring RFE Using RF

In this exercise, we will explore **recursive feature elimination** (**RFE**) using the random forest algorithm. RFE helps in selecting the best features with highest feature importance.

Perform the following steps to complete the exercise:

1. Import the **party** package:

    ```
    library(party)
    ```

2. Fit the random forest:

    ```
    cf1 <- cforest(pm2.5 ~ . , data=
    na.omit(PM25[,c("month","DEWP","TEMP","PRES","Iws","pm2.5")]),
    control=cforest_unbiased(mtry=2,ntree=50))
    ```

3. Calculate the variable importance, based on a mean decrease in MSE. The **varimp()** function implements the RFE technique:

    ```
    varimp(cf1)
    ```

    The output is as follows:

    ```
    ##    month     DEWP     TEMP     PRES      Iws
    ## 3736.679 5844.172 4080.546 1517.037 1388.532
    ```

In Step 2, the **party** package provides the method **cforest()**, which fits a random forest model using the parameter **mtry = 2** and **ntree = 50** and finds the best model where the **out-of-bag** (**OOB**) error is the least while training. The OOB error is the mean prediction error on each training sample **x**, using only the trees that did not have **x** in their bootstrap sample. The function **varimp()** returns the variable importance using the permutation principle (with values randomly shuffled) of the mean decrease in MSE. In other words, variable importance is measured as the mean decrease of the MSE over all out-of-bag cross-validated predictions, when a given variable is permuted after training but before prediction.

As a result of randomly shuffled (permuted) variables, we expect a *bad* variable to be created and inclusion of this shuffled variable to increase the MSE compared to when it is not included in the model. Hence, if the mean decrease in the MSE is high, the MSE of the model as a result of shuffling of the variable has got to be high. So, we can conclude the variable has higher importance.

Exercise 84: Exploring the Variable Importance using the Random Forest Model

In this exercise, we will explore the variable importance using the random forest model. We will again use the Beijing dataset to see which among the five variables (**month**, **DEWP**, **TEMP**, **PRES**, and **Iws**) predicts the PM2.5 the best.

Perform the following steps to complete the exercise:

1. Import the randomForest package using the following command:

    ```
    library(randomForest)
    ```

2. Now, create a new object using the following command:

    ```
    pm25_model_rf <- randomForest(pm2.5 ~ . , data =
    na.omit(PM25[,c("month","DEWP","TEMP","PRES","Iws","pm2.5")]),
    ntree=25,importance=TRUE, nodesize=5)
    ```

3. Print the model:

    ```
    pm25_model_rf
    ```

    The output is as follows:

    ```
    ##
    ## Call:
    ##  randomForest(formula = pm2.5 ~ ., data = na.omit(PM25[, c("month",
    "DEWP", "TEMP", "PRES", "Iws", "pm2.5")]), ntree = 25, importance = TRUE,
    nodesize = 5)
    ##                Type of random forest: regression
    ##                      Number of trees: 25
    ## No. of variables tried at each split: 1
    ##
    ##           Mean of squared residuals: 3864.177
    ##                     % Var explained: 54.39
    ```

4. Find the R-squared value for each tree:

    ```
    pm25_model_rf$rsq
    ```

The output is as follows:

```
##  [1] 0.2917119 0.3461415 0.3938242 0.4240572 0.4335932 0.4445404
0.4552216
##  [8] 0.4735218 0.4878105 0.4998751 0.5079323 0.5156195 0.5197153
0.5228638
## [15] 0.5286556 0.5305679 0.5312043 0.5341559 0.5374104 0.5397305
0.5421712
## [22] 0.5434857 0.5430657 0.5435383 0.5439461
```

5. Next, calculate the variable importance plot:

```
varImpPlot(pm25_model_rf)
```

The output is as follows:

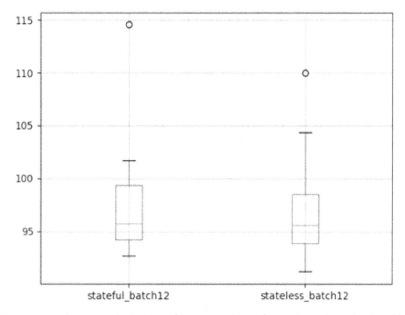

Figure 6.8: Percentage increase in MSE and increase in node purity value obtained by fitting the randomForest model on the Beijing PM2.5 data

The previous exercise demonstrates another way to look at the variable importance. Instead of the **party** package, we have used the **randomForest** package. **%IncMSE** is computed as described in the following steps:

1. Fit random forest (in our case, it's a regression random forest). Compute OOB-MSE and name this **MSE_Base**.

2. For each variable **j**: permute values of column **j**, then predict and compute **OOB_MSE_j**.

3. **%IncMSE** of the **jth** variable equals **(OOB_MSE_j - MSE_Base)/ MSE_Base * 100%**.

Figure 6.8 shows that inclusion of the variable **Iws** in the model increases the MSE by **22%** compared with the variable DEWP, which increases the MSE only by **15%**. We know that as a result of the shuffled values of the variable, the MSE is bound to increase, so the higher **%** implies a good variable. If we see the variable **TEMP**, the shuffling of values has not impacted the MSE that much compared with **Iws** and **DEWP**; hence, relatively, it is less important.

Node purity computes the value of loss function, which in this model is MSE. It helps in choosing the best split. Decrease in the MSE gives a higher node purity value. DEWP has the highest node purity followed by the feature month. In our dataset, both **%IncMSE** and **IncNodePurity** show similar results. However, keep in mind that **IncNodePurity** is often biased and should always be seen in conjunction with **%IncMSE**.

Feature Reduction

Feature reduction helps get rid of redundant variables that reduce the model efficiency in the following ways:

- Time to develop/train the model increases.
- Interpretation of the results becomes tedious.
- It inflates the variance of the estimates.

In this section, we will see three feature reduction techniques that help in improving the model efficiency.

Principal Component Analysis (PCA)

N. A. Campbell and William R. Atchley in their classic paper, *The Geometry of Canonical Variate Analysis*, Systematic Biology, Volume 30, Issue 3, September 1981, Pages 268–280, geometrically defined *a principal component analysis as a rotation of the axes of the original variable coordinate system to new orthogonal axes, called principal axes, such that the new axes coincide with directions of maximum variation of the original observation.* This forms the crux of what PCA does. In other words, it represents the original variable with principal components that explain the maximum variation of the original observations or data.

The paper elegantly presents the geometrical representation of principal components as shown in the following figure, which is a representation of the scatter diagram for two variables, showing the mean for each variable ($\bar{x}_1$ and $\bar{x}_2$), 95% concentration ellipse, and principal axes Y_1 and Y_2. The points y_{1m} and y_{2m} give the principal component scores for the observation $x_i = (x_{1m}, x_{2m})^T = $. The cosine of the angle θ between Y_1 and X_1 gives the first component u_{11} of the eigenvector corresponding to Y_1.

In linear algebra, an eigenvector of a linear transformation is a non-zero vector that changes by only a scalar factor when that linear transformation is applied to it.

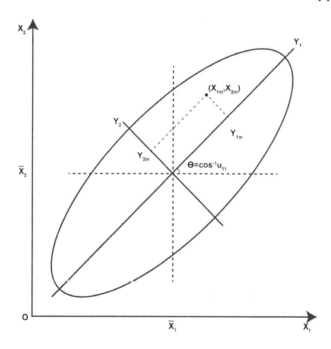

Figure 6.9: Shows the representation of the scatter diagram for two variables, showing the mean for each variable (x¯_1 and x¯_2), 95% concentration ellipse, and principal axes Y_1 and Y_2

Source: The Geometry of Canonical Variate Analysis, Systematic Biology, Volume 30, Issue 3, September 1981, Pages 268–280

Exercise 85: Performing PCA

In this exercise, we will perform PCA, which will help reduce the dimensionality of the feature space. In other words, fewer principal components that are the linear combination of input features will represent the entire dataset.

Perform the following steps to complete the exercise:

1. Import the **OzoneData** package:

    ```
    dim(OzoneData)
    ```

    The output is as follows:

    ```
    ## [1] 366   13
    ```

2. Print the column name using the **colnames** function:

    ```
    colnames(OzoneData)
    ```

    The output is as follows:

    ```
    ##  [1] "Month"                "Day_of_month"
    ##  [3] "Day_of_week"          "ozone_reading"
    ##  [5] "pressure_height"      "Wind_speed"
    ##  [7] "Humidity"             "Temperature_Sandburg"
    ##  [9] "Temperature_ElMonte"  "Inversion_base_height"
    ## [11] "Pressure_gradient"    "Inversion_temperature"
    ## [13] "Visibility"
    ## [1] 50   4
    ```

3. Find the means for all variables:

    ```
    apply(OzoneData,2,mean)
    ```

    The output is as follows:

    ```
    ##                  Month          Day_of_month             Day_of_week
    ##               6.513661             15.756831                4.002732
    ##          ozone_reading       pressure_height              Wind_speed
    ##              11.582020           5752.448016                4.868852
    ##               Humidity  Temperature_Sandburg     Temperature_ElMonte
    ##              58.295691             61.858629               57.219990
    ## Inversion_base_height     Pressure_gradient   Inversion_temperature
    ##            2596.265137             17.785440               61.005339
    ##             Visibility
    ##             123.300546
    ```

4. Find the variance of all variables:

```
apply(OzoneData,2,var)
```

The output is as follows:

```
##                Month          Day_of_month            Day_of_week
##            1.194365e+01          7.785578e+01           3.991773e+00
##           ozone_reading       pressure_height             Wind_speed
##            6.243605e+01          1.092618e+04           4.481383e+00
##              Humidity  Temperature_Sandburg   Temperature_ElMonte
##            3.861494e+02          2.039533e+02           1.109866e+02
## Inversion_base_height     Pressure_gradient Inversion_temperature
##            3.115312e+06          1.300448e+03           1.871074e+02
##             Visibility
##            6.444901e+03
```

Significant differences in variance of the variables will control the principal components. **prcomp()** will standardize the variables (mean **0** and variance **1**) before finding out the principal component.

```
pca.out<-prcomp(OzoneData,scale=TRUE)
```

5. Next, find the summary of the PCA:

```
summary(pca.out)
```

The output is as follows:

```
## Importance of components:
##                          PC1    PC2     PC3     PC4     PC5     PC6
## Standard deviation     2.2817 1.4288 1.05944 1.01842 1.00160 0.93830
## Proportion of Variance 0.4005 0.1570 0.08634 0.07978 0.07717 0.06772
## Cumulative Proportion  0.4005 0.5575 0.64386 0.72364 0.80081 0.86853
##                          PC7    PC8     PC9    PC10    PC11    PC12
## Standard deviation     0.74291 0.64513 0.54523 0.48134 0.33068 0.25908
## Proportion of Variance 0.04246 0.03202 0.02287 0.01782 0.00841 0.00516
## Cumulative Proportion  0.91099 0.94301 0.96587 0.98369 0.99211 0.99727
##                          PC13
## Standard deviation     0.18840
## Proportion of Variance 0.00273
## Cumulative Proportion  1.00000
```

6. Create a biplot using the **ggbiplot** function:

```
library(devtools)
install_github("vqv/ggbiplot", force=TRUE)
library(ggbiplot)
ggbiplot(pca.out)
```

The output is as follows:

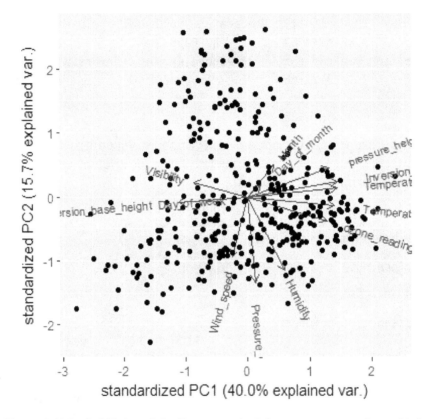

Figure 6.10 Scaled biplot of the first two principle components using ggbiplot

The biplot in the figure shows how **PC1** and **PC2** are the linear combination of features in the **Ozone** dataset. As shown in the output of **summary(pca.out)**, biplots depict the explained variance by using the various features in the dataset. The axes are seen as arrows originating from the center point. The figure also shows that the variables **pressure_height** and **inversion_temperature** contribute to **PC1**, with higher values in those variables moving the samples to the right on this plot. **Visibility** and **day_of_the_week** contribute to **PC2** with higher values.

If you find difficulty installing **ggbiplot**, you could also use the **biplot()** function from base R, as shown in the following plot. First, let's build a biplot to understand better:

```
biplot(pca.out,scale = 0, cex=0.65)
```

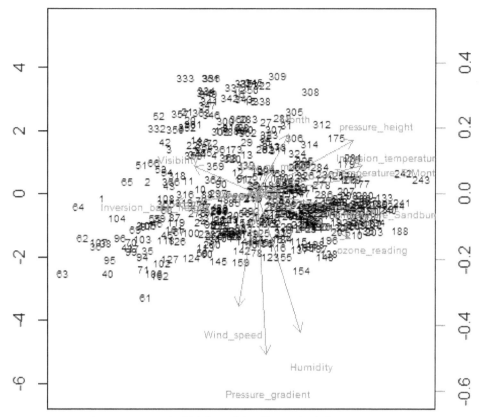

Figure 6.11 Scaled biplot of the first principle component

Observe that the maximum percentage of variance is explained by PC1 and all PCs are mutually uncorrelated. In particular, around **40%** of the variance is explained by PC1, and the first principal component (PC1-PC4) explains 70% of the variance. In other words, if we use the first four principal components, we should get a model almost similar to the one we would get when we use all the variables in the dataset. This should not be surprising as the principal component is a linear combination of the variables.

Variable Clustering

Variable clustering is used for measuring collinearity, calculating redundancy, and for separating variables into clusters that can be counted as a single variable, thus resulting in data reduction. Hierarchical cluster analysis on variables uses any one of the following: Hoeffding's D statistics, squared Pearson or Spearman correlations, or uses as a similarity measure the proportion of observations for which two variables are both positive. The idea is to find the cluster of correlated variables that are correlated with themselves and not with variables in another cluster. This reduces a large number of features into a smaller number of features or variable clusters.

Exercise 86: Using Variable Clustering

In this exercise, we will use feature clustering for identifying a cluster of similar features. From each cluster, we can select one or more features for the model. We will use the hierarchical cluster algorithm from the Hmisc package in R. The similarity measure should be set to "spear," which stands for the Pearson correlation, a robust measure for computing the similarity between two observations.

Perform the following steps to complete the exercise:

1. Install the **Hmisc** package using the following command:

    ```
    install.packages("Hmisc")
    ```

2. Import the **Hmisc** package and set the seed to **1**:

    ```
    library(Hmisc)
    set.seed(1)
    ```

3. Use variable clustering with Spearman correlation as the similarity measure:

    ```
    Ozone_var_clust <- varclus(as.matrix(OzoneData), similarity="spear")
    Ozone_var_clust
    ```

    The output is as follows:

    ```
    ## varclus(x = as.matrix(OzoneData), similarity = "spear")
    ##
    ##
    ## Similarity matrix (Spearman rho^2)
    ##
    ##                    Month Day_of_month Day_of_week ozone_reading
    ## Month               1.00         0.00        0.00          0.00
    ```

```
## Day_of_month           0.00          1.00          0.00          0.01
## Day_of_week            0.00          0.00          1.00          0.00
## ozone_reading          0.00          0.01          0.00          1.00
## pressure_height        0.12          0.00          0.00          0.36
## Wind_speed             0.04          0.01          0.00          0.00
## Humidity               0.01          0.00          0.00          0.20
## Temperature_Sandburg   0.05          0.01          0.00          0.63
## Temperature_ElMonte    0.07          0.00          0.00          0.59
## Inversion_base_height  0.00          0.01          0.00          0.32
## Pressure_gradient      0.03          0.00          0.00          0.06
## Inversion_temperature  0.04          0.01          0.00          0.54
## Visibility             0.04          0.02          0.01          0.20
##                        pressure_height Wind_speed Humidity
## Month                              0.12       0.04     0.01
## Day_of_month                       0.00       0.01     0.00
## Day_of_week                        0.00       0.00     0.00
## ozone_reading                      0.36       0.00     0.20
## pressure_height                    1.00       0.02     0.03
## Wind_speed                         0.02       1.00     0.03
## Humidity                           0.03       0.03     1.00
<Output Truncated for brevity>
## hclust results (method=complete)
##
##
## Call:
## hclust(d = as.dist(1 - x), method = method)
##
## Cluster method   : complete
## Number of objects: 13
```

4. Print the value:

```
print(round(Ozone_var_clust$sim,2))
```

The output is as follows:

```
##                  Month Day_of_month Day_of_week ozone_reading
## Month             1.00         0.00        0.00          0.00
## Day_of_month      0.00         1.00        0.00          0.01
## Day_of_week       0.00         0.00        1.00          0.00
```

```
## ozone_reading           0.00        0.01        0.00        1.00
## pressure_height         0.12        0.00        0.00        0.36
## Wind_speed              0.04        0.01        0.00        0.00
## Humidity                0.01        0.00        0.00        0.20
## Temperature_Sandburg    0.05        0.01        0.00        0.63
## Temperature_ElMonte     0.07        0.00        0.00        0.59
## Inversion_base_height   0.00        0.01        0.00        0.32
## Pressure_gradient       0.03        0.00        0.00        0.06
```

Based on the similarity matrix, the following figure shows the plot of variables in the same cluster. For example, `Temperature_ElMonte` and `Inversion_temperature` are both clustered into one cluster with a Spearman correlation score of 0.85. Similarly, `Humidity` and `Pressure_gradient` have a Spearman correlation of 0.25. A high similarity would entail the decision of dropping one of them. In addition to the top of the output of the cluster, one should also consider the model metrics before taking the final call of dropping the variable completely:

```
plot(Ozone_var_clust)
```

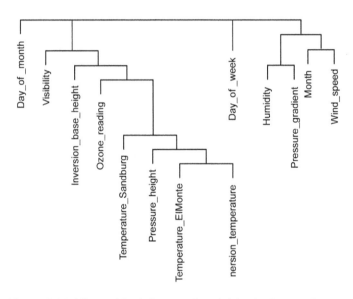

Figure 6.12: Hierarchical cluster of variables in Ozone dataset

Linear Discriminant Analysis for Feature Reduction

Linear discriminant analysis (**LDA**) helps in maximizing the class separation by projecting the data into a new feature space: lower dimensional space with good class separability in order to avoid overfitting (*curse of dimensionality*). LDA also reduces computational costs, which makes it suitable as a classification algorithm. The idea is to maximize the distance between the mean of each class (or category) and minimize the variability within the class. (This sounds certainly like how the clustering algorithm in unsupervised learning works, but we will not touch that here as it is not in the scope of this book.) Note that LDA assumes that data follows a Gaussian distribution; if it's not, the performance of LDA will be reduced. In this section, we will use LDA as a feature reduction technique rather than as a classifier.

For the two-class problem, if we have an m-dimensional dataset $\{X_1, X_2, ..., X_m\}$ with N observations, of which N_1 belongs to class c_1 and N_2 belongs to class c_2. In this case, we can project the data onto a line (with C=2, project into C-1 space):

$$Y = w^T X, \text{ where } X = \begin{bmatrix} x_1 \\ \vdots \\ x_m \end{bmatrix} \text{ and } w = \begin{bmatrix} w_1 \\ \vdots \\ w_m \end{bmatrix}$$

Such a projection is achieved by projecting the mean of X onto the mean of Y. Of all the lines possible, we would like to select the one that maximizes the separability of the scalars. In other words, where the projections of observation from the same class are projected very close to each other and, at the same time, the projected means are as far apart as possible.

It should be noted that while in LDA we use the class variable more like supervised learning, PCA does not need any class variable to reduce the feature size. That is why, while LDA preserves as much of the class discriminatory information as possible, PCA does not much care about it.

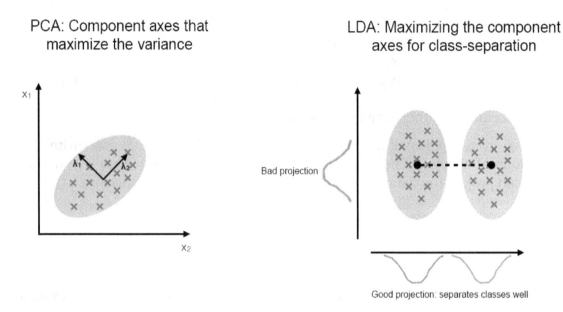

Figure 6.13: Comparing PCA and LDA

Source: https://sebastianraschka.com/Articles/2014_python_lda.html

Exercise 87: Exploring LDA

In this exercise, we will perform LDA for feature reduction. We will observe the difference in the model performance with all the features and the reduced features using LDA.

Perform the following steps:

1. Merge the two DataFrames on timestamp to stack other environmental variables along with PM2.5 into one DataFrame:

```
PM25_for_LDA <- merge(PM25_three_hour_pm25_avg,
PM25[,c("datetime","TEMP","DEWP","PRES","Iws","cbwd","Is","Ir")], by.x =
"timestamp",by.y = "datetime")
PM25_for_LDA = PM25_for_
LDA[,c("TEMP","PRES","DEWP","Iws","Is","Ir","pollution_level")]
```

2. Split the dataset into train and test:

```
index = sample(1:nrow(PM25_for_LDA), round(nrow(PM25_for_LDA)*0.6 ),
replace = FALSE)
LDA_train = PM25_for_LDA[ index, ]
LDA_test = PM25_for_LDA[ -index, ]
```

3. Import the **MASS** package:

```
library(MASS)
```

4. Fit the LDA model on the training dataset:

```
LDA_model = lda( pollution_level ~ ., data = LDA_train )
projected_data = as.matrix( LDA_train[, 1:6] ) %*%
  LDA_model$scaling
```

5. Plot 100 randomly selected projected values:

```
set.seed(100)
index <- sample(nrow(projected_data),100, replace = FALSE)
plot( projected_data[index], col = LDA_train[,7], pch = 19 )
```

The output is as follows:

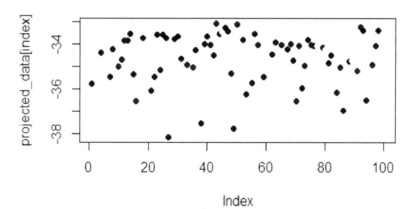

Figure 6.14: Plot of randomly selected 100 projected values

6. Perform the model testing:

```
LDA_test_reduced = LDA_test[, !( names( LDA_test ) %in% c( "pollution_
level" ) ) ]
LDA_model_results = predict( LDA_model, LDA_test_reduced )
```

7. Import the **caret** library and print the confusion matrix:

```
library( caret )
c_t = table( LDA_model_results$class, LDA_test$pollution_level )
print( confusionMatrix( c_t ) )
```

The output is as follows:

```
## Confusion Matrix and Statistics
##
##
##            0      1
##    0   2359    978
##    1   2257  11108
##
##                 Accuracy : 0.8063
##                   95% CI : (0.8002, 0.8123)
##      No Information Rate : 0.7236
##      P-Value [Acc > NIR] : < 2.2e-16
##
##                    Kappa : 0.4704
##    Mcnemar's Test P-Value : < 2.2e-16
##
##              Sensitivity : 0.5110
##              Specificity : 0.9191
##           Pos Pred Value : 0.7069
##           Neg Pred Value : 0.8311
##               Prevalence : 0.2764
##           Detection Rate : 0.1412
##     Detection Prevalence : 0.1998
##        Balanced Accuracy : 0.7151
##
##         'Positive' Class : 0
##
```

8. Find the dimension-reduced dataset:

```
new_LDA_train = as.matrix( LDA_train[,1:6] ) %*%
   LDA_model$scaling
new_LDA_train = as.data.frame( new_LDA_train )
new_LDA_train$pollution_level = LDA_train$pollution_level
```

9. Test the dataset:

```
new_LDA_test = as.matrix( LDA_test[,1:6] ) %*%
  LDA_model$scaling
new_LDA_test = as.data.frame( new_LDA_test )
new_LDA_test$pollution_level = LDA_test$pollution_level
```

10. Use the projected data. Let's fit a logistic model. You could use any other classification model as well:

```
PM25_logit_model_on_LDA <- glm(pollution_level ~ ., data = new_LDA_
train,family=binomial(link='logit'))
```

11. Perform the model evaluation on testing data:

```
predicted_LDA = predict(PM25_logit_model_on_LDA, newdata = new_LDA_
test,type="response")
```

12. Predict 1 if probability > 0.5:

```
predicted <- ifelse(predicted_LDA>0.5, 1,0)
actual <- new_LDA_test$pollution_level
```

13. Find the confusion matrix:

```
confusionMatrix(predicted, actual)
```

The output is as follows:

```
## Confusion Matrix and Statistics
##
##              Reference
## Prediction     0     1
##           0  2316   947
##           1  2300 11139
##
##                  Accuracy : 0.8056
##                    95% CI : (0.7995, 0.8116)
##       No Information Rate : 0.7236
##       P-Value [Acc > NIR] : < 2.2e-16
##
##                     Kappa : 0.4655
##   Mcnemar's Test P-Value : < 2.2e-16
##
##               Sensitivity : 0.5017
##               Specificity : 0.9216
##            Pos Pred Value : 0.7098
```

```
##           Neg Pred Value : 0.8289
##               Prevalence : 0.2764
##           Detection Rate : 0.1387
##     Detection Prevalence : 0.1954
##         Balanced Accuracy : 0.7117
##
##           'Positive' Class : 0
##
```

Note that the accuracy in **LDA_test** and the projected **new_LDA_test** are strikingly similar. This indicates that the projected values in the new lower dimensional space perform equally well compared with the original. It might always not be the case that the new space will result in the same performance as the original. Therefore, a thorough scrutiny is required before reducing the feature space.

Summary

In this chapter, we saw various feature selection and reduction techniques. The three main topics covered in this chapter were: Feature Engineering, Feature Selection, and Feature Reduction. The latter two have the same purpose of shrinking the number of features; however, the techniques used are completely different. Feature Engineering focuses on transforming variables into a new form that either helps in improving the model performance or makes the variable be in compliance with model assumption. An example is the linearity assumption in the linear regression model, where we typically could square or cube the variables and the skewness in data distribution, which could be addressed using log transformation. Feature Selection and Feature Reduction help in providing the best feature set or the best representation of the feature set, which improves model performance. Most importantly, both techniques shrink the feature space, which drastically improves the model training time without compromising the performance in terms of accuracy, **RMSE,** or any relevant model evaluation metric.

We also saw how some of the models themselves, such as random forest and **LDA,** could directly be used as feature selection and reduction techniques. While random forest works by selecting the best features through a method of random selection, LDA works by finding the best representation of features. Thus, the former is used in feature selection and the latter in reduction.

In the next chapter, we will explore more about model improvement, where some of the learnings from this chapter will be employed.

Model Improvements

Learning Objectives

By the end of this chapter, you will be able to:

- Explain and implement the concept of bias and variance trade-off in machine learning models.

- Perform model assessment with cross-validation.

- Implement hyperparameter tuning for machine learning models.

- Improve a model's performance with various hyperparameter tuning techniques.

In this chapter, we will focus on improving a model's performance using cross-validation techniques and hyperparameter tuning.

Introduction

In the previous chapter, we explored a few strategies that helped us build improved models using **feature selection** and **dimensionality reduction**. These strategies primarily focus on improving the model's computational performance and interpretability; however, to improve the model's performance with respect to performance metrics, such as overall accuracy or error estimates to build robust and more generalized models, we will need to focus on cross-validation and hyperparameter tuning.

In this chapter, we will walk you through the fundamental topics in machine learning to build generalized and robust models using cross-validation and hyperparameter tuning and implement them in R.

We will first study the topics in this chapter in detail with layman examples and leverage simple use cases to see the implementation in action.

Bias-Variance Trade-off

An interesting, arduous, and repetitive part of machine learning is the **model evaluation journey**. There is again, art and a different mindset required to build models that are robust. Throughout this book, we have simplified the model evaluation process with training and testing datasets that were derived by splitting the available data into a **70:30** or **80:20** ratio. Although this approach was effective in helping us understand how the model performs on unseen data, it still leaves several loopholes that might render the model futile for most other cases. We will need a more formal, thorough, and exhaustive method of validation for a machine learning model to be robust for future prediction events. In this chapter, we will study **cross-validation** and its various approaches to assess the performance of a machine learning model.

Before we delve into the specifics of the topic, we need to explore a crucial topic in machine learning called **bias-variance trade-off**. This topic has been much in discussion in most machine learning forums and academia. A crucial topic to the machine learning fraternity, it forms the foundation before studying model validation and improvements in depth. From the title of the topic, it may be easy to infer that in machine learning models, the bias-variance trade-off is a behavior exhibited by models, where models that showcase low bias in estimating model parameters, unfortunately, demonstrate higher variance in estimating model parameters, and vice versa. To understand the topic from a layman's perspective, let's first break down the topic into individual components, understand each component, and then reconstruct the larger picture with all components together.

What is Bias and Variance in Machine Learning Models?

In general, when a machine learning model fails to learn important (or sometimes complex) patterns exhibited in data, we say the model is **biased**. Such a model oversimplifies itself or only learns extremely simple rules that may not be helpful in making accurate predictions. The net outcome from such models is that the predictions tend to remain mostly the same (and incorrect), irrespective of the differences in input data. The patterns learned by the model are so simple or biased that the variations in the input data, unfortunately, don't yield the expected predictions.

On the other hand, if we reverse the rationale, we can easily define variance in machine learning models. Think about models that learn unnecessary patterns, such as noise from the data, such that even small variations in the input data lead to significantly large undesirable changes in the prediction. In such cases, we say that the model has a high variance.

The ideal scenario would be a model with low bias and low variance; that is, a model that has learned the necessary patterns from data. It successfully ignored the noise and delivers reasonable and desirable changes in predictive behavior with reasonable changes in the input data. Unfortunately, the ideal scenario is difficult to achieve and thus we arrive at the topic of **the bias-variance trade-off**.

Putting together all the individual components we studied, we can say every attempt to reduce bias or variance will lead to an increase in the other dimension, resulting in a situation where we would need to strike a balance between the desired bias and variance in model performance. The necessary changes that can be incorporated in machine learning models to strike the balance between bias and variance are achieved using a combination of hyperparameter tuning methods. We will study the concept of hyperparameter tuning in the upcoming sections. The following is a famous example used to demonstrate the bias-variance concept with a visual bullseye diagram:

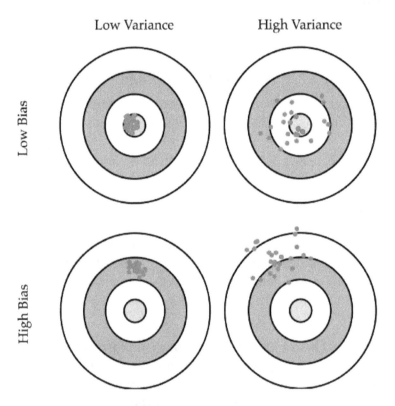

Figure 7.1: The bias-variance concept with a visual bullseye diagram

In the previous diagram, we can see four quadrants to specifically distinguish the bias-variance trade-off. The diagram is used to interpret the model bias and variance for a regression use case. Inferring a similar idea visually for a classification use case might be challenging; however, we get the bigger picture with the illustrated example.

Our ideal goal is to train a machine learning model with low bias and low variance. However, when we have low bias and high variance (the top-right quadrant in the preceding visualization), we see significantly large changes in the end outcome for a small variation in the input data. On the other hand, when we have high bias and low variance (the bottom-left quadrant in the visualization), we can see the end outcome getting concentrated in a region away from the target, demonstrating barely any variations for changes in the input. Lastly, we have high bias and high variance, that is, we hit far away from the target, as well as have large variations for small changes in the input. This would be the most undesirable state for a model.

Underfitting and Overfitting

In the previous scenario, where we have a high bias, we denote a phenomenon called **underfitting** in machine learning models. Similarly, when we have high variance, we denote a phenomenon called **overfitting** in machine learning models.

The following visual demonstrates the idea of **overfitting**, **underfitting**, and **ideal balance** for a regression model. We can see high bias resulting in an oversimplified model (that is, underfitting); high variance resulting in overcomplicated models (that is, overfitting); and lastly, striking the right balance between bias and variance:

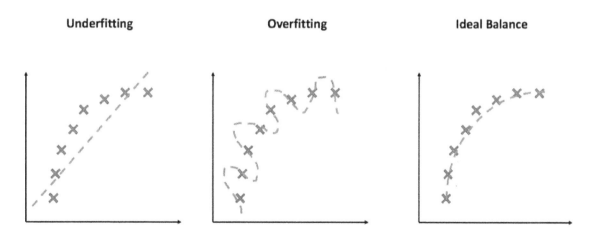

Figure 7.2: Visual demonstration of overfitting, underfitting, and ideal balance

To study bias and variance in machine learning models more effectively, we have cross-validation techniques. These techniques help us understand the model performance more intuitively.

Defining a Sample Use Case

For the purpose of exploring topics in this chapter with a practical dataset, we use a small dataset already available in the **mlbench** package, called **PimaIndiansDiabetes**, which is a handy dataset for classification use cases.

The dataset is originally from the National Institute of Diabetes and Digestive and Kidney Diseases. The use case that can be tailored from the dataset is when predicting if a patient has diabetes as a function of few medical diagnostic measurements.

> **Note**
>
> Additional information can be found at http://math.furman.edu/~dcs/courses/math47/R/library/mlbench/html/PimaIndiansDiabetes.html.
>
> The selection of the use case with a dataset size of less than 1000 rows is intentional. The topics explored in this chapter require high computation time on commodity hardware for regular use cases with large datasets. The selection of small datasets for the purpose of demonstration helps in achieving the outcome with fairly normal computational time for most readers using mainstream hardware.

Exercise 88: Loading and Exploring Data

To quickly study the overall characteristics of **PimaIndiansDiabetes** and explore the nature of the contents in each column, perform the following steps:

1. Use the following commands to load the **mlbench**, **randomForest**, and **dplyr** libraries:

    ```
    library(mlbench)
    library(randomForest)
    library(dplyr)
    ```

2. Use the following command to load data from the **PimaIndiansDiabetes** dataset:

    ```
    data(PimaIndiansDiabetes)
    df<-PimaIndiansDiabetes
    ```

3. Explore the dimensions of the dataset and study the content within each column using the **str** command:

```
str(df)
```

The output is as follows:

```
'data.frame':768 obs. of  9 variables:
 $ pregnant: num  6 1 8 1 0 5 3 10 2 8 ...
 $ glucose : num  148 85 183 89 137 116 78 115 197 125...
 $ pressure: num  72 66 64 66 40 74 50 0 70 96 ...
 $ triceps : num  35 29 0 23 35 0 32 0 45 0 ...
 $ insulin : num  0 0 0 94 168 0 88 0 543 0 ...
 $ mass    : num  33.6 26.6 23.3 28.1 43.1 25.6 31 35.3 30.5 0 ...
 $ pedigree: num  0.627 0.351 0.672 0.167 2.288 ...
 $ age     : num  50 31 32 21 33 30 26 29 53 54 ...
 $ diabetes: Factor w/ 2 levels "neg","pos": 2 1 2 1 2 1 2 1 2 2 ...
```

As we can see, the dataset has **768** observations and **9** variables, that is, 8 independent variables and 1 dependent categorical variable **diabetes** with values as **pos** for positive and **neg** for negative.

We will use this dataset and develop several classification models for the further topics in this chapter.

Cross-Validation

Cross-validation is a model validation technique that aids in assessing the performance and ability of a machine learning model to generalize on an independent dataset. It is also called **rotation validation**, as it approaches the validation of a model with several repetitions by drawing the training and validation data from the same distribution.

The cross-validation helps us:

- Evaluate the robustness of the model on unseen data.

- Estimate a realistic range for desired performance metrics.

- Mitigate overfitting and underfitting of models.

The general principle of cross-validation is to test the model on the entire dataset in several iterations by partitioning data into groups and using majority to train and minority to test. The repetitive rotations ensure the model has been tested on all available observations. The final performance metrics of the model are aggregated and summarized from the results of all rotations.

To study if the model has high bias, we can check the mean (average) performance of the model across all rotations. If the mean performance metrics say overall accuracy (for classification) or **mean absolute percentage error** (for regression) is low, then there is a high bias and the model is underfitting. To study if the model has a high variance, we can study the standard deviation of the desired performance metrics across rotations. A high standard deviation would indicate the model will have high variance; that is, the model will be overfitting.

There are several popular approaches in cross-validation:

- Holdout validation

- K-fold cross-validation

- Hold-one-out validation (LOOCV)

Let's explore each of these approaches in details.

Holdout Approach/Validation

This is the easiest approach (though not the most recommended) used in validating model performance. We have used this approach throughout the book to test our model performance in the previous chapters. Here, we randomly divide the available dataset into training and testing datasets. Most common split ratios used between the train and test datasets are **70:30** or **80:20**.

The major drawbacks of this approach are that the model performance is purely evaluated from a fractional test dataset, and it might not be the best representation for the model performance. The evaluation of the model will completely depend on the type of split, and therefore, the nature of the data points that end up in the training and testing datasets, which might then lead to significantly different results and thus high variance.

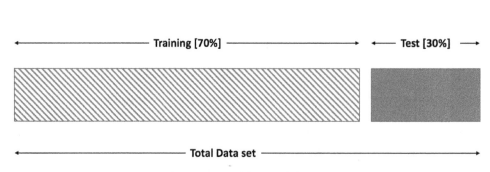

Figure 7.3: Holdout validation

The following exercise divides the dataset into 70% training and 30% testing, and builds a random forest model on the training dataset and then evaluates the performance using the testing dataset. This method was widely used in *Chapter 5, Classification*, so you shouldn't be surprised by the process.

Exercise 89: Performing Model Assessment Using Holdout Validation

In this exercise, we will leverage the data we loaded into memory in *Exercise 1: Loading and Exploring the Data*, to create a simple random forest classification model and perform model assessment using the holdout validation technique.

Perform the following steps:

1. First, import the **caret** package into the system using the following command. The **caret** package provides us with ready-to-use functions for model assessment, namely, **ConfusionMatrix**:

    ```
    library(caret)
    ```

2. Now, set up the seed for reproducibility as follows:

    ```
    set.seed(2019)
    ```

3. Create 70% **train** and a 30% **test** dataset using the following command:

    ```
    train_index<- sample(seq_len(nrow(df)),floor(0.7 * nrow(df)))
    train <- df[train_index,]
    test <- df[-train_index,]
    ```

4. Use the **print** function to display the output required:

    ```
    print("Training Dataset shape:")
    print(dim(train))
    print("Test Dataset shape:")
    print(dim(test))
    ```

5. Create a random forest model by fitting on the **train** dataset:

    ```
    model <-randomForest(diabetes~.,data=train, mtry =3)
    ```

6. Print the model using the following command:

    ```
    print(model)
    ```

7. Use the **predict** method on **test** dataset as illustrated here:

    ```
    y_predicted<- predict(model, newdata = test)
    ```

8. Create and print the **Confusion-Matrix** using the following command:

```
results<-confusionMatrix(y_predicted, test$diabetes, positive= 'pos')
print("Confusion Matrix  (Test Data)- ")
print(results$table)
```

9. Print the overall accuracy using the following command:

```
results$overall[1]
```

The output is as follows:

```
[1] "Training Dataset shape:"
[1] 537    9
[1] "Test Dataset shape:"
[1] 231    9

Call:
 randomForest(formula = diabetes ~ ., data = train, mtry = 3)
               Type of random forest: classification
                     Number of trees: 500
No. of variables tried at each split: 3

        OOB estimate of  error rate: 23.46%
Confusion matrix:
    neg pos class.error
neg 304  48   0.1363636
pos  78 107   0.4216216
[1] "Confusion Matrix  (Test Data)- "
          Reference
Prediction neg pos
       neg 133  37
       pos  15  46
```

Accuracy: 0.774891774891775

Figure 7.4: Model assessment using holdout validation

We can see the overall accuracy is 77%. This might not be the best representation of the model performance as we have only evaluated it on a random test sample. The results might be different if we use a different test sample. Let's now explore additional cross-validation approaches that overcome this trade-off.

K-Fold Cross-Validation

This technique is the most recommended approach for model evaluation. In this technique, we partition the data into k groups and use k-1 groups for training and the remainder (1 group) for validation. The process is repeated k times, where a new group is used for validation in each successive iteration, and therefore, each group is used for testing at one point of time. The overall results are the average error estimates across k iterations.

k-fold cross-validations, therefore, overcomes the drawbacks of the holdout technique by mitigating the perils associated with the nature of split as each data point is tested once over the book of k iterations. The variance of the model is reduced as the value of k increases. The most common values used for k are 5 or 10. The major drawback of this technique is that it trains the model k times (for k iterations). Therefore, the total compute time required for the model to train and validate is approximately k times the holdout method.

The following visual demonstrates a five-fold cross-validation and the aggregate results (hypothetical) from all rotations:

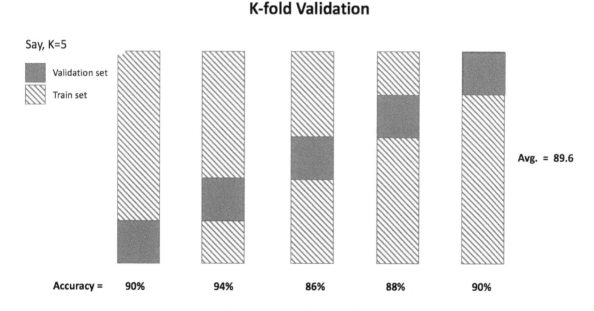

Figure 7.5: K-fold validation

The following code snippet implements the 5-fold cross-validation on the same dataset used in the previous example and prints the average accuracy across all folds.

Exercise 90: Performing Model Assessment Using K-Fold Cross-Validation

We will leverage the same dataset for the use case as from the previous two exercises and build a sample random forest classification model and evaluate the performance using k-fold cross-validation.

To perform model assessment using the k-fold cross validation approach, perform the following steps:

1. First, import the **caret** package into the system using the following command:

    ```
    library(caret)
    ```

2. Next, set the **seed** as **2019** using the following command:

    ```
    set.seed(2019)
    ```

3. Now, define a function for five-fold cross validation using the following command:

    ```
    train_control = trainControl(method = "cv", number=5, savePredictions =
    TRUE, verboseIter = TRUE)
    ```

4. Define the value of **mtry** as **3** (to match our previous example):

    ```
    parameter_values = expand.grid(mtry=3)
    ```

5. Fit the model using the following command:

    ```
    model_rf_kfold<- train(diabetes~., data=df, trControl=train_control,
                    method="rf",  metric= "Accuracy",
    tuneGrid = parameter_values)
    ```

6. Next, print overall accuracy (averaged across all folds):

    ```
    model_rf_kfold$results[2]
    ```

7. Now, print the detailed prediction dataset using the following command:

    ```
    print("Shape of Prediction Dataset")
    print(dim(model_rf_kfold$pred))

    print("Prediction detailed results - ")
    head(model_rf_kfold$pred) #print first 6 rows
    tail(model_rf_kfold$pred) #print last 6 rows

    print("Accuracy across each Fold-")
    model_rf_kfold$resample

    print(paste("Average Accuracy :",mean(model_rf_kfold$resample$Accuracy)))
    print(paste("Std. Dev Accuracy :",sd(model_rf_kfold$resample$Accuracy)))
    ```

The output is as follows:

```
+ Fold1: mtry=3
- Fold1: mtry=3
+ Fold2: mtry=3
- Fold2: mtry=3
+ Fold3: mtry=3
- Fold3: mtry=3
+ Fold4: mtry=3
- Fold4: mtry=3
+ Fold5: mtry=3
- Fold5: mtry=3
...
Accuracy: 0.7590782
"Shape of Prediction Dataset"
768    5
"Prediction detailed results - "
...
"Average Accuracy : 0.759078176725236"
"Std. Dev Accuracy : 0.0225461480724459"
```

As we can see, the overall accuracy has dropped a bit to **76% (rounded off from 75.9)**. This is the average accuracy from each fold. We have also manually calculated the mean and standard deviation of accuracy from each fold toward the end. The standard deviation for accuracy across each fold is **2%**, which is considerably low and therefore, we can conclude there is low variance. The overall accuracy is not low, so the model has a moderately low bias. There is scope for improvement in the overall performance, but our model is neither overfitting nor underfitting at the moment.

If you observe the code, we used the **trainControl** function that provides us with the necessary constructs to define the type of cross-validation with the **cv** method, and the number of folds as equal to **5**.

We use an additional construct to indicate the need to save the prediction, which we can later analyze in detail. The **trainControl** object is then passed to the **train** function in the **caret** package, where we also define the type of algorithm to be used as random forest with **rf** method, and the metric as **Accuracy**. The **tuneGrid** construct was ideally not necessary at this point; it is used for hyperparameter tuning that we will cover later. However, the **train** function in the **caret** package, by default, simplifies the function by using hyperparameter tuning. It tries different values of **mtry** in various iterations and returns the final prediction with the best value. In order to make apples to apple comparison with the previous example, we had to restrict the value of **mtry** to **3**. We, therefore, used the **expand.grid** object to define the value of **mtry** to be used in the cross-validation process.

The train function, when supplied with the `trainControl` object defined for cross-validation, divides the data into five partitions and leverages four partitions for training and one for testing. The process is repeated five times (k is set to **5**) and the model is tested on each partition in the dataset iteratively.

We can see the detailed results in the `pred` object (data frame) in the model results. Here, we can see the observed (actual) and predicted value of the data on each row. It additionally also annotates the value of the hyperparameter used in the fold, and the fold number it was a part of for testing.

The `resample` DataFrame in the `model` object records the accuracy and additional metrics across each fold in cross-validation. We can explore the average and standard deviation of the metrics of our interest to study bias and variance.

The final take-away from the k-fold cross validation is that the accuracy of the random forest model for the use case is 76% (that is, the average accuracy across all partitions).

Hold-One-Out Validation

In this technique, we take the k-fold validation to the logical extreme. Instead of creating k-partitions where, k would be 5 or 10, we choose the number of partitions as the number of available data points. Therefore, we would have only one sample in a partition. We use all the samples except one for training, and test the model on the sample which was held out and repeat this **n** number of times, where **n** is the number of training samples. Finally, the average error akin to k-fold validation is computed. The major drawback of this technique is that the model is trained n number of times, making it computationally expensive. If we are dealing with a fairly large data sample, this validation method is best avoided.

Hold-one-out validation is also called **Leave-One-Out Cross-Validation** (LOOCV). The following visual demonstrates hold-one-out validation for n samples:

Hold one out Validation

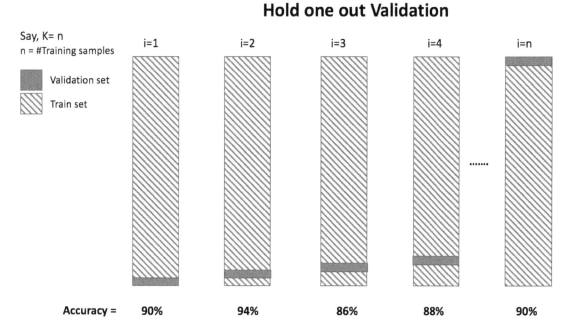

Figure 7.6: Hold-one-out validation

The following exercise performs **hold-one-out** or leave-one-out cross-validation on the same dataset using random forest with the same experimental setup.

Exercise 91: Performing Model Assessment Using Hold-One-Out Validation

Similar to *Exercise 2: Performing Model Assessment using Holdout Validation* and *Exercise 3: Performing Model Assessment using K-Fold Cross Validation*, we will continue to leverage the same dataset and perform hold-one-out validation to assess model performance.

To perform the model assessment using the hold-one-out validation approach, perform the following steps:

1. First, define function for hold-one-out validation using the following command:

    ```
    set.seed(2019)
    train_control = trainControl(method = "LOOCV", savePredictions = TRUE)
    ```

2. Next, define the value of **mtry** equals **3** (to match our previous example):

    ```
    parameter_values = expand.grid(mtry=3)
    ```

3. Fit the model:

```
model_rf_LOOCV<- train(diabetes~., data=df, trControl=train_control,
                    method="rf",  metric= "Accuracy",
tuneGrid = parameter_values)
```

4. Now, print the overall accuracy (averaged across all folds):

```
print(model_rf_LOOCV$results[2])
```

5. Print the detailed prediction dataset using the following commands:

```
print("Shape of Prediction Dataset")
print(dim(model_rf_LOOCV$pred))

print("Prediction detailed results - ")
head(model_rf_LOOCV$pred) #print first 6 rows

tail(model_rf_LOOCV$pred) #print last 6 rows
```

The output is as follows:

```
Accuracy
1 0.7721354
[1] "Shape of Prediction Dataset"
[1] 768    4
[1] "Prediction detailed results - "

"Shape of Prediction Dataset"
  768    4

"Prediction detailed results - "
  ...
```

As we can see, the overall accuracy at **77%** is almost the same as K fold cross-validation (a marginal increase of **1%**). The **LOOCV** construct here stands for **Leave-One-Out Cross-Validation**. The process is computationally expensive as it iterates the training process for as many times as there are data points (in this case, 768).

Hyperparameter Optimization

Hyperparameter optimization is the process of optimizing or finding the most optimal set of hyperparameters for a machine learning model. A hyperparameter is a parameter that defines the macro characteristics for a machine learning model. It is basically a metaparameter for the model. Hyperparameters are different from model parameters; model parameters are learned by the model during the learning process, however, hyperparameters are set by the data scientist designing the model and cannot be learned by the model.

To understand the concept more intuitively, let's explore the topic in layman terms. Consider the example of a decision tree model. The tree structure with the root node, decision nodes, and leaf nodes are (akin to the beta coefficients in logistic regression) are learned through training (fitting) of data. When the model finally converges (finds the optimal set of values for model parameters), we have the final tree structure that defines the traversal path for the end prediction. The macro characteristic for the model is however something different; in the case of decision tree, it would be the complexity parameter, denoted by **cp**. The complexity parameter, **cp**, restricts the growth of the tree with respect to depth; that is, doesn't allow branching of a node if the information gain or any other associated metric doesn't yield above a threshold. Applying this new rule restricts the depth of the tree beyond a point and helps in generalizing the tree better. The complexity parameter is therefore a parameter that defines a macro characteristic for the model that then tailors the book of the training process, which we call a hyperparameter.

Every machine learning algorithm will have a different set of hyperparameters associated that will help the model ignore errors (noise), and therefore improve generalizing capabilities. A few examples of hyperparameters in machine learning algorithms are illustrated in the following table:

Algorithm	Hyperparameters
Random Forest	• mtry: Number of features to be selected in each tree • ntree: Number of trees in the forest)
RPart	• cp: Complexity Parameter
XGBoost	• learning rate • max depth • nrounds (maximum number of iterations)

Figure 7.7: Hyperparameters in machine learning algorithms

Note

The number of hyperparameters is sometimes different in the implementations offered in R and Python. For example, the logistic regression implementation in R with the **caret** package doesn't tune the **c** parameter unlike the Python implementation in **sklearn**. Similarly, random forest implementation in **sklearn** of Python allows the use-of-depth of a tree as a hyperparameter.

Information on gradient-based hyperparameter optimization can be found at the following links:

https://arxiv.org/abs/1502.03492

http://proceedings.mlr.press/v37/maclaurin15.pdf

The process of hyperparameter tuning can be summarized as the iterative process of finding the optimal set of values for hyperparameters that results in the best machine learning model for our task of prediction. There are several approaches that can be taken to achieve this. With the fact that this process is iterative, we can affirm that there would be several approaches to optimize the path used to find the optimal set of values. Let's discuss in depth the broad strategies that can adopted for hyperparameter tuning.

Grid Search Optimization

The most naïve approach to find the optimal set of hyperparameters for a model would be to use **brute-force** methods and iterate with every combination of values for the hyperparameters and then find the most optimal combination. This will deliver the desired results, but not in the desired time. In most cases, the models we train will be significantly large and require heavy compute time for training. Iterating through each combination wouldn't be an ideal option. To improve upon the brute-force method, we have grid search optimization; as the name has already indicated, here, we define a grid of values that will be used for an exhaustive combination of values of hyperparameters to iterate.

In layman's terms, for grid search optimization, we define a finite set of values for each hyperparameter that we would be interested in optimizing for the model. The model is then trained for exhaustive combinations of all possible hyperparameter values and the combination with the best performance is selected as the optimal set.

The following diagram demonstrates the idea of grid search optimization for a hypothetical set of parameters. Using the hyperparameter grid, the combinations are defined, and the model is trained for each combination:

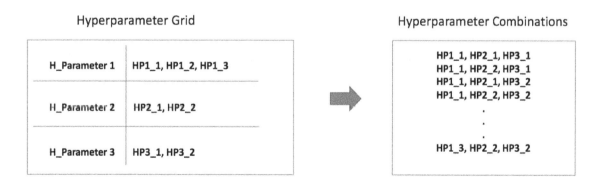

Figure 7.8: The hyperparameter grid and combinations

The advantage of grid search optimization is that it heavily reduces the time required to find the optimal set of hyperparameters given the limited set of candidate values to iterate upon (when compared to brute force). However, this comes with a trade-off. The grid search optimization model assumes that the optimal value of hyperparameter resides within the provided list of candidate values for each hyperparameter. If we don't provide the best value as a candidate value in the list (grid), we will never have the optimal set of values for the algorithm. Therefore, we would need to explore some suggestions for most recommended list of values for each hyperparameter before finalizing the list of candidate values. Hyperparameter optimization works best for experienced data science professionals, who have strong judgement for a variety of different machine learning problems.

We define hyperparameters for machine learning models that tailor the book of learning (fitting) for the models.

Exercise 92: Performing Grid Search Optimization – Random Forest

In this exercise, we will perform grid search optimization for the model using the **caret** package, where we define a grid of the values that we want to test and evaluate for the best model. We will use the random forest algorithm on the same dataset as was used in the previous topic.

Perform the following steps:

1. First, set the **seed** as **2019** using the following command:

    ```
    set.seed(2019)
    ```

2. Next, define the cross-validation method using the following command:

    ```
    train_control = trainControl(method = "cv",  number=5, savePredictions =
    TRUE)
    ```

3. Now, define **parameter_grid** as illustrated here:

    ```
    parameter_grid = expand.grid(mtry=c(1,2,3,4,5,6))
    ```

4. Fit the model with cross-validation and grid search optimization:

    ```
    model_rf_gridSearch<- train(diabetes~., data=df, trControl=train_control,
                    method="rf",  metric= "Accuracy",
    tuneGrid = parameter_grid)
    ```

5. Print the overall accuracy (averaged across all folds for each hyperparameter combination):

```
print("Accuracy across hyperparameter Combinations:")
print(model_rf_gridSearch$results[,1:2])
```

The output is as follows:

```
[1] "Accuracy across hyperparameter Combinations:"
mtry   Accuracy
1     1 0.7564893
2     2 0.7604108
3     3 0.7642730
4     4 0.7668704
5     5 0.7629658
6     6 0.7590697
```

6. Print the detailed prediction dataset:

```
print("Shape of Prediction Dataset")
print(dim(model_rf_gridSearch$pred))

[1] "Shape of Prediction Dataset"
[1] 4608     5

print("Prediction detailed results - ")
print(head(model_rf_gridSearch$pred)) #print the first 6 rows
print(tail(model_rf_gridSearch$pred)) #print the last 6 rows

[1] "Prediction detailed results - "
predobsrowIndexmtry Resample
1   neg pos      10    1    Fold1
2   neg pos      24    1    Fold1
3   neg neg      34    1    Fold1
4   neg pos      39    1    Fold1
5   neg neg      43    1    Fold1
6   neg neg      48    1    Fold1
```

```
predobsrowIndexmtry Resample
4603  neg neg    752  6    Fold5
4604  neg neg    753  6    Fold5
4605  pos pos    755  6    Fold5
4606  neg neg    759  6    Fold5
4607  neg neg    761  6    Fold5
4608  pos pos    762  6    Fold5
```

```
print("Best value for Hyperparameter 'mtry':")
print(model_rf_gridSearch$bestTune)
```

```
[1] "Best value for Hyperparameter 'mtry':"
mtry
4    4
```

```
print("Final (Best) Model ")
print(model_rf_gridSearch$finalModel)
```

```
[1] "Final (Best) Model "
Call:
randomForest(x = x, y = y, mtry = param$mtry)
               Type of random forest: classification
                     Number of trees: 500
No. of variables tried at each split: 4
```

```
OOB estimate of  error rate: 23.7%
Confusion matrix:
     neg pos class.error
neg 423  77    0.154000
pos 105 163    0.391791
```

7. Plot the grid metrics:

```
library(repr)
options(repr.plot.width=8, repr.plot.height=5)
plot(model_rf_gridSearch)
```

The output is as follows:

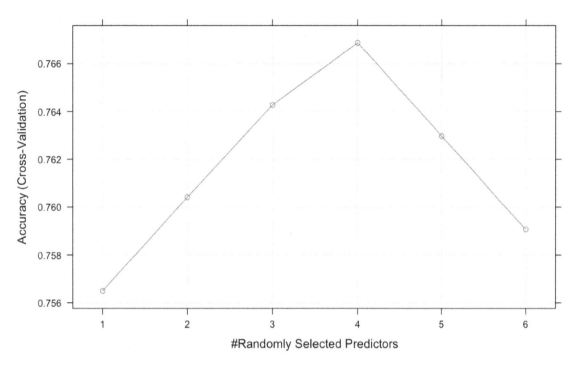

Figure 7.9: The accuracy of the random forest model across various values of hyperparameter

As we can see, the best results in terms of accuracy were delivered using the `mtry` hyperparameter with the value of 4. The highlighted portion of the output will help you in understanding the overall takeaway process. We used a 5-fold cross-validation along with grid search optimization, where we defined a grid for the `mtry` hyperparameter with the values of (1,2,3,4,5, and 6). The accuracy from each value is also shown, and we can see that the results from `mtry` equal to **4** are a notch higher than the others. Lastly, we also printed the final model that was returned by the grid search optimization process.

So far, we have only looked at random forest as a model to implement cross-validation and hyperparameter tuning. We can extend this to any other algorithm. Algorithms such as **XGBoost** have many more hyperparameters than random forest (with the R implementation), and therefore make the overall process a little more computationally expensive, as well as complicated. In the following exercise, we perform 5-fold cross validation, as well as grid search optimization for XGBoost, on the same dataset. The highlighted parts of the code are the changes for XGBoost.

> **Automated hyperparameter tuning:**
>
> https://towardsdatascience.com/automated-machine-learning-hyperparameter-tuning-in-python-dfda59b72f8a

Exercise 93: Grid Search Optimization – XGBoost

Similarly to the previous exercise, we will perform grid search optimization on the XGBoost model, instead of random forest, and on a larger set of hyperparameters to find the best model.

To perform grid search optimization on the XGBoost model, perform the following steps:

1. First, set the **seed** as **2019** using the following command:

   ```
   set.seed(2019)
   ```

2. Next, import the **dplyr** library using the following command:

   ```
   library(dplyr)
   ```

3. Define the cross-validation method using the following command:

   ```
   train_control = trainControl(method = "cv",  number=5, savePredictions = TRUE)
   ```

4. Next, define the parameter grid as illustrated here:

   ```
   parameter_grid = expand.grid(nrounds = c(30,50,60,100),
                                eta=c(0.01,0.1,0.2,0.3),
   max_depth = c(2,3,4,5),
                                gamma = c(1),
   colsample_bytree = c(0.7),
   min_child_weight = c(1)  ,
                                subsample = c(0.6)
                                )
   ```

5. Fit the model with cross-validation and grid search optimization:

```
model_xgb_gridSearch<- train(diabetes~., data=df, trControl=train_control,
            method="xgbTree", metric= "Accuracy",
tuneGrid = parameter_grid)
```

6. Print the detailed prediction dataset:

```
print("Shape of Prediction Dataset")
print(dim(model_xgb_gridSearch$pred))

"Shape of Prediction Dataset"
  49152   11

print("Prediction detailed results - ")
head(model_xgb_gridSearch$pred) #print the first 6 rows
tail(model_xgb_gridSearch$pred) #print the last 6 rows

[1] "Prediction detailed results - "
predobsrowIndex  eta max_depth gamma colsample_bytreemin_child_weight
subsample nrounds Resample
1  pos pos       3 0.01       2   1                0.7               1
0.6     100    Fold1
2  neg neg       6 0.01       2   1                0.7               1
0.6     100    Fold1
3  neg pos      20 0.01       2   1                0.7               1
0.6     100    Fold1
4  pos pos      23 0.01       2   1                0.7               1
0.6     100    Fold1
5  pos pos      25 0.01       2   1                0.7               1
0.6     100    Fold1
6  pos pos      27 0.01       2   1                0.7               1
0.6     100    Fold1

predobsrowIndex eta max_depth gamma colsample_bytreemin_child_weight
subsample nrounds Resample
49147  neg pos     732 0.3       5   1                0.7
1       0.6      60    Fold5
49148  neg pos     740 0.3       5   1                0.7
1       0.6      60    Fold5
49149  neg neg     743 0.3       5   1                0.7
1       0.6      60    Fold5
49150  pos pos     749 0.3       5   1                0.7
```

```
1         0.6      60      Fold5
49151  neg pos        751 0.3        5      1              0.7
1         0.6      60      Fold5
49152  neg neg        763 0.3        5      1              0.7
1         0.6      60      Fold5
```

```
print("Best values for all selected Hyperparameters:")
model_xgb_gridSearch$bestTune
```

```
[1] "Best values for all selected Hyperparameters:"
  nroundsmax_depth eta gamma colsample_bytreemin_child_weight subsample
27      60      4 0.1    1                  0.7                 1      0.6
```

7. Print the overall accuracy (averaged across all folds for each hyperparameter combination):

```
print("Average results across different combination of Hyperparameter
Values")
model_xgb_gridSearch$results %>% arrange(desc(Accuracy)) %>% head(5)
```

The output is as follows:

```
[1] "Average results across different combination of Hyperparameter
Values"
     eta max_depth gamma colsample_bytreemin_child_weight subsample nrounds
Accuracy      Kappa AccuracySD
1 0.10        4    1              0.7                1        0.6      60
0.7695612 0.4790457 0.02507631
2 0.01        3    1              0.7                1        0.6      30
0.7695442 0.4509049 0.02166056
3 0.01        2    1              0.7                1        0.6      100
0.7695187 0.4521142 0.03373126
4 0.30        2    1              0.7                1        0.6      30
0.7682540 0.4782334 0.01943638
5 0.01        5    1              0.7                1        0.6      30
0.7682455 0.4592689 0.02836553
KappaSD
1 0.05067601
2 0.05587205
3 0.08038248
4 0.04249313
5 0.06049950
```

8. Plot the graph:

```
plot(model_xgb_gridSearch)
```

The output is as follows:

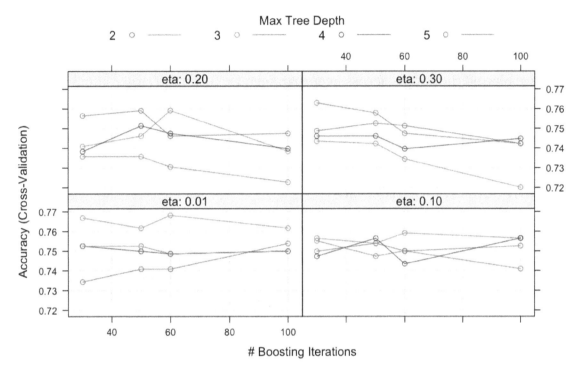

Figure 7.10: Visualizing the accuracy across various hyperparameter values for the XGBoost model

The output from the exercise might seem quite lengthy, but let's quickly summarize the results. Since we are performing cross-validation and hyperparameter tuning on XGBoost, we would need to provide a grid for a larger number of hyperparameters. The first line in the output indicates that the size of the prediction dataset is 49152 x 11. This indicates the exhaustive predictions from each combination of hyperparameters across each fold in cross-validation. We have printed the head and tail of the prediction dataset (the first and last six rows of data), and we can see the predicted outcome for each instance of the model with the associated hyperparameters, as well as the corresponding fold.

The next table shows us the best set of values for hyperparameters based on the accuracy of the model. We can see that the values of **nrounds=60**, **max_depth=3**, **eta=0.01**, **gamma=1**, **colsample_bytree=0.7**, **min_child_weight=1**, and **subsample=0.6** returned the best performance for the model.

The next table displays the corresponding accuracy for each combination of hyperparameters in the descending order of performance. The best accuracy is in the first line of the table that was achieved using the best set of hyperparameters. We achieved an accuracy of **76.8%**.

Lastly, we plotted the results across hyperparameters. Given the larger number of hyperparameters, we have a denser plot showcasing the results. However, we can directly check the results for the quadrant with **eta=0.01**, and study the variation for max depth and **nrounds** and conclude the best performance is from the same combination of hyperparameters.

Random Search Optimization

In random search optimization, we overcome one of the disadvantages of grid search optimization, which is choosing the best set of optimal values within the candidate values for each hyperparameter in the grid. Here, we opt for random choices from a distribution (in case of a continuous value for hyperparameters), instead of a static list that we would define. In random search optimization, we have a wider gamut of options to search from, as the continuous values for a hyperparameter are chosen randomly from a distribution. This increases the chances of finding the best value for a hyperparameter to a great extent.

Some of us might have already started understanding how random choices can always have the possibility of incorporating the best values for a hyperparameter. The true answer is that it doesn't always have an absolute advantage over grid search, but with a fairly large number of iterations, the chances of finding a more optimal set of hyperparameter increases with random search over grid search. There might be instances where random search would return less optimal values for hyperparameter tuning over grid search, given the random selection of values, however, most data science professionals have empirical validations of the fact that with a fairly decent number of iterations, random search trumps over grid search for most cases.

Implementation of random search optimization is simplified in the **caret** package. We have to define a parameter called **tuneLength**, which will set a maximum cap on the number of iterations for random search. The number of iterations would be equivalent to the number of times the model will be trained, and therefore the higher the number is, the higher the chances of getting the best set of hyperparameters and the associated performance boost. However, the higher the number of iterations, the higher the compute time required to execute.

In the following exercise, let's perform random search optimization on the random forest algorithm for the same dataset.

Exercise 94: Using Random Search Optimization on a Random Forest Model

We will extend the optimization process for machine learning models with random search optimization. Here, we only define the number of iterations that we would like to perform with random combinations of hyperparameter values for the model.

The aim of this exercise is to perform random search optimization on a random forest model.

Perform the following steps:

1. First, set the **seed** as **2019** using the following command:

```
set.seed(2019)
```

2. Define the cross-validation method as illustrated here:

```
train_control = trainControl(method = "cv",  number=5, savePredictions =
TRUE)
```

3. Fit the model with cross-validation and random search optimization:

```
model_rf_randomSearch<- train(diabetes~., data=df, trControl=train_
control,
                        method="rf",  metric= "Accuracy",tuneLength = 15)
```

4. Print the detailed prediction dataset:

```
print("Shape of Prediction Dataset")
print(dim(model_rf_randomSearch$pred))

[1] "Shape of Prediction Dataset"
[1] 5376    5

print("Prediction detailed results - ")
head(model_rf_randomSearch$pred) #print the first 6 rows
tail(model_rf_randomSearch$pred) #print the last 6 rows

[1] "Prediction detailed results - "
predobsrowIndexmtry Resample
1  pos pos      1    2    Fold1
2  neg neg      4    2    Fold1
3  pos pos      9    2    Fold1
4  neg pos     10    2    Fold1
```

```
5  neg neg      13   2   Fold1
6  pos pos      17   2   Fold1


predobsrowIndexmtry Resample
5371  neg neg     737   8   Fold5
5372  neg neg     742   8   Fold5
5373  neg neg     743   8   Fold5
5374  neg pos     758   8   Fold5
5375  neg neg     759   8   Fold5
5376  neg neg     765   8   Fold5


print("Best values for all selected Hyperparameters:")
model_rf_randomSearch$bestTune


[1] "Best values for all selected Hyperparameters:"
mtry
7    8
```

5. Print the overall accuracy (averaged across all folds for each hyperparameter combination):

```
model_rf_randomSearch$results %>% arrange(desc(Accuracy)) %>% head(5)
```

The output is as follows:

```
mtry  Accuracy      Kappa AccuracySDKappaSD
1     8 0.7838299 0.5190606 0.02262610 0.03707616
2     7 0.7773194 0.5047353 0.02263485 0.03760842
3     3 0.7760037 0.4945296 0.02629540 0.05803215
4     6 0.7734063 0.4964970 0.02451711 0.04409090
5     5 0.7720907 0.4895592 0.02618707 0.04796626
```

6. Plot the data for the random search optimization of the random forest model:

```
plot(model_rf_randomSearch)
```

The output is as follows:

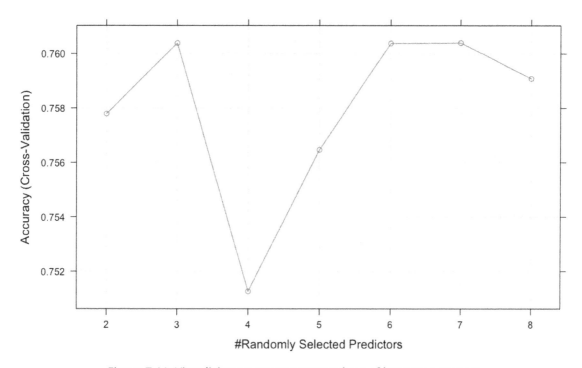

Figure 7.11: Visualizing accuracy across values of hyperparameters

We set the **tuneLength** parameter to **15**; however, since random forest in R only focuses on hyperparameter tuning for 1 parameter, that is, **mtry**, the number of iterations is exhausted at **7**. This is because we have only eight independent variables in the dataset. In most general cases, it would be advisable to set a higher number based on the number of features in the data. We can see the best value for **mtry** was found at 7. The plot showcases the differences between various values of **mtry**. The best accuracy we achieved with this model was 76%.

Let's now try the same experiment with XGBoost. Here, we will set **tuneLength** to **35**, which will be computationally expensive, that is, 15 x 5 (*folds*) = 75 model iterations. This would take significantly longer to execute than any of the previous iterations. If you want to see the results faster, you might have to reduce the number of iterations with **tuneLength**.

Exercise 95: Random Search Optimization – XGBoost

As with random forest, we will perform random search optimization on the XGBoost model. The XGBoost model has a larger number of hyperparameters to tune, and therefore is more suitable for random search optimization. We will leverage the same dataset as in previous exercises to build the XGBoost model and then perform optimization.

The aim of this exercise is to perform random search optimization on the XGBoost model.

Perform the following steps:

1. Set the **seed** as **2019** using the following command:

   ```
   set.seed(2019)
   ```

2. Define the cross-validation method using the following command:

   ```
   train_control = trainControl(method = "cv",  number=5, savePredictions =
   TRUE)
   ```

3. Fit the model with cross-validation and random search optimization:

   ```
   model_xgb_randomSearch<- train(diabetes~., data=df, trControl=train_
   control,
                                     method="xgbTree", metric=
   "Accuracy",tuneLength = 15)
   ```

4. Print the detailed prediction dataset:

   ```
   print("Shape of Prediction Dataset")
   print(dim(model_xgb_randomSearch$pred))

   print("Prediction detailed results - ")
   head(model_xgb_randomSearch$pred) #print the first 6 rows
   tail(model_xgb_randomSearch$pred) #print the last 6 rows

   print("Best values for all selected Hyperparameters:")
   model_xgb_randomSearch$bestTune
   ```

5. Print the overall accuracy (averaged across all folds for each hyperparameter combination):

```
model_xgb_randomSearch$results %>% arrange(desc(Accuracy)) %>% head(5)
```

The output is as follows:

```
"Shape of Prediction Dataset"
10368000        11


"Prediction detailed results - "
```

pred	obs	rowIndex	eta	max_depth	gamma	colsample_bytree	min_child_weight	subsample	nrounds	Resample
neg	pos	10	0.3	1	0	0.6	1	0.5	750	Fold1
neg	pos	24	0.3	1	0	0.6	1	0.5	750	Fold1
neg	neg	34	0.3	1	0	0.6	1	0.5	750	Fold1
neg	pos	39	0.3	1	0	0.6	1	0.5	750	Fold1
neg	neg	43	0.3	1	0	0.6	1	0.5	750	Fold1
neg	neg	48	0.3	1	0	0.6	1	0.5	750	Fold1

	pred	obs	rowIndex	eta	max_depth	gamma	colsample_bytree	min_child_weight	subsample	nrounds	Resample
10367995	neg	neg	752	0.4	15	0	0.8	1	1	700	Fold5
10367996	neg	neg	753	0.4	15	0	0.8	1	1	700	Fold5
10367997	pos	pos	755	0.4	15	0	0.8	1	1	700	Fold5
10367998	neg	neg	759	0.4	15	0	0.8	1	1	700	Fold5
10367999	neg	neg	761	0.4	15	0	0.8	1	1	700	Fold5
10368000	pos	pos	762	0.4	15	0	0.8	1	1	700	Fold5

```
[1] "Best values for all selected Hyperparameters:"
```

	nrounds	max_depth	eta	gamma	colsample_bytree	min_child_weight	subsample
7141	50	1	0.4	0	0.8	1	0.8928571

eta	max_depth	gamma	colsample_bytree	min_child_weight	subsample	nrounds	Accuracy	Kappa	AccuracySD	KappaSD
0.4	1	0	0.8	1	0.8928571	50	0.7682540	0.4729486	0.03702909	0.07153397
0.4	2	0	0.6	1	0.5714286	50	0.7669722	0.4814364	0.03387529	0.06442963
0.3	2	0	0.6	1	0.8214286	50	0.7656481	0.4690071	0.03393427	0.06244633
0.3	1	0	0.8	1	0.6785714	200	0.7643579	0.4664447	0.03483870	0.06367076
0.3	1	0	0.8	1	0.6071429	50	0.7643324	0.4635821	0.04090730	0.08065109

Figure 7.12: Detailed prediction results

Using *random search optimization*, we can see a different set of parameters selected as the optimal combination for the XGBoost model. Here, notice that the accuracy of grid search and random search are the same (the differences are marginal), however, the parameter values are completely different. The learning rate (`eta`) is 0.4, `max_depth` is 1 instead of 3, `colsample_byTree` is 0.8 instead of 0.7, and `nrounds` is 50 instead of 60. We have not passed any of these values as candidate values for grid search. In random search, given the wider gamut of options to select from, we may have promising results when compared to grid search. This, however, comes at a cost of *higher computation time*.

Also, the current dataset used is a small one (~800 samples). As the use case becomes a more compelling one (with more features and more data), the performance difference between random search and grid search might be wider.

As a rule of thumb, it is highly recommended to opt for random search over grid search, especially in cases where our judgement about the problem space is insignificant.

Bayesian Optimization

One of the major trade-offs within grid search and random search is that both techniques do not keep track of the past evaluations of hyperparameter combinations used for the model training. Ideally, if there was some artificial intelligence were induced in this path that could indicate the process with the historic performance on the selected list of hyperparameters and a mechanism to improve performance by advancing iterations in the right direction, it would drastically reduce the number of iterations required to find the optimal set of values for the hyperparameters. Grid search and random search, however, miss on this front and iterate through all provided combinations without considering any cues from previous iterations.

With **Bayesian optimization**, we overcome this trade-off by enabling the tuning process to keep track of previous iterations and their evaluation by developing a probabilistic model that would map the hyperparameters to a probability score of the selected loss function (an objective function) for the machine learning model. This probabilistic model is also called a **surrogate model** to the primary loss function in the machine learning model and in contrast is far easier to optimize than the loss function.

Discussing the mathematical context and derivations for the process will be beyond the scope of the chapter. The overall process in Bayesian optimization for hyperparameter tuning can be simplified as follows:

- Define a surrogate model (a probabilistic mapping of hyperparameters to the loss function).
- Find the optimal parameters for the surrogate model.

- Apply the parameters on primary loss function and update the model in the right direction based on results.

- Repeat until defined performance of iterations has been reached.

Using this simplistic framework, Bayesian optimization has in most cases delivered the ideal set of hyperparameters with the least number of iterations. As this approach keeps track of the past iterations and associated performance, its practices being more accurate with increasing amount of data. Bayesian methods are efficient and more practical to use as they operate in many ways like the human brain; for any task to be performed, we try understanding the initial view of the world, and then we improve our understanding based on new experiences. Bayesian hyperparameter optimization leverages the same rationale and enables an optimized path in tuning the hyperparameters for a model using informed decisions. A paper by *Bergstra et al.* (http://proceedings.mlr.press/v28/bergstra13.pdf) neatly explains the advantages of Bayesian optimization over random search optimization.

There are several techniques within Bayesian optimization that can be applied to hyperparameter tuning in the machine learning domain. A popular formalization of the Bayesian approach is **Sequential Model-Based Optimization** (**SMBO**), which again has several variations within. Each approach within SMBO varies based on the way the surrogate model is defined and the criteria used to evaluate and update parameters. A few popular choices for the surrogate model are **Gaussian Processes**, **Random Forest Regressions**, and **Tree Parzen Estimators** (**TPE**). Similarly, the criteria based on each successive iteration is evaluated in the optimization process and leveraged using **UCB**, that is, GP **Upper Confidence Bound**, for example, **Expected Improvement** (EI) or **Probability of Improvement** (**POI**).

To implement Bayesian optimization in R, we already have a handful of well-written libraries that abstract the entire process for us. `MlBayesOpt` is a popular package implemented by Yuya Matsumura in R. It is based on the **Gaussian Process** in SMBO for Bayesian optimization and allows the use of several functions to update the surrogate model.

The following exercise performs Bayesian optimization on the random forest model for the **mtry** and minimum node size hyperparameters. The output of the optimization process returns the best combination evaluated for each hyperparameter. We would then need to implement a regular model using the same combination for hyperparameter values.

> **Bayesian optimization:**
>
> https://towardsdatascience.com/the-intuitions-behind-bayesian-optimization-with-gaussian-processes-7e00fcc898a0
>
> https://papers.nips.cc/paper/7838-automating-bayesian-optimization-with-bayesian-optimization.pdf
>
> https://towardsdatascience.com/a-conceptual-explanation-of-bayesian-model-based-hyperparameter-optimization-for-machine-learning-b8172278050f

Exercise 96: Performing Bayesian Optimization on the Random Forest Model

Perform Bayesian optimization for the same dataset and study the output. In this optimization technique, we will leverage Bayesian optimization to intuitively select the best value for the **mtry** hyperparameter by iterating with the knowledge/context of previous iterations.

The aim of this exercise is to perform Bayesian optimization for the random forest model.

Perform the following steps:

1. First, set the **seed** as **2019** using the following command:

    ```
    set.seed(2019)
    ```

2. Import the **MlBayesOpt** library using the following command:

    ```
    library(MlBayesOpt)
    ```

3. Perform Bayesian optimization for random forest model using the **rf_opt** function from the **MlBayesOpt** package:

    ```
    model_rf_bayesain<- rf_opt(train_data = train,
    train_label = diabetes,
    test_data = test,
    test_label = diabetes,
    ```

```
        mtry_range = c(1L, ncol(df)-1),
        num_tree = 50,
        init_points = 10,
        n_iter = 10,
        acq = "poi", eps = 0,
        optkernel = list(type = "exponential", power =2))
```

The output is as follows:

```
elapsed = 0.02  Round = 1      mtry_opt = 6.3893     min_node_size = 18.0000 Value = 0.7706
elapsed = 0.02  Round = 2      mtry_opt = 5.9899     min_node_size = 16.0000 Value = 0.7576
elapsed = 0.02  Round = 3      mtry_opt = 3.1235     min_node_size = 6.0000  Value = 0.7706
elapsed = 0.02  Round = 4      mtry_opt = 5.3277     min_node_size = 5.0000  Value = 0.7619
elapsed = 0.01  Round = 5      mtry_opt = 1.3534     min_node_size = 16.0000 Value = 0.7619
elapsed = 0.01  Round = 6      mtry_opt = 1.3025     min_node_size = 15.0000 Value = 0.7576
elapsed = 0.02  Round = 7      mtry_opt = 6.7412     min_node_size = 2.0000  Value = 0.7619
elapsed = 0.01  Round = 8      mtry_opt = 1.0673     min_node_size = 16.0000 Value = 0.7532
elapsed = 0.02  Round = 9      mtry_opt = 1.7174     min_node_size = 9.0000  Value = 0.7662
elapsed = 0.02  Round = 10     mtry_opt = 5.2600     min_node_size = 11.0000 Value = 0.7532
elapsed = 0.02  Round = 11     mtry_opt = 1.9861     min_node_size = 9.0000  Value = 0.7489
elapsed = 0.02  Round = 12     mtry_opt = 2.8969     min_node_size = 2.0000  Value = 0.7706
elapsed = 0.02  Round = 13     mtry_opt = 7.0398     min_node_size = 2.0000  Value = 0.7532
elapsed = 0.01  Round = 14     mtry_opt = 5.1122     min_node_size = 21.0000 Value = 0.7532
elapsed = 0.02  Round = 15     mtry_opt = 2.2301     min_node_size = 2.0000  Value = 0.7619
elapsed = 0.02  Round = 16     mtry_opt = 6.1871     min_node_size = 8.0000  Value = 0.7576
elapsed = 0.02  Round = 17     mtry_opt = 6.1291     min_node_size = 17.0000 Value = 0.7879
elapsed = 0.02  Round = 18     mtry_opt = 4.7581     min_node_size = 6.0000  Value = 0.7576
elapsed = 0.02  Round = 19     mtry_opt = 5.0363     min_node_size = 11.0000 Value = 0.7576
elapsed = 0.01  Round = 20     mtry_opt = 1.1660     min_node_size = 4.0000  Value = 0.7446

Best Parameters Found:
Round = 17        mtry_opt = 6.1291        min_node_size = 17.0000 Value = 0.7879
```

Figure 7.13: Output for Bayesian optimization for random forest

The output displays the iterations computed for model evaluation and returns the result at the end of each iteration. You can increase the number of iterations by increasing the value of **n_iter**. The **init_points** variable defines the number of randomly chosen points to sample the target function before Bayesian optimization fits the Gaussian process. Additionally, we define the criteria function as **POI**. The **eps** parameter is an additional parameter that can be used to tune **EI** and **POI**, to balance exploitation against exploration, increasing epsilon will make the optimized hyperparameters more spread out across the whole range.

Lastly, we also define the kernel, that is, the correlation function for the underlying Gaussian process. This parameter should be a list that specifies the type of correlation function along with the smoothness parameter. Popular choices are square exponential (the default) or **Matern 5/2**.

The result of the Bayesian optimization process returned the best value for `mtry` as 6.12 (this needs to be truncated to 6, as `mtry` in **Random Forest** doesn't accept decimal values) and the best minimum node size as 17. We can use these parameter settings in the regular implementation of random forest and evaluate the model results.

Let's now use the same approach for the XGBoost model on the same use case.

Exercise 97: Performing Bayesian Optimization using XGBoost

Similar to the previous exercise, we will perform Bayesian optimization for the same dataset and study the output, albeit this time for the XGBoost model. Given that XGBoost has a larger set of hyperparameters to optimize, we would need to provide a range of values for each hyperparameter of interest to the optimization process.

To perform Bayesian optimization on the XGBoost model, carry out the following steps:

1. First, set the **seed** as **2019** using the following command:

    ```
    set.seed(2019)
    ```

2. Perform Bayesian optimization for the XGBoost model using the **xgb_opt** function from the **MlBayesOpt** package:

    ```
    model_xgb_bayesian<- xgb_opt(train, diabetes, test, diabetes,
    objectfun ='binary:logistic',
    evalmetric='logloss',
    eta_range = c(0.1, 1L),
    max_depth_range = c(2L, 8L),
    nrounds_range = c(70, 160L),
    bytree_range = c(0.4, 1L),
    init_points = 4, n_iter = 10,
    acq = "poi",
    eps = 0,
    optkernel =
    list(type = "exponential", power =2))
    ```

The output is as follows:

```
elapsed = 0.03   Round = 1        eta_opt = 0.9148      max_depth_opt = 8.0000  nrounds_opt = 115.1094  subsample_opt
= 0.3888         bytree_opt = 0.5484      Value = 0.0043
elapsed = 0.04   Round = 2        eta_opt = 0.1373      max_depth_opt = 7.0000  nrounds_opt = 126.0005  subsample_opt
= 0.7891         bytree_opt = 0.4742      Value = 0.0043
elapsed = 0.02   Round = 3        eta_opt = 0.8938      max_depth_opt = 7.0000  nrounds_opt = 100.7565  subsample_opt
= 0.4746         bytree_opt = 0.5072      Value = 0.2251
elapsed = 0.04   Round = 4        eta_opt = 0.6600      max_depth_opt = 8.0000  nrounds_opt = 130.9514  subsample_opt
= 0.5860         bytree_opt = 0.7261      Value = 0.0866
elapsed = 0.03   Round = 5        eta_opt = 0.9961      max_depth_opt = 7.0000  nrounds_opt = 100.6617  subsample_opt
= 0.3764         bytree_opt = 0.5078      Value = 0.0043
elapsed = 0.04   Round = 6        eta_opt = 0.8321      max_depth_opt = 5.0000  nrounds_opt = 153.3735  subsample_opt
= 0.4748         bytree_opt = 0.9643      Value = 0.5195
elapsed = 0.03   Round = 7        eta_opt = 0.8007      max_depth_opt = 5.0000  nrounds_opt = 107.0961  subsample_opt
= 0.4751         bytree_opt = 0.9671      Value = 1.0000
elapsed = 0.03   Round = 8        eta_opt = 0.9119      max_depth_opt = 3.0000  nrounds_opt = 106.9755  subsample_opt
= 0.4750         bytree_opt = 0.9673      Value = 0.1255
elapsed = 0.03   Round = 9        eta_opt = 0.7998      max_depth_opt = 5.0000  nrounds_opt = 106.4644  subsample_opt
= 0.4758         bytree_opt = 0.4203      Value = 0.0043
elapsed = 0.03   Round = 10       eta_opt = 0.7108      max_depth_opt = 5.0000  nrounds_opt = 106.8204  subsample_opt
= 0.4751         bytree_opt = 0.9671      Value = 0.1212
elapsed = 0.03   Round = 11       eta_opt = 0.7763      max_depth_opt = 4.0000  nrounds_opt = 105.2274  subsample_opt
= 0.1117         bytree_opt = 0.8938      Value = 0.0043
elapsed = 0.03   Round = 12       eta_opt = 0.5409      max_depth_opt = 6.0000  nrounds_opt = 108.1153  subsample_opt
= 0.2629         bytree_opt = 0.7986      Value = 0.0519
elapsed = 0.03   Round = 13       eta_opt = 0.7997      max_depth_opt = 4.0000  nrounds_opt = 125.8476  subsample_opt
= 0.4751         bytree_opt = 0.9674      Value = 1.0000
elapsed = 0.03   Round = 14       eta_opt = 0.9734      max_depth_opt = 2.0000  nrounds_opt = 102.1554  subsample_opt
= 0.4847         bytree_opt = 0.4069      Value = 0.0043

Best Parameters Found:
Round = 7        eta_opt = 0.8007         max_depth_opt = 5.0000  nrounds_opt = 107.0961  subsample_opt = 0.4751  bytre
e_opt = 0.9671   Value = 1.0000
```

Figure 7.14: Output for Bayesian Optimization using XGBoost

Like random forest, the **xgb_opt** function returns the optimal list of hyperparameters with the candidate values. Unlike **Random Forest**, we have a larger list of hyperparameters for XGBoost. We need to define the range for which we want the Bayesian optimization process to operate for each hyperparameter.

We can see that the best combination of hyperparameters from Bayesian optimization is different from what we found for **Random Search Optimization**. Again, the values of **nrounds** would need to be truncated (as a decimal value won't make sense) when we implement a standard XGBoost Tree model the parameters evaluate above namely: **nrounds**, **max_depth**, **eta**, and **subsample**.

In the chapter, we studied various cross-validation techniques to perform model assessment. A small amendment to the k-fold cross-validation helps us perform an improved validation of model performance. Before moving from k-fold to LOOCV, we can instead perform repeated k-fold to get a more robust evaluation of the model. The process repeats cross-validation multiple times where the folds are split in a different way in each repetition. Performing repeated k-fold is a better approach than LOOCV.

Activity 12: Performing Repeated K-Fold Cross Validation and Grid Search Optimization

In this activity, we will leverage the same dataset (as used in previous exercises), train a random forest model, perform repeated k-fold validation 10 times, and study the model performance. Within each fold iteration, we can try the different grid values of the hyperparameter and have a robust validation for the best model.

The aim of the activity is to perform repeated k-fold cross-validation and grid search optimization on the same model.

Perform the following steps:

1. Load the required packages (`mlbench`, `caret`, and `dplyr`).

2. Load the `PimaIndianDiabetes` dataset into memory from `mlbench` package.

3. Set a seed value for reproducibility.

4. Define the k-fold validation object using the `trainControl` function from `caret` package and define `method` as `repeatedcv` instead of `cv`.

5. Define an additional construct in the `trainControl` function for the number of repeats in the validation of `repeats` = `10`.

6. Define the grid for the `mtry` hyperparameter of a random forest model as `(3,4,5)`.

7. Fit the model with the grid values, cross-validation objects, and random forest classifiers.

8. Study the model performance by plotting the accuracy across different values of the hyperparameter.

The final output should be as follows:

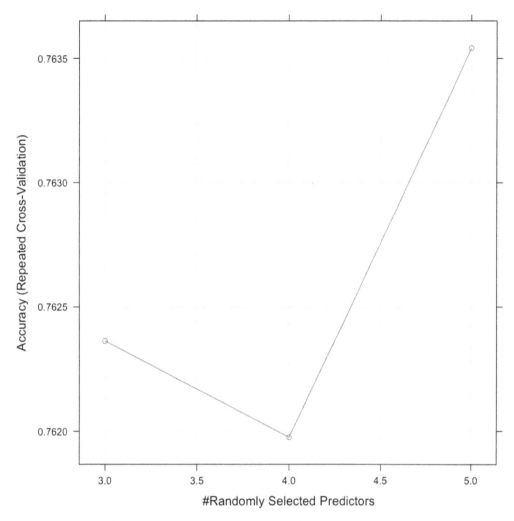

Figure 7.15: Model performance accuracy across different values of the hyperparameter

Note

The solution for this activity can be found on page 461.

Summary

In this chapter, you learned a few important aspects of model performance improvement techniques. We started with **Bias-Variance Trade-off** and understood it impacts a model's performance. We now know that high bias will result in underfitting, whereas high variance will result in overfitting of models, and that achieving one comes at the expense of the other. Therefore, in order to build the best models, we need to strike the ideal balance between bias and variance in machine learning models.

Next, we explored various types of cross-validation techniques in R that provide ready-to-use functions to implement the same. We studied holdout, k-fold, and hold-one-out validation approaches to cross-validation and understood how we can perform robust assessment of performance of machine learning models. We then studied hyperparameter tuning and explored grid search optimization, random search optimization, and Bayesian optimization techniques in detail. Hyperparameter tuning of machine learning models helped us to develop more generalized models with better performance.

In the next chapter, we will explore the process of deploying a machine learning model in the cloud.

Model Deployment

Learning Objectives

By the end of this chapter, you will be able to:

- Deploy an ML model as an API using the R plumber package

- Develop serverless APIs using AWS SageMaker, AWS Lambda, and AWS API Gateway

- Create infrastructure from scratch using AWS CloudFormation

- Deploy an ML model as an API using Docker containers

In this chapter, we will learn how to host, deploy, and manage models on AWS and Docker containers.

Introduction

In the previous chapter, we studied model improvements and explored the various techniques within hyperparameter tuning to improve model performance and develop the best model for a given use case. The next step is to deploy the machine learning model into production so that it can be easily consumed by or integrated into a large software product.

Most data science professionals assume that the process of developing machine learning models ends with hyperparameter tuning when we have the best model in place. In reality, the value and impact delivered by a machine learning model is limited (mostly futile) if it isn't deployed and (or) integrated with other software services/ products into a large tech ecosystem. Machine learning and software engineering are definitely two separate disciplines. Most data scientists have limited proficiency in understanding the software engineering ecosystem and, similarly, software engineers have a limited understanding of the machine learning field. Thus, in large enterprises where they build a product where a machine learning use case evolves into a major feature for a software product, there is a need for data scientists and software engineers to collaborate. However, collaboration between software engineers and data scientists in most cases is extremely challenging, as both find each other's fields highly overwhelming to comprehend.

Over the years, there has been a lot of effort invested in developing tools and resources by large corporations to aid data scientists to easily embrace a few software engineering components and vice versa. These tools have enabled easier collaboration between the two disciplines, accelerating the process of developing large-scale, enterprise-grade machine learning products.

In this chapter, we will learn about a few approaches to deploying machine learning models as web services that can easily integrate with other services in a large software ecosystem. We will also discuss the pros and cons of the different approaches and best practices for model deployment.

What is an API?

Before delving into the specifics of model deployment, we need to study an important software engineering topic that simplifies the entire process of model deployment, that is, an **Application Program Interface**, commonly referred to as an **API**. An API is a set of clearly defined methods for communication between various software components. Software development has been made significantly easier with the advent of APIs. If a developer, say, wanted to develop an iPhone app that would add some filters to an image, they need not write the entire code to capture the image from the phone's camera, save it to the library, and then apply their app-specific filters to it. Instead, they can use the phone camera API, which provides an easy way to communicate with the camera and only focus on writing code that would add filters to an image. In a nutshell, an API is the means for heterogeneous software components to communicate with each other.

In a large software product, there would be several components that are responsible for a specific task. These components interact with each other through a defined language that ensures the smooth communication of data, events, and alerts.

Here are some salient features of APIs:

* APIs help in **modularizing** software applications and enable the building of better products.

* APIs are commonly known by software engineers and are **language agnostic**. Thus, heterogenous applications developed in a completely different language or system can also effectively communicate with each other.

* Communication between services is also enabled using a common language, that is, **JavaScript Object Notation** (short for, **JSON**). However, there are other popular languages too, for example, XML.

* They also support HTTP, which means APIs are accessible through web browsers (such as Google Chrome or Mozilla Firefox) or a tool such as *Postman*.

> **Note**
>
> Postman is a free tool that offers easy-to-use services in the entire life cycle of an API, such as designing, debugging, testing, documenting, monitoring, and publishing. It is available for download on the Windows, Linux, and macOS platforms. You can learn more about Postman at https://www.getpostman.com/.

We are particularly interested in the development of RESTful APIs, that is, APIs that communicate over HTTP. RESTful APIs are also called **REST APIs** and have two main types of methods:

- **GET method**: This is used when we want to read data from a service.

- **POST method**: This is used when we want to send data to a service.

A few other methods are **head**, **put**, and **delete**.

Deploying machine learning models as (web service) REST APIs eases the process of integrating a service with other services. Software engineers are fond of using REST APIs and since the service is language-agnostic, we have a tremendous advantage in developing the model in the language of our choice. The software engineer could use Python, Java, Ruby, or one of many other languages for the development of other services, whereas we can develop the model in R, Python, Julia, and so on, and yet effectively and effortlessly integrate services into a large software product.

Now that we have a fair understanding of APIs, let's understand how we can deploy an ML model in R as an API.

Introduction to plumber

Plumber is an R package that helps in translating R functions into an HTTP API that can be invoked from other machines within a network, enabling communication between systems. By using R plumber, we will be able to achieve the advantages discussed, such as developing modularized, language agnostic, common communication language (JSON) based HTTP rest APIs that provide a defined path of communication between systems. Using plumber is extremely straightforward. With a few lines of code, we can convert our existing R functions into a web service that can be served as an endpoint.

In this chapter, we will extend the same model and use case we built in *Chapter 7, Model Improvements*, to classify whether a patient is diabetic using the `PimaIndiasDiabetes` dataset in the `mlbench` library. Later, we will extend the same use case to deploy the model as a web service using a Docker container and serverless applications.

Exercise 98: Developing an ML Model and Deploying It as a Web Service Using Plumber

In this exercise, we will develop a logistic regression model using three independent variables and deploy it as a REST API using Plumber. We will create a simple binary classification model and use the `plumber` package's services to wrap the model as an API by defining the HTTP get and post methods.

Perform the following steps to complete the exercise:

1. Create an R script named **model.R** using RStudio or Jupyter Notebook.

2. Load the required libraries and build a logistic regression model. Now, define the **get** methods that accept the input parameters and return the prediction as an outcome:

```
#----------Code listing for model.R----------------------------
library(mlbench)
data(PimaIndiansDiabetes)
df<-PimaIndiansDiabetes
```

> **Note**
>
> This data has been taken from the UCI Repository Of Machine Learning Databases from the following URLs:
>
> ftp://ftp.ics.uci.edu/pub/machine-learning-databases
>
> http://www.ics.uci.edu/~mlearn/MLRepository.html
>
> It was converted to the R format by Friedrich Leisch.

3. Train a logistic regression model with the **df** DataFrame object:

```
model<-glm(diabet-es~pregnant+glucose+pressure, data=df,
           family=binomial(link='logit'))
```

4. Define the API endpoint as a function with the additional **#' @get /** construct:

```
#' @get /predict_data
function(pregnant, glucose, pressure){
```

5. Within the function, convert the parameters into **numeric** values using the **as.numeric** command:

```
pregnant <- as.numeric(pregnant)
glucose <- as.numeric(glucose)
pressure <- as.numeric(pressure)
```

6. Then, create a DataFrame with the same column names as we did in the previous step:

```
sample <- data.frame(pregnant=pregnant,
                     glucose=glucose,
                     pressure=pressure)
```

7. Use the newly created **sample** DataFrame to make predictions on the trained model:

```
y_pred<-ifelse(predict(model,newdata=sample)>0.5,"yes","no")
```

8. Package the result as a **list** for the function's return call and complete/close the function definition with **}** parentheses:

```
list(Answer=y_pred)
}
```

The previous exercise demonstrates regular R model code with one additional construct. The model we developed is rather a simple one with only three independent variables and one dependent variable (unlike the eight independent variables we saw in *Chapter 7, Model Improvements*). We also created a function that will accept three input parameters, each representing one independent variable for the model. This function will be used as the endpoint when we deploy the model as a REST API. We added one additional construct just before the function (refer to the fourth step of the previous exercise):

```
#' @get /predict_data
```

This construct defines that the **predict_data** endpoint will be serving the GET requests. The function we defined for this endpoint accepts three parameters with no default values. Let's now install the **plumber** package and make a call using the web server.

The final complete **model.R** file should look like this:

```
#----------Code listing for model.R----------------------------
library(mlbench)
data(PimaIndiansDiabetes)
df<-PimaIndiansDiabetes

model<-glm(diabet-es~pregnant+glucose+pressure, data=df,
           family=binomial(link='logit'))

#' @get /predict_data
function(pregnant, glucose, pressure){
  pregnant <- as.numeric(pregnant)
```

```
        glucose <- as.numeric(glucose)
        pressure <- as.numeric(pressure)

        sample <- data.frame(pregnant=pregnant,
                            glucose=glucose,
                            pressure=pressure)

        y_pred<-ifelse(predict(model,newdata=sample)>0.5,"yes","no")

        list(Answer=y_pred)
    }
```

> **Note**
>
> You can also refer to the GitHub URL: https://github.com/TrainingByPackt/Applied-Supervised-Learning-with-R/blob/master/Lesson08/Docker/model.R.

9. Create another R script called **main.R**. Now, install the **plumber** package and load it into memory, and then deploy the R function using the **plumb** function, as illustrated here:

```
#-------main.R-----------------
install.packages("plumber")
library(plumber)
# (The previous code snippet is supposed to be save as 'model.R')
```

10. Use the following command to pass the R file to the **plumb** function:

```
pr <- plumber::plumb("model.R")
pr$run(port=8080,host='127.0.0.1')
```

11. After executing the previous code, the plumber library creates a web server within your **localhost** and responds to the requests. To test whether the endpoint functions we wrote are functioning in the expected way, we will invoke the endpoint from the browser.

> **Note**
>
> The following format is used to call the API endpoint:
>
> **[host]:[port]/endpoint_name?parameter1=Value1&Parameter2=Value2[&ParameterN=ValueN]**

The name of the **predict_data** endpoint corresponds to the definition in our code snippet:

```
#' @get /predict_data
```

The parameters are passed to the endpoint after the ? symbol, and multiple parameters are separated by the **&** symbol.

12. Since we deployed the endpoint to localhost, that is, **127.0.0.1** on the **8080** port, we will have the following API definition for the endpoint. Invoke the API using the browser:

```
http://127.0.0.1:8080/predict_data?pregnant=1&glucose=3&pressure=1
```

13. Execute the previous API definition, which will return the following prediction value:

```
{"Answer":["no"]}
```

To test the APIs, we can use a better tool, such as Postman, instead of the browser. Postman (https://www.getpostman.com/) is currently one of the most popular tools used in API testing. It is available for free on the Windows, Mac, and Linux platforms. Using Postman is relatively simple and doesn't include any new learning.

> **Note**
>
> In case you would like to explore additional details about Postman, you can explore the learning resources provided at https://learning.getpostman.com/docs/postman/launching_postman/installation_and_updates/.

14. After you download and install Postman for your system, you can test the API endpoint by pasting it in the input window, as shown in the following screenshot:

Figure 8.1: Plumber UI

We can execute the API by clicking on the **Send** button, and the results are displayed in the highlighted area of the previous screenshot. Observing the output from Postman, we can see that our machine learning model has been deployed successfully as an API endpoint.

Challenges in Deploying Models with plumber

We can see that deploying the model as an API using plumber is simple and can be done easily with a few additional lines of code. The `plumber` package provides additional features that we have not explored in this exercise. Some important topics that might be interesting to explore are as follows:

- **Filters**: Filters can be used to define a *pipeline* with a flow of incoming requests. This functionality helps to further modularize the deployment logic and workflow. You can read more at https://www.rplumber.io/docs/routing-and-input. html#filters.

- **Error handling**: With larger applications, the code base and the complexity of applications increase exponentially. It becomes increasingly important to add exception handlers and ease the process of debugging applications. You can read more about it at https://www.rplumber.io/docs/rendering-and-output. html#error-handling.

These methods have a major drawback. While it is relatively easy to set up an endpoint in a single host, there might be issues faced when deploying the same solution on a different system. These issues might arise due to the difference in the system architecture, software version, operating system, and so on. To mitigate the conflicts that you may face when deploying the endpoint, one technique is to make the process environment-agnostic, that is, a solution developed in one host system can be deployed without any issues in any other host with a different architecture, platform, or operating system. This can be achieved using **Docker containers** along with plumber for deployment instead of directly using plumber.

A Brief History of the Pre-Docker Era

Before diving deep into the Docker tool, let's understand some background and history.

The challenge of deploying an application in an environment-agnostic framework was achieved earlier using virtualization, that is, the entire application, dependencies, libraries, necessary frameworks, and the operating system itself was virtualized and packaged as a solution that could be deployed on a host. Multiple virtual environments could run on an infrastructure (called a **hypervisor**), and applications became environment-agnostic. However, this approach has a major trade-off. Packaging the entire operating system into the **virtual machine (VM)** of an application made the package heavy and often resulted in wasting memory and computing resources.

A more intuitive approach to this problem was to exclude the operating system from the package and only include the application-related libraries and dependencies. Additionally, enable a mechanism such that the package becomes infrastructure-agnostic, keeping the app lightweight. This is when Docker was introduced. The following visual sheds light on the high-level view of how Docker was improvised to solve problems previously solved by virtual machines:

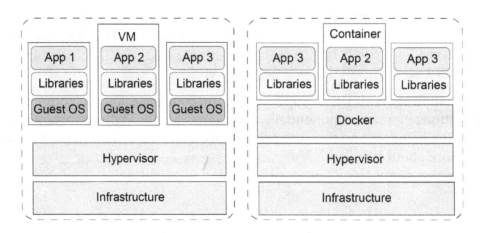

Figure 8.2: The architectural difference between a virtual machine and a Docker container

Let's now understand Docker containers in more detail.

Docker

Docker is a simple tool that eases the process of developing, deploying, and executing software applications using containers. A **container** is analogous to a shipping industry container, and allows a developer to package an entire application with its dependencies, and ship it all out as one package. Once built on a system, the package will work on any other system as well, regardless of the differences in the infrastructure.

With Docker, we can create a single document (called a **Dockerfile**) that defines a simplified step for setting up the required environment for the application. The Dockerfile is then used to build a **Docker image**. A container is an instance of a Docker image. For the same application, we might sometimes have multiple containers that will help in load balancing for high-traffic applications.

Deploying the ML Model Using Docker and plumber

We will leverage the same plumber application with Docker for environment- and infrastructure-agnostic deployment. First, we will need to download and install Docker on our system. It's free and easy. Create an account and download Docker for your system from https://www.docker.com/get-started. Once installed, you can verify whether Docker is running by executing the **docker** command in the terminal or Windows PowerShell.

Exercise 99: Create a Docker Container for the R plumber Application

In this exercise, we will extend the previously created plumber application as a Docker container. In order to develop environment-agnostic models that can be deployed to any production system without any issues, we can deploy a plumber app using Docker containers. These containers can then be deployed on any other machine that supports Docker Engine.

Perform the following steps to complete the exercise:

1. Define a Dockerfile, as illustrated here:

   ```
   FROM rocker/r-ver:3.5.0
   ```

2. Now, install the libraries for the **plumber** package using the following command:

   ```
   RUN apt-get update -qq && apt-get install -y  libssl-dev  libcurl4-gnutls-dev
   ```

3. Next, install the **plumber** package, as shown:

    ```
    RUN R -e "install.packages(c('plumber','mlbench'))"
    ```

4. Now, use the following command to copy all files from the current directory into the current folder for the container. This will copy our **model.R** and **plumber.R** file into a container:

    ```
    COPY / /
    ```

5. Next, define a port to be exposed where the container will be deployed:

    ```
    EXPOSE 8080
    ```

6. Define the first script to run when the container starts after the build:

    ```
    ENTRYPOINT ["Rscript", "main.R"]
    ```

We now have three files in our project folder, as shown in the following diagram. Note that the Dockerfile is a simple text file with no extensions. On running a **build** command from the terminal within this folder, **Docker Engine** searches for the Dockerfile and prepares the environment based on the instructions provided within the document:

Dockerfile   main.R   model.R

Figure 8.3: Project files

The final Dockerfile with all the commands, as defined in the previous steps, will look like this:

```
FROM rocker/r-ver:3.5.0

RUN apt-get update -qq && apt-get install -y  libssl-dev  libcurl4-gnutls-
dev

RUN R -e "install.packages(c('plumber','mlbench'))"

COPY / /

EXPOSE 8080

ENTRYPOINT ["Rscript", "main.R"]
```

7. We can now build the Docker image from the Dockerfile using the **docker build** command, as follows:

```
docker build -t r_ml_demo .
```

The . after the **r_ml_demo** indicates that the Dockerfile is present in the current folder. The build process takes a while as it creates the container image with all the necessary dependencies. Once the image is built, we can run the Docker image using the following command by mapping the machine's **8080** port to the container's published **8080** port.

8. Run the Docker image using the following command:

```
docker run --rm -p 8080:8080 r_ml_demo
```

> **Note**
>
> You can refer to the complete code from GitHub at https://github.com/ TrainingByPackt/Applied-Supervised-Learning-with-R/tree/master/Lesson08/ Docker.

The container can be tested again in the same way we tested our plumber application using Postman, and we will get exactly the same result. We can, therefore, deploy an R application using plumber and Docker on any other system, regardless of the operating system and missing libraries.

> **Note**
>
> Docker cannot be installed on Windows Home edition. Only Windows Pro editions support Hypervisor.

Disadvantages of Using plumber to Deploy R Models

While this process comes with a few advantages of easy and fast implementation, it also comes with some disadvantages. The major disadvantage of plumber is scaling the application endpoint for large complex use cases. The scale here refers to the number of times the endpoint is invoked as well as the amount of data that can be invoked through the endpoint.

One of the major drawbacks of using plumber is that it doesn't directly support passing JSON objects or arrays or lists to the endpoint. This becomes a bottleneck when we are dealing with bigger models with more than 20 independent variables. The previous use case, in *Exercise 2, Create a Docker Container for the R Plumber Application*, was a fairly small and lightweight model with three independent variables. Therefore, the API definition was short and sweet. However, as the number of parameters increases (which is definitely bound to happen for real production models), plumber model endpoint definitions will not be the best ones to use. Also, the plumber framework is not ideal for large complex software use cases. The small community around the framework, lack of proper documentation, and limited support makes it a risky choice for deploying a model into a large scale machine learning product or service.

Let's take a look at leveraging cloud services for deploying R ML models.

Amazon Web Services

Amazon Web Services (**AWS**) is the leading provider of cloud services. With the advent of the cloud, the tech industry has seen a dramatic shift in the process of building large-scale enterprise applications leveraging cloud services rather than self-hosted services. Other prominent players in the cloud services market are Microsoft, Google, and IBM. While all leading cloud providers have an exhaustive suite of services to build all kinds of software applications, we will focus only on AWS for the scope of this chapter. You are highly encouraged to explore alternative services for similar use cases from other cloud providers (not restricted to Google or Microsoft).

AWS has a ton of services readily available that can be used to make large, complex enterprise applications of any scale with no upfront commitments. You pay as you go, and there are also a large number of services that you can explore and test for free for one year (with certain limits). For the scope of the set of experiments we will perform in the upcoming exercises, the free tier should suffice. In case you do not already have an AWS account, create one at https://aws.amazon.com/free/activate-your-free-tier-account/.

You will need a valid credit/debit card for the signup process. We will only leverage the free tier service from AWS for the exercises.

There are several approaches that we could take to deploy a machine learning model using cloud services. Some may be well-suited for small applications, some for medium-sized and moderately complex applications, and others for large and very complex applications. We will explore the approach that has the least amount of software engineering yet provides effective flexibility and can easily scale into large-scale applications while easily integrating into complex applications.

The use of an API and delivering the machine learning model as an API makes the entire process of integrating the service into other applications fairly straightforward.

Introducing AWS SageMaker

Amazon SageMaker is a cloud service that provides developers and data scientists with a platform to build, train, and deploy machine learning models quickly. It is an extremely effective service in aiding data scientists with limited development knowledge to deploy highly scalable ML models while abstracting the entire complexities of the infrastructure and underlying services.

SageMaker automates the entire process of deploying a model as an API with the defined resources and creates an *endpoint* that can be used for inferencing within the other AWS services. To enable the endpoint to be inferenced by other external applications, we would need to orchestrate the flow of requests using two other AWS services, called **AWS API Gateway** and **AWS Lambda**. We will explore these new services later in the chapter.

Now, let's begin deploying our model using AWS SageMaker.

Deploying an ML Model Endpoint Using SageMaker

SageMaker, by default, doesn't provide a direct way to create R models, but there is an easy alternative provided by Amazon. AWS provides the functionality of **Infrastructure as Code** with **AWS CloudFormation**, that is, a service where we can codify the entire flow of provisioning and the setup of infrastructure resources for a project. With CloudFormation templates, we can automate the process of provisioning a tech stack as per our needs and reuse it any number of times. Amazon has provided a lucid and elaborate guide to get started with R notebooks on SageMaker using the CloudFormation template.

To find out more, you can refer to the guide at https://aws.amazon.com/blogs/machine-learning/using-r-with-amazon-sagemaker/ for a detailed understanding of the process.

Exercise 100: Deploy the ML Model as a SageMaker Endpoint

In this exercise, we will deploy an ML model as a SageMaker endpoint.

Perform the following steps to complete the exercise:

1. Log in to your AWS account and launch the CloudFormation script to create an R notebook.

2. Now, access the CloudFormation template from https://amzn.to/2ZzUM28 to create the R Notebook on SageMaker.

   Next, we will create and launch the stack in AWS using the previous CloudFormation template.

3. Click on the template; it directly navigates you to the CloudFormation service, as shown in the following screenshot. The cloud formation template (which is a YAML file) is hosted in a public S3 bucket and has already been added to the input box under **Specify an Amazon S3 template URL**. Click on the **Next** button and navigate to the **Details** page:

Figure 8.4: CloudFormation—Create Stack page

4. On the next page, specify the SSH key pair that you will use to log in to the EC2 instance. This is a secure way to access the cloud instance or virtual machine that we provision in the cloud. If you do not have a key already created for your account, you can create one using the steps provided on the Amazon website: https://docs.aws.amazon.com/AWSEC2/latest/UserGuide/ec2-key-pairs.html#having-ec2-create-your-key-pair.

5. Once the key pair is created or if you already have a pair, it will appear in the dropdown in the highlighted box, as shown in the following screenshot. Select your key pair and click on the **Next** button:

Specify Details

Specify a stack name and parameter values. You can use or change the default parameter values, which are defined in the AWS CloudFormation template. Learn more.

Stack name   rstudio-sagemaker

Parameters

KeyName   Search ▼   *Select a SSH key pair to login into the instance*

SSH key pair to use for instance login

Cancel   Previous   Next

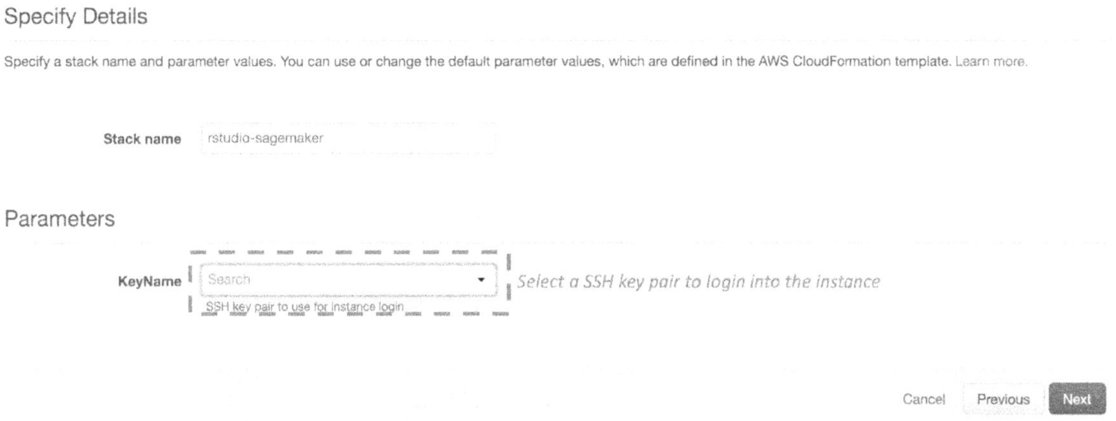

Figure 8.5: Creating a key pair

6. On the next **Option** page, we can directly click on the **Next** button and navigate to the next page.

7. Lastly, on the review page, select the **I acknowledge that AWS CloudFormation might create IAM resources with custom names** checkbox and click on the **Next** button.

8. The process will create the stack (it might take a while to show on the screen—refresh the screen after 1-2 minutes). Once created, you will see the stack ready under CloudFormation, as shown in the following screenshot. The output tabs will have the SSH command to be used to log in; copy the value in the highlighted section and run the command in a terminal or Command Prompt:

Figure 8.6: Stacks—SSH key

9. On running the SSH command from the terminal, it forwards port **8787** to your computer while connecting to the new instance. Once connected, open a browser window and type **https://127.0.0.1:8787** in the address bar to open the RStudio login page. The default username and password is set to **rstudio**. Enter the username and password and click on the **Sign In** button:

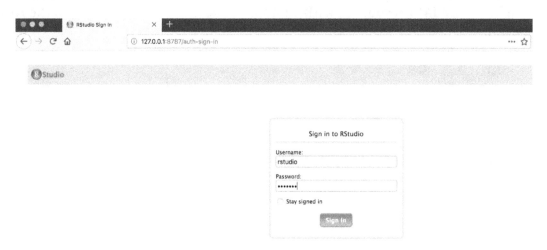

Figure 8.7: RStudio—Sign In page

10. Log in to RStudio and create a new R script with any name, say **Sagemaker.R**, load the necessary libraries, and get the SageMaker session ready:

```
library(reticulate)
library(readr)
```

11. Start the SageMaker session and define the default bucket as well as the role to be used for the session:

```
sagemaker <- import('sagemaker')
session <- sagemaker$Session()
bucket <- session$default_bucket()
role_arn <- session$expand_role('sagemaker-service-role')
```

12. Install the **mlbench** package and load the data for our use case. In the following command, we'll first set the **seed** for reproducibility:

```
set.seed(2019)

install.packages("mlbench")
library(mlbench)
data(PimaIndiansDiabetes)

df<- PimaIndiansDiabetes
```

13. To explore SageMaker's automated hyperparameter tuning, we will be developing an XGBoost model instead of a logistic regression model on the same use case as the previous one. Therefore, we need the target variable and all the independent variables in a numeric type. Also, SageMaker expects the data in a form where the first column is the target variable:

```
df$diabetes <- ifelse(df$diabetes == "yes",1,0)
```

14. Place the target variable as the first column in the dataset:

```
df<- df[,c(9,1:8)]
```

15. Create 70% train and 30% test datasets using the following command:

```
train_index <- sample(seq_len(nrow(df)),floor(0.7 * nrow(df)))
train <- df[train_index,]
test <- df[-train_index,]
```

16. Write the train and test data created from the **df** DataFrame into memory and upload the CSV files into an S3 bucket on AWS. The session has been defined with a default bucket, therefore, we can directly use the **upload_data** command with the path and the required constructs to upload the dataset on our default S3 bucket:

```
write_csv(train, 'diabetes_train.csv', col_names = FALSE)
write_csv(test, 'diabetes_test.csv', col_names = FALSE)

s3_train <- session$upload_data(path = 'diabetes_train.csv',
                                bucket = bucket,
                                key_prefix = 'data')
s3_test <- session$upload_data(path = 'diabetes_test.csv',
                               bucket = bucket,
                               key_prefix = 'data')
```

17. Define the train and test dataset (validation data) for the SageMaker session:

```
s3_train_input <- sagemaker$s3_input(s3_data = s3_train,
                                     content_type = 'csv')
s3_test_input <- sagemaker$s3_input(s3_data = s3_test,
                                    content_type = 'csv')
```

SageMaker provides AWS optimized pre-configured containers that can be leveraged directly for model training. We would need to choose a container base from the same region that our resources are hosted in. In this case, it is **us-east-1**.

18. Define the container for the estimator and the output folder in S3:

```
containers <- list('us-west-2' =
'433757028032.dkr.ecr.us-west-2.amazonaws.com/xgboost:latest',
                   'us-east-1' =
'811284229777.dkr.ecr.us-east-1.amazonaws.com/xgboost:latest',
                   'us-east-2' =
'825641698319.dkr.ecr.us-east-2.amazonaws.com/xgboost:latest',
                   'eu-west-1' =
'685385470294.dkr.ecr.eu-west-1.amazonaws.com/xgboost:latest')
```

19. Select the container for the estimator using the following command:

```
container <- containers[session$boto_region_name][[1]]
```

20. Define the output folder as illustrated here:

```
s3_output <- paste0('s3://', bucket, '/output')
```

21. Define the SageMaker estimator, the job, and the input data. Here, we would need to provide the type of instance that we would like to use for the model training process, and we will choose `ml.m5.large`:

```
estimator <- sagemaker$estimator$Estimator(image_name = container,
                                            role = role_arn,
                                            train_instance_count = 1L,
                                            train_instance_type = 'ml.
m5.large',
                                            train_volume_size = 30L,
                                            train_max_run = 3600L,
                                            input_mode = 'File',
                                            output_path = s3_output,
                                            output_kms_key = NULL,
                                            base_job_name = NULL,
                                            sagemaker_session = NULL)
```

22. Set the hyperparameters of interest for the model and define the training and validation datasets for the model as a list:

```
estimator$set_hyperparameters(num_round = 100L)
job_name <- paste('sagemaker-train-xgboost', format(Sys.time(), '%H-%M-
%S'),
                  sep = '-')

input_data <- list('train' = s3_train_input,
                   'validation' = s3_test_input)
```

> **Note**
>
> You can read more about the different types of instances that can be used for the purpose of model training at https://aws.amazon.com/sagemaker/pricing/instance-types/.

23. Train/fit the model we defined. The model training process will take a while (~10-12 minutes). In the background, SageMaker will provision an instance that was defined by us in the model definition, trigger the necessary background operations to orchestrate the training process, and finally, train the model:

```
estimator$fit(inputs = input_data, job_name = job_name)
```

24. Deploy the train model as an endpoint. We will have to, again, provide the type of instance we would want SageMaker to provision for the model inference. Since this is just a sample model, we can choose the instance with the lowest configuration. This process will also take some time, as SageMaker will orchestrate a series of services in the background to deploy the model as an endpoint:

```
model_endpoint <- estimator$deploy(initial_instance_count = 1L,
                                   instance_type = 'ml.t2.medium')

model_endpoint$content_type <- 'text/csv'
model_endpoint$serializer <- sagemaker$predictor$csv_serializer
```

After the model endpoint is created, we can test it by invoking it with the right form of test data. Since we are saving the test data as CSV files, we will pass comma-separated text to be serialized into JSON format. Therefore, we specify **text/csv** and **csv_serializer** for the endpoint. Let's prepare a sample test data feed for a quick test.

25. First, make a copy of the test dataset using the following command:

```
one_test <- test
```

26. Next, delete the target variable:

```
one_test$diabetes<-NULL
```

27. Create a single test sample using the following command:

```
test_sample <- as.matrix(one_test[7, ])
```

28. Now, delete the column names:

```
dimnames(test_sample)[[2]] <- NULL
```

29. Make a prediction using the model endpoint on the sample data that we created in the previous step. Invoke the SageMaker endpoint and pass the test data:

```
predictions <- model_endpoint$predict(test_sample)
```

30. Now, print the result using the **print** command:

```
print(ifelse(predictions>0.5,"yes",'no'))
```

The output is as follows:

```
1] "no"
```

This output helps us to understand that the model has been correctly deployed and is functioning as expected. We can check whether the endpoint is created by navigating to the SageMaker service in the AWS account and opening the *Endpoint* section from the right-hand-side sidebar:

Figure 8.8: Endpoint page

This endpoint can be used directly by other services within AWS to invoke and get predictions. The only requirement is that the input data should be provided as expected. To enable our model endpoint to be accessible by other services outside AWS, we would need to orchestrate the API request using AWS API Gateway and AWS Lambda.

> **Note**
>
> You can access the complete code file on GitHub at https://github.com/TrainingByPackt/Applied-Supervised-Learning-with-R/blob/master/Lesson08/RStudio_SageMaker.R.

Now, let's study these services a bit before delving into the solution.

What is Amazon Lambda?

AWS Lambda is an event-driven, serverless computing platform provided by Amazon as a part of Amazon Web Services. It is a computing service that runs code in response to events and automatically manages the computing resources required by that code. The service enables us to develop serverless applications. The term serverless indicates that we do not actually need to manage and provision the infrastructure resources; instead, they are managed by the cloud service provider, and we only pay for what we use, say, pay per event or execution. AWS Lambda can be configured to execute a defined function in response to a specific event, say, when someone uploads a new file to a defined S3 bucket or invokes another function or another service in AWS.

What is Amazon API Gateway?

Amazon API Gateway is a fully managed service that makes it easy for developers to create, publish, maintain, monitor, and secure APIs at any scale. With this service, we can develop REST as well as WebSocket APIs that act as a *front door* for applications to access data, business logic, or functionality from other backend services, while protecting the backend services within the private network. These backend services could be any applications that are running on AWS.

The overall flow of our service can be represented as in the following diagram:

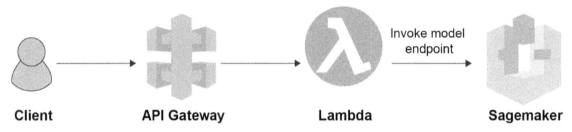

| Client | API Gateway | Lambda | Invoke model endpoint | Sagemaker |

Figure 8.9: Workflow of API Gateway, AWS Lambda, and SageMaker

The client (say, a web browser), calls an Amazon API Gateway's defined action and passes the appropriate parameter values. API Gateway passes the request to AWS Lambda, while it also seals the backend so that AWS Lambda stays and executes in a protected private network.

In our case, we will use Lambda to help us tailor the data received from API Gateway into an appropriate form that can be consumed by the SageMaker endpoint. This is necessary because there is a difference between the structure of data passed through a REST API and that of what SageMaker expects. The SageMaker model performs the prediction and returns the predicted value to AWS Lambda. The Lambda function parses the returned value and sends it back to API Gateway, after which API Gateway responds to the client with the result. This entire flow is orchestrated without us actually provisioning any infrastructure; it is entirely managed by AWS.

> **Note**
>
> This workflow is explained in further detail in a blog post by Amazon. You can read more at https://aws.amazon.com/blogs/machine-learning/call-an-amazon-sagemaker-model-endpoint-using-amazon-api-gateway-and-aws-lambda/.

There is one additional challenge that we will need to tackle. As of today, AWS Lambda doesn't support R for defining functions. It supports Python, Java, Go, and a few others, but R is not on the list as of now. The lambda function will be in charge of transforming the data passed by the API into the required form. We will leverage Python scripts for this task. In the future, we can expect R to be supported by AWS Lambda.

Now that we have the required context about the necessary services, let's deploy our model on a serverless application.

Building Serverless ML Applications

Serverless computing is the new paradigm within cloud computing. It allows us to build and run applications and services without thinking about servers. In reality, the application we build still runs on a cloud server, but the entire process for server management is done by the cloud service provider, such as AWS. By leveraging the serverless platform, we can build and deploy robust, large-scale, complex applications by only focusing on our application code instead of worrying about provisioning, configuring, and managing servers.

We have explored some important components of the AWS serverless platform such as AWS Lambda in this chapter, and we can now leverage these solutions to build a machine learning application where we can only focus on the core ML code and forget about provisioning infrastructure and scaling applications.

Exercise 101: Building a Serverless Application Using API Gateway, AWS Lambda, and SageMaker

In this exercise, we will build a machine learning model using AWS SageMaker and deploy it as an endpoint (using automated SageMaker functions). To enable the model endpoint to be invoked by any service (within or outside AWS) we define an AWS Lambda function and expose the endpoint to public networks through API Gateway.

The aim of this exercise is to create a serverless application that will use the SageMaker model endpoint we created in the previous exercise.

Perform the following steps:

1. Create an IAM role in AWS that will allow Lambda to execute endpoints from the SageMaker service. From the AWS dashboard, search for **IAM**, and click on the **Roles** option on the IAM page:

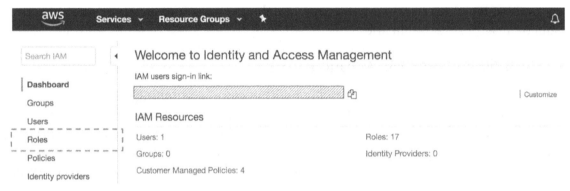

Figure 8.10: Creating IAM roles

2. Once the **Roles** page loads, click on the **Create role** option.

3. On the **Create role** page, select **AWS Service** as the type of trusted entity and **Lambda** as the service that will use this role. Click on the **Next: Permissions** button to proceed:

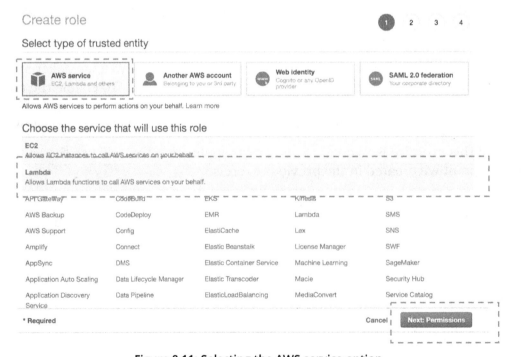

Figure 8.11: Selecting the AWS service option

4. On the **Permissions** page, filter policies using the **sagemaker** keyword, select the **AmazonSageMakerFullAccess** policy, and click on the **Next: Tags** option:

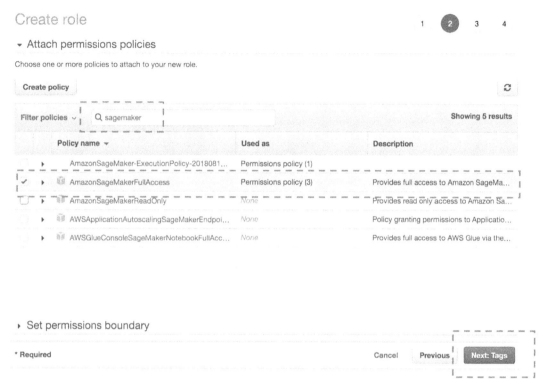

Figure 8.12: The Create role screen

5. On the **Tags** page, you can directly click on **Next** and proceed to the final page to name the **Role**.

6. Now, on the final page, add a suitable name (say, `lambda_sagemaker_execution`) and click on **Create role**. The role will be created for us to use:

Figure 8.13: Review page—creating role

7. In the AWS console, search for AWS Lambda and click on the **Create function** button. The create function page will have some inputs that need to be defined.

8. Select the **Author from scratch** option and give a name to the function (say, `lambda_sagemaker_connection`).

9. Next, select **Python 3.6** from the **Runtime** dropdown. For the **Execution role**, select the **Use an existing role** option and then select the role we created in the previous step, that is, `lambda_sagemaker_execution`. Click on the **Create function** button:

Figure 8.14: Creating a function form

10. Define a Python function that will accept the input request from the API, parse the payload, and invoke the SageMaker endpoint:

```
import os, io, boto3, json, csv

# grab environment variables
ENDPOINT_NAME = os.environ['ENDPOINT_NAME']
runtime= boto3.client('runtime.sagemaker')
```

> **Note**
>
> The endpoint name will be available in the SageMaker page under the endpoint section.

11. We will additionally define the environment variable for the function that will store the SageMaker endpoint:

```
def lambda_handler(event, context):
    print("Received event: " + json.dumps(event, indent=2))

    #Load JSON data from API call
    data = json.loads(json.dumps(event))
    payload = data['data']
    print(payload)

    #Invoke Sagemaker endpoint and pass Payload
    response = runtime.invoke_endpoint(EndpointName=ENDPOINT_NAME,
                                       ContentType='text/csv',
                                       Body=bytes(str(payload),'utf'))

    result = json.loads(response['Body'].read().decode())
    predicted_label = 'yes' if result >0.5 else 'no'
    return predicted_label
```

> **Note**
>
> You can refer to the complete code on GitHub at https://github.com/TrainingByPackt/Applied-Supervised-Learning-with-R/blob/master/Lesson08/Amazon_Lambda_Function.py.

12. Click on **Save**, and the Amazon Lambda function is ready. Now, create an API using Amazon API Gateway by searching for `API Gateway` in the AWS console, and create a new API function by selecting the following highlighted options in the screenshot. Give the API a suitable name, say, `api_lambda_connect`:

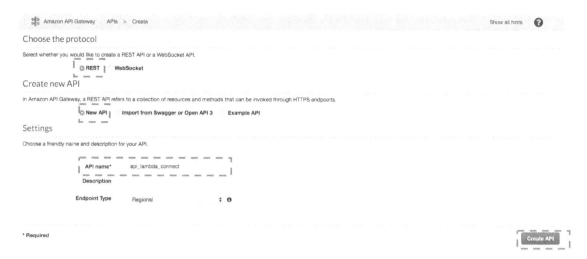

Figure 8.15: Amazon API Gateway

13. From the **Actions** dropdown, select **Create Resource**, add a suitable resource name, and then click on the **Create Resource** button:

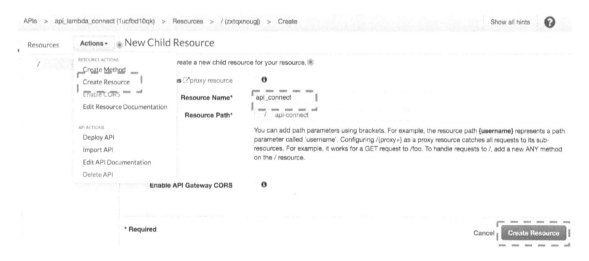

Figure 8.16: Creating a new child resource

14. Again, from the **Actions** dropdown, select **Create Method** and select the method type as **POST**.

15. Select the **Integration Type** as **Lambda Function** and mention the **Lambda Function** name in the input label, as shown in the following screenshot. Next, click on the **Save** button:

Figure 8.17: Creating a Lambda function

16. Next, select **Deploy API** from the **Actions** dropdown. A small window will open asking for details about the deployment stage to be used. Select **New Stage** as the deployment stage, provide a suitable name, (say, **test**) and click on the **Deploy** option. The API will now be deployed and will be ready to use.

17. Once the API is deployed, we can find the URL of the API to be invoked by navigating to the **test** deployment stage we created and clicking on the innermost member of the tree under the **test** deployment stage. Click on the **Save Changes** button and copy the URL to test:

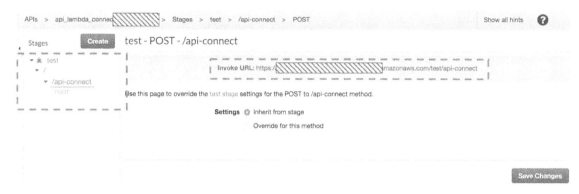

Figure 8.18: API-Connect stage

> **Note**
>
> The structure of the URL will be `https://****amazonaws.com/[deployment-stage]/[resource-name]/`.

18. Call the API from Postman. Open Postman, select a **POST** call, and paste the URL we copied from the API Gateway stage. Then, click on **Body** and add raw data, that is, the JSON formatted test data, in the body, as shown in the following screenshot:

Figure 8.19: Calling the API via Postman

19. Click on the **Send** button to invoke the API with the provided raw data. The result is showcased in the lower window.

We received a prediction of "no," which indicates that the model has been successfully deployed as a serverless application. We can now invoke the API from anywhere in the world in a browser or Postman and get predictions for the model. This API call be integrated with other services in a larger product and can be scaled as and when there is more demand.

Deleting All Cloud Resources to Stop Billing

All the resources we have provisioned will need to be deleted/terminated to ensure that they are no longer billed. The following steps will need to be performed to ensure that all resources created in the book of the exercise are deleted:

1. Log in to CloudFormation and click on **Delete** stack (the one we provisioned for RStudio).

2. Log in to SageMaker, open Endpoints from the right-hand-side sidebar, check the endpoint we created for the exercise, and delete it.

3. Log in to AWS Lambda and delete the Lambda function we created for the exercise.

4. Log in to AWS API Gateway and delete the API we created for the exercise.

Further notes on AWS SageMaker

We leveraged the existing containers of the algorithm provided by Amazon to train the model. This step was followed to keep things simple. We can bring our own custom trained algorithms to SageMaker and leverage the platform to deploy the model as a service. SageMaker takes care of the entire process of orchestrating the background resources to provision instances, configure model artefacts, and build the endpoint. We would, however, need to provide the data and model artifacts in a specific format for SageMaker to deploy it.

> **Note**
>
> Additional details on the process of building custom models can be found at https://docs.aws.amazon.com/sagemaker/latest/dg/build-model.html.

Activity 13: Deploy an R Model Using plumber

In this activity, we will develop a regression model in R and deploy it as an API endpoint using plumber. We will be using another use case for supervised learning in R, and we will build a regression model using a different dataset, that is, **Boston Housing**. The dataset is available within R's Mlbench library, which we already installed and provides information on the median price of a house within Boston when given a number of house attributes.

We will write two R scripts: `model.r` to house the regression model as well as the prediction function and `plumber.R` to house the necessary functions to deploy the model as an API endpoint.

> **Note**
>
> Additional details about the dataset can be explored at https://www.rdocumentation.org/packages/mlbench/versions/2.1-1/topics/BostonHousing.

Perform the following steps:

1. Create a `model.r` script, which will load the required libraries, data, and fit a regression model and the necessary functions to make predictions on unseen data.

2. Load the `mlbench` library, which has the data for this activity.

3. Load the `BostonHousing` data into a DataFrame, `df`.

4. Create a train dataset using the first `400` rows of `df` and test with the remaining.

5. Fit a logistic regression model using the `lm` function with the dependent variable as `medv` (median value) and `10` independent variables, such as, `crim`, `zn`, `indus`, `chas`, `nox`, `rm`, `age`, `dis`, `rad`, and `tax`.

6. Define a model endpoint as `predict_data`; this will be used as the API endpoint for plumber.

7. Within the function, convert the parameters to `numeric` and **factor** (since the API call will pass them as a string only).

8. Wrap the 10 independent features for the model as a DataFrame named `sample`, with the same name for the columns.

9. Pass the **sample** DataFrame to the predict function with the model (created in step 4), and return the predictions.

10. Load the **plumber** library.

11. Create a plumber object using the **plumb** function and pass the **model.r** file (created in part 1).

12. Run the plumber object by passing the hostname as **localhost** or **127.0.0.1** and a port, say **8080**.

13. Test the deployed model using the browser or Postman and invoke the API.

    API invocation:

    http://127.0.0.1:8080/predict_data?crim=0.01&zn=18&indus=2.3&chas= 0&nox=0.5&rm=6&age=65&dis=4&rad=1&tax=242

    The final output is as follows:

    ```
    {"Answer":[22.5813]}Note
    ```

    > **Note**
    >
    > The solution for this activity can be found on page 463.

Summary

In this chapter, we studied how to deploy our machine learning models with traditional server-based deployment strategies using R's plumber, and enhanced approaches using plumber for R with Docker containers. We then studied how serverless applications can be built using cloud services and how we can easily scale applications as needed with minimal code.

We explored various web services, such as Amazon Lambda, Amazon SageMaker, and Amazon API Gateway, and studied how services can be orchestrated to deploy our machine learning model as a serverless application.

In the next chapter, we will work on a capstone project by taking up one of the latest research papers based on a real-world problem and reproducing the result.

Capstone Project - Based on Research Papers

Learning Objectives

By the end of this chapter, you will be able to:

- Apply end-to-end machine learning workflow on a problem using mlr and OpenML, which involves identifying research articles.

- Train machine learning model and, subsequently, predict and evaluate using the model on a test dataset.

- Perform resampling on the dataset.

- Design experiments for building various models.

- Build benchmarks for choosing the best model.

In this chapter, we will take up the latest research paper based on a real-world problem and will reproduce the result.

Introduction

In this final chapter, we will focus on working on a research-based capstone project. The ideas from all the previous chapters such as designing the problem using the SCQ framework, identifying the source of data, preprocessing the dataset, training a machine learning model, evaluating a model, applying resampling techniques, and many other concepts will be used. Additionally, this chapter will also focus on benchmarking models, designing experiments in machine learning, collaborating in open source platforms, and making a research work reproducible for the benefits of the larger community.

The abundance of online resources, computation power, and out-of-the-box toolkit solutions has made the entry barrier in becoming a machine learning professional minimum. Today, we have plenty of quickstart algorithms provided as a function in a package in programming languages such as R and Python, or even as a drag and drop in platforms such as Google Cloud AutoML or Microsoft Azure Machine Learning Studio. However, what is often missing in many such quick start Hello World models is the keen focus on problem solving and the ability to go beyond the available tools.

Apart from the extravagant toolkits, there exists a world of research-oriented work produced by many leading practitioners from academia and industry. The importance of such research work is immense when it comes to producing breakthrough and high-quality outcomes. However, the accessibility of such research work is limited and hence prevents the widespread adoption among machine learning practitioners. Another reason why one does not pursue research-based work is because of the lack of reproducibility (mostly because of code not being available in public domain, unclear research finding, or poor quality of the research work) and jargon-filled theory (many written in mathematical language) found in research articles or papers.

This chapter is dedicated to such research work, which often goes unnoticed by many learners who endeavor into machine learning but limit themselves to using only specific tools and packages advocated in blogs or online books. We will focus on two significant research works, which, fortunately, also found a place in R packages. The next section will introduce the work and set the flow of the rest of this chapter.

Exploring Research Work

In this chapter, we will explore the two most significant research works that eventually also became an open source offering. The emphasis in this chapter is given onto a top-down approach, where we will start from the origin of excellent research work and see how it became a mainstream toolkit for everyone to use. While emphasizing on research work, we would like to highlight that a lot of research work does not find its place in the standard toolkit available in the market, but some gems could be found if one works slightly harder.

We recommend following the fantastic effort put by the creators of https:// paperswithcode.com. The **Papers With Code** team has created a free and open resource platform with machine learning papers, code, and evaluation tables with the help from the community and powered by automation. They have already automated the linking of code to papers, and they are now working on automating the extraction of evaluation metrics from papers. The work is commendable because it will bring the best research work to stand out amid the noise and abundance.

The following table will highlight five cases of research work, which we found through the Papers With Code website. Throughout this book, you would have seen a lot of R code using various packages for each stage of the machine learning workflow. The work done by the researchers of mlr and OpenML is now packaged in R, and in particular, OpenML is a complete platform. We will learn how to leverage the mlr and OpenML platforms to produce the best machine learning model, beyond just the quickstart **Hello World** examples. For reference, review the following table:

S.No.	Title	Authors	Published In	Code Link
1	Learning multi-label scene classification	Matthew R. Boutella, Jiebo Luob, Xipeng Shena, Christopher M. Brown	Pattern Recognition 37 (2004) 1757 – 1771	https://figshare.com/articles/Multilabel_classification_with_R_package_mlr/3384802/5
2	MLR: Machine Learning in R	Philipp Probst, Quay Au, Giuseppe Casalicchio, Clemens Stachl, and Bernd Bischl	Journal of Machine Learning Research 17 (2016) 1-5	https://github.com/mlr-org/mlr
3	Multilabel Classification with R Package MLR	Philipp Probst, Quay Au, Giuseppe Casalicchio, Clemens Stachl, and Bernd Bischl	The R Journal 9/1 (2017) 352-369	https://github.com/mlr-org/mlr

Figure 9.1: Research papers used in this chapter for demonstration (Part 1)

4	OpenML: networked science in machine learning	Joaquin Vanschoren, Jan N. van Rijn, Bernd Bischl, and Luis Torgo	SIGKDD Explorations 15(2), pp 49-60, 2013	https://github.com/openml/openml-r
5	OpenML: An R Package to Connect to the Machine Learning Platform OpenML	Giuseppe Casalicchio Jakob Bossek Michel Lang Dominik Kirchhoff Pascal Kerschke Benjamin Hofner Heidi Seibold Joaquin Vanschoren Bernd Bischl	Computational Statistics 32 (3), pp 1-15, 2017	https://github.com/openml/openml-r

Figure 9.2: Research papers used in this chapter for demonstration (Part 2)

The mlr Package

Now, we shall go into learning how the mlr package offers a complete framework to work with many machine learning models and problem. Often, in many ML projects, one has to manage an overwhelming amount of detailing around numerous experiments (also called **trial-and-error iterations**). Each experiment consists of many pieces of training using different machine learning algorithms, performance measures, hyperparameters, resampling techniques and predictions. Unless we do not systematically analyze the information obtained in each experiment, we will not be able to come out with the best combination of parameter values.

Another advantage of using the mlr package comes from its rich collection of machine learning algorithms from various packages. We do not have to install multiple packages for different implementation of the machine learning algorithm anymore. Instead, mlr offers everything in one place. To understand this better, refer to the following table:

S.No	Class	Name	Package
1	classif.ada	ada Boosting	ada
2	classif.binomial	Binomial Regression	stats
3	classif.blackboost	Gradient Boosting With Regression Trees	mboost,party
4	classif.boosting	Adabag Boosting	adabag,rpart
5	classif.C50	C50	C50
6	classif.cforest	Random forest based on conditional inference trees	party
7	classif.ctree	Conditional Inference Trees	party
8	classif.cvglmnet	GLM with Lasso or Elastic net Regularization (Cross Validated Lambda)	glmnet
9	classif.earth	Flexible Discriminant Analysis	earth
10	classif.featureless	Featureless classifier	mlr

Figure 9.3: The mlr Package (Part 1)

Multilabel Classification Algorithms

The following models are available in the mlr package for multilabel classification, where one observation could be assigned to more than one class. These models are useful in solving many useful problems, such as, in Netflix, you will see that each movie could be tagged as Action, Adventure and Fantasy. Alternatively, in YouTube, where millions of videos are posted every day, an automatic algorithm could tag the videos into multiple class and hence help in content filtering and better search.

We will use these algorithms along with the classifiers defined in the previous table:

S.No	Class	Name	Package
1	multilabel.cforest	Random forest based on conditional inference trees	party
2	multilabel.randomForestSRC	Random Forest	randomForestSRC
3	multilabel.rFerns	Random ferns	rFerns

Figure 9.4: Multilabel classification with the mlr package

OpenML Package

OpenML, a collaboration platform through which researchers from academia and industry can automatically share, organize, and deliberate machine learning experiments, data, algorithms, and flows. The platform brings efficient collaboration and results in reproducibility.

The OpenML package in R comes with various features that allow users to search, upload, and download the datasets and perform Machine Learning related operations. A user can upload the output of ML experiments, share them with other users, and download the output results. This enhances the reproducibility of work, speeds up the research work, and brings people from different domains together.

Problem Design from the Research Paper

In this chapter, we will understand, analyze, and reproduce the results from the *Learning multi-label scene classification* paper. We will effectively use the mlr and OpenML packages to reproduce the result. Before that, let's write the **Situation-Complication-Question** from the paper using the **SCQ framework**:

Situation Define the current situation. We can simplify this by answering the question – What happened?	Scene classification has applications in the following areas: 1. Context-sensitive image enhancement algorithm is often applied on the entire image base. However, the enhancement might be only required to let us say, images with ocean 2. In scene classification applications, such as image retrieval and organization, the images often belong to multiple semantic classes, for example, beach and mountain.
Complication Define the roadblock faced by the team in achieving their desired outcomes.	Classification errors occur when the classes overlap in the feature space. Binary classification model might not be sufficient for the multilabel classification task.
Question Define the question that would need answers to solve the problem.	1. Can we apply the image enhancement algorithm only on a selected category of images and not all? 2. Is it possible to tackle the multi-class belongingness problem using any classification algorithm from machine learning?

Figure 9.5: SCQ from the paper Learning multi-label scene classification

Features in Scene Dataset

The paper uses the **scene** dataset for semantic scene classification task. The dataset is a collection of images of natural scenes, where a natural scene may contain multiple objects, such that multiple class labels can describe the scene. For example, a field scene with a mountain in the background. From the paper, we have taken the first figure, which shows two images that are multilabel images depicting two different scenes in a single image. *Figure* 9.6 is a beach and urban scene, whereas *Figure* 9.7 shows mountains:

Figure 9.6: A beach and urban scene.

Figure 9.7: A mountains scene.

From the given images, we could use the following:

- **Color information**: This information is useful when differentiating between certain types of outdoor scenes.

- **Spatial information**: This information is useful in various cases. For example, light, warm colors at the top of the image may correspond to sunrise.

The paper uses CIE L*U*V*, such as space, denoted as Luv. Luv space proposes the anticipated perceptual uniformity. After adaptation (a mathematical transformation from the XYZ space to the L*U*V space) to Luv spaces, the image is divided into 49 blocks using a 7 x 7 grid. Then, the authors calculate the first and second moment (mean and variance) of each band (RGB), which corresponds to a low-resolution image and to computationally low-cost quality features, respectively. In total, we obtain 49 x 2 x 3 = 294 features vector per image.

The remaining six columns in the dataset correspond to the six labels represented in a true/false encoded value. If an image belongs to two classes, the respective column will have true value.

> **Note**
>
> In colorimetry, the CIE 1976 L*, u*, v* color space, was adopted by the **International Commission on Illumination** (**CIE**) in 1976, as a simple-to-compute transformation of the 1931 CIE XYZ color space, but which attempted perceptual uniformity, which is the difference or distance between two colors.

Implementing Multilabel Classifier Using the mlr and OpenML Packages

We will now see how to train a multilabel classifier using the mlr and OpenML packages. First, we will download the scene dataset from OpenML.

Exercise 102: Downloading the Scene Dataset from OpenML

In this exercise, we will download the scene dataset and set it up for further analysis.

Perform the following steps to complete the exercise:

1. In order to download the scene dataset through OpenML API, first create an account in the OpenML website at https://www.openml.org/register. The registration process involves verifying your email address, post which you will get the access to the API keys.

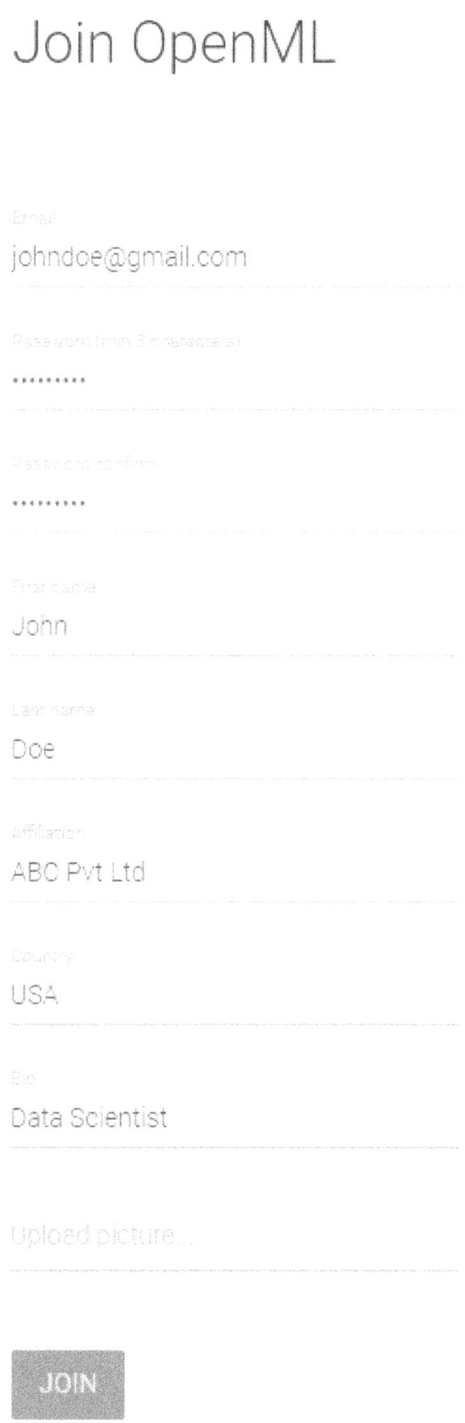

Join OpenML

Email
johndoe@gmail.com

Password (min 8 characters)
....

Password confirm
....

First name
John

Last name
Doe

Affiliation
ABC Pvt Ltd

Country
USA

Bio
Data Scientist

Upload picture...

JOIN

Figure 9.8: The OpenML registration page.

2. After logging in to your account, navigate to your account and select the API AUTHENTICATION option.

3. On the API Authentication page, select and copy-paste the API key from the API key section. The authors of the Multilabel Classification with R Package mlr paper uploaded a bunch of datasets with a 2016_multilabel_r_benchmark_paper tag, which we can now download from OpenML and start reproducing their results. We will specifically use the scene dataset (with ID 40595).

4. Open RStudio and install all the required packages before proceeding.

5. Import the required packages and libraries:

```
library(mlr)
library(BBmisc)
library(OpenML)
library(batchtools)
library(parallelMap)
```

6. Use the API key from the OpenML and register the API key using the following command:

```
setOMLConfig(apikey = "627394a14f562f0fa8bcc9ec443d879f")
```

The output is as follows:

```
## OpenML configuration:
##    server          : http://www.openml.org/api/v1
##    cachedir        : C:\Users\Karthik\AppData\Local\Temp\Rtmp6bSgE4/
cache
##    verbosity       : 1
##    arff.reader     : farff
##    confirm.upload  : TRUE
##    apikey          : ****************************d879f
```

7. Use the following command to download the dataset from the source:

```
ds.list = listOMLDataSets(tag = "2016_multilabel_r_benchmark_paper")
```

The output is as follows:

```
## Downloading from 'http://www.openml.org/api/v1/json/data/list/tag/2016_
multilabel_r_benchmark_paper/limit/5000/status/active' to '<mem>'.
```

8. Next, we will use the ID 40595 to get the scene dataset:

```
oml.data = lapply(40595, getOMLDataSet)
df.oml.data.scene <- data.frame(oml.data)
```

Note

Ensure that you install the farff package before proceeding with the previous two commands.

9. Create the DataFrame using the following command:

```
df_scene = df.oml.data.scene
labels = colnames(df_scene)[295:300]
scene.task = makeMultilabelTask(id = "multi", data = df_scene, target = labels)
```

The output is as follows:

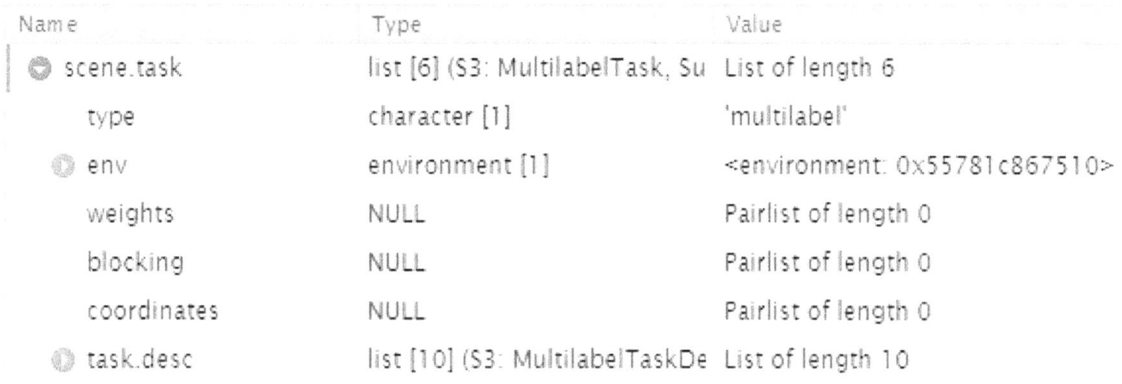

Name	Type	Value
scene.task	list [6] (S3: MultilabelTask, Su	List of length 6
type	character [1]	'multilabel'
env	environment [1]	<environment: 0x55781c867510>
weights	NULL	Pairlist of length 0
blocking	NULL	Pairlist of length 0
coordinates	NULL	Pairlist of length 0
task.desc	list [10] (S3: MultilabelTaskDe	List of length 10

Figure 9.9: Environment setting of the scene.task variable.

In this exercise, we registered an account in OpenML and obtained an API key. Using the API key, we were able to download the scene dataset, which has a 2016_multilabel_r_benchmark_paper tag in OpenML. Finally, we converted the dataset into data frame. OpenML provides many such features to collaborate. One can share their code, experiments, and flow with a larger community by assigning a tag.

Constructing a Learner

A **learner** is a machine learning algorithm implementation in the mlr package. As highlighted in the previous section on the mlr package, there is a rich collection of such learner functions in mlr.

For our scene classification problem, the mlr package offers building a multilabel classification model in two possible ways:

- **Adaptation method**: In this, we adapt an explicit algorithm on the entire problem.

- **Transformation method**: We transform the problem into a simple binary classification problem and then apply the available algorithm for the binary classification.

Adaptation Methods

The mlr package in R offers two algorithm adaption methods. First, the multivariate random forest algorithm that comes from the **randomForestSRC** package, and second, the random ferns multilabel algorithm built in the **rFerns** package.

The **makeLearner()** function in mlr creates the model object for the **rFerns** and **randomForestSRC** algorithms, as shown in the following code:

```
multilabel.lrn3 = makeLearner("multilabel.rFerns")

multilabel.lrn4 = makeLearner("multilabel.randomForestSRC")

multilabel.lrn3
```

The output is as follows, which shows the information such as name and predict-type about the multilable.rFerns model:

```
## Learner multilabel.rFerns from package rFernsd

## Type: multilabel

## Name: Random ferns; Short name: rFerns

## Class: multilabel.rFerns

## Properties: numerics,factors,ordered

## Predict-Type: response

## Hyperparameters:
```

> **Note**
>
> Ensure that you install the *rFerns* and *randomForestSRC* packages before proceeding with the previous two commands.

Transformation Methods

The second method for constructing a learner is to use the **problem transformation** methods. The mlr package comes with a wrapped multilabel learner, which creates a multilabel or binary classification learner using the `makeLearner()` function, and then any one of the five wrapper functions (described in the following section) could be utilized for problem transformation.

Binary Relevance Method

In multilabel classification problems, each label could be transformed as a binary classification problem. In the process, any one observation could have multiple labels assigned to it. In the mlr package, the `makeMultilabelBinaryRelevanceWrapper()` method converts the binary learner method to a wrapped Binary Relevance multilabel learner.

Classifier Chains Method

The classifier chain wrapper method implements a multilabel model, where the binary classifiers are arranged into a chain. Each model comes out with a prediction in the order specified by the chain. The model uses all the features in the given dataset, along with all the predictions of the model that are before in the chain. The `makeMultilabelClassifierChainsWrapper()` method in mlr is used to create the classifier chain wrappers.

Nested Stacking

Like classifier chain, however, the class (or label) of the observation are not the actual class but are based on estimations of the class obtained by the trained model (learner) from the previous model in the chain. The `makeMultilabelNestedStackingWrapper()` method in the mlr package is used to create the nested stacking wrappers.

Dependent Binary Relevance Method

The **Dependent Binary Relevance** (**DBR**) method combines both the learning strategies of chaining and stacking, in which each label goes through training with the actual values of all other labels. During the prediction phase for a label, the other required labels are obtained in a previous step by a base learner (like Binary Relevance method). The `makeMultilabelDBRWrapper` method in the mlr package is used to create the dependent Binary Relevance wrappers.

Stacking

Like the dependent Binary Relevance method, however, in the training phase, the labels used as input for each label are obtained by the Binary Relevance method instead of using the actual labels. The **makeMultilabelStackingWrapper** method in the mlr package is used to create the stacking wrappers.

In the following exercise, we will see how to generate decision tree model using the **classif.rpart** method.

Exercise 103: Generating Decision Tree Model Using the classif.rpart Method

In this exercise, we will generate the decision tree model using the **classif.rpart** method and then transform it using *Binary Relevance* and nested *Stacking* wrappers.

Perform the following steps to complete the exercise:

1. First, use the **makeLearner** method to create the object for **classif.rpart**:

   ```
   lrn = makeLearner("classif.rpart", predict.type = "prob")
   ```

2. Next, create the stacking wrappers using the **makeMultilabelBinaryRelevanceWrapper** method:

   ```
   multilabel.lrn1 = makeMultilabelBinaryRelevanceWrapper(lrn)
   multilabel.lrn2 = makeMultilabelNestedStackingWrapper(lrn)
   ```

3. Next, print the model:

   ```
   lrn
   ```

   The output is as follows:

   ```
   Learner classif.rpart from package rpart
   Type: classif
   Name: Decision Tree; Short name: rpart
   Class: classif.rpart
   Properties: twoclass,multiclass,missings,numerics,factors,ordered,
   prob,weights,featimp
   Predict-Type: prob
   Hyperparameters: xval=0
   ```

4. Print the stacking wrappers, as illustrated here:

```
multilabel.lrn1
```

The output of the previous command is as follows, which shows the information such as the type of model, properties available as part of the model output, and the predict-type:

```
Learner multilabel.binaryRelevance.classif.rpart from package rpart
Type: multilabel
Name: ; Short name:
Class: MultilabelBinaryRelevanceWrapper
Properties:
numerics,factors,ordered,missings,weights,prob,twoclass,multiclass
Predict-Type: prob
Hyperparameters: xval=0
```

Train the Model

We can train a model as usual with a multilabel learner and a multilabel task as input; use the **multilabel.lrn1** object.

Exercise 104: Train the Model

In this exercise, we will first randomly split the data into train and test datasets and then train the model using the **tain()** function from mlr package and the **multilabel. lrn1** object defined in the previous section.

Perform the following steps to complete the exercise:

1. Use the following command to train, predict, and evaluate the dataset:

```
df_nrow <- nrow(df_scene)
df_all_index <- c(1:df_nrow)
```

2. Create the **train_index** and **test_index variable** using the following command:

```
train_index <- sample(1:df_nrow, 0.7*df_nrow)
test_index <- setdiff(df_all_index,train_index)
```

3. Use the **train** function, which takes model object `multilabel.lrn1` (**BinaryRelevanceWrapper**), dataset `scene.task` with only randomly selected **train_index** to train the model:

```
scene_classi_mod = train(multilabel.lrn1, scene.task, subset = train_
index)
scene_classi_mod
```

The output is as follows:

```
Model for learner.id=multilabel.binaryRelevance.classif.rpart; learner.
class=MultilabelBinaryRelevanceWrapper
Trained on: task.id = multi; obs = 1684; features = 294
Hyperparameters: xval=0
```

The **scene_classi_mod** model using the **1684** randomly chosen observations from **scene** dataset is trained using the **rpart** package in R, which is an implementation of the **Classification and Regression Tree** (**CART**) algorithm in machine learning wrapped with the Binary Relevance method for multilabel classification.

Predicting the Output

Prediction can be done as usual in mlr with the **predict** function. The input arguments are trained models; the scene.task dataset is assigned to the **task** and **test_index** arguments, which correspond to the **test** dataset is assigned to the **subset** argument:

```
pred = predict(scene_classi_mod, task = scene.task, subset = test_index)

names(as.data.frame(pred))
```

```
[1] "id"                  "truth.Beach"         "truth.Sunset"
"truth.FallFoliage"

 [5] "truth.Field"        "truth.Mountain"      "truth.Urban"
"prob.Beach"

 [9] "prob.Sunset"        "prob.FallFoliage"    "prob.Field"
"prob.Mountain"

[13] "prob.Urban"         "response.Beach"      "response.Sunset"
"response.FallFoliage"

[17] "response.Field"     "response.Mountain"   "response.Urban"
```

Performance of the Model

In order assess the performance of the prediction, the mlr package offers the **performance()** function, which takes as an input the prediction of the model along with all the measures we would like to compute. All available measures for multilabel classification can be listed by **listMeasures()**. As per the paper, we use measures such as **hamloss**, **f1**, **subset01**, **acc**, **tpr**, and **ppv** on our predictions:

```
MEASURES = list(multilabel.hamloss, multilabel.f1, multilabel.subset01,
multilabel.acc, multilabel.tpr, multilabel.ppv)

performance(pred, measures = MEASURES)
```

The output of the previous command is as follows:

```
multilabel.hamloss        multilabel.f1 multilabel.subset01        multilabel.
acc        multilabel.tpr

            0.1260950                 0.5135085              0.5878285
0.4880129                  0.5477178

        multilabel.ppv

            0.7216733
```

The following command will list down all the measures available for multilabel classification problem:

```
listMeasures("multilabel")
```

The output is as follows:

```
[1] "featperc"                 "multilabel.tpr"        "multilabel.hamloss"
"multilabel.subset01" "timeboth"

 [6] "timetrain"                 "timepredict"        "multilabel.ppv"
"multilabel.f1"         "multilabel.acc"
```

Resampling the Data

For evaluating the complete performance of the learning algorithm, we can do some resampling. To define a resampling strategy, either use **makeResampleDesc()** or **makeResampleInstance()**. After that, run the **resample()** function. Use the following default measure to calculate the hamming loss:

```
rdesc = makeResampleDesc(method = "CV", stratify = FALSE, iters = 3)

r = resample(learner = multilabel.lrn1, task = scene.task, resampling =
rdesc,measures = list(multilabel.hamloss), show.info = FALSE)

r
```

The output is as follows:

```
Resample Result

Task: multi

Learner: multilabel.binaryRelevance.classif.rpart

Aggr perf: multilabel.hamloss.test.mean=0.1244979

Runtime: 4.28345
```

Binary Performance for Each Label

We can calculate a binary performance measure, for example, the accuracy, or the **auc** for each label, the **getMultilabelBinaryPerformances()** function is useful. We can apply this function to any multilabel prediction, for example, also on the resampled multilabel prediction. For calculating **auc**, we need predicted probabilities:

```
getMultilabelBinaryPerformances(r$pred, measures = list(acc, mmce, auc))
```

The output is as follows:

##	acc.test.mean	mmce.test.mean	auc.test.mean
## Beach	0.8728708	0.12712921	0.7763484
## Sunset	0.9335272	0.06647279	0.9066371
## FallFoliage	0.9148317	0.08516826	0.8699105
## Field	0.9077690	0.09223099	0.8895795
## Mountain	0.7922725	0.20772746	0.7670873
## Urban	0.8213544	0.17864562	0.7336219

Benchmarking Model

In a benchmark experiment, different learning methods are applied to one or more than a few datasets with the purpose of comparing and ranking the algorithms concerning one or more performance measures. The **mlr()** method offers a very robust framework to conduct such experiments and helps in keeping track of all the results of the experiment to compare.

Conducting Benchmark Experiments

In our first experiment, we use the multilabel **randomForestSRC** and **rFerns** learners of the **mlr()** package and various measures to get our first benchmark.

In the following exercise, we will explore how to conduct a benchmarking on various learners.

Exercise 105: Exploring How to Conduct a Benchmarking on Various Learners

In this exercise, we will see how to conduct a benchmarking on various learners we created so far and compare the results to select the best learner (model) for the multilabel scene classification problem. This helps us organize all the results in a structured format to select the best performing model.

Perform the following steps to complete the exercise:

1. First, list all learners using the following command:

    ```
    lrns = list(makeLearner("multilabel.randomForestSRC"),
                makeLearner("multilabel.rFerns")
                )
    MEASURES = list(multilabel.hamloss, multilabel.f1, multilabel.subset01,
    multilabel.acc, multilabel.tpr, multilabel.ppv)
    ```

2. Conduct the benchmark experiment:

    ```
    bmr = benchmark(lrns, scene.task, measures = MEASURES)
    ```

    The output is as follows:

    ```
    ## Exporting objects to slaves for mode socket: .mlr.slave.options
    ## Mapping in parallel: mode = socket; cpus = 2; elements = 2.
    ```

3. Now, execute the **bmr** object:

```
bmr
```

Iterations of the model train will look something like the following for each learner:

```
Task: multi, Learner: multilabel.rFerns

[Resample] cross-validation iter 9: multilabel.hamloss.test.
mean=0.183,multilabel.f1.test.mean=0.653,multilabel.subset01.test.
mean=0.768,multilabel.acc.test.mean=0.54,multilabel.tpr.test.mean=
0.9,multilabel.ppv.test.mean=0.564
...

[Resample] Aggr. Result: multilabel.hamloss.test.mean=0.183,multilabel.
f1.test.mean=0.663,multilabel.subset01.test.mean=0.756,multilabel.acc.
test.mean=0.549,multilabel.tpr.test.mean=0.916,multilabel.ppv.test.
mean=0.566
```

The following table demonstrates the mean of various measures on the test data:

No	learner.id	Hamloss mean	f1 mean	subset01 mean	acc mean	tpr mean	ppv mean
1	randomForestSRC	0.08988	0.56023	0.46822	0.55310	0.55372	0.92914
2	rFerns	0.18266	0.66424	0.75987	0.54944	0.92017	0.56520

Figure 9.10: Mean of various measures on the test data.

This table shows that the **randomForestSRC** model does a slightly better job than **rFerns** on all the measures, primarily in the **hamloss mean measure**.

Accessing Benchmark Results

The **mlr()** method provides many **getBMR** functions to extract useful information such as performance, predictions, leaners, and many more from the benchmark experiment object.

Learner Performances

The **getBMRPerformances** function gives all values of all the measures defined in the benchmark in each iteration of the training. The following table lists the values for each measure using the **randomForestSRC** and **rFerns** learners.

```
getBMRPerformances(bmr, as.df = TRUE)
```

learner.id	iter	hamloss	f1	subset01	acc	tpr	ppv
randomForestSRC	1	0.096127	0.543568	0.497925	0.533195	0.533195	0.918919
randomForestSRC	2	0.080221	0.615491	0.406639	0.609959	0.609959	0.937888
randomForestSRC	3	0.091978	0.54426	0.485477	0.536653	0.538728	0.908784
randomForestSRC	4	0.080556	0.575	0.45	0.56875	0.570833	0.968966
randomForestSRC	5	0.079167	0.622222	0.4	0.616667	0.616667	0.95
randomForestSRC	6	0.089903	0.540802	0.473029	0.537344	0.537344	0.923077
randomForestSRC	7	0.090595	0.539419	0.493776	0.53112	0.53112	0.943662
randomForestSRC	8	0.099306	0.527778	0.508333	0.51875	0.51875	0.909722
randomForestSRC	9	0.089903	0.578147	0.460581	0.568465	0.570539	0.925806
randomForestSRC	10	0.094744	0.554633	0.481328	0.545643	0.545643	0.896104

Figure 9.11: Learner performances randomForestSRC

learner.id	iter	hamloss	f1	subset01	acc	tpr	ppv
rFerns	1	0.183956	0.659889	0.759336	0.547026	0.908714	0.565752
rFerns	2	0.166667	0.681604	0.746888	0.567773	0.929461	0.589007
rFerns	3	0.19018	0.660304	0.775934	0.541494	0.928769	0.553819
rFerns	4	0.183333	0.666111	0.7625	0.549653	0.929167	0.560321
rFerns	5	0.160417	0.709306	0.6875	0.604167	0.94375	0.611345
rFerns	6	0.192254	0.645781	0.792531	0.525934	0.923237	0.533821
rFerns	7	0.19018	0.64592	0.746888	0.537344	0.896266	0.56339
rFerns	8	0.190972	0.644722	0.758333	0.534722	0.877083	0.556373
rFerns	9	0.182573	0.65325	0.767635	0.539765	0.900415	0.563559
rFerns	10	0.185339	0.660996	0.763485	0.544952	0.921162	0.561625

Figure 9.12: Learner performances rFerns

Predictions

We could also get the predictions on the test dataset using the **getBMRPredictions** function. The two tables in this section show the actual and the predicted labels of a few images represented by the ID column. Observe that the predictions are not perfect, just as we would expect from the relatively low overall accuracy.

Predictions using randomForestSRC:

```
head(getBMRPredictions(bmr, as.df = TRUE))
```

ID	Actual					
	Beach	Sunset	FallFoliage	Field	Mountain	Urban
9	TRUE	FALSE	FALSE	FALSE	FALSE	FALSE
20	TRUE	FALSE	FALSE	FALSE	FALSE	FALSE
26	TRUE	FALSE	FALSE	FALSE	FALSE	FALSE
32	TRUE	FALSE	FALSE	FALSE	FALSE	TRUE
42	TRUE	FALSE	FALSE	FALSE	FALSE	FALSE
54	TRUE	FALSE	FALSE	FALSE	FALSE	FALSE

Figure 9.13: The actual labels.

ID	Predicted					
	Beach	Sunset	FallFoliage	Field	Mountain	Urban
9	FALSE	FALSE	FALSE	FALSE	FALSE	FALSE
20	FALSE	FALSE	FALSE	FALSE	FALSE	FALSE
26	TRUE	FALSE	FALSE	FALSE	FALSE	FALSE
32	TRUE	FALSE	FALSE	FALSE	FALSE	FALSE
42	TRUE	FALSE	FALSE	FALSE	FALSE	FALSE
54	FALSE	FALSE	FALSE	FALSE	FALSE	FALSE

Figure 9.14: The predicted labels.

Learners and measures

The **getBMRLearners** function gives details about the learners used in the benchmark. Information such as hyperparameter and predict-type could be obtained using this function. Similarly, the **getBMRMeasures** function provides details such as best about the performance measures. The following table shows the details about the measures we used in our benchmark experiment:

```
getBMRLearners(bmr)
```

The output is as follows:

```
## $multilabel.randomForestSRC
## Learner multilabel.randomForestSRC from package randomForestSRC
## Type: multilabel
## Name: Random Forest; Short name: rfsrc
## Class: multilabel.randomForestSRC
## Properties: missings,numerics,factors,prob,weights
## Predict-Type: response
## Hyperparameters: na.action=na.impute
##
##
## $multilabel.rFerns
## Learner multilabel.rFerns from package rFerns
## Type: multilabel
## Name: Random ferns; Short name: rFerns
## Class: multilabel.rFerns
## Properties: numerics,factors,ordered
## Predict-Type: response
## Hyperparameters:
```

Run the **getBMRMeasures(bmr)** function:

```
getBMRMeasures(bmr)
```

No	Name	Detail	Best Value	Worst Value	Minimize
1	Hamming loss	The proportion of labels that are predicted incorrectly	0	1	TRUE
2	F1 measure (multilabel)	The harmonic mean of precision and recall on a per-instance basis (Micro-F1)	1	0	FALSE
3	Subset-0-1 loss	The proportion of observations where the complete multilabel set (all 0-1-labels) is predicted incorrectly	0	1	TRUE

Figure 9.15: Learners and measures (part 1).

Figures 15 and 16 summarize the result of the **getBMRMeasures(bmr)** command:

No	Name	Detail	Best Value	Worst Value	Minimize
4	Accuracy (multilabel)	The averaged proportion of correctly predicted labels concerning the total number of labels for each instance	1	0	FALSE
5	TPR (multilabel)	Also called a recall. Averaged proportion of predicted labels which are relevant for each instance	1	0	FALSE
6	Positive predictive value (multilabel)	Also called precision. The averaged ratio of correctly predicted labels for each instance	1	0	FALSE

Figure 9.16: Learners and measures (part 2).

Merging Benchmark Results

Often, we run multiple experiments and would like to see all the benchmarks coming from the experiments into one consolidated list of values to compare the results. The **mergeBenchmarkResults** function helps in combining the results.

Here's the benchmark:

```
lrns = list(makeLearner("multilabel.randomForestSRC"),
            makeLearner("multilabel.rFerns")
       )
bmr = benchmark(lrns, scene.task, measures = MEASURES)
lrn.classif.randomForest = makeLearner("classif.randomForest")
bmr.BR.rf = benchmark(lrn.classif.randomForest, scene.task, measures =
MEASURES)
mergeBenchmarkResults(list(bmr, bmr.BR.rf))
```

	Learner.id	Hamloss mean	F1 mean	subset01	ACC mean	TPR mean	PPV mean
1	randomForestSRC	0.08988	0.56023	0.46822	0.55310	0.55372	0.92914
2	rFerns	0.18266	0.66424	0.75987	0.54944	0.92017	0.56520
3	BR.rf	0.08372	0.6140	0.42378	0.60454	0.61229	0.90919
4	CC.rf	0.08156	0.6356	0.397597	0.62727	0.63080	0.89797
5	STA.rf	0.08123	0.6308	0.408415	0.62095	0.62850	0.90910
6	NST.rf	0.08573	0.6055	0.432510	0.59595	0.60315	0.90161

Figure 9.17: Merging benchmark results.

Clearly, using **classif.randomForest** with the classifier chain wrapper produces the highest accuracy and performs well in all the other measures as well.

Activity 14: Getting the Binary Performance Step with classif.C50 Learner Instead of classif.rpart

In this activity, we will revisit the entire process flow of building a model, in which we will use the `makeLearner` function to specify the `rpart` model, replacing `C50`. Specifically, we will rerun the entire machine learning flow, starting from the problem transformation step to getting the binary performance step with the classif.C50 learner instead of `classif.rpart`.

Perform the following steps to complete the activity:

1. Define the algorithm adaptation methods.

2. Use the problem transformation method, and change the `classif.rpart` learner to `classif.C50`.

> **Note**
>
> You need to install the `C50` package for this code to work.

3. Print the learner details.

4. Print the multilabel learner details.

5. Train the model using the same dataset with training dataset.

6. Print the model details.

7. Predict the output using the C50 model we created earlier on the test dataset.

8. Print the performance measures.

9. Print the performance measures for the `listMeasures` variable.

10. Run the resampling with the cross validation method.

11. Print the binary performance.

Once you complete the activity, you should see the following output:

```
##                 acc.test.mean mmce.test.mean auc.test.mean
## Beach              0.8608226     0.13917740     0.8372448
## Sunset             0.9401745     0.05982551     0.9420085
## FallFoliage        0.9081845     0.09181554     0.9008202
## Field              0.8998754     0.10012464     0.9134458
## Mountain           0.7710843     0.22891566     0.7622767
## Urban              0.8184462     0.18155380     0.7837401
```

> **Note**
>
> The solution for this activity can be found on page 466.

Working with OpenML Upload Functions

In order to improve collaboration and version control the experiments, we can upload the flows we create into OpenML using the **uploadOMLFlow** function:

```
flow.id = uploadOMLFlow(makeLearner("multilabel.randomForestSRC"))
```

The output is as follows:

```
Downloading from 'http://www.openml.org/api/v1/flow/exists/mlr.multilabel.
randomForestSRC/R_3.2.2-v2.b955a5ec' to '<mem>'.

Do you want to upload the flow? (yes|no)

Uploading flow to the server.

Downloading response to: C:\Users\Karthik\AppData\Local\Temp\Rtmpe4W4BW\
file3f044abf30f2.xml

Uploading to 'http://www.openml.org/api/v1/flow'.

Flow successfully uploaded. Flow ID: 9708
```

We encourage students to explore the OpenML platform to find many more such functionalities, as the platform helps researchers all around the world to collaborate and share their work, making good work spread fast and help build the best model with the collective wisdom of researchers.

Summary

In this chapter, we used the mlr and OpenML packages from R to build an entire machine learning workflow for solving a multilabel semantic scene classification problem. The mlr package offered a rich collection of machine learning algorithms and evaluation measures that helped us in quick implementation and facilitated a faster experimentation process to get the best model for the problem. The package also offered many wrapper functions to handle the multilabel problem. Building real-world machine learning models using a robust framework such as the one in mlr helps in speeding the implementation and provides a structure to the complete project. Further, using OpenML, we could reproduce a research work using the already available dataset and code, and then modify it according to our need. Such a platform offers the ability to collaborate at scale with researchers all over the world. At the end, we could also upload our own machine learning flows with others for them to pick it up from where we left.

In this book, our focus was to teach supervised learning in R programming language. Supervised learning is a class of algorithms where we are provided with labeled observation of data. Exploratory Data Analysis (EDA) methods help in understanding the dataset well, and the SCQ framework is used to design the problem precisely. The features are chosen on the basis of the problem design and an appropriate supervised learning model is selected after many rounds of experiments and evaluation. We then learned how to deploy machine learning models in production environment, which could be used by an application team in a business. Also, in cases where the dataset has hundreds of features, we used feature reduction and selection techniques.

We would like to emphasize that in any machine learning project, beyond a certain point (could be defined such as 3 months of effort from the start of project or 100 trial runs with different combinations), we should stop and ask whether or not what we have done so far could be deployed in a production environment. If the answer is yes, deploy it and keep monitoring the response for any abnormality and improvements. If it's a no, go back to the drawing boards and start over (obviously if such a luxury is given). Machine learning in stages such as hyperparameter fine-tuning and model selection is an art. A lot of trial-and-error experiments are required to come out with the best model.

Appendix

About

This section is included to assist the students to perform the activities present in the book. It includes detailed steps that are to be performed by the students to complete and achieve the objectives of the book.

Chapter 1: R for Advanced Analytics

Activity 1: Create an R Markdown File to Read a CSV File and Write a Summary of Data

1. Start the RStudio and navigate to **Files** | **New Files** | **R Markdown**.

2. On the New R Markdown window, provide the **Title** and **Author** name, as illustrated in the following screenshot. Ensure that you select the **Word** option under the **Default Output Format** section:

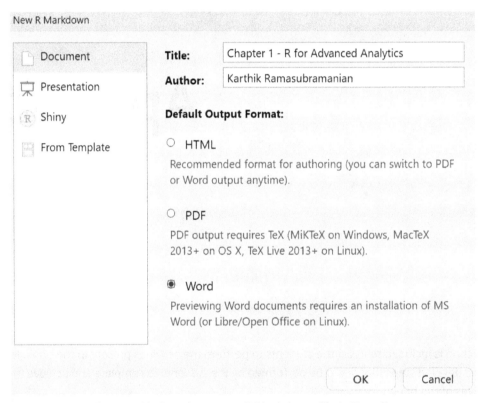

Figure 1.13: Creating a new R Markdown file in Rstudio

3. Now, use the **read.csv()** method to read the **bank-full.csv** file:

```
RStudio
File  Edit  Code  View  Plots  Session  Build  Debug  Profile  Tools  Help
        Go to file/function          Addins

Chapter 1 - R for Advanced Analytics.Rmd
        Knit       Insert          Run
14   destinationFileName <- "bank.zip"
15
16   #download.file(url, destinationFileName,method = "auto",
     quiet=FALSE)
17
18   #zipFile<-file.choose() # lets you choose a file and save its
     file path in R (at least for windows)
19
20   outputDir <- wd # Define the folder where the zip file should
     be unzipped to
21
22   #unzip(zipFile,exdir=outputDir)  # unzip your file
23
24   setwd(wd)
25   df_bank_detail <- read.csv("bank-full.csv", sep = ';')
26
```

Figure 1.14: Using the read.csv method to read the data

4. Finally, print the summary into a word file using the **summary** method:

```
##       age                 job            marital            education
##   Min.   :18.00   blue-collar:9732   divorced: 5207   primary  : 6851
##   1st Qu.:33.00   management :9458   married :27214   secondary:23202
##   Median :39.00   technician :7597   single  :12790   tertiary :13301
##   Mean   :40.94   admin.     :5171                    unknown  : 1857
##   3rd Qu.:48.00   services   :4154
##   Max.   :95.00   retired    :2264
##                   (Other)    :6835
##   default          balance         housing        loan           contact
##   no :44396   Min.   : -8019   no :20081   no :37967   cellular :29285
##   yes:  815   1st Qu.:    72   yes:25130   yes: 7244   telephone: 2906
##               Median :   448                           unknown  :13020
##               Mean   :  1362
##               3rd Qu.:  1428
##               Max.   :102127
##
```

Figure 1.15: Final output after using the summary method

Activity 2: Create a List of Two Matrices and Access the Values

1. Create two matrices of size **10 x 4** and **4 x 5** by randomly generated numbers from a binomial distribution (use **rbinom** method). Call the matrix **mat_A** and **mat_B**, respectively:

```
mat_A <- matrix(rbinom(n = 40, size = 100, prob = 0.4),nrow = 10, ncol=4)
mat_B <- matrix(rbinom(n = 20, size = 100, prob = 0.4),nrow = 4, ncol=5)
```

2. Now, store the two matrices in a list:

```
list_of_matrices <- list(mat_A = mat_A, mat_B =mat_B)
```

3. Using the list, access the row 4 and column 2 of **mat_A** and store it in variable **A**, and access row 2 and column 1 of **mat_B** and store it in variable **B**:

```
A <- list_of_matrices[["mat_A"]][4,2]
B <- list_of_matrices[["mat_B"]][2,1]
```

4. Multiply the **A** and **B** matrices and subtract from row 2 and column 1 of **mat_A**:

```
list_of_matrices[["mat_A"]][2,1] - (A*B)
```

The output is as follows:

```
## [1] -1554
```

Activity 3: Create a DataFrame with Five Summary Statistics for All Numeric Variables from Bank Data Using dplyr and tidyr

1. Import the **dplyr** and **tidyr** packages in the system:

```
library(dplyr)
library(tidyr)
Warning: package 'tidyr' was built under R version 3.2.5
```

2. Create the **df** DataFrame and import the file into it:

```
df <- tbl_df(df_bank_detail)
```

3. Extract all numeric variables from bank data using **select()**, and compute min, 1st quartile, 3rd quartile, median, mean, max, and standard deviation using the **summarise_all()** method:

```
df_wide <- df %>%
   select(age, balance, duration, pdays) %>%
   summarise_all(funs(min = min,
                       q25 = quantile(., 0.25),
                       median = median,
                       q75 = quantile(., 0.75),
                       max = max,
                       mean = mean,
                       sd = sd))
```

4. The result is a wide data frame. 4 variable, 7 measures:

```
dim(df_wide)
## [1]  1 28
```

5. Store the result in a DataFrame of wide format named **df_wide**, reshape it using the **tidyr** functions, and, finally, convert the wide format to deep, use the gather, separate, and spread functions of the **tidyr** package:

```
df_stats_tidy <- df_wide %>% gather(stat, val) %>%
   separate(stat, into = c("var", "stat"), sep = "_") %>%
   spread(stat, val) %>%
   select(var,min, q25, median, q75, max, mean, sd) # reorder columns
print(df_stats_tidy)
```

The output is as follows:

```
## # A tibble: 4 x 8
##          var   min   q25 median   q75    max        mean          sd
## *      <chr> <dbl> <dbl>  <dbl> <dbl>  <dbl>       <dbl>       <dbl>
## 1        age    18    33     39    48     95    40.93621    10.61876
## 2    balance -8019    72    448  1428 102127 1362.27206  3044.76583
## 3   duration     0   103    180   319   4918  258.16308   257.52781
## 4      pdays    -1    -1     -1    -1    871   40.19783   100.12875
```

Chapter 2: Exploratory Analysis of Data

Activity 4: Plotting Multiple Density Plots and Boxplots

1. First, load the necessary libraries and packages in the RStudio:

```
library(ggplot2)
library(cowplot)
```

2. Read the **bank-additional-full.csv** dataset in a DataFrame named **df**:

```
df <- read.csv("bank-additional-full.csv",sep=';')
```

3. Define the **plot_grid_numeric** function for density plot:

```
plot_grid_numeric <- function(df,list_of_variables,ncols=2){
  plt_matrix<-list()
  i<-1
  for(column in list_of_variables){
    plt_matrix[[i]]<-ggplot(data=df,aes_string(x=column)) +
      geom_density(fill="red",alpha =0.5)  +
      ggtitle(paste("Density Plot for variable:",column)) + theme_bw()
    i<-i+1
  }
  plot_grid(plotlist=plt_matrix,ncol=2)
}
```

4. Plot the density plot for the **campaign**, **pdays**, **previous**, and **emp.var.rate** variables:

```
plot_grid_numeric(df,c("campaign","pdays","previous","emp.var.rate"),2)
```

The output is as follows:

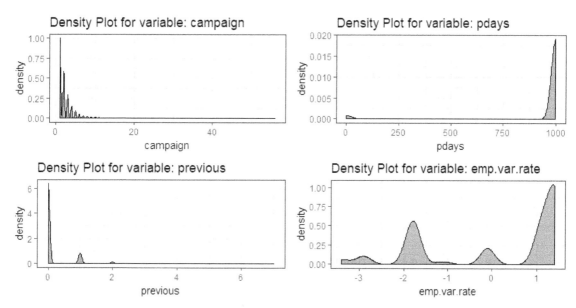

Figure 2.27: Density plot for the campaign, pdays, previous, and emp.var.rate variables

Observe that the interpretations we obtained using the histogram are visibly true in density plot as well. Hence, this serves as another alternative plot for looking at the same trend.

5. Repeat step 4 for boxplot:

```
plot_grid_numeric <- function(df,list_of_variables,ncols=2){
  plt_matrix<-list()
  i<-1
  for(column in list_of_variables){
    plt_matrix[[i]]<-ggplot(data=df,aes_string(y=column)) +
      gcom_boxplot(outlier.colour="black") +
      ggtitle(paste("Boxplot for variable:",column)) + theme_bw()
    i<-i+1
  }
  plot_grid(plotlist=plt_matrix,ncol=2)
}
plot_grid_numeric(df,c("campaign","pdays","previous","emp.var.rate"),2)
```

The output is as follows:

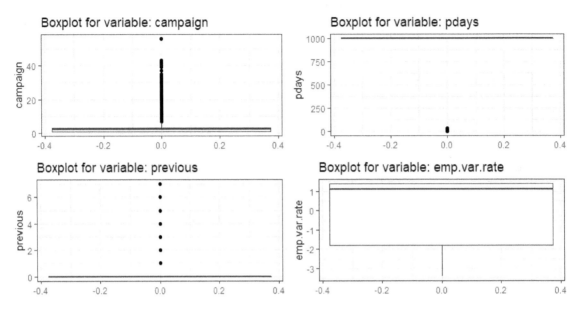

Figure 2.28: Boxplot for the campaign, pdays, previous, and emp.var.rate variables

Now, let's explore the last four numeric variable of the dataset, that is, `nr.employed`, `euribor3m`, `cons.conf.index`, and `duration`, and see whether we could derive some meaningful insights.

Chapter 3: Introduction to Supervised Learning

Activity 5: Draw a Scatterplot between PRES and PM2.5 Split by Months

1. Import the **ggplot2** package into the system:

    ```
    library(ggplot2)
    ```

2. In **ggplot**, assign the component of the **a()** method with the variable **PRES**.

    ```
    ggplot(data = PM25, aes(x = PRES, y = pm2.5, color = hour)) +    geom_
    point()
    ```

3. In the next layer of the **geom_smooth()** method, passing **colour = "blue"** to differentiate.

    ```
    geom_smooth(method='auto',formula=y~x, colour = "blue", size =1)
    ```

4. Finally, in the **facet_wrap()** layer, use the **month** variable to draw a separate segregation for each month.

    ```
    facet_wrap(~ month, nrow = 4)
    ```

    The final code will look like this:

    ```
    ggplot(data = PM25, aes(x = PRES, y = pm2.5, color = hour)) +
            geom_point() +
            geom_smooth(method='auto',formula=y~x, colour = "blue", size =1) +
            facet_wrap(~ month, nrow = 4)
    ```

The plot is as follows:

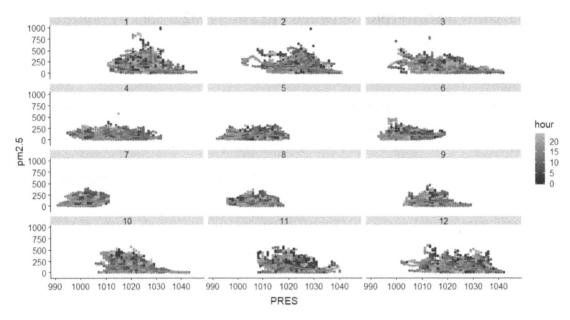

Figure 3.19: Scatterplot showing the relationship between PRES and PM2.5

Activity 6: Transforming Variables and Deriving New Variables to Build a Model

Perform the following steps for building the model:

1. Import the required libraries and packages into the system:

```
library(dplyr)
library(lubridate)
library(tidyr)
library(ggplot2)
library(grid)
library(zoo)
```

2. Combine the year, month, day, and hour into a **datetime** variable:

```
PM25$datetime <- with(PM25, ymd_h(sprintf('%04d%02d%02d%02d', year, month,
day,hour)))
```

3. Remove the rows with missing values in any column:

```
PM25_subset <- na.omit(PM25[,c("datetime","pm2.5")])
```

4. Use the **rollapply()** method from the package **zoo** to compute the moving average of PM2.5; this is to smoothen any noise from a reading of PM2.5:

```
PM25_three_hour_pm25_avg <- rollapply(zoo(PM25_subset$pm2.5,PM25_
subset$datetime), 3, mean)
```

5. Create two levels of the PM25 pollution, **0-Normal**, **1-Above Normal**. We can also create more than two levels; however, for logistic regression, which works best with binary classification, we have used two levels:

```
PM25_three_hour_pm25_avg <- as.data.frame(PM25_three_hour_pm25_avg)
PM25_three_hour_pm25_avg$timestamp <- row.names(PM25_three_hour_pm25_avg)
row.names(PM25_three_hour_pm25_avg) <- NULL
colnames(PM25_three_hour_pm25_avg) <- c("avg_pm25","timestamp")
PM25_three_hour_pm25_avg$pollution_level <- ifelse(PM25_three_hour_pm25_
avg$avg_pm25 <= 35, 0,1)
PM25_three_hour_pm25_avg$timestamp <- as.POSIXct(PM25_three_hour_pm25_
avg$timestamp, format= "%Y-%m-%d %H:%M:%S",tz="GMT")
```

6. Merge the resulting data frame (PM25_three_hour_pm25_avg) with the values of other environmental variables such as **TEMP**, **DEWP**, and **Iws**, which we used in the linear regression model:

```
PM25_for_class <- merge(PM25_three_hour_pm25_avg,
PM25[,c("datetime","TEMP","DEWP","PRES","Iws","cbwd","Is","Ir")], by.x =
"timestamp",by.y = "datetime")
```

7. Fit the generalized linear model (**glm**) on **pollution_level** using the TEMP, DEWP and Iws variables:

```
PM25_logit_model <- glm(pollution_level ~ DEWP + TEMP + Iws, data = PM25_
for_class,family=binomial(link='logit'))
```

8. Summarize the model:

```
summary(PM25_logit_model)
```

The output is as follows:

```
Call:
glm(formula = pollution_level ~ DEWP + TEMP + Iws, family = binomial(link
= "logit"),
    data = PM25_for_class)

Deviance Residuals:
    Min      1Q   Median       3Q      Max
-2.4699  -0.5212   0.4569   0.6508   3.5824

Coefficients:
               Estimate Std. Error z value Pr(>|z|)
(Intercept)   2.5240276  0.0273353   92.34   <2e-16 ***
DEWP          0.1231959  0.0016856   73.09   <2e-16 ***
TEMP         -0.1028211  0.0018447  -55.74   <2e-16 ***
Iws          -0.0127037  0.0003535  -35.94   <2e-16 ***
---
Signif. codes:  0 '***' 0.001 '**' 0.01 '*' 0.05 '.' 0.1 ' ' 1

(Dispersion parameter for binomial family taken to be 1)

    Null deviance: 49475  on 41754  degrees of freedom
Residual deviance: 37821  on 41751  degrees of freedom
AIC: 37829

Number of Fisher Scoring iterations: 5
```

Chapter 4: Regression

Activity 7: Printing Various Attributes Using Model Object Without Using the summary Function

1. First, print the coefficient values using the following command. Make sure the output is like the output of the **summary** function using the **coefficients** option. The coefficients are the fitted values from the model that uses the OLS algorithm:

   ```
   multiple_PM25_linear_model$coefficients
   ```

   The output is as follows:

   ```
   (Intercept)        DEWP         TEMP          Iws
   161.1512066    4.3841960   -5.1335111   -0.2743375
   ```

2. Find the residual value (difference) of the predicted and actual values of PM2.5, which should be as small as possible. Residual reflects how far the fitted values using the coefficients are from the actual value.

   ```
   multiple_PM25_linear_model$residuals
   ```

   The output is as follows:

   ```
        25              26              27              28
   17.95294914    32.81291348    21.38677872    26.34105878
                29              30              31              32
   ```

3. Next, find the fitted values that should be closer to the actual PM2.5 for the best model. Using the coefficients, we can compute the fitted values:

   ```
   multiple_PM25_linear_model$fitted.values
   ```

   The output is as follows:

   ```
        25          26          27          28          29
   111.047051  115.187087  137.613221  154.658941  154.414781
                30          31          32          33          34
   ```

4. Find the R-Squared values. They should look the same as the one you obtained in the output of the **summary** function next to the text Multiple R-squared. R-Square helps in evaluating the model performance. If the value is closer to 1, the better the model is:

    ```
    summary(multiple_PM25_linear_model)$r.squared
    ```

    The output is as follows:

    ```
    [1] 0.2159579
    ```

5. Find the F-Statistic values. Make sure the output should look same as the one you obtained in the output of the **summary** function next to the text F-Statistics. This will tell you if your model fits better than just using the mean of the target variable. In many practical applications, F-Statistic is used along with p-values:

    ```
    summary(multiple_PM25_linear_model)$fstatistic
    ```

    The output is as follows:

    ```
       value     numdf     dendf
    3833.506     3.000 41753.000
    ```

6. Finally, find the coefficient p-values and make sure the values should look the same as the one you obtained in the output of the **summary** function under Coefficients for each variable. It will be present under the column titled `Pr(>|t|):`. If the value is less than 0.05, the variable is statistically significant in predicting the target variable:

    ```
    summary(multiple_PM25_linear_model)$coefficients[,4]
    ```

    The output is as follows:

    ```
      (Intercept)            DEWP            TEMP             Iws
    0.000000e+00    0.000000e+00    0.000000e+00    4.279601e-224
    ```

The attributes of a model are equally essential to understand, especially in linear regression than to obtain the prediction. They help in interpreting the model well and connect the problem to its real use case.

Chapter 5: Classification

Activity 8: Building a Logistic Regression Model with Additional Features

1. Create a copy of the **df_new** data frame into **df_copy** for the activity:

    ```
    df_copy <- df_new
    ```

2. Create new features for square root, square power, and cube power transformations for each of the three selected numeric features:

    ```
    df_copy$MaxTemp2 <- df_copy$MaxTemp ^2
    df_copy$MaxTemp3 <- df_copy$MaxTemp ^3
    df_copy$MaxTemp_root <- sqrt(df_copy$MaxTemp)

    df_copy$Rainfall2 <- df_copy$Rainfall ^2
    df_copy$Rainfall3 <- df_copy$Rainfall ^3
    df_copy$Rainfall_root <- sqrt(df_copy$Rainfall)

    df_copy$Humidity3pm2 <- df_copy$Humidity3pm ^2
    df_copy$Humidity3pm3 <- df_copy$Humidity3pm ^3
    df_copy$Humidity3pm_root <- sqrt(df_copy$Humidity3pm)
    ```

3. Divide the **df_copy** dataset into train and test in 70:30 ratio:

    ```
    #Setting seed for reproducibility
    set.seed(2019)

    #Creating a list of indexes for the training dataset (70%)
    train_index <- sample(seq_len(nrow(df_copy)),floor(0.7 * nrow(df_copy)))

    #Split the data into test and train
    train_new <- df_copy[train_index,]
    test_new <- df_copy[-train_index,]
    ```

4. Fit the logistic regression model with the new training data:

    ```
    model <- glm(RainTomorrow~., data=train_new
    ,family=binomial(link='logit'))
    ```

5. Predict the responses using the fitted model on the train data and create a confusion matrix:

```
print("Training data results -")
pred_train <-factor(ifelse(predict(model,newdata=train_new,
type = "response") > 0.5,"Yes","No"))
#Create the Confusion Matrix
train_metrics <- confusionMatrix(pred_train, train_
new$RainTomorrow,positive="Yes")
print(train_metrics)
```

The output is as follows:

```
"Training data results -"
Confusion Matrix and Statistics

          Reference
Prediction    No   Yes
       No  58330  8650
      Yes   3161  8906

               Accuracy : 0.8506
                 95% CI : (0.8481, 0.8531)
    No Information Rate : 0.7779
    P-Value [Acc > NIR] : < 2.2e-16

                  Kappa : 0.5132
 Mcnemar's Test P-Value : < 2.2e-16

            Sensitivity : 0.5073
            Specificity : 0.9486
         Pos Pred Value : 0.7380
         Neg Pred Value : 0.8709
             Prevalence : 0.2221
         Detection Rate : 0.1127
   Detection Prevalence : 0.1527
      Balanced Accuracy : 0.7279

       'Positive' Class : Yes
```

6. Predict the responses using the fitted model on test data and create a confusion matrix:

```
print("Test data results -")
pred_test <-factor(ifelse(predict(model,newdata=test_new,
type = "response") > 0.5,"Yes","No"))
#Create the Confusion Matrix
test_metrics <- confusionMatrix(pred_test, test_
new$RainTomorrow,positive="Yes")
print(test_metrics)
```

The output is as follows:

```
"Test data results -"
Confusion Matrix and Statistics

          Reference
Prediction    No    Yes
       No   25057  3640
       Yes   1358  3823

               Accuracy : 0.8525
                 95% CI : (0.8486, 0.8562)
    No Information Rate : 0.7797
    P-Value [Acc > NIR] : < 2.2e-16

                  Kappa : 0.5176
 Mcnemar's Test P-Value : < 2.2e-16

            Sensitivity : 0.5123
            Specificity : 0.9486
         Pos Pred Value : 0.7379
         Neg Pred Value : 0.8732
             Prevalence : 0.2203
         Detection Rate : 0.1128
   Detection Prevalence : 0.1529
      Balanced Accuracy : 0.7304

       'Positive' Class : Yes
```

Activity 9: Create a Decision Tree Model with Additional Control Parameters

1. Load the **rpart** library.

    ```
    library(rpart)
    ```

2. Create the control object for decision tree with new values **minsplit** =15 and **cp** = **0.00**:

    ```
    control = rpart.control(
        minsplit = 15,
        cp = 0.001)
    ```

3. Fit the tree model with the train data and pass the control object to the **rpart** function:

    ```
    tree_model <- rpart(RainTomorrow~.,data=train, control = control)
    ```

4. Plot the complexity parameter plot to see how the tree performs at different values of **CP**:

    ```
    plotcp(tree_model)
    ```

    The output is as follows:

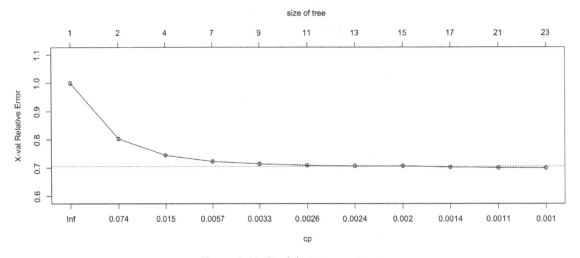

Figure 5.10: Decision tree output

5. Use the fitted model to make predictions on train data and create the confusion matrix:

```
print("Training data results -")
pred_train <- predict(tree_model,newdata = train,type = "class")
confusionMatrix(pred_train, train$RainTomorrow,positive="Yes")
```

The output is as follows:

```
"Training data results -"
Confusion Matrix and Statistics

          Reference
Prediction    No    Yes
       No  58494   9032
       Yes  2997   8524

               Accuracy : 0.8478
                 95% CI : (0.8453, 0.8503)
    No Information Rate : 0.7779
    P-Value [Acc > NIR] : < 2.2e-16

                  Kappa : 0.4979
 Mcnemar's Test P-Value : < 2.2e-16

            Sensitivity : 0.4855
            Specificity : 0.9513
         Pos Pred Value : 0.7399
         Neg Pred Value : 0.8662
             Prevalence : 0.2221
         Detection Rate : 0.1078
   Detection Prevalence : 0.1457
      Balanced Accuracy : 0.7184

       'Positive' Class : Yes
```

6. Use the fitted model to make predictions on test data and create the confusion matrix:

```
print("Test data results -")
pred_test <- predict(tree_model,newdata = test,type = "class")
confusionMatrix(pred_test, test$RainTomorrow,positive="Yes")
```

The output is as follows:

```
"Test data results -"
Confusion Matrix and Statistics

          Reference
Prediction    No    Yes
       No   25068   3926
       Yes   1347   3537

               Accuracy : 0.8444
                 95% CI : (0.8404, 0.8482)
    No Information Rate : 0.7797
    P-Value [Acc > NIR] : < 2.2e-16

                  Kappa : 0.4828
 Mcnemar's Test P-Value : < 2.2e-16

            Sensitivity : 0.4739
            Specificity : 0.9490
         Pos Pred Value : 0.7242
         Neg Pred Value : 0.8646
             Prevalence : 0.2203
         Detection Rate : 0.1044
   Detection Prevalence : 0.1442
      Balanced Accuracy : 0.7115

       'Positive' Class : Yes
```

Activity 10: Build a Random Forest Model with a Greater Number of Trees

1. First, import the **randomForest** library using the following command:

```
library(randomForest)
```

2. Build random forest model with all independent features available. Define the number of trees in the model to be 500.

```
rf_model <- randomForest(RainTomorrow ~ . , data = train, ntree = 500,
                                           importance = TRUE,
                                           maxnodes=60)
```

3. Evaluate on training data:

```
print("Training data results -")
pred_train <- predict(rf_model,newdata = train,type = "class")
confusionMatrix(pred_train, train$RainTomorrow,positive="Yes")
```

The output is as follows:

```
"Training data results -"
Confusion Matrix and Statistics

          Reference
Prediction    No   Yes
       No  59638 10169
       Yes  1853  7387

               Accuracy : 0.8479
                 95% CI : (0.8454, 0.8504)
    No Information Rate : 0.7779
    P-Value [Acc > NIR] : < 2.2e-16

                  Kappa : 0.4702
 Mcnemar's Test P-Value : < 2.2e-16

            Sensitivity : 0.42077
            Specificity : 0.96987
         Pos Pred Value : 0.79946
         Neg Pred Value : 0.85433
```

```
          Prevalence : 0.22210
     Detection Rate : 0.09345
Detection Prevalence : 0.11689
  Balanced Accuracy : 0.69532

       'Positive' Class : Yes
```

4. Evaluate on test data:

```
print("Test data results -")
pred_test <- predict(rf_model,newdata = test,type = "class")
confusionMatrix(pred_test, test$RainTomorrow,positive="Yes")
```

The output is as follows:

```
"Test data results -"
Confusion Matrix and Statistics

              Reference
Prediction    No    Yes
       No   25604   4398
      Yes     811   3065

               Accuracy : 0.8462
                 95% CI : (0.8424, 0.8501)
    No Information Rate : 0.7797
    P-Value [Acc > NIR] : < 2.2e-16

                  Kappa : 0.4592
 Mcnemar's Test P-Value : < 2.2e-16

            Sensitivity : 0.41069
            Specificity : 0.96930
         Pos Pred Value : 0.79076
         Neg Pred Value : 0.85341
             Prevalence : 0.22029
         Detection Rate : 0.09047
   Detection Prevalence : 0.11441
      Balanced Accuracy : 0.69000

       'Positive' Class : Yes
```

Chapter 6: Feature Selection and Dimensionality Reduction

Activity 11: Converting the CBWD Feature of the Beijing PM2.5 Dataset into One-Hot Encoded Columns

1. Read the Beijing PM2.5 dataset into the DataFrame **PM25**:

    ```
    PM25 <- read.csv("PRSA_data_2010.1.1-2014.12.31.csv")
    ```

2. Create a variable **cbwd_one_hot** for storing the result of the **dummyVars** function with ~ **cbwd** as its first argument:

    ```
    library(caret)
    cbwd_one_hot <- dummyVars(" ~ cbwd", data = PM25)
    ```

3. Use the output of the **predict()** function on **cbwd_one_hot** and case it as DataFrame:

    ```
    cbwd_one_hot <- data.frame(predict(cbwd_one_hot, newdata = PM25))
    ```

4. Remove the original **cbwd** variable from the **PM25** DataFrame:

    ```
    PM25$cbwd <- NULL
    ```

5. Using the **cbind()** function, add **cbwd_one_hot** to the **PM25** DataFrame:

    ```
    PM25 <- cbind(PM25, cbwd_one_hot)
    ```

6. Print the top 6 rows of **PM25**:

    ```
    head(PM25)
    ```

    The output of the previous command is as follows:

    ```
    ##    No year month day hour pm2.5 DEWP TEMP PRES    Iws Is Ir cbwd.cv cbwd.
    NE
    ## 1  1 2010     1   1    1     0   NA  -21  -11 1021  1.79  0  0       0
    0
    ## 2  2 2010     1   1    1     1   NA  -21  -12 1020  4.92  0  0       0
    0
    ## 3  3 2010     1   1    2     NA  -21  -11 1019  6./I  0  0       0
    0
    ## 4  4 2010     1   1    3     NA  -21  -14 1019  9.84  0  0       0
    0
    ```

```
## 5  5 2010     1   1    4    NA  -20  -12 1018 12.97  0  0        0
0
## 6  6 2010     1   1    5    NA  -19  -10 1017 16.10  0  0        0
0
##     cbwd.NW cbwd.SE
## 1       1        0
## 2       1        0
## 3       1        0
## 4       1        0
## 5       1        0
## 6       1        0
```

Observe the variable **cbwd** in the output of the **head(PM25)** command: it is now transformed into one-hot encoded columns with the **NE**, **NW**, and **SE** suffixes.

Chapter 7: Model Improvements

Activity 12: Perform Repeated K-Fold Cross Validation and Grid Search Optimization

1. Load the required packages **mlbench**, **caret**, and **dplyr** for the exercise:

```
library(mlbench)
library(dplyr)
library(caret)
```

2. Load the **PimaIndianDiabetes** dataset into memory from **mlbench** package:

```
data(PimaIndiansDiabetes)
df<-PimaIndiansDiabetes
```

3. Set a **seed** value as **2019** for reproducibility:

```
set.seed(2019)
```

4. Define the K-Fold validation object using the **trainControl** function from the **caret** package and define **method** as **repeatedcv** instead of **cv**. Define an additional construct in the **trainControl** function for the number of repeats in the validation **repeats = 10**:

```
train_control = trainControl(method = "repeatedcv",
                             number=5,
                             repeats = 10,
   savePredictions = TRUE,
   verboseIter = TRUE)
```

5. Define the grid for hyperparameter **mtry** of random forest model as **(3,4,5)**:

```
parameter_values = expand.grid(mtry=c(3,4,5))
```

6. Fit the model with the grid values, cross-validation object, and random forest classifier:

```
model_rf_kfold<- train(diabetes~.,
data=df, trControl=train_control,
                 method="rf", metric= "Accuracy",
   tuneGrid = parameter_values)
```

7. Study the model performance by printing the average accuracy and standard deviation of accuracy:

```
print(paste("Average Accuracy :",mean(model_rf_kfold$resample$Accuracy)))
print(paste("Std. Dev Accuracy :",sd(model_rf_kfold$resample$Accuracy)))
```

8. Study the model performance by plotting the accuracy across different values of the hyperparameter:

```
plot(model_rf_kfold)
```

The final output is as follows:

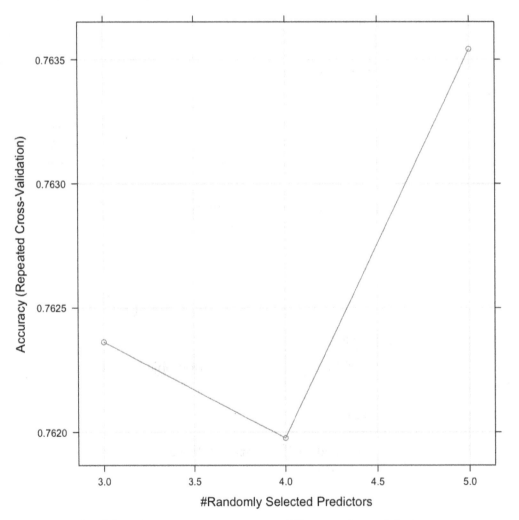

Figure 7.17: Model performance accuracy across different values of the hyperparameter

In this plot, we can see that we perform repeated k-fold cross-validation and grid search optimization on the same model.

Chapter 8: Model Deployment

Activity 13: Deploy an R Model Using Plumber

1. Create a **model.r** script that will load the required libraries, data, fit a regression model and necessary function to predict on unseen data.

2. Load the **mlbench** library that has the data for this activity:

   ```
   library(mlbench)
   ```

3. Load **BostonHousing** data into a DataFrame **df**:

   ```
   data(BostonHousing)
   df<-BostonHousing
   ```

4. Create train dataset using the first **400** rows of df and test with the remaining:

   ```
   train <- df[1:400,]
   test <- df[401:dim(df)[1],]
   ```

5. Fit a logistic regression model using the **lm** function with dependent variable as **medv** (median value) and 10 independent variables, such as, **crim**, **zn**, **indus**, **chas**, **nox**, **rm**, **age**, **dis**, **rad**, and **tax**.

   ```
   model <- lm(medv~crim+zn+indus+chas+
     nox+rm+age+dis+rad+tax,data=train)
   ```

6. Define a model endpoint as **predict_data**; this will be used as the API endpoint for Plumber:

   ```
   #' @get /predict_data
   function(crim,zn,indus,chas,nox,rm,age,dis,rad,tax){
   ```

7. Within the function, convert the parameters to numeric and factor (since the API call will pass them as string only):

   ```
   crim <- as.numeric(crim)
   zn <- as.numeric(zn)
   indus <- as.numeric(indus)
   chas <- as.factor(chas)
   nox <- as.numeric(nox)
   rm <- as.numeric(rm)
   age <- as.numeric(age)
   dis <- as.numeric(dis)
   rad <- as.numeric(rad)
   tax <- as.numeric(tax)
   ```

8. Wrap the 10 independent features for the model as a DataFrame named **sample**, with the same name for the columns:

```
sample <- data.frame(crim  = crim,   zn  = zn,   indus  = indus,
                      chas  = chas,   nox = nox,  rm  = rm,
                      age  = age,   dis  = dis,  rad  = rad,
                      tax  = tax )
```

9. Pass the **sample** DataFrame to the predict function with the model (created in the 4th step) and return predictions:

```
y_pred<-predict(model,newdata=sample)

    list(Answer=y_pred)
}
```

The entire **model.r** file will look like this:

```
library(mlbench)
data(BostonHousing)
df<-BostonHousing
train <- df[1:400,]
test <- df[401:dim(df)[1],]

model <- lm(medv~crim+zn+indus+chas+nox+rm+age+dis+rad+tax,data=train)

#' @get /predict_data
function(crim,zn,indus,chas,nox,rm,age,dis,rad,tax){

  crim <- as.numeric(crim)
  zn <- as.numeric(zn)
  indus <- as.numeric(indus)
  chas <- as.factor(chas)
  nox <- as.numeric(nox)
  rm <- as.numeric(rm)
  age <- as.numeric(age)
  dis <- as.numeric(dis)
  rad <- as.numeric(rad)
  tax <- as.numeric(tax)
```

```
    sample <- data.frame(crim  = crim,   zn  = zn,   indus  = indus,
                         chas  = chas,   nox  = nox,   rm  = rm,
                         age  = age,   dis  = dis,   rad  = rad,
                         tax  = tax )

    y_pred<-predict(model,newdata=sample)

    list(Answer=y_pred)
}
```

10. Load the **plumber** library.

    ```
    library(plumber)
    ```

11. Create a plumber object using the **plumb** function and pass the **model.r** file (created in part 1).

    ```
    r <- plumb(model.r)
    ```

12. Run the plumber object by passing the hostname as **localhost** or **127.0.0.1** and a port, say **8080**.

    ```
    http://127.0.0.1:8080/
    ```

13. Test the deployed model using the browser or Postman and invoke the API.

    API invoke:

    http://127.0.0.1:8080/predict

    ata?crim=0.01&zn=18&indus=2.3&chas=0&nox=0.5&rm=6&

    age=65&dis=4&rad=1&tax=242

    ```
    {"Answer":[22.5813]}
    ```

Chapter 9: Capstone Project - Based on Research Papers

Activity 14: Getting the Binary Performance Step with classif.C50 Learner Instead of classif.rpart

1. Define the algorithm adaptation methods:

```
multilabel.lrn3 = makeLearner("multilabel.rFerns")
multilabel.lrn4 = makeLearner("multilabel.randomForestSRC")
multilabel.lrn3
```

The output is as follows:

```
## Learner multilabel.rFerns from package rFerns
## Type: multilabel
## Name: Random ferns; Short name: rFerns
## Class: multilabel.rFerns
## Properties: numerics,factors,ordered
## Predict-Type: response
## Hyperparameters:
```

2. Use the problem transformation method, and change the **classif.rpart** learner to **classif.C50**:

```
lrn = makeLearner("classif.C50", predict.type = "prob")
multilabel.lrn1 = makeMultilabelBinaryRelevanceWrapper(lrn)
multilabel.lrn2 = makeMultilabelNestedStackingWrapper(lrn)
```

> **Note**
>
> You need to install the **C50** package for this code to work.

3. Print the learner details:

```
lrn
```

The output is as follows:

```
## Learner classif.C50 from package C50
## Type: classif
## Name: C50; Short name: C50
## Class: classif.C50
## Properties: twoclass,multiclass,numerics,factors,prob,missings,weights
## Predict-Type: prob
## Hyperparameters:
```

4. Print the multilabel learner details:

```
multilabel.lrn1
```

The output is as follows:

```
## Learner multilabel.binaryRelevance.classif.C50 from package C50
## Type: multilabel
## Name: ; Short name:
## Class: MultilabelBinaryRelevanceWrapper
## Properties: numerics,factors,missings,weights,prob,twoclass,multiclass
## Predict-Type: prob
## Hyperparameters:
```

5. Train the model using the same dataset with training dataset:

```
df_nrow <- nrow(df_scene)
df_all_index <- c(1:df_nrow)
train_index <- sample(1:df_nrow, 0.7*df_nrow)
test_index <- setdiff(df_all_index,train_index)
scene_classi_mod = train(multilabel.lrn1, scene.task, subset = train_
index)
```

6. Print the model details:

```
scene_classi_mod
```

The output is as follows:

```
## Model for learner.id=multilabel.binaryRelevance.classif.C50; learner.
class=MultilabelBinaryRelevanceWrapper
## Trained on: task.id = multi; obs = 1684; features = 294
## Hyperparameters:
```

7. Predict the output using the **C50** model we created for the test dataset:

```
pred = predict(scene_classi_mod, task = scene.task, subset = test_index)
names(as.data.frame(pred))
```

The output is as follows:

```
##  [1] "id"                  "truth.Beach"        "truth.Sunset"
##  [4] "truth.FallFoliage"   "truth.Field"        "truth.Mountain"
##  [7] "truth.Urban"         "prob.Beach"         "prob.Sunset"
## [10] "prob.FallFoliage"    "prob.Field"         "prob.Mountain"
## [13] "prob.Urban"          "response.Beach"     "response.Sunset"
## [16] "response.FallFoliage" "response.Field"    "response.Mountain"
## [19] "response.Urban"
```

8. Print the performance measures:

```
MEASURES = list(multilabel.hamloss, multilabel.f1, multilabel.subset01,
multilabel.acc, multilabel.tpr, multilabel.ppv)

performance(pred, measures = MEASURES)
```

The output is as follows:

```
##   multilabel.hamloss        multilabel.f1 multilabel.subset01
##            0.1258645            0.5734901            0.5532503
##         multilabel.acc        multilabel.tpr        multilabel.ppv
##            0.5412633            0.6207930            0.7249104
```

9. Print the performance measures for the **listMeasures** variable:

```
listMeasures("multilabel")
```

The output is as follows:

```
##  [1] "featperc"            "multilabel.tpr"       "multilabel.hamloss"
##  [4] "multilabel.subset01" "timeboth"             "timetrain"
##  [7] "timepredict"         "multilabel.ppv"       "multilabel.f1"
## [10] "multilabel.acc"
```

10. Run the resampling with cross-validation method:

```
rdesc = makeResampleDesc(method = "CV", stratify = FALSE, iters = 3)
r = resample(learner = multilabel.lrn1, task = scene.task, resampling =
rdesc,measures = list(multilabel.hamloss), show.info = FALSE)
r
```

The output is as follows:

```
## Resample Result
## Task: multi
## Learner: multilabel.binaryRelevance.classif.C50
## Aggr perf: multilabel.hamloss.test.mean=0.1335695
## Runtime: 72.353
```

11. Print the binary performance:

```
getMultilabelBinaryPerformances(r$pred, measures = list(acc, mmce, auc))
```

The output is as follows:

```
##              acc.test.mean mmce.test.mean auc.test.mean
## Beach            0.8608226     0.13917740     0.8372448
## Sunset           0.9401745     0.05982551     0.9420085
## FallFoliage      0.9081845     0.09181554     0.9008202
## Field            0.8998754     0.10012464     0.9134458
## Mountain         0.7710843     0.22891566     0.7622767
## Urban            0.8184462     0.18155380     0.7837401
```

Index

About

All major keywords used in this book are captured alphabetically in this section. Each one is accompanied by the page number of where they appear.